298558

D1766856

Risk and Hazard Management
for Festivals and Events

Events of all types are produced every day for all manner of purposes, attracting all sorts of people. To provide a safe and secure setting in which people gather is imperative. Event risk and hazard management must be fully integrated into all event plans and throughout the event management process.

Hazard management is the planning process required for the effective management of potential adverse incidents and areas of uncertainty. It involves intensive, detailed planning and cooperation to apply control systems to minimise hazards associated with venues, outdoor sites, work procedures, facilities, equipment and crowds of spectators. It involves planning for emergencies and security, and compliance with legal constraints and requirements.

Risk and Hazard Management for Festivals and Events provides students with a comprehensive, fully integrated planning and management mechanism that can be applied to events of all types and size. The Event Safety Management System provides guidelines and processes for proactive methods to identify, assess and control hazardous conditions and practices. The system incorporates design of festival venues and sites, and unites the operational functions of crowd control, communications, security, terrorism prevention processes and emergency response protocols.

Explanation of the causes of crowd disasters and studies into crowd behaviour are supported with international case studies. Written in an accessible, practical way, this book is essential reading for all events students and event managers.

Peter Wynn-Moylan is a Lecturer on Special Events and Conventions Management at the School of Business and Tourism, Southern Cross University, Australia. He has had a 40-year career in event management covering all aspects of the industry.

Risk and Hazard Management for Festivals and Events

Peter Wynn-Moylan

Routledge
Taylor & Francis Group

LONDON AND NEW YORK

First published 2018
by Routledge
2 Park Square, Milton Park, Abingdon, Oxon OX14 4RN

and by Routledge
711 Third Avenue, New York, NY 10017

Routledge is an imprint of the Taylor & Francis Group, an informa business

British Library Cataloguing-in-Publication Data
A catalogue record for this book is available from the British Library

Library of Congress Cataloging-in-Publication Data
A catalog record for this book has been requested

ISBN: 978-1-138-67838-5 (hbk)
ISBN: 978-1-138-67839-2 (pbk)
ISBN: 978-1-315-55897-4 (ebk)

Typeset in Frutiger
by Keystroke, Neville Lodge, Tettenhall, Wolverhampton

Visit the companion website: www.routledge.com/cw/wynn-moylan

MIX
Paper from
responsible sources
FSC
www.fsc.org   FSC™ C013985

Printed in the United Kingdom
by Henry Ling Limited

This book is dedicated to the memory of my brother, Raymond Badger, 1951–2013, Fire Brigade Captain, Policeman and Highway Emergency Controller.

Contents

List of figures   xvii
Preface   xix
Acknowledgements   xxiii

1   Event hazard and risk management: regulations and legislation   1

Chapter objectives   1
Duty of care   2
  *ALARP: managing hazard to a level that is 'as low as reasonably
     practicable' 4*
Occupational health and safety   4
  Defining occupational health and safety (OH&S) 5
  Information sources 6
Workplace health and safety responsibilities   7
  Persons conducting a business or undertaking 7
  Consultation 8
  Definition of worker 8
  Other persons at an event 9
Laws, regulations and codes of practice   9
  Regulations – prescriptive standards 10
  Performance-based standards 10
  Process standards 11
  Codes of practice 11
  Administration of legislation 12
  Inspections 12
  Notification 13
Waivers   13
  Manage the risk 14
  Transfer the risk 14
  Process 15
Summary   15
Bibliography   16

Contents

2   **Event Safety Management System (ESMS)**   **18**

Chapter objectives   18
Event safety policy   20
Organisational structure and allocation of responsibilities 21
Health and safety officer 22
Partnerships 22
Multi-agency teamwork 24
Implementing a safety planning process   25
Identifying activities 26
Hazard and risk management process   26
Hazard management definitions 27
Hazard evaluation   29
Establish the context 29
The main steps in identifying hazardous conditions 30
Checklists 30
Evaluation of hazards 33
Priority 34
Software   35
Control of hazards   35
Protocols   37
Public 37
Basic 37
Specific 40
Comprehensive 40
Monitoring and evaluation   41
Monitor and review 41
Information management 42
Summary   42
Bibliography   44

3   **Understanding crowd disasters**   **45**

Chapter objectives   45
Death and injury in crowds at festivals and events   46
Crowd crush   47
Crowd turbulence or crowd quake   47
Defining crowds   49
One crowd or many 51
Crowd behaviour theory   52
Crowding perception 53
Place scripts (habitual behaviour in a place) 55
Crowd behaviour in an emergency   56
Summary   59
Bibliography   59

4   Crowd management planning   **64**

Chapter objectives   64
Managing crowds   66
Crowd management or crowd control   67
Planning and preparation   68
Good practice manuals for crowd management planning   69
What if...? Simulation modelling   69
Modelling techniques   71
Various models for simulating crowd behaviours   71
Evacuation simulation software   73
'What if' exercises   75
DIM-ICE model   75
Summary   77
Bibliography   77

5   Space and flow in public areas   **80**

Chapter objectives   80
Space   82
Density and movement   82
Crowd flow   84
Crowd processing   86
Early opening and delayed closing   86
Ticketing   87
Queueing theory   88
Flow charts   88
Crowd monitoring and control   90
Crowd characteristics   91
Crowd control staff   93
Assessing required staff numbers   94
Stewarding and ushering   95
Crowd monitoring tasks   97
Monitoring points   97
Closed circuit television (CCTV)   98
Post-event dispersal of the crowd   99
Staff crowd management training   100
Communicating with the crowd   100
Pre-event communication   101
During the event   102
Communication messages   102
Site administration office – communications centre   102
On-site communication systems   103
Summary   103
Bibliography   104

Contents

6   Safe site design   106

  Chapter objectives   106
  Estimates of audience numbers   107
  Site and venue safety evaluation   108
    Pre-event inspection   109
    Environmental hazards   110
    Swimming and water areas   111
  Site layout and design   111
    Separation issues   112
    Crowd/traffic-related issues   112
    Access entry   113
    Emergency services access   113
  Street and unconfined events   114
  Site maps   115
    Creating the site map   115
  Computer Aided Design (CAD)   117
  Vehicle traffic management   117
    Crowd/traffic-separation related issues   118
  Parking   120
    Secure parking   121
    Traffic and parking controls   121
  Public transport   121
  Event signage   122
  Entrances and perimeters   124
    Barriers and fences   124
    Entrances and exits   125
  Internal site movement control   125
    Stairways, gangways and ramps   126
    Auditorium   126
    Seating   127
    Location of stages   127
    Accommodating special needs   127
    Facilities and stalls   128
  Restricted areas   128
    Backstage   129
    Green room   131
    Stage   131
  On-site facilities and services   132
    Site lighting and power requirements   132
    Power supply   132
    Stages, platforms and other performance facilities   133
    Temporary structures   134
    Doors and windows   134
    Seating   134
    Loading   135

Toilet facilities 135
    Food vendors and staff toilets 137
    Maintenance 137
Campgrounds 138
Water 139
Waste management 139
    Litter management 140
On-site first aid – emergency medical aid 141
    Medical teams 142
    First aid facilities 142
    Ambulance services 144
Summary 144
Bibliography 146

7 Site management: production and operational work practice hazards 148

Chapter objectives 148
Production – overseeing and coordinating the site/venue set-up 149
Site construction scheduling 150
    Production scheduling 150
    Schedule of resource supply 151
Site construction 151
    Precinct control 151
    Sub-contractor management 152
    Safety monitoring 153
    Weather impacts 153
On-site operations and facility control 154
Site operations 154
    Immediate pre-opening activities 154
    Supervision of the event operation and venue services 155
    Compliance 156
On-site staff communications 157
    Communications within the venue 157
Overseeing of the event breakdown 159
Safe work practices and equipment use 160
Violence 160
    Assessing the risk 161
    Controlling the risk 161
    Response to violent incidents 162
Stress 162
    Identifying stress 163
    Assessing the risk 163
    Controlling the risk 163
Ergonomics 164
    Identifying and managing ergonomic hazards 166

Personal protective clothing and equipment 166
Performance area and stage safety 168
  Performer misbehaviour 170
Hazardous equipment 170
  Registration, licensing, certification, permit to work 171
  Hazard identification and assessment process 171
  Overseeing equipment use work processes 171
  Common types of controls associated with equipment 172
  Stop work 174
  Key information transfer and feedback 174
Staging equipment 175
Hazardous substances and dangerous goods 176
  Control 176
Fireworks and flares 177
Fire safety 177
Summary 178
Bibliography 179

8 Food, alcohol and drugs **181**

Chapter objectives 181
Food 182
Food vans or stalls 182
  Refuse disposal 183
  Hand washing 183
  Food supplies 184
  Food handling 184
  Thawing, cooking, heating and cooling 184
  Cleaning and sanitising 184
  Chemical storage 185
  Food storage – temperature control 185
  Food handling staff considerations 185
  Gas cylinders 185
Other stall holders 186
  Tattooing and body piercing 186
Alcohol and drug use at festivals 186
  Safe partying 186
Alcohol 187
  Adverse health and social effects 188
  Implementing strategies to assist guests to drink responsibly 189
  Harm minimisation benefits 189
  Responsible service of alcohol 190
  Staff 190
  Alcohol-free events 191
  Selling alcohol 191

Time   192
Designated area   192
Age   193
Wristbanding   193
Food   194
Signage   194
Monitoring guests for intoxication   195
Refusing to serve alcohol to intoxicated guests   196
Removal of patrons from licensed premises   196
Assisted removals   196
Multiple assisted removals   197
Other considerations   197
On-site breathalysers   197
Illicit drugs   198
Mixing alcohol and drugs   198
Overdoses   200
Pill testing   201
Support for testing   202
Arguments against testing   203
Water   204
Chill-out space   204
Health promotion   204
Infection control and personal hygiene issues   205
Sexual assault at music festivals   205
Offensive behaviour   205
Summary   206
Bibliography   207

9   Security and law enforcement on-site   210

Chapter objectives   210
Police   212
General security staff   213
Screening and patrolling   214
Briefing   214
Security procedures   215
Passes   216
Media passes   217
Temporary passes   218
Searching of persons entering the event   218
Bag checks   218
Body searches   218
Warning notices   218
Confiscated items   219
Staff   219

Contents

Selecting a security contractor 219
Security screening of staff 221
  Controls 221
  Pre-employment screening 221
  Pre-employment checks 222
  Identity 222
  Qualifications and employment history 222
  Employment checks 222
  Criminal convictions 223
  Security checks for contractor staff 223
Performer, celebrity and VIP security 223
  Shared responsibilities 224
  Celebrity behaviour 225
  Liaison with VIP security 225
High profile events 225
  Enhanced security provision at high profile events 226
  Extra measures to be considered 226
  VIP area passes 226
  Security passes 227
Summary 227
Bibliography 228

10 Counter terrorism protective security 229

Chapter objectives 229
Counter terrorism protective security advice for major events 230
Managing the terrorism risks 232
  Protective measures 232
  Step one: identify the threats 232
  Step two: protecting and identifying vulnerabilities 233
  Step three: identify measures to reduce risk 233
  *Step four: review security measures and rehearse and review security
    and contingency plans 234*
Threat levels 234
  Response levels 234
Protective security planning 235
  Creating the security plan 236
  Staff security awareness 237
Improvised explosive devices 237
  Explosive effects of a bomb 237
  Causes of fatalities, injuries and damage from blasts 238
  Controls 238
  Protocols applicable to most incidents 238
  Site search 239
  Search plans 239

Bomb threat   239

Suicide bomb attacks   240
   Controls   240

Firearm attacks   241
   Controls   241
   Staff protocols for a firearms/weapons incident   242
   Police response   243

Protected spaces   244
   Open air events   244

Suspicious deliveries   245
   Controls   245

Chemical, biological or radiological material attacks   246
   Controls   246

Heavy vehicle attacks   246
   Controls   247

Hostile reconnaissance   247
   What to look for   248
   Controls   248

Summary   248
Bibliography   249

11   Emergency response   **251**

Chapter objectives   251
Cancelling the event   253
   Suspending or re-scheduling   254
   Cancellation process   254

Emergency Operations Centre (EOC)   254
   Documented procedures   255
   Staff   256
   Transition considerations   256
   Emergency power   256

Emergency communications procedures   257
   Informing the public of an emergency   257
   Staff communications during an emergency   258

Emergency communications planning   258
Interagency communications   259
   Use of social media   261

Protocols for responding to an emergency   261
Emergency grab bags   263
Evacuation   265
Planning   265
Decision to evacuate   267
Delayed warnings   268
Instructions to the public   269

Contents

    Warning interpretation   269
    Information and instruction   269
  Crowd behaviours in emergencies   270
  Evacuation guidance   271
    Emergency signs   272
    Leadership   272
  Evacuation assembly areas   273
    Evacuation and assembly areas   273
    Actions within the assembly area   273
  Post-emergency recovery phase   274
    When to re-open the venue   274
  Staff training   275
    Emergency drills   276
    Equipment testing   276
  Summary   276
  Bibliography   277

12   Incident reporting and investigation   **281**

  Chapter objectives   281
  Incident investigation processes   282
    Incident protocols   282
    Investigations   284
    Gathering information   284
    Investigating the incident cause   285
  Causal analysis tree model of an investigation   286
    Incident report   286
  Post-event hazard control review and report   287
    Recording issues   287
    Debriefing   288
    Revising plans and procedures   288
  Summary   289
  Bibliography   290

Appendix: case studies   **292**
Index   **302**

Figures

2.1	Rigging lighting – note safety harness.	34
2.2	Safety instruction notice to staff.	38
3.1	Fencing used as queuing control.	55
4.1	Small entry gates enable easy ticket checking but could become bottlenecks.	66
4.2	Congestion caused by bag checks, note PA speaker.	74
5.1	Bag check and wrist-banding entrance.	85
5.2	Temporary fencing defining different access areas.	87
5.3	Three flow charts for the same event.	89
5.4	Security guard at vulnerable border fencing.	95
6.1	Site plan of street event showing location of fences, barriers, stalls, stage and amenities.	116
6.2	Side stage access control fencing – note covering to prevent public view of backstage.	130
6.3	Portaloos and restricted service areas.	135
6.4	Toilet queue – ideally the wait should be no more than 10 minutes.	138
6.5	Industrial waste bins.	140
6.6	First aid post.	143
7.1	Water filled barriers used to define emergency access road.	156
7.2	Wrist-banding – note workers' poor posture.	165
7.3	Phase 3 to 2 phase power supply box.	175
8.1	Food stalls – public area.	183
8.2	Easily undermined method of restricting alcohol by selling tickets limited by age and amount.	187
8.3	Age restricted alcohol drinking area.	193
9.1	Mobile police station.	212
9.2	Police assisting members of the public.	215
9.3	Security guard.	220
11.1	Emergency protocols and equipment in a temporary location.	264
12.1	Sub-contractors with the best seat in the house.	289

Preface

No man ever steps in the same river twice, for it's not the same river and he's not the same man.

Heraclitus

It's never the same festival twice, variables of audience, staff, sub-contractors, performers, equipment, weather, social and economic situations mean that each event generates its own unique set of circumstances, even if held in the same location and date year after year. This ever-changing combination of elements creates hazards and risk.

Special events and festivals are particularly prone to hazardous factors that create a possibility of harm to both the crowd and the event personnel. Hazards may be posed by the layout and condition of the event site or venue work environment and abnormal conditions such as power failures, breakdowns or, in the case of outdoor events, extreme weather. Factors such as site design and large crowds and movement of equipment, create risks that can lead to disasters if not managed properly.

Each event is a unique combination of elements – contracted suppliers, paid and volunteers staff, attendees and locations – combined for a one-off occasion and brought together in a short time period, creating uncertainty and unfamiliarity, and consequential insecurity. An event manager must spend time and effort to reduce that insecurity. The role of hazard management is to discover the causes of uncertainty and reduce them to as low as reasonably possible.

Emergencies come in a variety of forms, by management failure or oversight – stage collapse, crowd crush, collisions, electrocutions; or by weather events – storms, extreme heat; by incidents in the venue or site – fire, flood, power failure; or by the actions of others – fights, theft, substance abuse.

For a terrorist, a festival or special event can represent a high value, newsworthy target. They can achieve their strategic objectives by destroying lives and infrastructure. By attacking events, terrorists are highlighting the clash of culture and values.

All of these occurrences and situations will require a planned response and prearranged procedures for handling large numbers of confused and frightened people. Emergency procedures are also required for individuals suffering injury, overdose or crime. Plans will also be needed for crisis management liaison in the case of a regional disaster external to the event such as an earthquake, a cyclone or political rioting.

As a result of the increasing economic importance of events, particularly festivals, within the tourism sector and the increasing awareness of the range of possibilities for injury and harm to attendees at events from traffic accidents to food poisoning, from crowd crush to drug overdose, from storms and fire to terrorist attack, it is clear that the level of expected professionalism has become higher and the penalties for not meeting requirements will, no doubt, increase in frequency and severity. Hazard management planning is increasingly being demanded by event stakeholders such as the government and their agencies, insurance companies, sponsors, law and the courts.

This is not to say that professional event organizers have ignored their responsibilities. They have been actively seeking from relevant government organisations guidance material and codes of practice, and industry accreditation of event organizers.

In August 2005 a two-day risk management workshop was held in Johannesburg, South Africa that brought together representatives from the event industry and regulatory authorities to examine and discuss the obligations and opportunities for effective and efficient compliance and quality assurance in the area of safe and secure planned public events. The attendees reviewed existing legalities and the proposed legislation related to the production of public events, and discussed the compliance challenges faced by event organizers and the enforcement challenges faced by regulatory agencies. An outcome of the workshop was a draft of a ten point charter for a Code of Professional Conduct for Safe Events.

1 Do no harm
2 Conduct business in a safe and responsible manner
3 Meet or exceed the standard of care exemplified by best practices in the worldwide events industry
4 Identify and access all appropriate reference resources
5 Require training, research and continuous professional development from all role players, including but not limited to staff, volunteers, suppliers, sponsors and others
6 Cause a risk assessment to be performed by a competent person for all events
7 Require prior to the start of any live event a public announcement describing appropriate egress and evacuation steps
8 Each and every event will maintain a life safety plan
9 Safety plans will be reviewed, updated and communicated prior to the event
10 Continually develop and maintain currency in all of the above

This proposed Code of Professional Conduct for Safe Events requires that a commitment to safety must be made by everyone involved in the planning and production of the event project.

Source: Julia Rutherford Silvers (2008) *Risk Management for Meetings and Events* Butterworth-Heinemann

---

Event hazard and risk management and Event Safety Management System

Event hazard risk management is a comprehensive process that must be fully integrated and embedded into all the event plans and throughout the event management process. It involves the protection of people, property, information and other event assets to ensure a safe, successful and sustainable event. It is the duty of every event organizer, producer, manager, supplier and participant, to be proactive in preventing risk of injury from occurring by dealing with hazards before they can cause any harm.

The importance of event hazard management cannot be overstated. If an event's marketing is ineffective the worst that happens is no one comes to the event. If event safety is ineffective, people die.

This book, *Risk and Hazard Management for Festivals and Events*, focuses on managing hazard risk by examining how events managers can implement policies and procedures to safely manage the numerous hazards associated with public events. It concentrates on the hazards and risks in venues and work practices used by the events industry. From an operational perspective, it investigates how festivals can plan and construct facilities and venues in order to make them safe.

Risk and Hazard Management for Festivals and Events is intended to be an instruction text for a management system for the control of hazards at festivals and special events. It provides a comprehensive, fully integrated planning and management mechanism appropriate for major event organisations, festival community committees and individual event managers. The flexible harm minimisation and control system can be applied to events of all types and size – from community run music for children in the park, street parades of vintage cars, all day food and wine fairs, to enormous five-day outdoor music festivals.

An Event Safety Management System (ESMS) is the methodical identification of hazards, assessment of risk posed by the hazards, and the control of those risks, either by eliminating the hazard entirely or by minimising the risk. The `hazard' is the dangerous situation. The `risk' is the likelihood and consequence of the hazard affecting people and properly.

The system encompasses how an event is designed and the policies and procedures used in production and operations to achieve a pre-determined standard of safety. It involves intensive, detailed planning and cooperation to apply control systems to minimise hazards associated with venues, outdoor sites, work procedures, facilities, equipment, and crowds of spectators. It involves planning for emergencies and security, and compliance with legal constraints and requirements.

The ESMS encompasses the processes required for planning consultation and partnerships, and instituting a safety policy. It is proactive, aiming to prevent injury from occurring by dealing with hazards before they can cause any harm by providing methods to identify, assess and control hazardous conditions and practices, including design of venues and festival sites. The system also incorporates and unites the operational functions of crowd control, traffic management, communications, security and emergency protocols.

It does this by first establishing the hazard identification, evaluation and control process. And then examines various areas of risk to further assess particular hazards in those areas. The process begins with the most significant area of event safety concern – the crowd of attendees. The next area of concern is the work practices of the event's staff and contractors. Both these areas can be said to have preventable hazards. But other safety planning concerns are reactive, the response to an emergency. The actions by the event organiser in preparing for emergencies has a direct relationship to its outcome. The various preparatory actions are examined in the second half of the book.

Dr. Peter Wynn-Moylan. Southern Cross University. February 2017.

Acknowledgements

There are some key texts used constantly throughout the completion of this work. The chapters on Occupational Health and Safety, and Safety Management Systems would not be coherent without the work of Liz Bluff, John Toohey, Kerry Borthwick and Richard Archer. Rose Challenger's *Understanding Crowd Behaviours* provided a comprehensive and cogent overview of Crowd Behaviour theory both past and present that has been used throughout the book.

There was an obvious need to have the best advice possible for the sections on emergency response and terrorism prevention measures. Government agencies in Australia and the United Kingdom provide excellent manuals and guidelines. I have heavily incorporated and adapted material from the Australian Emergency Manuals Series, Worksafe Victoria, and the remarkably comprehensive *Counter Terrorism Protective Security Advice for Major Events* from the UK National Counter-Terrorism Security Office (NaCTSO).

The photography is by Karena Wynn-Moylan taken at festivals in Byron Shire NSW. The festival capital of the world.

Chapter 1

Event hazard and risk management

Regulations and legislation

Chapter objectives

This chapter explores:

- Who is responsible for event safety
- Laws enforcing event safety
- Extent of responsibility

An event manager has a responsibility to develop the event organisation's policy and procedures for the safe conduct of its activities to make sure that the event site or venue is free from hazards that could cause injury or illness to their employees or to event attendees. Occupational Health and Safety laws in most countries require employers to use a risk management approach to ensure that their workplaces are safe for everyone who enters them. For an event, the event workplace is defined as the site or the venue in which it is held. Everyone includes the attendees at the event, all service contractors and all staff.

In all aspects of public life there is a heightened tendency towards litigation and many and various insurances are now required for events. While larger events with more creditability and financial backing may be able to obtain insurance with relative ease, smaller community events can sometimes face daunting costs of securing adequate liability cover. The danger for the event manager is that if an incident occurs they may be personally liable.

Criminal prosecution and heavy penalties under health and safety laws for companies and individuals who manage or are responsible for events are a real possibility in the wake of a terrorist incident, particularly if it emerges that core standards and statutory duties have not been met. Particularly relevant to protective security at events are the specific requirements of the UK Health and Safety at Work Act 1974 and Regulations.

The need to focus on proper preparation and prevention to guard against criminal prosecution for safety and security lapses has sharpened in the UK with the introduction of the Corporate Manslaughter Act 2008 and Corporate Homicide Act 2007 and the Regulatory Enforcement and Sanctions Act 2008.

Duty of care

Hazard and risk management planning is increasingly being demanded by event stakeholders such as the government and their agencies, insurance companies, sponsors, law and the courts. Failure to do so is considered a breach of 'duty of care'.

Duty of care is a legal principle that regards the event organiser as a responsible person who must take all reasonable care to avoid acts of omissions that could injure another. It means taking actions that will prevent any foreseeable hazard of injury to the people who are directly involved, or affected by the event: staff, volunteers, performers, audience, host community etc.

It covers not only employees, but also extends to third parties at the workplace, such as drivers making deliveries, food sellers, merchandise stall holders, performers, participants, contestants and all subcontractors. And, perhaps most of all, the audience at the event.

In general, event organisers as employers must ensure the health, safety and welfare of their employees when at the event workplace by:

- maintaining places of work under their control in a safe condition and ensuring safe entrances and exits
- making arrangements for ensuring the safe use, handling, storage and transport of equipment and materials
- providing and maintaining systems of work and working environments that are safe and without risks to health
- providing the information, instruction, training and supervision necessary to ensure the health and safety of employees.

Duty of care has been given a wide interpretation by the courts. In most legislation, duties, for example, are 'unqualified', that is, they are absolute. The event manager, as a representative of the event organising body, must absolutely guarantee a safe and healthy workplace. While the legal system clearly takes extenuating circumstances into account in particular cases, the onus of proof is on the manager to demonstrate that everything was done to prevent an injury occurring.

A test of what is reasonably practicable is usually applied in defence against prosecution in most jurisdictions and usually takes into consideration factors such as:

- foreseeability
- preventability
- reasonableness (for example, cost, administration)
- due diligence.

Causality is a complex legal issue in the context of crowd related accidents and incidents. For example, the definitions of 'reasonably foreseeable' and a 'competent person' performing the risk assessment, approving the site and signing off on the safety aspects of a major event, needs to be fully understood by an event's management.

The basis for imposing a duty of care on a person is that the 'duty of care holder' makes a specified contribution to, and has involvement in and/or manages:

- the activity, place of work, systems or arrangements whereby work is undertaken
- things used in undertaking the work (such as equipment, services or structures)
- the capability (instruction and supervision) of those undertaking the work.

The primary 'duty of care holders' are the persons conducting a business or undertaking. There are also 'specified classes' of duty holders who are:

- those with management or control of event workplace areas
- suppliers of equipment, services and materials
- erectors, installers and suppliers of structures.

A 'duty of care holder' is not allowed to relinquish or pass on their duties to anyone else (Bluff 2009).

A person can have more than one duty, and more than one person may concurrently have the same duty. Each 'duty holder' must comply with the required standard (e.g. reasonably practicable) to the extent of their control over relevant matters, and they must consult, cooperate and coordinate activities with all persons having a duty in relation to the same matter.

In practice this means for example, that the event manager must ensure that a stall holder selling food must do so in accordance with relevant regulations, and is supplied with power, water and waste handling facilities. In turn, the food seller has a duty of care to ensure the facility is clean and safe for staff, the food is correctly stored, cooked and served, and waste is correctly removed.

ALARP: managing hazard to a level that is 'as low as reasonably practicable'

A key principle is that all duty of care holders must eliminate or reduce hazards or risks *so far as is reasonably practicable*. Accordingly, the duties of persons conducting a business or undertaking and other 'duty holders' are to be qualified by *reasonably practicable* defined as meaning:

> that which is, or was, at a particular time reasonably able to be done in relation to health and safety, taking into account and weighing up all relevant matters including:
>
> (a) the likelihood of the hazard or risk eventuating
> (b) the degree of harm that may result if the hazard or risk eventuated
> (c) what the duty of care holder knows, or a person in their position ought reasonably to know about:
>
> > i. the hazard, the potential harm and the risk
> > ii. ways of eliminating or reducing the hazard, the harm or the risk
>
> (d) the availability and suitability of ways to eliminate or reduce the hazard, the harm or the risk
> (e) the costs associated with the available ways of eliminating or reducing the hazard, the harm or the risk, including whether the cost is grossly disproportionate to the degree of harm and the risk.

A test of what is reasonably practicable is usually applied in defence against prosecution under workplace safety legislation in most countries. This takes into consideration factors such as:

- foreseeability
- preventability
- reasonableness (for example, cost, administration)
- due diligence.

In effect, complying with the 'duty of care' so far as is reasonably practicable requires 'duty of care holders' to implement workplace safety management to identify hazards, assess risks (the degree and likelihood of harm) and eliminate or reduce the risk.

Occupational health and safety

There are specific acts of law in almost every country to secure the health and safety of employees and the public. However, legislation and regulations vary widely from country to country and jurisdiction to jurisdiction. For instance, in federal systems such as Germany, Australia and the USA, the laws vary from state to state. The laws have varying degrees of potency, for instance, in Scandinavian countries they cannot be overridden by any other law, whereas in some states in the USA the constitutional right to carry a gun (clearly an issue for event safety) can prevail over safety regulations, although almost all mass gathering events prohibit weapons.

Many of the occupational health and safety (OH&S) issues found in the building and construction industry are those encountered in event management during the production operations phase of an event, particularly if the event is being conducted in a temporary venue or site rather than in a purpose-built facility. There are also similar security and public order issues occurring at events to those found in the licensed premises field.

The event manager must address these legal requirements regardless of the event size. The various laws cover an event manager's responsibilities towards persons who are employees and contractors, as well as non-employees (including volunteers, contestants, participants, performers and, most of all, attendees) when in control of premises used by persons as a place of work. An event's location, whether it is in one place or many, a purpose-built venue, a street festival site, or a parade route, is considered as a place of work.

Therefore, it is unconditionally necessary for event managers to be acquainted with the provisions of the various laws and processes. Event locations must comply with OH&S regulations contained in development application approvals. There are severe penalties for breaches and events can be immediately shut down by compliance officers or police.

Defining occupational health and safety (OH&S)

Before going any further, it is probably necessary to be clear about just what occupational health and safety means. The following definition of 'health' by the World Health Organization is a good place to start.

> ### Definition box 1.1
>
> Health is a state of complete physical, mental and social well-being and not merely the absence of disease and infirmity.
>
> The enjoyment of the highest attainable standard of health is one of the fundamental rights of every human being without distinction of race, religion, political belief, economic or social condition.

The Australian National Occupational Health and Safety Commission Act refers to occupational health and safety matters as relating to one or more of the following:

(a) physiological and psychological needs and well-being of persons engaged in occupations
(b) work-related death
(c) work-related trauma
(d) prevention of work-related death or work-related trauma
(e) protection of persons from, or from risk of, work-related death, or
(f) rehabilitation and retraining of persons who have suffered work-related trauma.
(Toohey et al. 2005)

Occupational health and safety focuses on work practices and has a different focus to other forms of health and safety-related activities, such as public health, environmental protection, traffic safety, consumer protection, fire safety and personal health. However, the boundaries are not always clear cut and there is often overlap. Workplace safety legislation requires, for example, employers and employees to ensure that their work activities do not put third parties, such as visitors and contractors, at risk. There are elements of public safety in workplace safety law, for example, environment and health and safety are connected when production involves waste, or traffic control is required in the public roads and areas surrounding an event precinct.

OH&S objectives usually include:

- protecting third parties at a workplace
- protecting people at work from injury and illness
- providing for consultation and cooperation between employers and employees ensuring that risks are identified, assessed, eliminated or controlled
- providing for continuous monitoring of health and safety standards.

It is possible to simply define workplace safety as activities preventing injuries or illness at work or removing or reducing the risk of such injuries or illness. The emphasis of such definitions is on being 'safe from'. This concentration on the safety aspect of OH&S ignores the health aspect from the larger perspective of human needs that extend beyond physical safety and security to include psychological and social needs and promote the health, safety and welfare of people at work (Thompson and Marks 2001).

In legislation, 'safety' refers to being secure from harm, injury, danger or risk. 'Welfare' refers to the provision of proper event workplace facilities, such as first aid rooms, toilets and washrooms. 'Health', is a state of complete physical, mental and social wellbeing, not merely the absence of disease or infirmity. In effect this is saying that workers need much more than safety from danger, accident or disease to be healthy, thriving human beings. They must have quality of life.

This means, then, that the various safety laws deal not only with protecting people from injuries and fatalities, but also with illnesses and diseases, physical and psychological. If, for example, an employee or group of employees is being harassed, the stress associated with such harassment may lead to health problems. More obvious psychological aspects of work health may include the effects of armed hold-ups or assaults on employees. Less obvious are organisational factors, such as inappropriate shift or roster arrangements and the often excessive workloads common to festivals and events.

Information sources

OH&S information exists in many forms: textual, numerical, graphic, spatial or audiovisual and can be found in sources external and internal to the organisation.

External

- National and state OH&S legislation, codes of practice and guidance material
- Industry standards
- Information provided by OH&S authorities
- Union and industry bodies
- OH&S professional bodies
- Internet, books, journals and magazines

- Manufacturers' specifications, technical information and data
- Research literature
- Manufacturers' manuals
- Safety handbooks

Internal

- Employees
- OH&S policies and procedures
- Work instructions, job and work system analysis
- Risk assessments (past and present)
- Insurance and incident investigation records
- Workers' compensation data
- OH&S reports including workplace inspections

Workplace health and safety responsibilities

The positive, proactive duty of care of senior managers of event organisations, e.g. executive and directors, means they must exercise due diligence to ensure an event's compliance (Bluff 2009). Due diligence means:

- understanding the nature of the operations or undertakings of events
- understanding the hazards and risks within those operations or undertakings
- ensuring the event manager has appropriate resources and processes available to work safely
- ensuring that the event manager has appropriate processes for receiving, considering and responding to information regarding incidents, accidents and hazards
- verifying the implementation of those processes through regular audits and verifying legal compliance.

Persons conducting a business or undertaking

The event manager is known as a 'person conducting a business or undertaking', or PCBU and has a duty to ensure, so far as is reasonably practicable, the health and safety of:

- workers engaged, or caused to be engaged by the event manager
- workers whose activities in carrying out work are influenced or directed by the event manager while the workers are at work at the event.

The event manager also has a duty to ensure that the health and safety of other persons is not put at risk from work carried out as part of the conduct of the event. These duties include requiring the event manager to ensure, so far as is reasonably practicable:

- the provision and maintenance of a work environment that is without risk to health and safety
- the provision and maintenance of safe plant, structures and safe systems of work

7

- the safe use, handling including transport and storage of plant, structures and substances
- the provision of any information, training, instruction or supervision that is necessary to protect all persons from risk to their health and safety arising from work carried out as part of the conduct of the event
- the provision of, and access to, adequate facilities for the welfare of workers at the event workplace
- the monitoring of health of workers and the conditions at the event workplace, for purpose of preventing work-related illness or injury.

The event manager is required to eliminate the risk to health and safety, so far as is reasonably practicable and can be prosecuted for a breach of their duty even if there is no incident or injury, e.g. inaction over an identified hazard can lead to a prosecution.

Consultation

Consultation is a key element in any event workplace health and safety programme. The event manager is required to consult with all workers who will be present at the event and not just the employees of the event organisation. Where there are overlapping duties with other PCBUs such as a 'duty of care holder' from a contractor or service provider, both the Event Manager and the relevant PCBU must consult, cooperate and coordinate activities with each other.

Definition of worker

Workers must comply, so far as they are reasonably able, with any reasonable instruction given by the event manager that allows them to comply with laws and regulations; and cooperate with any reasonable policy or procedure of the event manager that relates to work health and safety.

Effectively, anyone carrying out work for the event is considered to be a worker, including:

- staff employees
- short-term labour
- volunteers and participants
- apprentices/trainees/interns
- sub-contractors and contractors (including performers)

These workers have both rights and duties. These are the right to work in a safe and healthy event workplace (including physical as well as psychological aspects of work) and to have access to information to assist them in working safely and avoiding exposure to unhealthy situations. This means they should have access to the event's safety policies and procedures and the expectations placed on them by these policies and programmes, including having available safety data sheets that provide information on the use of hazardous equipment and work practices.

The significant duties and obligations of workers include refraining from taking any action that would place others at risk, including refusing to act on instructions to carry out an act that they consider to be dangerous or to behave in a way that frivolously disregards common sense caution; and to not wilfully place at risk the workplace health and safety of any person at the workplace. Workers must use safety controls on equipment properly and correctly and not interfere with the workings of safety equipment, and to use personal protective equipment if the equipment is provided by the worker's employer and the worker is properly instructed in its use.

Other persons at an event

Suppliers of equipment and materials for use by people at an event must make sure that these items are safe for use without risks. They must also provide adequate information to ensure their safe use. Likewise, those who erect, install, or operate equipment at an event workplace have an obligation to make sure that the equipment is safely erected or installed and is safe to use when properly used.

Attendees and visitors must take reasonable care for their own health and safety and take reasonable care that their acts or omissions do not adversely affect the health and safety of others. They must comply with any reasonable instruction given by the event manager that complies with laws or regulations.

Overall, employees, volunteers, sub-contractors and all other service suppliers on an event site must cooperate with the event manager to ensure that all the event's safety policies and procedures requirements are met.

Laws, regulations and codes of practice

Apart from the instinctive human concern for our own health and safety and that of others, there are many other reasons for making event workplace safety a priority (Toohey et al. 2005). They include:

- community standards or expectations that organisations have a responsibility for those that work for them
- the loss of staff morale and potential industrial relations problems in the event of death, injury or disease
- legal obligations that require workplaces to be safe and healthy for employees as well as for contractors and visitors
- costs associated with event workplace injury, such as lost time, reduced productivity, staff replacement and retraining costs, as well as loss of business reputation
- costs to employees through reduced quality of life as a result of event workplace injury and disease, reduced income for the injured and their family and the grief endured by everyone involved.

Legislation, regulations and, in some cases, standards together make up what can be described as 'OH&S law'. Most workplace safety laws have regulations that specify in more detail how to comply. Beneath regulations, some jurisdictions have standards that are also mandatory. It is important to note that courts treat breaches of regulations and some mandatory standards in the same way that they treat breaches of a law. Managers need to be aware of both.

At a lower legal level are codes of practice, rules that should be followed unless there is an alternative course of action that achieves the same or better standard of health and safety in the workplace. Some jurisdictions produce guidance material that does not carry the force of law, but which can provide useful information.

While workplace safety laws in each jurisdiction are relatively uniform, the supporting rules present a different picture. These differences reflect the fact that each jurisdiction's workplace safety legislation has been developed separately. Differences in terminology and drafting procedures have created marked differences in the supporting rules. For example, there may be different conditions for breach of a standard as opposed to a regulation. Managers with responsibilities in more than one jurisdiction should compare requirements and draft policies and procedures to meet the most stringent requirements.

Regulations – prescriptive standards

Over time, standards and regulations have developed in their approach. Historically, standards or regulations were prescriptive, detailing what to do in order to make the event workplace safe and comply with the law. There are many such prescriptive or specification standards. For example:

- *Occupational violence*. Public contact workstations must be designed to include an escape route to enable retreat to a safe place in the event of a violent incident.

- *Work at heights*. Where there is a risk that a person could fall at least 2.4 metres or the pitch on a roof is more than 26 degrees, the risk of falling must be prevented by:

  - edge protection
  - a fall protection cover placed over an opening, or
  - a travel restraint system.

- If prevention of falling is not practicable the risk of death or injury due to falling must be prevented or minimised by:
  - use of a fall-arrest harness system, or
  - an industrial safety net.

- There are many other standards applicable to events.

The chief advantage of a prescriptive standard is that it is clear what actions must be taken. Such definite guidelines can be valuable for training as well as planning and managing work.

At the same time, the standards can become complex in detail, requiring manuals to explain how to implement them. They are also not easily applicable to certain hazards, such as organisational stressors. Prescriptive standards can also become out of date when, for example, there are rapid changes to technology affecting work processes and new information on hazards is discovered. Finally, they may often be seen as inflexible, especially when circumstances prevent effective compliance and there are equally good or better ways to reduce the risk.

Performance-based standards

As a result of such shortcomings, a performance-based approach to standard setting is often applied. This means that the standards define the outcomes that must be achieved, not the specific actions to achieve them. Exposure standards are a good example of performance standards in which the outcome is usually expressed as a numeric target.

For example, the Australian National Standard for Occupational Noise limits the maximum permissible event workplace exposure to noise, under certain conditions, to a maximum of 85dB – a figure often exceeded on music festival stages. But there are no details in the standard about how these limits can be achieved.

The chief advantage of such performance-based standards is that they allow people to find ways of achieving the outcome appropriate to the technology being used, the level of resources and the individual workplace. In a word, they are flexible.

However, by themselves, they do not say what to do to achieve the outcome, but often event organisers need or expect such guidance. Additional guidance notes, training and advice are usually required to show how the required outcome might be achieved.

Process standards

Consequently, a third type of standard is adopted: the process standard. These standards identify a particular process or series of steps to be followed to remove or reduce risk in the workplace. Instead of being hazard-specific, this is a more general approach towards all the event workplace hazards, not just those highlighted by particular regulations and standards. It underpins proactive workplace safety law management systems.

The advantage of process standards is that they force employers to be systematic and thorough in the application of each step. They are also capable of being applied widely to different and changing workplaces. In addition, they require training in their application and do not provide definite answers that many look for in regulations or standards. Different people may, for example, come up with conflicting and potentially faulty risk assessments and controls for similar workplaces.

The lesson of all of this is that one type of standard is rarely sufficient. Each of them has its place. What is required to maximise event safety is an effective combination of all three types of standards or regulations in workplace safety law as well as up-to-date information and guidance in their application to assist their use in the event workplace.

Codes of practice

Codes of practice are written to assist with the application of the standards by providing practical guidance at the workplace. Each code of practice provides information about one or more ways of achieving legal requirements. Event managers still have the option of implementing different control measures if these better suit their event, but the onus is on the employer to show how an alternative system meets laws or regulations.

Non-compliance with codes of practice is not illegal. However, in court proceedings, workplace safety inspectors may use non-compliance as evidence of a breach of duty of care on the basis that the information about controlling a particular risk was readily available (in the form of a code of practice) and that the event manager should have complied. Conversely, event managers could use their compliance with a code of practice as evidence to support their meeting duty of care requirements. Because of their role in court proceedings, codes of practice are sometimes referred to as 'evidentiary standards'.

Finally, it is important to remember that 'duty of care' requires the employer to provide a safe and healthy event workplace and not just to comply with the existing regulations or mandatory standards. It may be that some hazardous situations in the event workplace are not addressed by specific regulations, standards or codes of practice. In which case, guidance may be needed from others such as workplace safety law professionals, government event workplace inspectors or other experts such as engineers, scientists, ergonomists or doctors. Failure to seek and use such guidance may result in a breach of the law resulting in fines or imprisonment.

Administration of legislation

Administration of workplace safety legislation rests with a government authority or department depending on the law in that particular country or jurisdiction. It normally involves:

- ensuring compliance through inspections, investigations and enforcement activity
- promoting workplace safety law education and awareness through training, publications and campaigns
- collecting information on and providing analysis of event workplace injuries and illnesses, and for example, safety alerts
- providing advice to government, industry, employees, unions, workplace safety law professionals
- developing regulations, standards and codes of practice.

Workplace safety law authorities sometimes certify tradespeople in high-risk occupations such as electricians, pyrotechnicians, forklift drivers and riggers. Some also have specific responsibilities for approving temporary amusement structures such as big dippers and merry-go-rounds.

Inspections

The main inspection powers usually include:

- making searches, inspections, examinations and tests
- taking samples of any substance or thing (in particular foodstuffs)
- requiring people to answer questions or furnish information
- requiring the event manager to provide assistance and facilities
- gathering and inspecting any documents.

Inspectors may issue:

- investigation notices to stop plant or prevent disturbance of premises in order to allow investigations to proceed effectively
- improvement notices to correct hazardous situations
- prohibition notices to stop hazardous activity.

Inspectors in some jurisdictions may also issue infringement notices, also known as 'penalty notices' or 'on-the-spot fines', but the circumstances vary.

Inspectors use a mixture of proactive inspections, usually targeting high-risk aspects of an event, such as traffic and crowd control processes, erection of temporary structures, food handling, waste processing; and reactive investigations, which are investigations into serious incidents or complaints from employees or the public. Proactive investigations look at either the workplace safety management system and its application or specific systems of work, rather than being random and arbitrary, and are often linked to approval or licencing for the use of public spaces or temporary sites.

Notification

Workplace safety laws and regulations require:

- immediate notification of incidents involving fatalities and serious injuries and illnesses; the regulations define what 'serious' means
- notification of less serious incidents, for example, where workers' compensation is payable.

Again, the regulations identify the types of incidents and the timeframe for notification. Some jurisdictions require notification of incidents involving near misses and damage or potential damage to dangerous items of plant such as generators, or temporary structures such as stages or scaffolded seating.

The regulations specify the details required in the notification and who is to be contacted – the workplace safety law authority and/or the workers' compensation insurer. They also specify the nature of any record keeping.

Waivers

Participation in events, as a competitor or partaker in activities such as a parade or a performance workshop has the potential for an adverse occurrence that could result in a legal action. Consider the following scenario: an event includes a 'Fire Challenge' involving volunteers from the audience twirling fire sticks. Joe Smith burns his arm and sues the event organisation for damages relating to his injury. Scenarios like this are all too common. But is it fair? Joe volunteered to do the activity.

Many individuals, live in a 'sue or be sued' society in which it's a natural reaction to blame someone other than themselves for their injuries. But since participation in many event activities is voluntary, more and more organisations are seeking to shift the risk of liability that may arise out of participation in the activity to the participants themselves. In other words, if a person wants to participate in the activity, he or she must assume the risk of any potential liability.

Some event programmes offer potentially dangerous activities that increase the risk that a participant will get injured and try to hold the event organiser liable. In such instances, every participant in an event activity should be required to sign a carefully drafted release. While a fairly detailed document is best, a more general release, sometimes referred to as 'assumption of risk', may suffice.

Manage the risk

Part of risk management is risk avoidance. Certain activities simply should not be offered. It's not a good idea, for example, to conduct a 10K run for senior citizens, in the tropics, with no nearby medical facilities.

Most events use outside contractors to conduct such activities. While many activities are usually not considered dangerous, accidents can, and do, occur. If the participant's injury is severe enough and if the negligence is somewhat obvious (e.g., selecting a highly rigorous course for a 'fun run'), the event organiser can be swept into any resulting litigation on a theory of negligent selection of the contractor.

Accordingly, event organisers should exercise due care in selecting their contractors. Before signing a contract, investigate the company's precautionary systems and safety record. Are the employees experienced? Do they have the required licenses?

A well-written agreement with contractors is required that carefully spells out duties and responsibilities. To the extent possible, the agreement should minimise the indemnification the event organisation must give to the contractor and maximise the indemnification obtained from the contractor. Also, be sure that the contractor has adequate insurance and have the event named as an additional insured party on the contractor's insurance policy.

The event organisation will still retain a certain amount of risk. It is prudent to prepare for any circumstances that reasonably can be anticipated and to inform, warn and educate attendees about the risks.

Transfer the risk

A form of risk transfer is to ask participants to sign a waiver and release, a document by which the signer agrees to give up any right to recover damages from the other entity, and to release that entity from all potential liability, in return for the right to participate in the activity. If well drafted, it can discourage potential claimants from the outset, and if a claim is brought, can facilitate a quick dismissal.

While not providing a guarantee against liability, release and waiver documents provide an excellent layer of protection. The document states that the participant knows that the activity he or she is electing to do is potentially hazardous, and that he or she releases the organisation from liability due to any resulting injuries and waives any claims against the organisation for liability. In other words, the individual is taking sole responsibility and liability for any injuries arising out of participation in the activity.

In order to be legally enforceable, a release and waiver must be voluntarily entered into, and the participant must have full knowledge of the potential risks associated with the activity. As to the voluntary element, participants make their own choices as to whether to participate in the activity and to sign the release. Regarding the 'knowledge' element, participants must be made aware of the potential dangers associated with the activity beforehand so that they can sign the release with full awareness of associated risks.

When the document meets these elements, protection from liability is extended to the organisation for injuries that are inherent in the activity (e.g. getting hit by a golf ball during a golf tournament). If the injury is caused by something other than an inherent risk (e.g. a golf buggy accident), the protection may not apply.

The release can be written to be specific to one activity, or it can be written broadly to cover all activities occurring during the event. Keep in mind that a minor (anyone under age 18) cannot sign a release; rather, a parent or guardian must sign the release on the minor's behalf.

The form, content and scope of the release and waiver must be carefully considered. A broad release to relieve the organisation of liability for any personal injury or property damage arising out of participation in an event is not sufficient. The attendee must be aware and understand the risks involved in the specific activity and detail all of the risks that could occur. So, there is a need to be explicit about what potential legal claims are being waived. Releases should be for a specific activity to take place at a specific time and place. Generally speaking, the more narrowly focused the waiver and release, the more likely that it will be enforceable.

Event organisers need to be sensitive about when they ask participants to sign releases. Sufficient time must be provided for the participant to consider the release. It is good practice to send early notice of the requirement to sign a release as a condition of participation (and even a copy of the release), then, as participants arrive at the event, have them sign the releases. If a participant does not want to sign a release and waiver, a 'zero tolerance' rule is best, meaning that everyone signs the release and waiver or they do not participate.

Process

First, provide each participant with a comprehensive and well-drafted release prior to the start of the event. The release should detail, with specificity, the risks to be faced inherent in the activity (e.g., bad weather, treacherous terrain). Inserting detail may possibly frighten participants, but in the end it can eliminate or substantially reduce an event organiser's liability in the event that something goes wrong.

Second, think about having an activity leader (e.g., a marathon running coach) provide a safety discussion for the participants before detailing what can go wrong and how to deal with it.

Third, give the participants ample time to review the release prior to signing it and the opportunity to ask questions of the guide or activity leader. If advance sign-up for the activity is required, provide the release as part of the online registration process.

Fourth, conduct due diligence when hiring subcontractors to run an activity. Require that the company have all necessary licences and training, and demand that they carry liability insurance in an appropriate amount.

Finally, insure against the risk. Not all risks can be managed or transferred. Consider the scope of planned activities and the degree and likelihood of exposure. Then, balance that against the cost of insurance. Based on that analysis, purchase adequate additional insurance for the event. Most commercial general liability policies for conferences will not cover 'unusual' activities, such as rock climbing, horseback riding, and others. Securing sufficient backup insurance for a few additional dollars could prove to be well worth the investment.

Summary

- The event manager is responsible for ensuring the event site or venue, and the activities conducted at an event, is free from hazards that could cause injury or illness to their employees or to event attendees.

- 'Duty of care' is a legal principle that regards the event organiser as a responsible person who must take all reasonable care to avoid acts of omissions that could injure another, taking actions that will prevent any foreseeable hazard of injury to the people who are directly involved or affected by the event: staff, volunteers, performers, audience, host community etc.
- The primary 'duty of care holders' are the people conducting a business or undertaking. There are also 'specified classes' of duty holders, who are those with management or control of event workplace areas, suppliers of equipment, services and materials, erectors, installers, and suppliers of structures. A 'duty of care holder' is not allowed to relinquish or pass on their duties to anyone else.
- ALARP – is controlling a hazard to a level that is 'as low as reasonably practicable'. The associated key principle is that all duty of care holders must eliminate or reduce hazards or risks to as far as is *reasonably practicable*.
- Complying with the 'duty of care' so far as is reasonably practicable requires 'duty of care holders' to implement workplace safety management to identify hazards, assess risks (the degree and likelihood of harm), and eliminate or reduce the risk.
- There are specific acts of law in almost every country to secure the health and safety of employees and the public. However, legislation and regulations vary widely from country to country and jurisdiction to jurisdiction.
- Occupational Health and Safety laws in most countries require employers to use a risk management approach to ensure that their workplaces are safe for everyone who enters them. This means that attendees to an event are covered under these and the other safety laws that protect people from injuries and fatalities, illnesses and diseases. For an event, the workplace is defined as the site or the venue in which it is held.
- Other safety-related legislation, such as public health, environmental protection, traffic safety, consumer protection, fire safety and personal health, also apply to events and compliance is also the event manager's responsibility.
- Most workplace safety laws have regulations and standards that are mandatory. Courts treat breaches of regulations and standards as breaches of a law. Codes of practice are rules that should be followed unless there is an alternative course of action that achieves the same or better standard of health and safety in the workplace.
- A Waiver and Release is a document in which the signer agrees to release an event from all potential liability, in return for the right to participate in an activity.

Bibliography

ACT Occupational Health and Safety Council (2005) *The Scope and Structure Review of the Occupational Health and Safety Act 1989*. Australian Capital Territory Government.

Allen, J., O'Toole, W., McDonnell, I. and Harris, R. (2011) *Festival & Special Event Management*, 5th edn. Milton, QLD: John Wiley and Sons.

Bluff, E., Gunningham, N. and Johnstone, R. (2004) *OHS Regulation for a Changing World of Work*. Sydney: Federation Press.

Bluff, L. (2009) *The National Review into Model OHS Laws: A Paper Examining the 'Specified Classes' of Duty Holders; Reasonably Practicable and Risk Management; and Access to OHS Advice*. National Research Centre for OHS Regulation. Australian National University.

Mellor, N. and Veno, A. (1998) *Public Events: Safety and Security Strategies*. Victoria: Centre for Police and Justice Studies, Monash University.

Rodgers, T. (2013) *Conferences and Conventions*. Oxford: Butterworth-Heinemann.

Sherriff, B. (2003) Workplace OHS consultation: legal and practical issues, in *Australian Master OHS and Environmental Guide*. Sydney: CCH.

Silvers, J.R. (2008) Risk Management for Meetings and Events. Oxford: Butterworth-Heinemann.

Thompson, W. and Marks, F. (2001) *Understanding New South Wales Occupational Health and Safety Legislation*, 3rd edn. North Ryde: CCH Australia.

Toohey, J., Borthwick, K. and Archer, R. (2005) *OH&S in Australia*. Melbourne: Thomson.

Worksafe Victoria. (2006) *Advice for Managing Major Events Safely*, 1st edn. Victoria: Government of Victoria.

Chapter 2

Event Safety Management System (ESMS)

Chapter objectives

This chapter identifies and discusses:

- An Event Safety Management System
- Processes to evaluate and control Hazards

An Event Safety Management System (ESMS) is a coordinated and documented set of planning activities undertaken by an event organiser that lead to a formalised set of procedures for the effective management of safety at the venue or event by integrating safety practices into all event production and operational activities.

An ESMS is centred on the notion of 'continual improvement'. One of the advantages of cyclical or annual events is the capacity to learn from event to event and improve the standard of safety performance. One-off events, however, often do not have this luxury and are more reliant on the expertise of the event team and contractors to learn and improve from safety incidents at prior events.

The ESMS planning and management process should assist an event organiser to make planning decisions informed by risk management, and reduce all safety hazards to ALARP. This will include:

- the organisational structure and allocation of responsibilities
- an event safety policy
- work procedures and processes
- crowd and traffic control
- terrorism prevention measures
- emergency response
- monitoring and review.

An ESMS plan process communicates and consults with all relevant stakeholders in order to:

- establish the event's context
- identify significant safety hazards
- analyse safety hazards in terms of likelihood and consequence considering current controls
- evaluate the risks against a pre-determined risk criteria
- assess possible treatment options (controls)
- implement selected controls through use of protocols
- monitor and review hazard management processes to make any necessary changes.

The general structure of an ESMS is:

- OHS policy and the event organisation's safety policy
- senior management leadership and commitment
- structure and responsibility
- objectives and targets
- hazard management action plans
- implementation procedures and protocols
- training and competency
- communication, consultation and reporting
- emergency response preparedness
- measurement and management review.

Event safety policy

An event safety policy defines the commitment that the event organiser makes towards hosting a safe event. The event safety policy is a document that communicates the values, objectives and broad commitments of the event organiser to conducting a safe event. It represents a high-level commitment by the event organiser that sets the tone for how, and to what degree, the system for managing safety will be supported.

Ultimately the entire ESMS should be designed to support and achieve the commitments made under the event safety policy. Without 100 per cent commitment from the event's executive and senior management, the risk management process will not be effective. The same applies to an event's safety culture. It may be more difficult for staff to develop a positive safety culture if the senior managers are not actively communicating and embracing the concept themselves. If an event organiser wants the event team to have a high-quality ESMS, senior management must openly and actively communicate and practise a safety policy.

Practical ways in which an event's senior management can convey strong leadership and commitment include:

- ensuring adequate budget is available for addressing safety issues
- hazard management items are regularly put on the agenda for discussion at senior event management meetings
- establishing safety performance and reporting targets for each functional area manager
- setting specific hazard management tasks in individual operational area managers' job descriptions and employment contracts
- ensuring safety issues are raised and discussed during event debriefs
- checking that specific safety obligations are included in contracts of suppliers
- placing the highest priority on safety when making decisions, above other potentially conflicting agendas.

Some suggested items and themes for inclusion in an event safety policy are:

- statements conveying management commitment signed by the CEO
- objectives or targets for personal injury performance (e.g. number of medical treatments per 1,000 spectators, injury free bump-in phase)
- compliance with OHS legislation
- a commitment towards a high level of event security
- a reference to the safety of participants, entertainers, members of the public, event staff and contractors; competent and trained staff.

Example: event safety policy

- We are committed to ensuring the health and safety of all participants in the staging of our event.
- All stakeholders participate through consultation to deliver a safe and successful event, each sharing responsibility for one another.

- We will endeavour to identify and manage all hazards and where possible eliminate them in our workplace.
- We will work with all regulatory and all other authorities to ensure compliance with relevant legislation.
- Where no guidelines exist, we will actively work with our partners and stakeholders to achieve best practices.
- The ultimate goal is to stage a successful event with no harm to people or damage to the environment.

Once developed and signed off by the relevant senior executive, the policy must be communicated across the organisation to ensure all internal (e.g. staff and volunteers) and relevant external (e.g. contractors and stall traders) stakeholders are familiar with it. Ways to communicate the event safety policy to relevant internal and external stakeholders include:

- placing copies of the event safety policy within all tender documentation for procurement of goods and services
- prescribing compliance with the event safety policy, event SMS and hazard management plan within all contracts (for higher risk contractors, further prescription will be required within their terms and conditions of their contract)
- inserting copies of the event safety policy and hazard management plan in staff and training manuals
- before the event, displaying the event safety policy and hazard management protocols in visible locations throughout the event management office
- posting highly visible copies of the event safety policy and hazard management protocols in key locations during the event for staff, contractors and workforce to notice (e.g. staff break areas, event management offices, etc.)
- referring to the event safety policy and hazard management plans during staff and contractor inductions
- providing access to the event safety policy and hazard management plans and protocols on the event website.

Organisational structure and allocation of responsibilities

Hazard management activity begins by establishing staff roles of responsibility, accountability and authority. Some positions will have specific regulatory responsibilities attached to them, for example, traffic controller, while others will be more general.

Each person involved with the event production and operations phases needs to know their responsibilities and duties, who they are accountable to, and what they are accountable for. The standards by which their outcomes are measured, and, what authority they have to carry out their responsibilities, need to be documented in the job description or contract, and fully understood.

How responsibilities, accountabilities and authority are identified will depend on:

- the position held and the tasks carried out
- what corporate hazard management policy and the law requires
- the hazards associated with the job.

Responsibility, accountability and authority begin with the event manager and cascade through the organisation, including to contractors. Everyone should know what they are supposed to do as part of their hazard management responsibility, to what standard, and what actions they may take to ensure that their safety duties are fulfilled. This needs to be documented, regularly reviewed and checked to see that everyone with a hazard management responsibility is complying with the event's safety policy and the law.

As a good test, imagine an accident has occurred and it has reached court. Can it be demonstrated clearly that everything had been done to ensure that everyone knew what their hazard management responsibilities were, what standards had been met, and what ability they had to carry out their responsibilities?

Health and safety officer

Large events often employ a specialist health and safety officer to assist the organisation, its managers and employees, supervise health and safety in the workplace in line with corporate policy and the law. This normally includes:

- reporting to the senior management team on hazard management matters by conducting safety inspections
- providing administrative support for consultative arrangements
- preparing the hazard management programme
- developing risk management strategies and monitoring their progress establishing appropriate information and training programmes reporting and assisting in the investigation of incidents.

As part of the management team, a safety officer also has obligations to inform other managers and the event manager of changes to legislation and codes of practice.

Even so, the responsibility for health and safety lies with the organisation and all its employees – managers, supervisors and staff – not just with the health and safety officer. This should be made clear in the policy. It is a major error to solely identify one person or a small team with complete health and safety responsibility and the (impossible) task of implementing it by themselves. Hazard management activity must be owned by all managers involved and not be or be seen to be owned by the health and safety officer or any other individual.

Partnerships

No event manager can create a safety management system and a set of procedures without consultation with a range of stakeholders. It is essential to consult staff, police, emergency services, traffic authorities, ambulance services, local government, sub-contractor facilities and service suppliers, and representatives of each stakeholder group to conduct an assessment of the potential hazards associated with an event's programme of activities, production operations, the venue and/or the site, and establish the required processes to minimise the identified hazards.

An awareness of the nearest emergency services and their working requirements is mandatory for the event management. In addition to the crucial relationship with police and emergency services, there are other significant partners for event managers in the area of hazard management, such as providers of training for volunteers in traffic management, serving of alcohol, materials handling, etc., and health and drug agencies.

A consultation process, in which everyone's knowledge and cooperation is required, is critical to the success of safety planning. The objective is to gain greater understanding by and agreement between all parties involved in a potential hazard issue. Formal consultative arrangements allow all parties and stakeholders to see that information sharing and clear communication are genuine and two-way so that decision making in general is informed and applicable. Consultation is typically required in the following instances:

- when risks are to be assessed or assessments are being reviewed
- when decisions are to be made on control measures
- when monitoring procedures are to be introduced or altered
- when decisions are to be made about the adequacy of facilities
- when changes are being proposed to premises, systems of work, to equipment or substances used for work
- when decisions are to be made about the consultative procedures.

Early planning consultation with police, emergency and government authorities will require access to key event planning documentation – site layout, crowd control measures, traffic management plans; and key information – size and demographics of expected crowd, types of performance, duration. Often this information is required when gaining approvals to conduct the event and involve compliance with regulations and laws. All safety aspects of the event should be included in the preliminary event planning discussions, and continue throughout all subsequent production and operational planning.

Consultation must be reciprocal in which everyone affected is given the opportunity to consider the issues and have their opinions heard and valued. A formal consultation is one that is conducted with advance notice given of the issues to be examined, where everyone has the opportunity to contribute, and where decisions and actions are recorded and distributed. These procedures ensure that the event operations are conducted with a systematic approach to health and safety. The meetings can be used to gather input for safety audits, hazard identification and risk assessment processes, communicating hazard alerts, carrying out surveys using checklists and conducting research.

Formal consultation is only part of the picture, informal, day-to-day consultation in its broadest form should be standard management practice. Consultation outside formal meetings needs to occur as part of day-to-day planning processes, provided everyone is alerted to deal with issues and has sufficient information to do so. Informal safety consultation can be included in staff and sub-contractor meetings particularly for obtaining feedback on procedures.

Complacency is an issue to be aware of during event preparation, plans should be context and location specific. Also, successful execution of an annual event in previous years does not negate the need to thoroughly plan and prepare for the forthcoming event. Similarly, just because an event has been successful in one location, it should not be assumed that it will be successful with the same preparation and control measures in another location. For example, an event taking place in London will have different requirements to the same event taking place in Melbourne.

It is important to strike a balance between operational practicalities and creativity. Often, a large proportion of the budget is allocated to artistic elements, to make the event look impressive. However, the operational element, i.e., making the event run effectively and safely, is of equal importance.

An event should be considered from a system-wide perspective, i.e., taking not only the event itself into account, but also factors in the surrounding area, in order to fully understand the wider implications of the event being organised. For instance, it is important to consider whether other events are happening at the same time in the same area or close by, as this will alter the profile of the event and the likely crowds expected. It is beneficial to avoid a clash of events wherever possible. Adopting this approach necessitates interaction with other agencies from other geographical areas, e.g., councils, transport authorities.

A crucial area of joint agency collaboration which currently appears to be lacking is that between venue architects/designers and event organisers/managers. Crowd event personnel are rarely involved in the design stage and, therefore, venues are often constructed against the best practices of crowd management and, instead, are designed to look aesthetically appealing. To avoid this, those commissioned to design venues for large crowd events should communicate with, and listen to, the expert advice of event organisers in the initial planning stages. This should better enable architects and designers to create crowd-friendly venues.

Multi-agency teamwork

A multi-agency approach, drawing on the expertise of police, fire and ambulance services, local authorities and event organisers, for example, should be promoted and adopted. In addition, a hierarchical model, comprising chief executives, senior officers, a safety advisory group, and a team of event planners should be utilised. This will enable the event to be considered from multiple perspectives which should increase the likelihood of all potential problems being covered.

Included as part of the multi-agency event team should be disabled individuals – e.g., people in wheelchairs, since they are best placed to advise what disabled access and facilities will be most appropriate for a crowd event. Reliance on able-bodied advisors is much less satisfactory.

All agencies to be involved should be introduced on site as early in the process as possible. This should help to build a sense of team solidarity, enable all individuals to learn from each other and create a common body of knowledge, and allow the various strengths and weaknesses of different parties to be assessed.

If an event is to be successful, it is important that the multi-agency event team continues to work together as a united team throughout the whole event, from the early planning and table top exercises through to event delivery. This should enable a bond to develop between all involved increasing levels of trust.

It is critical to identify early in the process the key personnel, and assign their individual roles and responsibilities. All parties should be aware of their own roles and responsibilities, and of the roles and responsibilities of others, to ensure successful integration of all agencies. It is important to be aware of the weaknesses of different members of the event team – e.g., who is more risk averse, who is more likely to take bigger risks, who will need more support. This awareness should develop over time as the team work together, and should enable the team to know, for instance, when people will need additional support, when more consideration needs to be given to taking certain risks, and when information received may be more cautious.

For a multi-agency approach to be successful, all parties must be prepared to work alongside one another and compromise when necessary. Similarly, it is important to trust the judgements and opinions of fellow team members in their specific areas of expertise. Other parties may have concerns about certain issues, but providing those concerns are addressed during event preparation and contingencies are in place to manage incidents should they arise, this should be sufficient.

All meetings should be structured and documented, with actions noted and followed up as appropriate. Consistency of terminology between all agencies involved in a particular crowd event – and within the crowd event industry more generally, is a key issue for the smooth running of an event. At present, however, terminology used is not consistent. For example, there is inconsistency in official guidelines, regarding safe crowd densities and capacities for different venues. The concept of 'a crowd' differs considerably between individuals and, therefore, it is difficult to ensure all parties are working from the same baseline.

Fundamental crowd event terms, such as 'major incident', 'stampede', 'crush', which are highly emotive and carry serious consequences, are often perceived differently by distinct agencies. What one party believes to be a major incident, another more experienced party may not, and this can have subsequent effects on the level of action taken.

'Stampede' is a particular trigger term that can be used to transfer blame from an authority's poor crowd control procedures onto the victims by claiming panic was the prime cause of a disaster. Case study 4 in the Appendix, the Koh Pich Bridge disaster, is an example.

Different authorities often have different approaches to crowd event management. This can be particularly problematic when one event spans several authority regions, as there is then inconsistency within the same event. A multi-agency approach, drawing on the expertise and perspectives of a wide range of individuals, should be used.

All parties must be prepared to work together as a united team, and be aware of their own roles and responsibilities, and those of the other agencies. The agency members who will comprise the event team should meet as early as possible in the event preparations, to enable team-working throughout the process and to build a sense of team solidarity. Consistency of crowd event terminology between all agencies is key.

Implementing a safety planning process

With all hazard management roles specified, planning the implementation of the event safety policy can commence. A documented plan or process based on an understanding of what is required is needed to direct implementation. Everything flows from the policy which should state what the general requirements are, which can include:

- complying with the law
- meeting any company-specific standards
- enterprise agreements with unions
- standards
- industry best practice.

Where the organisation spans a number of jurisdictions and providing there is no conflict, the highest standards should be used. Jurisdictions provide regulations, codes and guidance material to explain in greater detail what is required. Industry standards will have specific requirements. Due to special site or programme content issues, an event's policy may have even more stringent standards. In addition to having a hazard management policy and organising hazard management responsibilities and consultation, previously discussed, the following requirements are found in a hazard management process:

- training management and workers in hazard management
- gathering hazard management information, collecting data, analysing data and managing records
- identifying hazards and managing risk
- health and safety policies and procedures to deal with hazards peculiar to the specific workplace, for example, manual handling, stress, alcohol, motor vehicles, confined spaces, and for inspecting workplaces
- preparing for emergencies
- notifying, reporting and investigating incidents
- providing medical facilities and first aid resources
- compensating and rehabilitating injured workers.

Training in hazard management needs to be given to all workers appropriate to their position. As with all jobs, competencies need to be identified and procedures put in place to make sure that workers have the necessary competencies at the level required.

Identifying activities

The next step is to assess how current organisational arrangements and activities match the requirements. Managers, supervisors, employees and contractors need to be involved to provide information on their ability to conform to specific regulations, codes of practice and guidance material.

There will be requirements that are being met and requirements that need further attention and gaps between what should be and what is. The size of the gap will vary and some will be able to be fixed relatively easily. Others may suggest a need of special attention. In discussion with those affected, identify how the gap can best be closed and if hazard specialists or technical advisers are required to help close it. If closing the gap involves significant costs, set out all the options, their comparative effectiveness and full costing to provide reasons for the preferred option. In this process, investigate if the proposed safety activities are likely to achieve their objectives.

Hazard and risk management process

The terms 'hazard' and 'risk' need to be defined and understood. A hazard is any one thing or situation with the potential to cause harm to people, and a risk is the likelihood of a hazard causing harm and the seriousness of the potential harm. There is a need to distinguish between accepted and commonly used definitions of hazard and risk as there is empirical evidence to suggest these terms are far from well understood by many persons with OHS responsibilities. In fact every day expressions such as 'safety problems' and 'safety issues' are in more common usage, and safety problems and solutions are often intermixed. To the extent that the terms hazard and risk are used, they are often mistakenly used interchangeably.

> ### Definition box 2.1
>
> The 'hazard' is the dangerous situation.
> The 'risk' is the likelihood and consequence of the hazard affecting people and property.

'Hazard management' is the systematic identification of hazards, the assessment of risk posed by the hazards and the control of those risks, either by eliminating the hazard entirely or by minimising the risk. It encompasses how event safety is designed and operated, and the policies and procedures event managers use in operations to maintain facilities and work processes to a pre-determined standard of safety, serviceability and appearance.

Hazardous risks should be detected during the design planning phase of an event project. Every attempt should be made to eliminate hazards by designing them out when temporary structures, equipment and work systems are planned. Specific strategies should be developed to deal with certain crises or risks which may occur before, during as well as after the event.

The management process consists of well-defined steps in which, when taken in sequence, support better decision making by contributing to a greater insight into risks and their impacts, and involves methodically:

- analysing the real life framework surrounding an activity (the chance of something happening that will impact on the event, its audience, or the location)
- rating the likelihood and consequence of a particular negative event occurring
- implementing avoidance and/or mitigation strategies to ensure that aims can be achieved regardless of a particular risk or hazard.

The principles of hazard management are to treat or tolerate hazards through the application of appropriate controls to a pre-determined acceptable level. Risks that are analysed as being above this level and unacceptable are terminated. There are four key steps:

1 establishment of an event safety management system policy
2 assessment of hazards
3 application and implementation of preventative measures – controls and protocols
4 monitoring and reporting.

Hazard management definitions

Hazard management processes are directed towards the effective management of potential opportunities for harm to employees and attendees. An important feature of the processes is understanding and applying common terminology. The following OH&S terms provide a list of standard words and expressions that can describe the possible problems and at the same time analyse them.

Definition box 2.2

Hazard: A source of potential injury or illness; or a situation with a potential to cause injury or illness.

Incident: Any unplanned event that either caused or had potential to cause injury or illness.

Risk: The chance of something happening that will impact on objectives. It is usually measured in terms of likelihood and consequence.

Safety hazard: The likelihood and consequence of an injury or illness occurring.

Consequence: A consequence is the outcome or impact of an incident. It can be measured either in qualitative or quantitative terms. There is often more than one consequence to a specific incident.

Likelihood: A form of qualitative description of frequency and probability.

Stakeholders: People and organisations that may affect, or be affected by, or perceive themselves to be affected by, a decision or activity that relates to an event.

Hazard management: The application of a systematic approach to identifying, assessing and controlling hazard across the event.

Control policies: Procedures, processes, practices or devices that minimise or eliminate harm.

Residual risk: The remaining level of risk once a hazard treatment measure has been applied.

Documentation: Proof of hazard management is not just an incident free, successful event, it is the documents that recorded the hazards that are an integral part of the management of the event. These include incident report sheets and a hazard register. They make up the hazard management planning document.

Hazard audit: The aim of the hazard audit is to allow the event organisation to know where they are with respect to the standard in the industry. It helps to identify the gaps.

> Australian Standard: Risk Management (AS/NZS 4360-2004) and
> Australian Standard: Occupational Health and Safety
> Management Systems: Specification (AS 4801-2000).

Hazard management is the process to apply control systems to minimise the risk of injury by providing methods to identify, assess and control hazardous conditions and practices. The outcome is to manage the risk presented by a hazard to a level that is 'as low as reasonably practicable' – a process known as **ALARP**. ALARP applies the concept of Hazard Management by treating or tolerating hazards through the application of appropriate controls to a pre-determined acceptable level. Risks that are analysed as being above this level and unacceptable are terminated.

Hazard evaluation

Hazard evaluation is the starting point of the process to apply control systems to mini-mise the risk of injury. For planning purposes event risks can be simply divided into two categories: *Control* and *Respond*.

Control risks are those hazards associated with venues, outdoor sites, work pro-cedures, facilities, equipment and crowds of spectators, which can be controlled by proactive intervention to prevent injury from occurring by minimising the risk before it can cause any harm.

Respond hazards are those that cannot be controlled, emergencies caused by natu-ral causes – extreme weather, earthquake, illness; by accident – fire, collision; and by malevolence – riot, terrorist attack; that can only be responded to with emergency procedure training, protocols and facilities.

Establish the context

Consult staff, suppliers and representatives of each stakeholder group to conduct a hazard assessment. This involves analysing each activity of the event to determine what and how things can go wrong. Existing contingency and emergency action plans should be reviewed to ensure their relevance and be updated if required. Similar events can be assessed to gain an understanding of how to implement new procedures or technology.

The programme design of the event is the first and foremost subject for investiga-tion. What elements of the programme contain potential hazards. Artistic designers constantly seek to incorporate creativity into their events to deliver the wow factor for their clients and audiences. They will propose exciting event concepts not imagined could occur in a venue, they may want to put a gigantic entertainment stage in front of a bank of fire exit doors, use pyrotechnics in conjunction with helium-filled bal-loons on the dinner tables, drape the walls or ceiling with flammable fabric, or create a giant maze with bales of hay. Such artistic elements not only have the potential to captivate the audience, but also the potential to jeopardise attendees and the venue if not properly managed.

This is why it's imperative that the event's safety personnel liaise with the artistic designer in the earliest stages of planning a site or venue's usage. This ensures the site or venue limitations can educate the designer regarding what can and can't be done, and why. This also offers the opportunity to discover alternatives that will still meet the designer's vision within the compliance restrictions of the venue. In many cases, an exemption may be possible, given that sufficient safeguards are incorporated into the event plan.

The next element of the process involves six distinct areas of hazard identification:

1. the site or venue in which the event is to be held
2. the production equipment and facilities, and work practices
3. crowd control
4. the operational work practices
5. security and first aid
6. emergencies.

The characteristics of each hazard needs to be identified and described – how it occurs and how it affects people, such as the extent of damage and long term effects. Also factors relating to concentration and time should be recorded. A reliable measure of exposure as well as a standard to compare it against is needed. Exposure can vary greatly in different locations and with differing processes.

The main steps in identifying hazardous conditions

Hazard identification does not only involve identifying the hazards themselves but should also include identification of 'contributory events' or problem scenarios which contribute to the hazards, the assessment of how likely they are to occur and what happens when they do.

- Identify the hazardous nature of the condition.
- Select a suitable measuring technique.
- Determine from regulations/standards whether monitoring is required.
- Determine whether any exposure standard is involved.
- Assess workplace environmental conditions.
- Collect and document data, analyse, evaluate.
- Report findings and recommendations.

Checklists

A set of safety checklists is a useful tool for the evaluation of the facilities and operational processes used to conduct an event. Each checklist should contain questions about hazard and risk issues that can be examined by using on-site personal observation about a particular aspect of the event work practices or venue facilities. For examples, see the checklist resources on the companion website.

Generic checklists are useful, but often contain items that are either superfluous or lack specificity. It is preferable that customised checklists are created for each event based on generic lists, modified for an event's particularities of location, activities and attendance.

An example might be:

	Yes	No
Are the entrances, exits, stairways, gangways and ramps adequate for the expected attendance?		
Is the venue in a clean and sanitary condition?		
Does the venue have adequate lighting?		
Can it be ensured that crowds queuing do not block entrances, exits or pedestrian flow?		
Can non-drinking areas be cordoned off from drinking areas?		

Are equipment, installations and components essential to the safety of persons using the venue maintained in a condition that ensures their proper performance?		
Are all electrical items working properly and regularly maintained?		
Are there clear instructions and training in the use of appliances and equipment?		
Are all electrical cords regularly inspected to ensure they are in good condition?		
Are electrical items protected by a safety switch?		
Are stair, carpet and floor coverings firmly fastened?		
Does the seating enable people to move freely between rows?		
Are entrances, car parks and paths all well-lit and maintained?		
Are stairs and floors in good repair?		
Are exits clear of obstructions?		
Are exit doors easily opened from inside?		
Have adequate arrangements been made to ensure toilets are kept clean and serviceable during the event?		

A simple checklist such as the one above can identify a deficiency or a hazard, but fails to provide the detail required for hazard management planning. A more useful checklist would include a hazard description and evaluation rating, and an action instruction. For example:

What potential risks have you identified?	Date inspected	What problem was detected (if any)?	Likelihood A,B,C,D,E	Impact A,B,C,D	Risk rating H,M,L priority	Who will fix the problem?	When will it be fixed?	Completed (signed off)
Is the car park and the surrounding area adequately lit?								
Are the entrance and exit areas clear and free of obstructions?								
Is there adequate access for emergency vehicles?								
Are parking spots clearly marked?								
Is there a separate entrance and exit to encourage a directional flow of traffic?								
Are there rules for pedestrians in the car park?								
Are shrubs and trees trimmed to minimise the risk of physical injury and ensure maximum visibility?								
Is there a separate parking area for staff?								
Are surfaces well maintained?								
Is signage visible and able to be seen at night?								
Are there sufficient spaces for disabled people?								

This form of checklist not only identifies the hazard but allocates a risk rating and a planning priority level. You can find an example in the checklist resources on the companion website.

Evaluation of hazards

Once the hazard is identified it must be ranked or classified according to its probability of occurrence and the potential consequence of its impact should it occur. Establish a classification system to rank the impact as high, medium or low – thereby assigning priority to certain hazards for further action based on a criteria of probability of occurrence and consequence of impact.

The hazard should be evaluated on its impact – the effect on a person or persons; and the likelihood of it happening. For example, falling into a deep hole in a pathway would cause either a level B critical injury or a level C marginal injury. The likelihood of a person falling in the hole depends on a range of factors, such as the number of people on the pathway, and how avoidable it is, but the likelihood could be either frequent or probable. The hazard is accordingly rated as high.

Likelihood		A. Frequent	B. Probable	C. Occasional	D. Remote	E. Improbable
	Impact					
	A. Catastrophic	High	High	High	High	High
	B. Critical	High	High	High	Medium	Low
	C. Marginal	High	Medium	Medium	Low	Low
	D. Negligible	Medium	Low	Low	Low	Low

Likelihood description:

A	Frequent:	Will occur regularly: day to day
B	Probable	Will occur on most occasions, circumstances
C	Occasional	Will occur from time to time
D	Remote	May occur but not regularly or often
E	Improbable	Unlikely to ever occur

Impact effect/description

A	Catastrophic	Death/severe injury (e.g. loss or crushed limb, brain damage)
B	Critical	Major injuries – require medical assistance (including concussions)
C	Marginal	Minor injuries, cuts, treated internally (including minor sprains)
D	Negligible	No injury, but distress caused

A hazard classified as high represents a highly probable occurrence with catastrophic consequences. This warrants immediate control strategies to be developed and applied to avoid or reduce the impact and occurrence of the hazard eventuating.

Priority

- **High** Preventative measures must be included in all planning
- **Medium** Preventative measures must be considered in all planning
- **Low** Preventative measures to be managed at the time

An example of using this process might be as follows:

Example

Take the case of rigging from the roof of a stage. In the event of an accident and the rigger falls, the severity of the accident would possibly be a single death. Hence you are looking at a catastrophic impact.

Now you must consider the likelihood of such an accident happening. Choosing from your range of options, is it more *possible* that it will happen, than *unlikely* or *improbable*?

Hence the risk assessment indicates that the level of risk is high, and you should make every effort to reduce it.

In order to try and reduce the risk you might, for example, instruct that a safety harness must be worn; that the driver of the hoist vehicle must be present at all times when someone is aloft; that protective headgear must be worn etc.

This is taking the necessary action to reduce the hazard, and if you re-assessed the situation, the likelihood of a death occurring would have dropped to *remote* indicating that the level of risk is acceptable requiring low level risk management.

Figure 2.1 Rigging lighting – note safety harness.

Software

EHS is an acronym for Environment, Health and Safety. The term 'EHS Software' refers to a database driven enterprise software application that covers data from the various broad fields of environment and waste management, occupational health and medical, safety and industrial hygiene. There is a range of general safety management software platforms available, but none specifically designed for the events industry. It would be possible to adapt those with a capability for hazard identification, occurrence reporting, risk assessment and performance monitoring.

A platform that can be satisfactorily modified for event use is Integrum QHSE Risk & Compliance Software that provides all functions in one application, not modules, and can be used both in offline and application modes. It is particularly useful for incident management, compliance, and contractor management. It comes with a training and eLearning system. Another modifiable platform is Synergi Life by DNV GL. This software provides separate modules for incidents, risk analyses, audits, and assessments. It has practical utilities for reporting, processing, analysing, corrective actions, communication, experience transfer, trending and KPI monitoring.

There is a huge volume of EHS software packages that promote themselves as an 'all in one or complete'. These commonly have features and modules that are either not relevant to events, or are very difficult to adapt. For large events it would be preferable to contact a software provider and have a program designed for the event. A useful site that provides assessments of ESE software is: www.capterra.com/ehs-management-software

Control of hazards

Once the hazards have been ranked it is possible to devise and implement control strategies. There is a hierarchy of hazard control:

1 Elimination of the hazard at source: discontinue event or parts of the event.
2 Substitution: replacing hazard with a safe option, contingency plans – backups/ alternatives.
3 Isolation or engineering: removing the link between the hazard and persons at risk.
4 Reduction of hazard: minimise the danger if it cannot be eliminated, undertaking any necessary work to ensure compliance.
5 Administration: training, policies and procedures for safe work practices, adherence to rules and regulations, permits and licenses.
6 Personal protective equipment: hard hats, gloves, first aid kits.

The event safety plan should start the consideration of the control method of an identified hazard at the top of the hierarchy – elimination, and if that is not possible, move to the next level of control. It may be that a particular hazard requires a number of levels of control for different interactions – trained operator, informed staff, member of the public.

Using the example of the high hazard deep hole mentioned above, the controls range from filling the hole in, placing boards or cover over it, putting a fence or barrier around it, using a person or flashing light to warn people about the hole. The choice of control is also determined by factors of cost, time and available resources.

Example of assessment and controls for rubbish collection hazards:

Task	Picking up of litter and food waste on site and placing in bins
Where	Public areas of the site
Who	Volunteers
When	Constantly during event, and after the crowd has left the site
How	Picking up of items from the ground, tables, seating, walkways
Environmental conditions	Weather, day/night activity, crowd interaction
Possible hazards	Cuts from broken glass, metal; burns from batteries, lighters; health risk from needle-stick, used bandages, tissues, condoms, babies' nappies, faeces; confrontation with aggressive/drunken crowd members
Likelihood	Probable/frequent
Impact	Marginal/minor
Rating	Medium
Controls – levels 4 and 5	Volunteers to wear thick-soled boots, leather gloves, hats, hi-vis vests, identity badges or uniforms. Equipment to include trash pickers and grabbers, brooms, small wheeled bins. Flashlight. A first aid kit must be available at short notice

Task	Transfer of contents of rubbish bins to dumpsters; emptying collection bins into dumpsters; sorting into organic, recycle and land fill classifications; identification and storing of lost property.
Where	From public areas, backstage and food stalls to dumpster sorting area
Who	Volunteers
When	Constantly during event, and after the crowd has left the site
How	Wheeling bins to dumpsters, sorting during emptying. The dumpster has three compartments: one for each kind of rubbish. Note: food stalls are responsible themselves for the disposal of their used cooking oil and it is not to be taken to the dumpster area.
Environmental conditions	Weather, day/night activity, crowd interaction
Possible hazards	Cuts from broken glass, metal; burns from batteries, lighters; health damage from needle-stick, used bandages, tissues, condoms, babies' nappies, faeces; confrontation with aggressive/ drunken crowd members; manipulation and lifting of bins
Likelihood	Probable/frequent
Impact	Marginal/minor
Rating	Medium
Controls – levels 4 and 5	Volunteers to wear thick-soled boots, leather gloves, hats, hi-vis vests, identity badges or uniforms. Equipment to include trash pickers and grabbers, brooms, trollies. Flashlight. A first aid kit must be available at short notice.

Task	Collection of dumpsters' contents by garbage truck
Where	Dumpsters' sorting area
Who	Sub-contractors
When	Twice daily 5pm and 10pm
How	For recyclable waste – trucks deliver empty dumpsters and remove full dumpsters; for general ground fill waste dumpsters are emptied into a garbage truck
Environmental conditions	Weather, day/night activity, traffic and crowd interaction
Possible hazards	Collisions with pedestrians and staff, other traffic and infrastructure during arrival and departure of trucks, and the exchange or emptying of dumpsters. Spillage
Likelihood	Occasional
Impact	Critical
Rating	High
Controls – levels 3 and 4	Dumpster area to be isolated from public access; entry and exit separate to public traffic entry and exit and parking areas. Sufficient room for manoeuvring trucks. Sufficient lighting.

Protocols

Protocols are the event's policy and procedures for the hazard management actions, liaison and communication. Protocols identify the duties and tasks of each staff member in a range of safety aspects of the staging of the event/programme. They ensure personnel know and implement the most effective processes to effectively manage and anticipate emergencies.

Protocols identify the chain of command and who has responsibility for the safety aspects of the event and are intended to ensure personnel, procedures and equipment are in place to effectively deal with an emergency. In most cases event protocols incorporate standard and recommended Occupational Health and Safety (OH&S) and hazard management technical requirements and procedures.

Each event will have its own set of protocols that have been created specifically for that event based on the hazard assessment process and the control measures required. There are four levels of protocols – public, basic, specific and comprehensive.

Public

Signage regarding emergency exits, evacuation routes, security and first aid locations, traffic system, and prohibited behaviour, for example see Figure 2.2.

Basic

Issued to all staff, contractors and service suppliers. Basic procedures in the simplest form. A laminated, wallet-sized card outlining those procedures is a useful way of ensuring that everyone knows what to do. The card could also be fixed to workstations, or attached to a neck lanyard. Basic protocols should provide all personnel with:

Figure 2.2 Safety instruction notice to staff.

- details of the venue layout, including entrances, exits, first-aid points and any potential hazards
- communication guidelines and procedures
- procedures for responding to emergency incidents – accident, fire, first aid, violence, criminal activity, such as first response, raising alarms, requesting assistance
- details of emergency and evacuation plans.

Protocols should be clearly communicated to all staff and updated regularly. They should be distributed to everyone at their induction into the organisation as part of their induction training; and be provided to sub-contractors.

Sample of a basic set of protocols:

ACCIDENT

1 Care for the patient
2 Don't do more than you are trained for
3 Call first aid on Channel 3
4 Keep crowd away from patient
5 Identify friends/family of patient

EVACUATION

On hearing the fire alarm and verbal instruction or on being instructed to evacuate, remain calm and:

1 Collect personal belongings only if immediately and safely accessible and portable e.g. briefcases, carry bags.
2 Do not attempt to return to usual workplace/unit
3 Follow instructions of Emergency Wardens
4 Unless otherwise instructed, leave via nearest safe exit and proceed to designated Assembly Area
5 Remain at Assembly Area and report any missing persons to Security

FIRE

1 Assist persons in immediate danger
2 Operate alarm system
3 Clear and restrict the danger area
4 Phone 000 and ask for fire service. Give operator clear details of location and type of fire
5 Report actions to Security on Channel 2
6 Attend to fire if trained in appropriate actions
7 Evacuate the immediate area

EMERGENCY

1 The person discovering the emergency should immediately notify Security on Channel 2
2 The person receiving the initial report should obtain the following information:

  a Type of emergency
  b Location
  c Actions being taken by persons at the scene
  d Any persons injured
  e Whether relevant emergency services have been notified or are required
  f Name
  g Contact details (where applicable)

3 On discovering an actual or potential emergency, the relevant emergency service/s must be advised via the '000' telephone number.

WT CHANNELS

1 Site management
2 Security
3 First aid

ALWAYS

1 Maintain communications
2 Preserve the scene
3 Exclude any media involvement
4 Keep a record

Specific

Instructions for distinct areas of responsibility – e.g. traffic control protocols, will include instructions for traffic stop/go signs, content of electronic sign messages, location and method of display of directional and prohibitive signage, rules for efficient movement in the public transport drop-off and pick-up areas, controlling pedestrian passageways and road crossings, ensuring separation of public and event service vehicles.

The event box office and entrance will require protocols on selling and inspecting tickets, for refunds and pass-outs, for inspecting bags, for confiscating prohibited items, for refusing entry and for ejecting gate-crashers.

In the auditorium protocols will be needed for entry and exiting, for ushering to seats, to deal with unruly or offensive behaviour, for stage invasions and attempts to touch performers.

Dangerous equipment will necessitate protocols for production staff for the operation, deactivation and isolation of any on-site machinery and utility supply in case of emergency, e.g., lock out procedures, danger tags, storage and handling.

Security staff, bar staff selling alcohol, and on-site first aid personnel will all require a set of protocols for their responsibilities.

The variety of events prevents the provision of a comprehensive list. For example, consider the protocols required for bull riding at a rodeo, or those needed for a marathon fun run. Each event will need to create its own set of protocols in response to the demands and activities of the event.

In the following chapters, specific hazards and their control methods will be examined. Each will have a set of associated protocols.

Comprehensive

A manual containing all the event's safety plans for communications, evacuation, first aid, traffic control; plus details of safety systems for site lay-out and production construction, operations, security arrangements and contacts; and, site maps, contractor agreements, and contact details for all staff.

The manual should be permanently located in the emergency control room and easily accessible to all control room staff. Several hard copies are required.

Monitoring and evaluation

It is worth emphasising that a monitoring and evaluation process applies to all activities that threaten safety, not simply hazard identification and risk management activities. So the process requires monitoring to assess how well information is shared and decisions acted upon. The allocation of hazard management responsibilities, accountabilities and authority also need to be monitored to see that they are appropriate, reflect changes to the work being undertaken and to the regulations.

The method of monitoring and evaluating will vary according to the nature of the activities and the associated objectives discussed, agreed upon and documented. The main considerations are:

- Who will do the monitoring (technical assistance may be required)?
- What equipment, data, information or procedures are required?
- When will it be done and how often?
- How will it be reported, by whom and to whom?

Monitoring and evaluation reports are then made directly up the line to more senior management for any comment. The point of such procedures should be clear – to ensure that safety remains the ultimate responsibility of management.

Monitor and review

For hazard management to be effective it must be implemented by everyone in the event organisation. The effectiveness of the control strategies should be monitored and reviewed to determine success. Documentation should be filed for reference at future events and as evidence that all reasonable care was taken in staging a safe event. A post event de-briefing that includes all stakeholders to document the operation of the event.

As monitoring and evaluation will provide information on how the particular hazard management practices were implemented, it will also reveal whether the larger hazard management goals for the organisation as a whole are being met or are likely to be met. It will be necessary to develop a strategy for identifying the specific actions that need to be taken to meet any system shortcomings – ineffectiveness, unsuitability – and realistic ways of improving upon current levels of performance.

The event manager or the health and safety officer can assist by gathering information on best practice in similar firms or industries, while managers and workers can be encouraged to come up with their own recommendations. Providing they are done professionally, techniques such as brainstorming can be useful. The use of external third-party facilitators can also be effective in opening people's imagination to possible improvements.

The most important point is that there should be no performance complacency as that is precisely the time things go wrong. It is important to continue to question the way things are done and find ways to do them better. The process of change and improvement never stops. Therefore managing hazard management information is critical to a systematic approach.

Information management

Information and data are required to design and make the hazard management system work. An event manager not only needs to know about the legal and corporate requirements, but also information about the organisation itself, the hazards associated with the work, the measures available to control those hazards and to monitor and evaluate them and assess the performance of the system. The information must be reliable, up to date, readily accessible and in a form people can use. Some information, such as identifying trends and hot spots, will require constant attention.

With all these factors to consider, the prospect of managing hazard management information and data looks overwhelming. Without a strategy it can be, but with one it can be managed in an ordered and effective way.

Information management

'Information management' describes the measures required for the effective collection, storage, distribution/access, use, maintenance and disposal of information to support business processes. This process includes considerations such as the following:

- To what level of detail will information be defined?
- Who should be made responsible for it?
- How will its sensitivity be protected and its quality preserved?
- How can it be made more accessible?

Summary

- An Event Safety Management System (ESMS) is a formalised set of procedures for the effective management of safety at the venue or event. It is used to make planning decisions informed by risk management, and reduce all safety hazards to ALARP by integrating safety practices into all event event production and operational activities.
- The ESMS allocates roles of responsibility, accountability and authority. A specialist health and safety officer supervises health and safety in the workplace in line with event policy and the law, and develops risk management strategies, monitoring and training programmes.
- It is essential to consult staff, police, emergency services, traffic authorities, ambulance services, local government, sub-contractor facilities and service suppliers, and representatives of each stakeholder group to conduct an assessment of the potential hazards associated with event programme of activities, production operations, the venue and/or the site, and establish the required processes to minimise the identified hazards.
- A multi-agency approach, drawing on the expertise of police, fire and ambulance services, local authorities and event organisers, for example, should be promoted and adopted.

- An event safety policy defines the commitment to hosting a safe event. The event safety policy is a document that communicates the values, objectives and broad commitments of the event organisation to conducting a safe event.
- Hazard management is the systematic identification of hazards, the assessment of risk posed by the hazards and the control of those risks, either by eliminating the hazard entirely or by minimising the risk. The principles of hazard management are to treat or tolerate hazards through the application of appropriate controls to a pre-determined acceptable level.
- A hazard is any one thing or situation with the potential to cause harm to people, and a risk is the likelihood of a hazard causing harm and the seriousness of the potential harm.
- Hazardous risks should be detected during the design planning phase of an event project. Every attempt should be made to eliminate hazards by designing them out when temporary structures, equipment and work systems are planned. Hazard identification does not only involve identifying the hazards themselves but should also include identification of 'contributory events' or problem scenarios which contribute to the hazards.
- Event risks can be simply divided into two categories: *Control* risks are those hazards that can be controlled by proactive intervention to prevent injury from occurring by minimising the risk before they can cause any harm. *Respond* hazards are those that cannot be controlled, emergencies caused by natural causes, by accident and by malevolence that can only be responded to with emergency procedure training, protocols and facilities.
- Once the hazard is identified it must be ranked or classified according to its probability of occurrence and the potential consequence of its impact should it occur.
- Once the hazards have been ranked it is possible to devise and implement control strategies. The hierarchy of hazard controls are:

  - elimination, substitution, isolation, reduction
  - training, policies, procedures and adherence to rules and regulations, permits and licences
  - personal protective equipment.

- A set of safety checklists is a useful tool for the evaluation of the facilities and operational processes used to conduct an event.
- Protocols identify the duties and tasks of each staff member in a range of safety aspects of the staging of the event/programme. They ensure personnel know and implement the most effective processes to effectively manage and anticipated emergencies and the chain of command and responsibilities.
- Each event will have its own set of protocols that have been created specifically for that event based on the hazard assessment process and the control measures required. There are four levels of protocols public, basic, specific and comprehensive.
- The effectiveness of the ESMS strategies should be monitored and reviewed to determine success.

Bibliography

Bajaj, B. (2003) Risk Management. In R. Best, C. Langston & G. Valence (Eds), *Workplace Strategies and Facilities Management: Building in Value*. Oxford: Elsevier Butterworth-Heinemann, pp. 128–145.

Borger, H. (2009) *Bullying One and All*. National Safety Vol.77. No 2.

Department for Culture, Media and Sport (2008) *Guide to Safety at Sports Grounds*, London: DCMS.

Health and Safety Executive (HSE) (1999) *The Event Safety Guide: A Guide to Health, Safety and Welfare at Music and Similar Events*. Norwich: HSE Books.

Health and Safety Executive (HSE) (2003) *Working Together to Reduce Stress at Work: A Guide for Employees*. Norwich: HSE Books.

Reason, J. (1990) *Human Error*. Cambridge: Cambridge University Press.

Reason, J. (1997) *Managing the Risks of Organisational Accidents*. London: Ashgate.

Seton (2007) *Solutions for a Safe, Secure Workplace*. Regents Park, NSW: Seton Australia.

Tarlow, P. (2002) *Event Risk Management and Safety*. New York: John Wiley & Sons.

Taylor, G., Easter, K. and Hegney, R. (2004) *Embracing Occupational Safety and Health*. Oxford: Elsevier Butterworth-Heinemann.

Toohey, J., Borthwick, K. and Archer, R. (2005) *OH&S in Australia*. Melbourne: Thomson.

Worksafe Victoria (2006) *Advice for Managing Major Events Safely*. 1st edn. Victoria: Government of Victoria.

Chapter 3

Understanding crowd disasters

Chapter objectives

This chapter discusses:

- The causes of death and injury in crowd disasters at events
- Definitions of crowds
- Theories of crowd behaviour

Major events range in focus from sport to entertainment and even cultural gatherings. They can be hosted in permanent purpose-built venues or adapted to temporary environments. They can be commercial ventures or a not-for-profit event conducted by the local community. They may use existing infrastructure or add additional overlay. They may provide their own event team or outsource functions to contractors. Each event is unique and poses its own specific safety risks. Major events, however, have one thing in common – they attract large crowds – and those crowds require expert management.

A major 2010 report, *Understanding Crowd Behaviours, Volume 1: Practical Guidance and Lessons Identified*; and, *Volume 2: Supporting Theory and Evidence*, was commissioned by the British Cabinet Office. It forms part of the civil protection literature and guidance, published on the UK Resilience website (www.cabinetoffice.gov.uk/ukresilience). The research was carried out by Challenger, Clegg and Robinson, organisational psychologists at the Centre for Socio-Technical Systems Design (CSTSD) at Leeds University Business School. The material in this chapter is mostly sourced from their report, and a subsequent 2013 paper by Rose Challenger, *Understanding Crowd Behaviours*.

Death and injury in crowds at festivals and events

When attending major events the community has an expectation that they do so without risk of injury and that the event host has systems to ensure their safety. But an alarming and tragic feature of festivals and events is the disturbingly frequent incidents of death and injury due to crowd crushes.

A major cause of injury and death are slips, trips and falls in the crowd hurry or rush that often occurs in multi-venue festivals where programmes conflict, or where desirable attractions quickly follow one another in different venues. Stumbling or loss of footing can lead to trampling, the crushing of people underneath others. "When people lose their balance and fall down, the mass tramples them, as the pushing crowd is not controllable. The injured people may turn into obstacles for others, which can produce piles of fallen people" (Helbing et al. 2005: 3). Investigations show that virtually all crowd deaths are due to compressive asphyxia and not the 'trampling' or 'stampeding' often reported by media.

A commonly held view of crowd disasters is the panic stampede. During, and in the aftermath of a disaster, in line with early crowd behaviour theories espousing irrational behaviour and loss of control (Le Bon 1908), the crowd itself is often blamed for causing the calamity by pushing, shoving and exhibiting inexcusable behaviour. However, this view is completely discredited and current research argues that crowds are rarely irrational (Hughes 2003; Mawson 2005; Lee and Hughes 2007) and often remain organised and cooperative in an emergency situation (Drury and Winter 2004; Drury and Cocking 2007; Cocking and Drury 2008).

It is essential for crowd management, in both normal and emergency situations, that event managers have a clear understanding of crowds and crowd behaviour based on research and not on commonly held erroneous concepts

Crowd crush

In *The causes and prevention of crowd disasters*, John Fruin (1993) outlined the basic principles for understanding risks to crowds at mass gatherings, such as festivals, sporting events and religious ceremonies.

Fruin asserts that a moving crowd mass of people has its own energy. When that energy is impeded by obstacles or funnelled into bottlenecks in a venue (such as narrow passages or gateways) the crowd mass compacts as it slows, creating more energy. As the compacting continues from the rear of the mass, the compacting energy increases to critical density levels at the front of the crowd mass where the blockage has occurred. People at the back of a crowd or queue are often unaware of what is occurring at the front of the crowd and continue to move into available space while being pushed themselves from behind by people following them into the stoppage. If this increasing energy cannot be dispersed to the sides by the release of lateral space, i.e., temporary fences falling or being removed, crushing begins. If the blockage is suddenly removed, the released energy behaves as a powerful spring and the people in the very front rows of the crowd are often swept off their feet by those behind, and are trampled.

In *Crowd Density – Advice for Managing Major Events Safely* (Worksafe Victoria 2006) event organisers are warned that although unlikely, a crowd crush can occur at any event. The authors state that the most common causes of crowd crush hazards are:

- overcrowding – excessive numbers of people for the space available
- crushing – pressing of a mass of people against a fixed solid object.

And that there are a number of crowd actions that may contribute to the overcrowding or crushing, including:

- surging – a sudden spontaneous pressure wave of people in the same direction
- pushing – one or more individuals thrusting their way through a crowd
- swaying – a lateral movement of a crowd
- rushing – running or rapid movement in one direction.

Crowd turbulence or crowd quake

Helbing et al. (2007) describe crowd turbulence as enormous physical forces that occur when people are packed so tightly that their bodies are touching. Turbulence begins usually at an accumulation of more than 3 persons per square metre. As density increases to 5 people per square metre or higher, the physical pressure is so high that basically people are squeezed in between the bodies of others, and then forces are transferred from one body to another. That means a little shaking of each single body adds up to a powerful force that pushes people around, and as a result of this, crowd turbulence happens. Because the sensations are a little bit like an earthquake, it is also called a crowd quake. When that happens it's very difficult for an individual to remain standing. It is easy to lose balance and fall to the ground. And that makes things even worse because all those people around lose balance and fall on top of others in a domino effect. And then those people on the ground have great difficulty breathing.

Helbing says it's really the physical forces that matter and it doesn't require people to panic to cause a crowd disaster. He advised authorities in Saudi Arabia on making the pilgrimage to Mecca safer, after the last disaster in 2006 at the Jamarat Bridge at Mina. After studying video footage of that event, it turned out to the investigators' great surprise that sudden turbulence motions in the crowd caused the disaster. This discovery led to the conclusion that crowd turbulence seems to be a standard mechanism causing crowd disasters. This was confirmed by Helbing's report on the crowd disaster at the Love Parade music festival in Germany where 21 people were killed and 510 injured (Helbing and Mukerji 2012). Although in early reports, as so often happens, the crowd was blamed for getting out of control, Helbing's analysis reveals otherwise – the injuries were not caused by crowd panic, but by crowd turbulence.

Helbing's discovery supported Fruin's earlier contention that the combined pressure of massed pedestrians and shockwave effects that run through crowds at critical density levels produces forces which are impossible for individuals, even small groups of individuals, to resist or control caused by pushing, and the domino effect of people leaning against each other. The extreme forces that are produced by a crowd mass once it reaches critical density are almost impossible to stop. Reports of persons being literally lifted out of their shoes and of clothes being torn off are common in uncontrolled crowd situations. "When crowd density equals the plan area of the human body, individual control is lost, as one becomes an involuntary part of the mass. At occupancies of about 7 persons per square meter the crowd becomes almost a fluid mass. Shock waves can be propagated through the mass sufficient to lift people off of their feet and propel them distances of 3m (10 ft) or more" Fruin (1993).

Survivors of crowd disasters report difficulty in breathing because of crowd pressures, and asphyxia, very likely accentuated by fear, is a more common cause of crowd deaths than trampling. Compressive asphyxia occurs when people are stacked up vertically, one on top of the other, or by horizontal pushing and leaning forces. In the Ibrox Park soccer stadium incident, police reported that the pile of bodies was 3m (10ft) high. At this height, people on the bottom would experience chest pressures of 800–900lbs. Horizontal forces sufficient to cause compressive asphyxia become more powerful as people push off against each other to obtain breathing space.

Experiments to determine concentrated forces on guardrails due to leaning and pushing have shown that a force of 30 per cent to 75 per cent of participant weight can occur. In a US National Bureau of Standards study of guardrails, three persons exerted a leaning force of 792N (178lbs) and 609N (137lbs) pushing. In a similar Australian Building Technology Centre study, three persons in a combined leaning and pushing posture developed a force of 1370N (306 lbs). This study showed that under a simulated 'crowd crush', 5 persons were capable of developing a force of 3430N (766lbs) (Fruin 1993). Bone fracture analysis indicates that a 20 per cent compression of the chest cavity can break ribs – this is a force of about 3000N confirming that it is possible for a 5 person deep push to break ribs (Viano and King 2000). Investigations into dangerous crowd pressures showed that "death was estimated to have occurred 15 seconds after a load of 1440 lbf (6227N) was applied. In another case it was estimated that death occurred after 4–6 minutes of applying a load of 250lbf (1112N)" (Fruin 1993).

When considering crowd forces and the impact they have on crowd movement, it is important to remember that:

- crowd forces are not random but occur for a reason (Henein and White 2005, 2007). For instance, people who want to move in a particular direction but are prevented from doing so may push in the desired direction. Alternatively, people may push in order to try to retain their personal space.

- forces are directed, or applied by one crowd member to another in a particular direction (Henein and White 2005).
- forces propagate through a crowd, often moving like a shockwave (Fruin 1993). This means that a force is not instantly felt by all crowd members and, therefore, the factor of time must be considered – i.e., how long it takes for a force to travel through the crowd. "Force applied at the rear of a crowd is not immediately felt at the front; instead it travels from person to person, and is experienced by all people as it is transmitted" (Henein and White 2007: 696).
- forces, once exerted, are outside an individual's control and, therefore, carry dangerous consequences (Henein and White 2007). For example, an individual who is subject to a force – i.e., to pushing – may become unable to move in the direction he or she desires, thereby losing control over his or her own actions, or, more seriously, may become injured (Henein and White, 2005).
- forces – as a result of being both propagated and additive in the direction in which they are exerted – are location specific (Henein and White 2005, 2007). Thus, most injuries occur at either the front of a crowd – where the forces are most concentrated – or in the centre of a crowd, where forces from individuals pushing off a wall from the front combine with forces from individuals pushing from the back (Fruin 1993).

Defining crowds

From the information given above, it is clearly a crucial imperative that all event managers must include crowd management considerations in all planning aspects of their event – site lay out, traffic and pedestrian movement, monitoring, security and emergency response. To do this successfully, the manager needs to be able to read and understand the crowd, and drawing on the knowledge, skills and experience of those individuals who are able to do so, is essential. Most of all it is vital to be able to understand crowd behaviour in any one of a range of situations and circumstances.

The first piece of basic information is that there is no one typical crowd, but a diversity of crowd types and crowd behaviours. Therefore, an event must be profiled according to its specific conditions, to ascertain the likely composition and behaviour of the crowd. The planning framework for the event must be developed in order to cope with diversity. For each event, this will involve determining who the crowd are, i.e., their likely composition and profile, and their purpose (their aims and objectives) in attending the event.

There are many different types of crowd, each with their own characteristics. Therefore, it is important to distinguish different crowd types, in order to successfully prepare for and manage a particular crowd at a particular event. It is also important to differentiate distinct crowd types within a larger crowd, and to treat each type appropriately. Specific crowd behaviour characteristics can be used to help assess likely actions, including how organised the crowd is, how cohesive and psychologically united the crowd is, and the levels of volatility and emotional intensity.

To constitute a crowd, individuals come together in an unfamiliar situation and behave in a socially coherent manner without prior awareness, or communication, of group norms and values to guide their behaviour (Turner 1982). Reicher (1996) contends that an ability to behave in a socially coherent manner, without any apparent pre-planning, communication or direction, is what makes a crowd.

Challenger (2013) says there is no agreed single definition of 'a crowd', but multiple, and often vague descriptions based around the concept of a crowd being 'a large gathering of people'. However, characteristics which appear common to the various definitions include: a sizeable number of people; at a specific location; for a measurable time period; with common goals; and displaying common behaviours. Key criteria which may jointly characterise a crowd include:

- **Size:** to be considered a crowd there must be a sizeable number of people.
- **Density:** crowd members must be co-located in a particular area with a sufficient, but safe, density distribution.
- **Time** (the fact of being together at a particular moment): some large gatherings of people, such as those inside an auditorium are relatively stable in membership for the duration of a prolonged event. But other gatherings, at the entrance gates for instance, are relatively transient, in that the membership of the crowd changes constantly as people arrive and depart.
- **Collectively** (the purpose of being together): In order to be considered a crowd, individuals come together as a group, in a specific location for a specific purpose, for a measurable amount of time. Individuals must share a social identity if they are to be thought of as a crowd, and crowd members should also share common goals and interests, and act in a coherent manner. Therefore, collectively – in terms of social identity, goals, interests and behaviours – would appear to be a crucial aspect of being a crowd.

Two examples:

> *Crowds at concerts* are usually of variable composition, primarily determined by the profile of the act. For instance, a pop concert may have a larger proportion of teenagers and family groups, while an operatic concert may have a larger proportion of couples and older individuals. The profile of both the crowd and the act will then have a subsequent impact on the amount of management needed. Concert crowds are typically compliant, providing they get to see what they wanted to see, but can become irate and tense if there are long queues or delays, particularly if there is no information or communication provided.

> *Crowds at celebrations* such as New Year's Eve are predominantly well-behaved party goers aged between 20 and 30 years old, although alcohol-initiated violence can be typically expected. There are generally few families or elderly people due to the nature of the event. A small percentage of the crowd will typically arrive early and congregate at the best viewing points, followed by a late surge just before the event begins.

Momboisse (1967) distinguishes four types of crowd:

1 **casual crowds:** ones which are not organised or unified, but comprise individuals who are simply in the same place at the same time
2 **conventional crowds:** ones which are gathered for a specific purpose or to observe a specific event, with crowd members who share common interests

3 **expressive crowds:** ones with members who are involved in some form of expressive behaviour, although not in a destructive way, for instance, dancing or singing

4 **aggressive or hostile crowds:** ones which are unorganised and lacking in unity, but with members who are willing to be enticed into disorder and unlawful behaviour.

Yet another perspective can be obtained by considering the 'crowd mood', the pervading atmosphere or tone of a venue or site. The mood (or temper) of a crowd is a combination of the purpose and function of the event, the environment in which it occurs, and the attending crowd itself. The crowd mood could be relaxed, happy, boisterous, aggressive or anxious. This can be influenced by:

- the environment (such as type of venue, weather, music, terrain, heat, cold, noise)
- the event (nature of the gathering: religious, festival, concert, public speech, demonstration, march, protest, performer)
- the crowd itself (demographics, character and composition of the crowd).

One crowd or many

A crowd is not homogeneous, but is comprised of a wide range of diverse individuals, with different wants, needs and expectations. This means there is no one, typical crowd, but a whole range of crowd types and crowd behaviours, depending on numerous factors, including the event type, its location, the time of day, the performance types, whether the event is free or ticketed, and all the variations of environmental situations. So, for successful crowd management, the audience at an event should not be treated as one mass, but as a collection of smaller groups, with crowd management planning appropriate to the composition and likely behaviours of each group.

Within one particular event, there will be many different types of crowd, including several variations of the crowd types described above, each with its own profile. For instance, some people will just want to be there for the atmosphere, some will want to be actively involved in the event, and some will want to simply observe the event. Crowds for special events, for example, can be thought of as comprising numerous smaller crowds, each of which can be considered to have its own 'personality' (Berlonghi 1995) or its own shared social identity (Reicher 2001).

In a major study, Crompton and McKay (1997) investigated the motives which stimulated people to attend festivals. They found that attendance at an event was rarely the result of a single motive. Crompton and McKay claimed that an individual may desire to satisfy several different needs through a single event attendance. For example, a need to interact with family or friends may be accompanied by a desire for cultural enrichment. At the same time, different individuals may engage in the same event and derive different benefits from their event experience. For one person listening to music may be a means of experiencing a cultural tradition, for another it may be a new and novel experience, while for yet another it may be a just a setting for socialising.

It is also possible to consider people reacting to circumstances transiting from one crowd type to another – for example people walking from their car as individuals, into an entrance as an ambulatory crowd, and then into an auditorium where the performers' energy changes the crowd from passive spectators into participants, causing density crushing perhaps, then leading to aggression followed by escape rushing.

This diversity makes event management difficult and, therefore, a flexible framework must be developed in order to accommodate the different crowd types. The mixture of crowd types, and their differing personalities and social identities, must be simultaneously managed if an event is to be effectively supervised.

Therefore, it is vital that each event be considered and profiled according to its specific conditions, drawing on knowledge and experience from previous events, concerning the likely crowd composition, expectations and probable behaviours.

Crowd behaviour theory

Most crowd management planning is based on police and security contractor control practices, in which crowds are generally perceived as troublesome, problematic and in need of control. However, although valuable and in part necessary, this approach should not dominate planning. If the crowd feels fairly treated and trusted by the event organisers, they should begin to self-manage and self-police, leading to a more successful outcome in emergency situations than simply demanding obedience. This trust can only occur if the crowd management planning is based on a clear understanding of the key theories of crowd behaviours that focus on the underlying assumptions and rules governing human behaviour, in both normal and emergency situations.

One of the earliest, and most highly influential theories of crowd behaviour was **Group Mind Theory** (Le Bon 1908), which proposed that individuals, when submerged in a crowd, lose all sense of self and responsibility. They no longer identify themselves as individuals with responsibility for their own actions, but instead become anonymous members of a group. As a member of the crowd, individuals are subject to panic contagion, which serves to quickly and unpredictably spread ideas and sentiments among the group, resulting in rapid and unpredictable shifts in behaviour. Consequently, unconscious, antisocial and uncivilised motives are released and the crowd behave according to primitive, savage instincts, for example panic flight or stampede.

Reicher (1996) contends that Le Bon's depiction of mindless crowd action considered crowd behaviours in isolation from the context in which the behaviours arise and are acted out. Consequently, behaviours which do occur as a result of contextual factors were incorrectly considered by Le Bon to be inherent attributes of the crowd and, therefore, are incorrectly considered to be predictable general crowd behaviours. Yet Le Bon's theory has dominated crowd control practice and continues to be supported by some security agencies.

Following on from the group mind tradition of Le Bon, a concept of 'deindividuation' was used by Festinger et al. (1952) to explain individuals' atypical behaviour when part of a crowd. **Deindividuation** describes the process whereby there is a loss of a sense of a socialised individual self-awareness and evaluation apprehension in crowd situations that foster anonymity and susceptibility to external cues and to the crowds' motives and emotions. Behaviour may range from a mild lessening of restraint, for example, screaming during a concert; to impulsive self-gratification, for example, vandalism or molestation; to destructive social explosions, for example, group violence or rioting.

These ideas are very similar to those proposed by 'mob sociology' (Momboisse 1967; Schweingruber 2000), which attempts to explain how a typically law abiding crowd can become transformed into a disorderly mob. According to this perspective, as tensions mount within the group, perhaps in reaction to an emergency, individuals are absorbed into the crowd, and become increasingly responsive only to the crowd itself. Subsequently, crowd members lose their sense of self-control and self-consciousness, making it easier for disorder and panic to occur. The theory suggests that as individuals become anonymous crowd members they leave behind their sense of self-awareness, self-observation, self-responsibility and individualised identity, resulting in weakened moral restraints and antisocial behaviours.

In contrast to the irrational behaviour of crowds advocated by these theories, Berk (1974) claimed crowd action to be rational and based on probabilities. He proposed a model of rational crowd behaviours, involving five key steps:

1 crowd members seek information
2 possible events are predicted from this information
3 behavioural options are listed
4 an order of preference for the probable outcomes of alternative options is established
5 a course of action is decided upon, aimed at maximising rewards while minimising costs.

Consequently, the probability of a crowd member behaving in a particular way is determined both by the likely payoff of the action, in terms of rewards outweighing costs, and the perceived likelihood of support for the action (Berk 1974). The difficulty of this approach for crowd management planning purposes is that a perceived payoff for individuals is almost impossible to determine in advance.

The **social identity model** of crowd behaviour, based on social identity theory and self-categorisation theory, offers an explanation for a crowd's ability to spontaneously behave in a socially coherent manner without any apparent pre-planning, communication or direction. This model proposes that when part of a crowd, individuals do not lose their identity, as theories such as deindividuation suggest, but simply shift from an individual identity to a shared social identity (Reicher 1996, 1997; Drury and Reicher 1999), and by defining and accepting an appropriate shared identity, the individual crowd members are able to act as a united group.

Through this process of defining an appropriate social identity for themselves within the crowd, individuals are able to act in accordance with that identity, which explains how crowds are able to spontaneously act in a socially coherent manner (Reicher 1984). It follows, therefore, that if a crowd's behaviour is based upon its social identity, the way in which its identity is defined will determine the basis of that crowd's behaviour (Reicher 1996).

There is much evidence, across multiple crowd events in multiple contexts, in support of the social identity approach to crowd behaviours (Drury and Reicher 1999, 2000; Reicher 1996; Stott and Drury 1999; Stott and Reicher 1998). This notion that crowd members act in terms of social identity is a key strength of this model and has remained as a core concept in most subsequent models of crowd behaviour.

Crowding perception

In *Crowding at an arts festival*, Hoon Lee and Alan R. Graefe (2003) defined 'crowding' as a negative assessment by a member of a crowd of the density level of the crowd in which they are. The perceptions of people in a crowd determine whether the crowd density will be just an unpleasant experience, or end in disaster. People in a crowd do not have a broad view of what is happening around them, and if the negative perception becomes an overwhelming dread of being severely crowded, or there is a perception of danger, the human flight response can cause an individual to panic.

An individual's perception of being crowded is subjective and generally based on the character and behaviour of other festival attendees. According to Shelby and Heberlein (1986), social psychological factors have a more powerful influence on crowding perception than actual crowd density levels or the number of encounters with other event attendees.

There are three specific theories related to crowding:

- **Expectancy:** an experiential state of perceived lack of space and resources.
- **Stimulus overload:** the results of excessive stimulation.
- **Social Interference:** experience of unwanted behavioural interference, the attribution of arousal to the invasion of personal space, and loss of control.

Expectancy

Expectations for crowd density contribute significantly and directly to perceived crowding than actual crowd density encountered. Seeing more people than expected cause people to feel more crowded. When festival attendees see fewer or the same number of other festival attendees as they expect to see, their perception of crowding levels is low. However, when more people than expected are encountered, the perceived crowding level increases.

Fruin's analysis of individual space occupancy showed that in waiting areas, 20 square feet per patron will allow relatively free movement; 10 square feet, movement on an 'excuse me' basis; and 5 square feet, standing without touching others but with little ability to move freely, the occupancy level usually found in most normal waiting situations, such as queues or approaches to ticket inspection points. At approximately 3 square feet per person, involuntary touching and brushing against others will occur, a psychological threshold that should generally be avoided in most public situations. Below 2 square feet per person, potentially dangerous crowd forces and psychological stresses may begin to develop.

Stimulus overload

Crowd stimulus overload occurs as people feel overwhelmed by the attendance of other festival attendees or by the condition of the physical environment in a given area. Overload occurs when there are too many unwanted and uncontrolled interactions, and unfamiliar or inappropriate social contacts in conditions of high crowd density, in which people meet more stimuli than they can handle. The crowd density interferes with an individual's ability to maintain control of their equilibrium and sense of self. Negative outcomes occur when the amount and rate of stimulation caused by density exceeds the individual's ability to deal with it.

The fundamental assumption of the stimulus-overload model is that the size, density, and cultural mixture of other people cause susceptible individuals to be exposed to excessive levels of psychic stress. The triggering factor in the experience of overload is the anxiety caused by uncertainty and uncontrollability.

People try to handle this overly stimulating state with various strategies, such as insulating or isolating themselves by closing down sensory input with earphones, looking only downward, or staying close to friends. If these adaptations are successful, they can lessen or cancel the negative effects of stress. However, if these strategies do not work or are not appropriate in reducing density-induced stress, then crowding is experienced and the sufferer could flee or panic, perhaps leading to injury.

Social interference

An attendee's behaviour at festivals is consciously or subconsciously motivated by the desire to accomplish a variety of outcomes, such as absorption, immersion, participation or social interaction. Because human behaviour is often goal directed, negative crowding perception occurs when the number, behaviour or proximity of other persons interferes with a person's attaining their goal, and their consequential lack or loss of control over the situation. This loss of situational control often results in disruptive behaviour such as pushing, jostling and rushing. Actions that can lead to arguments and violence, and if done by a group can cause trips, falls, and in the worst cases, crowd rush leading to crowd crush.

Figure 3.1 Fencing used as queuing control.

Place scripts (habitual behaviour in a place)

Donald and Canter's (1992) **social facilitation theory** proposes that, when part of a crowd, individuals may be motivated to perform their most habitual behaviour. For example, following the same routes or going out the same way they came in. Individuals' plans of action within a particular environment or place are often represented as scripts, sequences of behavioural patterns in which individuals automatically engage when in a particular environment or experiencing a particular event. Scripts are a coherent sequence of events expected by the individual, involving him either as a participant or as an observer.

Individuals often develop specific '**place scripts**' for the sequence of actions likely to take place when in a particular environment, for example, using the same entrance and exit each day. "People will define, understand or formulate a script in relation to where they are, and interpret the behaviour of others, and define what a place is by what happens there" (Donald and Canter 1992: 205).

Once ingrained, such scripts are remarkably resistant to change, even in extraordinary circumstances such as emergencies, as individuals are instinctively drawn towards the familiar (Sime 1983, 1985, 1993). In an emergency evacuation, for example, individuals are often reluctant to evacuate via an emergency exit, instead preferring to use the exit with which they are most familiar, typically their usual entrance and exit route despite the inappropriateness and probable danger (Canter 1990; Donald and Canter 1992). For instance, a report into 'The Station' nightclub fire in Rhode Island in February 2003 (Gosshandler et al. 2005) estimates that up to two thirds of people attempted to escape from the fire via the main entrance, i.e., the way they entered the nightclub.

Therefore, in emergencies, people must receive information and cues from several sources, e.g., from the behaviour of others, the presence of specialised staff such as police, or specific instructions from staff or authority figures, in order to diagnose a situation. They are then able to break from their place script and act as appropriate. "[W]hat people see as being the appropriate actions is shaped by a combination of what they expect of the circumstances and what figures of authority do and say to help re-define those circumstances" (Donald and Canter 1992: 19) with the provision of clear and appropriate information during such events.

The theory of place scripts has important practical implications for the management of emergency situations. In order to help people abandon their place scripts, clear and timely information must be provided, to override any inappropriate place scripts related to routine day-to-day behaviour. To ensure individuals are able to quickly break away from their scripts at the beginning of an emergency situation, clear, appropriate information must be provided during an evacuation, in order to override individuals' schema and encourage more appropriate behaviour.

Crowd behaviour in an emergency

Understanding crowd behaviour enables an event manager to plan for emergencies based on heavily researched principles. "[B]ehaviour in emergencies and disasters has a predictable and relatively consistent set of characteristics"(Donald and Canter 1992: 203–204). There are three main perspectives for understanding crowd behaviours in emergency evacuations and disasters (Drury and Cocking 2007; Cocking and Drury 2008):

1   theories of mass panic
2   affiliation and normative approaches
3   social identity approach

The notion of 'mass panic' or stampede is typically used to describe a crowd response to emergency situations. This explanation, drawn from Le Bon's (1908) conceptualisation of crowds as more emotional and less intelligent than individuals when acting alone, suggests that, when faced with an emergency or disaster situation, the social bonds between members of a crowd dissolve, resulting in mindless, instinctive, irrational and self-centred behaviour (Brown 1954; Quarantelli 1954; Smelser 1962). These antisocial behaviours then spread quickly through the crowd in the process of 'contagion' (Ross 1908; McDougall 1920). Indeed, the classic entrapment theory of panic (Quarantelli 1954, 1957, 1977; Killian 1972) proposes that when major physical danger is imminent but escape routes are limited, i.e., when individuals feel trapped, panic is more likely to occur, resulting in 'flight' behaviours, including pushing, trampling and crushing (Janis and Leventhal 1968).

Sime (1980, 1999) suggests that the concept of panic is often used as a way of blaming the crowd in the aftermath of a disaster, for example, 'the crowd panicked which led to crushing and death'. Indeed, the word 'panic' itself typically has negative connotations, reinforcing assumptions made about the irrational, selfish nature of crowd behaviours during an emergency (Sime 1980, 1995). "The term 'panic' refers to inappropriate (or excessive) fear and/or flight and highly intense fear and/or flight" (Mawson 2005: 96) in which individuals tend to behave en masse, i.e., to follow what other crowd members do, and sensible alternative routes or exits are typically overlooked or inefficiently used.

Mass panic theory claimed that a panicked crowd is one where individuals move, or attempt to move, considerably faster than they do normally. Interactions between individuals become more physical in nature, e.g., people start pushing and shoving. Movement becomes uncoordinated, particularly when moving through a bottleneck. Jams build up, causing dangerous crowd pressures. Clogging and 'arching' occur at exits. As the large, high density crowd rushes towards a narrow exit wanting to escape as quickly as possible the exit becomes clogged and the crowd form an arch-shape, radiating outwards behind the exit. Escape is slowed by fallen or injured individuals who act as 'obstacles' and are trampled (Helbing et al. 2000).

Yet, research conducted over the past 50 years argues to the contrary: that in most, if not all, emergency situations, crowd behaviours remain fairly organised and structured (Chertkoff and Kushigian 1999), while members of the crowd exhibit helping behaviours, alongside collective concern and cooperation (Johnson 1987). For example, the majority of the crowd at the Duisburg Love Parade crowd crush in 2010, did not panic or stampede but tried to help each other. Moreover, if panic does arise, it typically remains confined to individuals, as opposed to spreading through the crowd (Drury and Cocking 2007).

In other words, panic, and the selfish or antisocial stampede behaviours typically associated with it, is very rare and a misconception (Fischer 1998, 2002). "[T]he idea of mass panic occurring in emergencies, is largely a myth unsupported by evidence, and that the term is neither a helpful nor accurate description of human behaviour in emergencies" (Cocking and Drury 2008: 13).

Indeed, many studies of disasters report panic and irrational behaviour to be very rare. However, behaviour does appear to become more self-centred, although still relatively constrained, with social bonds intact, when escape, due to delayed warnings, becomes urgent and, therefore, there is insufficient time to evacuate in an orderly fashion (Sime 1983, 1999; Johnson 1988).

Nevertheless, in contrast to the traditional model of panic, during an emergency situation or evacuation, crowd behaviours are not reduced to irrational, selfish tendencies but rather the crowd retains its sociality. When faced with an emergency or threatening situation, individuals exhibit 'affiliative behaviour' i.e., they are motivated to move towards familiar places and towards familiar people (Sime 1983). This proximity to familiar places and people is thought to have a calming effect, reducing the fight or flight instinct (Mawson 2005). For instance, studies of mass evacuation have found that family groups do not break down in an emergency, but attempt to evacuate together and remain united as a group focusing on collective, rather than individual survival (Johnson 1988; Feinberg and Johnson 2001). People prefer to delay evacuating until all members of the group are able to leave together. However, the drawback of this is that families may be slower to begin evacuation which, ultimately, can threaten their survival (Mawson 2005).

The normative model (Aguirre 2005) proposes that behaviour in emergency situations is still governed by the same social rules as in normal situations. Hence, social, organisational and place-related roles and responsibilities appear to be maintained (Best 1977; Canter et al. 1980; Donald and Canter 1992).

Recent theories of group behaviour, such as the Elaborated Social Identity Model (Drury and Reicher 1999; Stott and Drury 1999) attempt to explain the mutual concern and helping behaviours observed during an emergency in large crowds, comprised of people who do not know each other and who have no pre-existing social bonds (Drury and Cocking 2007).

This is more fully identified in the social identity/self-categorisation approach (Drury and Winter 2004; Drury and Cocking 2007; Cocking and Drury 2008) which proposes a model of mass emergent sociality and collective resilience to offer an explanation of the collective sociality of crowds, i.e., helping, cooperation and coordination behaviours displayed by individuals who do not know each other in emergency situations. "[A]n approach which allows for co-ordination and co-operation amongst a crowd of strangers, and which can explain sociality in emergencies (such as instances of helping strangers at a cost to the personal self) in terms of their crowd membership itself" (Drury and Cocking 2007: 11).

This model suggests that the common experience of threat or emergency may transform a physical crowd into a psychological crowd, with a shared social identity (Reicher 2001; Drury and Cocking 2007; Cocking and Drury 2008). "[D]isasters can create a sense of 'we-ness' leading to a common bond of solidarity amongst participants, where co-operation and altruism predominate rather than selfish behaviour" (Cocking et al. 2009: 30). The experience of a shared social identity provides crowd members with perceptions of unity and expectations of mutual support (Cocking and Drury 2008) while also helping to reduce stress levels (Drury and Reicher 1999; Haslam and Reicher 2006). This enables the crowd as a whole to act as a source of strength for individual crowd members (Levine et al. 2005).

This theory helps explain the collective behaviours, i.e. coordination, cooperation, helping behaviours and personal sacrifices, frequently observed among unfamiliar crowd members during an emergency. In addition, research reports that increased social support in emergency situations is associated with reduced stress levels (Haslam et al. 2005), increased optimism (Dougall et al. 2001), and lowered levels of depression (Tyler and Hoyt 2000), while also moderating the damaging effects of disaster, such as post-traumatic stress disorder (Eustace et al. 1999).

Further research indicates that the presence of informed individuals acting as leaders within the crowd influences both the speed and accuracy of crowd movement (Dyer et al. 2008), particularly when their spatial positioning is optimal (Aube and Shield, 2004). More specifically, leaders positioned in the core rather than the periphery of the crowd, i.e., in close proximity to other crowd members, are more likely to influence crowd movement (Dyer et al. 2008). Crowds are able to make cohesive decisions regarding direction and speed of movement even if only a few members have the necessary information, with the degree to which they are influential dependent on their spatial position within the crowd.

This dominance of informed individuals over crowd movement is particularly important in emergency evacuations, when only a few crowd members typically have information about the unfolding situation. Thus, when planning a crowd event, careful consideration must be given to the number of individuals to be located within the crowd (whether these be stewards or crowd volunteers) who are aware of the location of emergency exits, and where these informed individuals should be positioned to most effectively act as leaders in the event of an emergency evacuation.

Summary

- Most death and injury in crowd disasters are caused by crush or crowd turbulence, not stampede (which is very rare).
- Crowds can be defined by their behaviour and there are many different ways of defining and describing crowds.
- Panic in an emergency situation, typically characterised by antisocial, irrational behaviours, is actually very rare. Instead, behaviours typically remain structured and organised, with helping, cooperation and coordination behaviours often displayed.
- Behaviours only become more self-centred when time to escape is limited and, therefore, orderly evacuation is not possible.
- Crowd members are typically motivated to move towards familiar people during an emergency. Family members or groups of friends prefer to evacuate together, and will often wait to exit until all members of the group are able to do so. However, this slows the rate of evacuation.
- Crowd members are also typically motivated to move towards familiar places during an emergency, e.g. people prefer to use the exit with which they are most familiar, rather than an emergency exit.
- Social, organisational and place-related norms appear to be maintained during an evacuation. For instance, gender roles are typically retained, with women generally receiving more help, and offering more emotional support, than men.
- When united by an emergency situation, a physical crowd may be transformed into a psychological crowd, sharing a social identity. This shared identity then enables crowd members to act as a source of strength for one another and exhibit collective behaviours, i.e., coordination, cooperation, helping behaviours and personal sacrifices.

Bibliography

Aguirre, B. E. (2005) 'Emergency evacuations, panic and social psychology', *Psychiatry: Interpersonal and Biological Processes*, 68, 121–129.

Aube, F. and Shield, R. (2004) *Modeling the effect of leadership on crowd flow dynamics*. Cellular Automata, Proceedings, 3305, 601-611.

Berlonghi, A. E. (1995) 'Understanding and planning for different spectator crowds', *Safety Science*, 18, 239–247.

Berk, R. (1974) *Collective Behaviour*. Dubuque, IA: Brown.

Best, R. L. (1977) *Reconstruction of a Tragedy: The Beverly Hills Supper Club Fire, Southgate, Kentucky*. Quincy, MA: National Fire Protection Association.

Brown, R. W. (1954) 'Mass phenomena'. In G. Lindzey (Ed.) *Handbook of Social Psychology* (pp. 833–876). Cambridge, MA: Addison-Wesley.

Canter, D. (1990) *Fires and Human Behaviour*, 2nd edn. London: David Fulton Publishers.

Canter, D., Breaux, J. and Sime, J. (1980) 'Domestic, multiple occupancy and hospital fires', In D. Canter (Ed.) *Fire and Human Behaviour*. Chichester. Wiley.

Challenger, R. (2013) *Understanding Crowd Behaviours*. Leeds: The Stationery Office (TSO).

Challenger, R., Clegg, C. W. and Robinson, M. A. (2010a) *Understanding Crowd Behaviours, Volume 1: Practical Guidance and Lessons Identified*. Leeds: The Stationery Office (TSO).

Challenger, R., Clegg, C. W. and Robinson, M. A. (2010b) *Understanding Crowd Behaviours, Volume 2: Supporting Theory and Evidence*. Leeds: The Stationery Office (TSO).

Chertkoff, J. M. and Kushigian, R. H. (1999) *Don't Panic: The Psychology of Emergency Egress and Ingress*. Westport, CT: Praeger.

Cocking, C. and Drury, J. (2008) 'The mass psychology of disasters and emergency evacuations: A research report and implications for the Fire and Rescue Service'. *Fire Safety, Technology and Management*, 10, 13–19.

Cocking, C., Drury, J. and Reicher, S. (2009) 'The psychology of crowd behaviour in emergency evacuations: Results from two interview studies and implications for the Fire & Rescue Services', *Irish Journal of Psychology. Special Edition: Psychology and the Fire & Rescue Services.*

Crompton, J. and McKay, S. (1997) 'Motives of visitors attending festival events', *Annals of Tourism Research*, Vol 24, No 2.

Donald, I. and Canter, D. (1992) 'Intentionality and fatality during the King's Cross underground fire', *European Journal of Social Psychology*, 22, 203–218.

Dougall, A. L., Hyman, K. B., Hayward, M. C., McFeeley, S. and Baum, A. (2001) 'Optimism and traumatic stress: The importance of social support and coping', *Journal of Applied Social Psychology*, 31, 223–245.

Drury, J. (2004) 'No need to panic', *The Psychologist*, 17, 118–119.

Drury, J. and Cocking, C. (2007) *The mass psychology of disasters and emergency evacuations: A research report and implications for practice*. Brighton: University of Sussex.

Drury, J. and Reicher, S. (1999) 'The intergroup dynamics of collective empowerment: Substantiating the social identity model of crowd behavior', *Group Processes & Intergroup Relations*, 2, 381–402.

Drury, J. and Reicher, S. (2000) 'Collective action and psychological change: The emergence of new social identities', *British Journal of Social Psychology*, 39, 579–604.

Drury, J. and Winter, G. (2004) 'Social identity as a source of strength in mass emergencies and other crowd events', *International Journal of Mental Health (special issue on 'Coping with disasters: The mental health component')*, 32, 77–93.

Dyer, J. R. G., Ioannou, C. C., Morrell, L. J., Croft, D. P., Couzin, I. D., Waters, D. A. and Krause, J. (2008) 'Consensus decision making in human crowds', *Animal Behavior*, 75, 461–470.

Emergency Management Australia (1999) *Safe and Healthy Mass Gatherings*. Manual Number 12. Australian Emergency Manuals Series. Commonwealth of Australia

Eustace, K., MacDonald, C. and Long, N. (1999) 'Cyclone Bola: A study of the psychological after-effects', *Anxiety, Stress and Coping: An International Journal*, 12, 285–298.

Feinberg, W. E. and Johnson, N. R. (2001) 'The ties that bind: A macro-level approach to panic', *International Journal of Mass Emergencies and Disasters*, 91, 269–295. 1162. New Vol 2. indd 183.

Festinger, L., Pepitone, A., & Newcomb, T.M. (1952) *Some consequences of deindividuation in a group*. Journal of Abnormal and Social Psychology, 47, 382–389.

Fischer, H. W. (1998) *Response to Disaster: Fact versus Fiction and its Perpetuation*, 2nd edn. Landam, MD: University Press of America.

Fischer, H. W. (2002) 'Terrorism and 11 September 2001: Does the behavioral response to disaster model fit?', *Disaster Prevention and Management*, 11, 123–127.

Fruin, J. J. (1993) 'The causes and prevention of crowd disasters'. In R. A. Smith and J. F. Dickie (Eds), *Engineering for Crowd Safety* (pp. 99–108). Amsterdam: Elsevier.

Gosshandler, W., Bryner, N., Madrzykowski, D. and Kuntz, K. (2005) *Report of the*

Technical Investigation of the Station Nightclub Fire, Volume 1. Boulder, CL: National Institute of Standards and Technology U.S. Department of Commerce.

Haslam, S. A. and Reicher, S. (2006) 'Stressing the group: Social identity and the unfolding dynamics of responses to stress', *Journal of Applied Psychology*, 91, 1037–1052.

Haslam, S. A., O'Brien, A., Jetten, J., Vormedal, K. and Penna, S. (2005) 'Taking the strain: Social identity, social support and the experience of stress', *British Journal of Social Psychology*, 44, 355–370.

Helbing. D. and Mukerji. P (2012) *Crowd Disasters as Systemic Failures: Analysis of the Love Parade Disaster*, EPJ Data Science, 1-7, London: Springer Open.

Helbing, D., Farkas, I. and Vicsek, T. (2000) 'Simulating dynamic features of escape panic', *Nature*, 407, 487–490.

Helbing, D., Johansson, A. and Al-Abideen, H. Z. (2007) 'Dynamics of crowd disasters: An empirical study', *Physical Review E*, 75, Article Number 046109.

Helbing, D., Buzna, L., Johansson, A. and Werner, T. (2005) 'Self-organized pedestrian crowd dynamics: Experiments, simulations, and design solutions', *Transportation Science*, 39, 1–24.

Henein, C. M. and White, T. (2005) 'Agent-based modelling of forces in crowds', *Multi-Agent and Multi-Agent-Based Simulation*, 3415, 173–184.

Henein, C. M. and White, T. (2007) 'Macroscopic effects of microscopic forces between agents in crowd models', *Physica A*, 373, 694–712.

Hughes, R. L. (2003) 'The flow of human crowds', *Annual Review of Fluid Mechanics*, 35, 169–182.

Janis, I. L. and Leventhal, H. (1968) Human reactions to stress. In E. F. Borgatta and W. Lambert (Eds) *Handbook of Personality Theory and Research*. Chicago, IL: Rand McNally.

Johnson, N. R. (1987) 'Panic at The Who concert stampede: An empirical assessment', *Social Problems*, 34, 362–373.

Johnson, N. R. (1988) 'Fire in a crowded theatre: A descriptive investigation of the emergence of panic', *International Journal of Mass Emergencies and Disasters*, 6, 7–26.

Killian, L. M. (1972) *Collective Behavior*. Prentice-Hall. NJ: Englewood Cliffs.

Le Bon, G. (1908) *The Crowd: A Study of the Popular Mind*. London: Unwin.

Lee. H, and Graefe, A. R. (2003) 'Crowding at an arts festival', *Tourism Management*, 24(1), 1–11.

Lee, R. S. C. and Hughes, R. L. (2005) 'Exploring trampling and crushing in crowds', *Journal of Transportation Engineering*, 131, 576–582.

Lee, R. S. C. and Hughes, R. L. (2007) 'Minimisation of the risk of trampling in a crowd', *Mathematics and Computers in Simulation*, 74, 29–37.

Levine, M., Prosser, A., Evans, D. and Reicher, S. (2005) 'Identity and emergency intervention: How social group membership and inclusiveness of group boundaries shape helping behavior', *Personality and Social Psychology Bulletin*, 31, 443–453.

Mawson, A. R. (1978) *Panic behavior: A review and a new hypothesis*. Paper presented at the 9th World Congress of Sociology. Uppsala, Sweden. August.

Mawson, A. R. (2005) 'Understanding mass panic and other collective responses to threat and disaster', *Psychiatry*, 68, 95–113.

McDougall, W. (1920) *The Group Mind*. London: Cambridge University Press.

Mellor, N. and Veno, A. (1998) *Public Events: Safety and Security Strategies*. Victoria: Centre for Police and Justice Studies Monash University.

Momboisse, R. (1967) *Riots, Revolts and Insurrections*. Springfield, IL: Charles C. Thomas.

Netten, N. and van Someren, M. (2011) 'Improving communication in crisis management by evaluating the relevance of messages', *Journal of Contingencies and Crisis Management* Volume 19 Number 2, 75–85.

Quarantelli, E. L. (1954) 'The nature and conditions of panic', *American Journal of Sociology*, 60, 267–275.

Quarantelli, E. L. (1957) 'The behavior of panic', *Sociology and Social Research*, 60, 187–194.

Quarantelli, E. L. (1977) Panic behavior: Some empirical observations. In D. J. Conway (Ed.) *Human Response to Tall Buildings*. Stroudsberg, PA: Dowden, Hutchinson and Ross, pp. 336–350.

Reicher, S. (1996) 'The Crowd century: Reconciling practical success with theoretical failure', *British Journal of Social Psychology*, 35, 535–553.

Reicher, S. (1997) 'Collective psychology and the psychology of the self', *BPS Social Section Newsletter*, 36, 3–15.

Reicher, S. (2001) The psychology of crowd dynamics. In M. A. Hogg and S. Tindale (Eds), *Blackwell Handbook of Social Psychology: Group Processes*. Oxford: Blackwell Publishing, pp. 182–208.

Reicher, S. (2004) 'The context of social identity: Domination, resistance, and change', *Political Psychology*, 25, 921–945.

Reicher, S. D. (1984) 'Social influence in the crowd – attitudinal and behavioural effects of de-individuation in conditions of high and low group salience', *British Journal of Social Psychology*, 23, 341–350.

Ross, E. A. (1908) *Social Psychology: An Outline and Source Book*. New York: Macmillan.

Schweingruber, D. (2000) 'Mob sociology and escalated force: Sociology's contribution to repressive police tactics', *The Sociological Quarterly*, 41, 371–389.

Shelby, B. and Heberlein, T. A. (1986) Carrying Capacity in Recreation Setting. Corvallis, OR: Oregon State University Press.

Sime, J. D. (1980) The concept of panic. In D. Canter (Ed.) *Fires and Human Behaviour*. Chichester: Wiley.

Sime, J. D. (1983) 'Affiliative behaviour during escape to building exits', *Journal of Environmental Psychology*, 3, 21–41.

Sime, J. D. (1985) 'Movement toward the familiar: Person and place affiliation in a fire entrapment setting', *Environmental Behavior*, 17, 697–724.

Sime, J. D. (1993) *Crowd psychology and engineering: Designing for people or ball-bearings.* International Conference on Engineering for Crowd Safety, March 1993, London, UK.

Sime, J. D. (1995) 'Crowd psychology and engineering', *Safety Science*, 21, 1–14.

Sime, J. D. (1999) 'Crowd facilities, management and communications in disasters', Facilities, 17, 313–324.

Smelser, N. J. (1962) *Theory of Collective Behaviour.* London: Routledge & Kegan Paul.

Stott, C. and Drury, J. (1999) The intergroup dynamics of empowerment: A social identity model. In P. Bagguley and J. Hearn (Eds) *Transforming Politics: Power and Resistance*. London: Macmillan.

Stott, C. and Reicher, S. (1998) 'Crowd action as intergroup process: Introducing the police perspective', *European Journal of Social Psychology*, 28, 509–529.

Toohey, J., Borthwick, K. and Archer. R. (2005) *OH&S in Australia*. Melbourne: Thomson.

Turner, J. C. (1982) Towards a cognitive redefinition of the social group. In H. Tajfel (Ed.) *Social Identity and Intergroup Relations*. Cambridge: Cambridge University Press.

Tyler, K.A. and Hoyt, D.R. (2000) 'The effects of an acute stressor on depressive symptoms among older adults: The moderating effects of social support and age', *Research on Aging*, 22, 143–164.

Viano, D. and King. A. (2000) *Biomechanics of Chest and Abdomen Impact*. Boca Raton, FL: CRC Press.

Worksafe Victoria. (2006) *Advice for Managing Major Events Safely.* 1st edn. Victoria: Government of Victoria.

Chapter 4

Crowd management planning

Chapter objectives

This chapter explores:

- Theory, techniques and processes for crowd management and crowd control planning

A great deal is known about crowds and how to plan for and manage crowd events. Disasters are predictable, given the knowledge available about human behaviours in emergency situations. Yet, Elliott and Smith (2006) suggest that despite the plentiful crowd disasters that have occurred, there is still an overall failure to learn the lessons identified. Disasters have continued to occur, in spite of official reports detailing key lessons. So why are these lessons not applied in event planning?

According to Elliott and Smith (2006) and Canter (1990), planning failure is partially due to the fragmented, piecemeal approach adopted in relation to crowd safety concerns, rather than consideration of the system as a whole.

Prof. Dr. G. Keith Still claims a common mistake is that officials often start with maps and plans (the BIG picture). Then they talk their way through all the detail and by the end of a planning meeting everyone has different pieces of the jigsaw (Still 2012). He recommends reducing the complexity into bite size chunks and tackling every section in part, then as a whole connected system of liabilities and responsibilities, that has to be managed on behalf of the crowd. "Successful crowd management isn't about chance. It's thorough planning, preparation and risk management. It's about information, communication and design. But most of all it is about understanding people" (Still 2012: 1).

There appears to be a technocratic emphasis on crowd safety and control. Thus, as issues regarding safety and control are conceptualised as technical considerations, the solutions sought are predominantly technical ones. "Sadly, purely technical solutions rarely take full account of the complexity of crowd-related disaster." And "a failure to search for the underlying causes of tragedy combined with a search for simple technical solutions as a panacea for ground safety problems and a complacent attitude among senior managers, inevitably leads to a certainty that disasters are not things of the past" (Elliott and Smith 2006: 387–398).

Challenger argues that there is a need to consider in parallel, and jointly optimise, both social and technical factors "if lessons are to be effectively learned and the occurrence of crowd disasters thereby reduced, a wide range of factors – such as culture, communication, and human behaviour – must be considered" (Challenger 2013: 4).

From his analyses of major crowd incidents and an engineer's knowledge of the basic principles of traffic flow, Fruin (1985, 1993) proposes four primary factors which can raise the probability of crowd disasters occurring:

1 **Increased force**: i.e., the pushing forces and pressures within a crowd, such as those produced by a crowd crush. The greater the forces, the greater the likelihood of crushing occurring and, consequently, the greater the risk of disaster.
2 **Lack of information**: i.e., insufficient provision of information (e.g., communications, signs or actions of personnel) to inform individuals in the crowd to act or react.
3 **Inappropriately designed and/or inadequate space**: i.e., the extent to which the layout and/or amount of space (e.g., standing and seating areas, stairs, doors or escalators) which comprise an event location are able to accommodate safe crowd movement.
4 **Unmanaged time**: i.e., lack of consideration given to how crowd flow and density can be successfully managed by controlling timings, e.g., mass crowd arrival leads to high densities as opposed to safer, staggered entry which results in gradual density increases.

Dickie (1995), identifies four different but related key factors which can be found in the majority of crowd disasters:

Figure 4.1 Small entry gates enable easy ticket checking but could become bottlenecks.

1 inadequate planning
2 excited crowd
3 lack of crowd management and control
4 a flaw or hazard in the facility.

Managing crowds

Rose Challenger (2013) interviewed British crowd management experts to create a list of the key risks involved with crowd events. Their perceptions echoed prior research but emphasised insufficient pre-planning, resulting in a lack of awareness and thorough consideration of what can go wrong and how it can be managed. Other significant factors itemised were:

● insufficient control system overseeing the whole event, with parties unaware of who is in charge
● lack of experienced personnel and lack of familiarity with the event environment
● external risks, such as terrorism and severe weather conditions
● complacency as result of past event success.

Successful crowd management involves thorough planning and preparation, and should consider issues such as event type, location, likely crowd profile, resources needed and contingencies, using a wide range of 'what if' scenarios that recognise that seemingly small problems occurring in combination can have a significant impact on event success. It is essential to organise full coordination between all agencies, including police intelligence, and personnel who have plentiful first-hand knowledge, skills and experience in planning for and managing crowd events. An indispensable component is leadership, communication and guidance to initiate crowd movement in emergencies.

Crowd management or crowd control

Although the two terms are often used interchangeably, it is important operationally to acknowledge the distinction between crowd management and crowd control, to enable more appropriate preparation for an event, along with more suitable action or intervention during the event (Sime 1993; Berlonghi 1995).

Crowd management concerns the facilitation of both the activities and crowd members at an event, to not only ensure that the crowd are able to safely enjoy the event which they came to observe or to be part of, but also to encourage the crowd to behave in the desired manner. "Crowd management includes all measures taken in the normal process of facilitating the movement and enjoyment of people" (Berlonghi 1995: 240). For example, ticket sales, seating, parking, noise control, public announcements, concession stands and communication are all aspects of crowd management.

Crowd control, on the other hand, concerns the actions taken to organise the crowd once they begin to exhibit undesirable behaviours, such as disorder. More forceful measures then need to be taken to quickly bring the crowd back under control, such as limiting access and controlling admissions (Berlonghi 1995). Crowd control should only be used as a last resort, since implementing it too soon can have adverse consequences (Stanton and Wanless 1995).

Berlonghi (1995) proposes that there are identifiable crowd catalysts which contribute to or trigger a crowd from needing to be managed to needing to be controlled, these include:

- **Operational circumstances**: e.g., lack of parking, cancellations or sold-out events.
- **Event activities**: e.g., music, loud noises or special effects.
- **Performers' actions**: e.g., violent, sexual or offensive gestures or comments.
- **Spectator factors**: e.g., crowd cheering, Mexican wave, rushing for seats, drinking alcohol, aggression or throwing objects.
- **Security or police factors**: e.g., abuse of authority, provocations, use of excessive or unreasonable force or arguments with crowd members.
- **Weather factors**: e.g., rain, heat, humidity or lack of ventilation.
- **Natural disasters**: e.g., floods, earthquakes or tornadoes.
- **Man-made disasters**: e.g., structure failures or toxic chemicals.

Berlonghi also claimed the causes of poor crowd behaviour are:

- queues, where delays create anxiety;
- cancellations cause anger;
- poor sightlines cause congestion, frustration;
- dissatisfaction with 'performance' leads to irritability;

Crowd management planning

- price sensitivity leads to value consideration and alienation through inequality leads to anger;
- size of the crowd, more people, more pressure, more obstacles, leads to frustration.

He added that

- good lighting increases accountability, poor lighting allows anonymity
- security presence and professionalism or lack of security or professionalism affects crowd behaviour
- cleanliness of venue/infrastructure – poor sense of order and organisation affects crowd behaviour
- signage – clear instructions affect crowd perception of how they should behave.

Crowd management is preferable to crowd control (Sime 1999; Stanton and Wanless 1995). If management is well-planned and well organised, it should be possible to prevent, or quickly resolve, most problems arising at crowd events. The key factors which experts believe to be central to successfully planning and managing crowd events can be grouped broadly into the following categories:

- planning and preparation
- communication and information
- understanding the crowd
- experienced personnel
- command and control
- observing and monitoring.

(Challenger 2013)

Planning and preparation

Thorough planning and preparation for a crowd event is essential. This should include careful consideration of:

- event type
- profile of the act
- location of the event
- timing of the event
- whether the event is free or paid entry
- event publicity and promotion
- the likely crowd composition, and their likely behaviours
- the scope and scale of the system to be planned and managed
- the range of 'what if' scenarios that need to be considered
- minor risks combining to create major problems
- the knock-on effects of an incident over consecutive days
- the agencies needing to be involved
- the resources that will be needed
- problems that could potentially arise
- contingencies to be implemented to deal with those problems if they occur.

It is not possible to over stress the importance of coordination between all agencies, and the need to ensure all personnel, from all agencies, are consistently and effectively educated, trained and briefed, for both normal and emergency circumstances. Police intelligence surrounding the event and the likely crowds it will attract, should be drawn on throughout the planning and preparation stages.

It is important not to rely too heavily on preconceptions about how a crowd will behave or what will go wrong at an event, e.g., to focus on terrorism or hooliganism, or the behaviours of non-ticket holders who will be attracted to the events for a range of motives (both legal and illegal).

Each event should be assessed on its own merits, and the atmosphere and crowd profile on the day of the event taken into account. Each event will have its own special circumstances likely to involve new or additional risks which will require careful analysis and mitigation. For instance, very large scale, multi-day, multi-site crowd events, will be very different to more frequent, one-off events in a great number of ways. Generic 'off the shelf' crowd management plans available online will require significant modification or input information loading to be worthwhile.

Good practice manuals for crowd management planning

A number of good practice guideline manuals have been published by government organisations designed for all professionals and practitioners involved in events, crowd management, crowd control and emergency services. They include:

Understanding Crowd Behaviours, Volume 1: Practical Guidance and Lessons Identified. Challenger, R., Clegg, C. W. and Robinson, M. A. Leeds: The Stationery Office (TSO).
Safe and Healthy Mass Gatherings. Australian Emergency Manuals Series. Emergency Management Australia.
The Event Safety Guide: A Guide to Health, Safety and Welfare at Music and Similar Events. Health and Safety Executive (UK).
Advice for Managing Major Events Safely. Government of Victoria.
Public Events: Safety and Security Strategies. Centre for Police and Justice Studies, Monash University, Victoria.

These manuals focus on thorough planning and preparation, multi-agency team-working, utilisation of experienced personnel, cross-agency coordination, strategies for communications, differentiation of different types of crowd and awareness of different behaviours from different types of crowd.

What if...? Simulation modelling

Crowd simulation modelling for crowd safety and risk analysis has one objective, to develop a safer crowd management plan. Crowd simulation techniques are concerned with modelling crowd movements, behaviours and interactions between crowds and between crowd members. Simulations assist in both understanding a specific scenario (as it develops) and planning the appropriate crowd management strategy, process and procedures. Still (2012) says it is not possible to develop a safe, robust crowd management plan without some form of crowd modelling (e.g. some idea of how the crowd will behave at an event/venue).

'What if' simulation tools can be used during planning throughout the planning stage, to consider strategies and contingency plans to deal with potential problems and to test out the suitability and sufficiency of crowd management plans under consideration. A wide range of scenarios should be tested, considering not only major risks such as bomb threats, panic – when a large number of people in a small space sense something is wrong it can lead to crushing, pushing, crowd collapse and serious injury. Less dramatic, but probably more likely, risks such as tripping hazards or software problems have the potential to contribute towards more major incidents. Moreover, scenarios should be extended to consider the wider event environment, along with the knock-on effects of incidents occurring in succession or combination.

Simulation modelling should provide information that can be used to coordinate the early stages of site planning, mostly involving the production and operations procedures. However, this is dependent on effective communications between the crowd management, site design and event operational teams.

Crowd behaviour should be modelled at three levels:

1   the individual,
2   interactions between individuals, and
3   the group – to mirror the behaviours of a crowd in reality.

The simulation can model the physical forces within a crowd that have a direct impact on movement and behaviour. These forces occur for a reason, are direction and location specific, propagate through the crowd, and, once exerted, are typically out of an individual's control, thereby carrying dangerous consequences. Self-organisation phenomena, which emerge because a crowd typically behaves according to the principle of least effort, can be accurately simulated with crowd behaviour models. These include the 'faster is slower' effect, lane formation, herding and queuing, and 'corner hugging'.

Additional observed crowd behaviours which can be realistically modelled include:

● Individuals prefer not to take detours or move in opposition to the main crowd flow, instead taking the fastest route or, if routes are of equal length, the route with the least changes in direction.
● Individuals try to maintain a distance from others and from obstacles, in order to avoid collisions.
● Group or family members prefer to move as a unit and will wait for one another if they become separated.

Initiatives which can be implemented to improve crowd flow, based on these observations, include:

● barriers and fences to encourage lane formation;
● entry and exit doors and gates;
● long line-of-sight paths;
● rounded rather than angular corners;
● monitoring and communication systems.

However, current crowd behaviour models do not adequately include important psychological aspects of human behaviour, such as memory, emotions and stress, and underestimate the ability of crowd members with limited knowledge of a situation to communicate with one another in order to exchange information, and the ability to then gain further knowledge from exploring the environment (Pelechano and Badler

2006). Nevertheless, they are very useful during planning and preparation for a crowd event. They provide an opportunity to consider potential problems from multiple perspectives, to share information from differing agencies, and to develop adequate contingency plans to manage and control these problems should they arise.

Modelling techniques

Crowd event modelling projects all follow a similar process, and all modelling techniques have limitations:

> Real-time crowd simulation is difficult because large groups of people exhibit behaviour of enormous complexity and subtlety. A crowd model must not only include individual human motion and environmental constraints such as boundaries, but also address a bewildering array of dynamic interactions between people. Further, the model must reflect intelligent path planning through this changing environment. Humans constantly adjust their paths to reflect congestion and other dynamic factors. Even dense crowds are characterized by surprisingly few collisions or sudden changes in individual motion. It has proven difficult to capture these effects in simulation, especially for large crowds in real-time.
> (Treuille et al. 2006: 1160)

To capture all the aspects of a complex dynamic environment where human factors are involved is impossible. Any attempt to model the full scope of reality would have to capture all the elements that may have an influence on reality. For example, how do frustration, aggression or delays affect each individual in the crowd? There are so many unknown factors that reliance on analysis by a single model is problematic. A more practical approach is to use appropriate models for each aspect of the event. For example statistical analysis would be appropriate for some projects (spreadsheet modelling) and some projects may require a virtual reality model of 3D interactions (through time).

Running one simulation is not enough to study many types of high density pedestrian environments. It is necessary to test the extremes of the spectrum of possible scenarios – groups of individuals not moving, and all individuals moving, low density and high density, cross flow, counter flow and congested spaces. By considering the extremes, the simulation can represent the conditions at which the risks of crowd injury can be assessed. By testing the extreme conditions (no-one moving, crowds building up, rates of flow, everyone moving, trips/falls, counter flows etc.) a contingency plan for the worst-case scenarios can be developed accordingly. For example, it is prudent to 'what if' test the plan and strategy for between 200 and 500 per cent (or more) people arriving over a shorter period of time than expected to test the robustness of the crowd management process.

Various models for simulating crowd behaviours

Challenger (2013) has surveyed the various models for simulating crowd movement, and says they fall into two categories:

1 macroscopic, which concern the behaviour of the crowd as a whole; and
2 microscopic, which concern the behaviour, decisions and interactions of individuals within the crowd.

Macroscopic models

Macroscopic models include: *regression models*, which use simple equations to calculate flow variables; and *fluid dynamics models*, which liken the movement of a crowd to the flow of a fluid.

Regression models predict pedestrian flow under specific circumstances, dependent on the infrastructure (e.g., stairs, corridors), from statistically established relations between flow variables (Milazzo et al. 1998). For example, simple spreadsheet models are useful means of measuring and predicting flow variables, such as ingress and egress rates, flow rate, speed of movement and density. This information can then be used to assist preparations for a crowd event. *Route choice models* describe pedestrian wayfinding, based on the premise that pedestrians chose their route in order to maximise utility, in terms of travel time, effort, comfort, etc. (Hoogendoorn and Bovy 2003).

A drawback of macroscopic models is that no individual features, such as physical abilities, direction of movement and individual positioning, can be considered (Wong and Luo 2005; Lerner et al. 2007). Fluid analogies of crowds are also weak, people do not behave according to laws of physics. "The laws of crowd dynamics have to include the fact that people do not follow the laws of physics, they have a choice in their direction, have no conservation of momentum and can stop and start at will. They cannot be reduced to equations which are appropriate for the movement of ball bearings through viscous fluids" (Still 2000: 16).

Microscopic models

Microscopic models include: *rule-based models*, e.g., Reynolds's (1987, 1999) 'boids' model which likens crowd behaviour to the movement of flocking birds; *social forces models*, where each individual is represented by a self-driven particle subject to social and physical forces; *cellular automata models*, which divide the environment into a uniform grid of discrete cells, with agents able to move between unoccupied neighbouring cells; and *agent-based models,* the most complex and realistic of the simulation models.

The 'boids' model (or rules-based model) likens crowd behaviours to the movement of herds of animals as being similar to the way in which a crowd typically moves. The model uses a 'flocking algorithm' to describe animal and crowd movement (Reynolds 1987; Saiwaki et al. 1999), comprising the elements of:

- **Separation**: keeping a minimum distance between individuals in the given environment.
- **Alignment**: consistency in the direction and movement speed of an individual in relation to others.
- **Cohesion**: gathering members into a unique crowd.
- **Avoidance**: preventing each individual colliding with others.

Rule-based models have been criticised for lacking realism by primarily determining an individual's choice of movement according to the speed, direction and proximity of other individuals, other important factors which may influence crowd behaviours are overlooked (Pelechano and Malkawi 2008).

Social forces model

The social forces model, a behavioural model of individual pedestrian dynamics, describes collective behaviour using a self-driven, multi-particle system framework (Helbing et al. 2000), wherein each self-driven particle has a target and is prepared to move at a given velocity to reach that target (Parisi and Dorso 2007). In other words, pedestrians like to move in a certain direction at a certain speed, adapting their velocity within a certain time period, while keeping their distance from other individuals and obstacles.

This model regards the crowd as populated by intelligent, autonomous agents capable of perceiving their environment, generating intentions, making independent decisions and performing rational, realistic behaviours, according to various sets of underlying simulation rules. Accordingly, individual attributes, such as age, gender, mobility, size and walking speed can be assigned randomly.

Within the simulation modelling, the motion of each crowd member is expressed as a result of combined socio-psychological and physical forces which attract or repel individuals. These 'social forces' reflect individuals' intentions to not collide with other people or obstacles, and to move in a specific direction at a specific speed. The simulation space is treated as continuous, thus individuals are able to move continuously in a two-dimensional environment. This enables realistic crowd phenomena – such as herding behaviour and mass queuing, to be generated.

Force effects

In line with the social forces model, Henein and White (2005, 2007) argue that force effects should be a basic element in models of crowd behaviours, since forces, such as pushing, or people leaning on one another, can have a direct effect on the way in which crowd members move and, ultimately, may result in injuries or death. The physical forces, i.e., pushing and shoving, characteristic of crowd movement under certain circumstances, influence crowd behaviours when crowd density becomes so high that individuals are forced to collide, such as during an emergency evacuation. Helbing and Molnar (1997) describe these forces as *acceleration* – the velocity of each individual varies over time, as he or she attempts to reach optimum speed, while avoiding obstacles; and, *repulsion* – a repulsive force from other individuals and from obstacles and edges.

> Force effects are particularly important in modelling crowd behaviours. Although people generally try to move toward goals, force effects can cause them to be pushed away from their desired trajectories and accurate models must reflect this. Also, the presence of crowd members injured by excessive force can significantly affect the ability of others to move freely. In an evacuation situation, increased desired walking speed leads to increased forces, and these forces tend to cause additional delays to those trying to exit. Models that do not represent pushing forces therefore cannot directly account for all these additional delays.
>
> (Henein and White 2005: 173–174)

Evacuation simulation software

Human crowd behaviour is complex and difficult to capture for computer mathematical equations used for crowd simulation programs. Nevertheless there are numerous models concerned with evacuation behaviour. These are either *cellular automata models*, or *agent-based models.* Two key evacuation models are: EXODUS and SIMULEX

Exodus18 is a suite of software tools which enables evacuation simulation for large numbers of people from within an enclosure, for example in mass transportation, such as aircraft, trains or ships. The basic cellular automata model tracks the trajectory of individuals either as they escape from an enclosure, or as they are overcome by fire or toxic gases. Each individual moves from one cell/node to the next, dependent on whether a node is occupied or empty.

EXODUS includes multiple social psychological attributes and characteristics which can be assigned to individual agents, such as age, name, sex, breathing rate, agility, mobility, running speed, response time and drive. It features an itinerary list, which enables each individual to perform certain tasks before evacuating, such as searching for a child, or returning to a location to collect a bag, along with a feature that enables the use of signage and communication between individuals to be modelled (Filippidis et al. 2003).

SIMULEX is an agent-based model, concerned with evacuation from complex buildings. It enables more realistic human behaviours to be modelled, since multiple factors are taken into account, including physical motions and gestures (e.g., swaying and twisting), proximity of other evacuees, shape of building structure, and influence of gender and age. Additionally, walking speed and the direction of each individual are assessed independently of group density, meaning that each individual is allowed to

Figure 4.2 Congestion caused by bag checks, note PA speaker.

decide on his or her own direction and speed, depending on environmental logistics, proximity of other people and obstacles. Thus, for example, an individual is able to slow down if obstacles are encountered.

A weakness of SIMULEX is that it relies on inter-person distances to specify individuals' walking speeds and directions, yet in reality, people are not equally spaced (Santos and Aguirre 2004). It is because of such issues that Still (2012) says caution is advised, as just one tool, one software system, one methodology or one technique cannot be used to solve large complex crowd problems.

'What if' exercises

'What if' scenarios are incredibly useful during planning and preparation for a crowd event. They provide an opportunity to test out the suitability and sufficiency of the plans in place, to observe potential problems from multiple perspectives, to share information from differing agencies, and to develop adequate contingency plans to manage and control problems when they arise.

'What if' exercises should be carried out throughout the planning stage, not just the end, and should be done in real time whenever possible, building incrementally from a relatively small incident. For example, all parties could consider what their most vulnerable area is, and scenarios could be developed around those. It is important to think about obscure incidents, such as a burst water main or an explosion, but there is little added value of considering highly unlikely events, such as a plane falling out of the sky.

If it is possible to conduct an evacuation drill, or practice traffic control, it is beneficial to have a few crowd control measures in place and to observe how individuals move. The nature and location of potential problems can then be better anticipated, enabling more appropriate control measures to be implemented.

DIM-ICE model

Developed over two decades by Prof. Dr. G. Keith Still FIMA Professor of Crowd Dynamics and Crowd Management at Bucks New University, the DIM-ICE risk model was developed from the analysis of accidents and incidents from around the world. Its intention is to create an understanding of how particular site design limitations (capacity, throughput), information provision (social media, signage, PA announcements, news) elements and the management systems (processes and procedures) are key to understanding how to influence crowd behaviour in places of public assembly.

The DIM-ICE model is a systematic check list for risk assessment and crowd management. It defines an event in phases, influences and modes.

- **Three primary influences on crowd behaviour**: design, information and management
- **Three primary phases of crowd behaviour**: ingress, circulation and egress
- **Two primary modes of crowd behaviour**: normal and emergency.

This can be expressed in a matrix (see p.76) which is populated with the specifics of the event being modelled.

The process asks planners to consider the three ways a crowd can be influenced: DIM (design of site, information provided to the crowd, and management systems of queuing, ushering, ticketing), outlining these features against the three different phases of behaviour, coming in to the event, circulating around the event site, and leaving – ingress, circulation and egress – ICE, in a matrix of nine boxes.

Normal crowd flow	Ingress	Circulation	Egress
Site design			
Information			
Management			

Planners are then asked to consider the same matrix for extreme or emergency situations – asking what changes will occur.

Emergency crowd flow	Ingress	Circulation	Egress
Site design			
Information			
Management			

Colours are added to the description to highlight where risks are high (red), medium (orange) or low (green). This is to draw the users' attention to the underlying elements that give rise to crowd risks. It is primarily a checklist to ensure the crowd management plan has considered both the phases and influences of crowd behaviour. The colours assist in both understanding (red needs to improve, orange needs to be monitored, green is the things thought to be done well).

Beginning with simple grids and calculations, the process then explores how many people in a moving crowd can fit into any confined space on the event site, working out upper safety limits and discussing the implications for assessment, before looking at the maths in more detail. The numerical analysis of flow rates, fill times and capacity are potentially the primary elements where improvements to crowd safety would have had most impact.

This type of analysis focusses on improving crowd safety through the principles and applications of numerical techniques (not involving computer simulations). To further understand the phases, influences and modes of crowd behaviour, the process of meta-modelling the event is used. Using a range of crowd modelling tools, the DIM-ICE model is able to predict the time of critical density, and understand the early warning signs of a crowd in distress. See www.GKStill.com

Summary

- There is a difference between crowd management and crowd control.
- Crowd management includes all measures taken in the normal process of facilitating the movement and enjoyment of the event.
- Crowd control concerns the actions taken to organise the crowd once they begin to exhibit undesirable behaviours or in emergencies.
- There are identifiable crowd catalysts which contribute to or trigger a crowd from needing to be managed to needing to be controlled.
- The key factors for managing crowd events are: planning and preparation; communication and information; understanding the crowd; experienced personnel.
- Crowd simulation techniques are used for modelling crowd movements, behaviours, and interactions between crowds and between crowd members. Simulations assist in both understanding a specific scenario and planning the appropriate crowd management strategy, process and procedures.
- 'What if' simulation tools, can be used during planning throughout the planning stage, to consider strategies and contingency plans to deal with potential problems and to test out the suitability and sufficiency of crowd management plans under consideration.
- There are various models for simulating crowd movement. They fall into two categories:

  - macroscopic, which concern the behaviour of the crowd as a whole; and
  - microscopic, which concern the behaviour, decisions and interactions of individuals within the crowd.

- 'What if' scenarios test out the suitability and sufficiency of the plans in place, and provide observation of potential problems from multiple perspectives, enabling the developing of plans to manage and control problems when they arise.

Bibliography

Berlonghi, A. (1994) *The Special Event Risk Management Manual*. Dena Point, CA: Alexander Berlonghi.

Berlonghi, A. (1995) 'Understanding and planning for different spectator crowds', *Safety Science*, 18, 239–247.

Canter, D. (1990) *Fires and Human Behaviour*, 2nd edn. London: David Fulton Publishers.

Challenger, R. (2013) *Understanding Crowd Behaviours*. Leeds: The Stationery Office (TSO).

Challenger, R., Clegg, C. W. and Robinson, M. A. (2010) *Understanding Crowd Behaviours, Volume 1: Practical Guidance and Lessons Identified*. Leeds: The Stationery Office (TSO).

Challenger, R., Clegg, C. W. and Robinson, M. A. (2010) *Understanding Crowd Behaviours, Volume 2: Supporting Theory and Evidence*. Leeds: The Stationery Office (TSO).

Dickie, J. F. (1995) 'Major crowd catastrophes', *Safety Science*, 18, 309–320.

Elliott, D. and Smith, D. (2006) Football stadia disasters in the United Kingdom: Learning from tragedy? In D. Smith and D. Elliott (Eds) *Key Readings in Crisis Management: Systems and Structures for Prevention and Recovery*. London: Routledge, pp. 369–392.

Fruin, J. J. (1985) Crowd dynamics and the design and management of public places. In J. Pauls (Ed.) *International Conference on Building Use and Safety Technology*. Washington: National Institute of Building Sciences, pp. 110–113.

Fruin, J. J. (1993) The causes and prevention of crowd disaster. In R. A. Smith and J. F. Dickie (Eds) *Engineering for Crowd Safety*. Amsterdam: Elsevier, pp. 99–108.

Filippidis, L., Gwynne, S., Galea, E. R. and Lawrence, P. (2003) *Simulating the interaction of pedestrians with way finding systems*. Proceedings of the 2nd International Conference Pedestrian and Evacuation Dynamic 2003.

Helbing, D. and Molnar, P. (1997) Self-organization phenomena in pedestrian crowds. In F. Schweitzer (Ed.) *Self-organization of Complex Structures: From Individual to Collective Dynamics*. London: Gordon and Breach, pp. 569–577.

Helbing, D., Farkas, I. and Vicsek, T. (2000) 'Simulating dynamic features of escape panic', *Nature*, 407, 487–490.Henein, C. M. and White, T. (2005) 'Agent-based modelling of forces in crowds', *Multi-Agent and Multi-Agent-Based Simulation*, 3415, 173–184.

Henein, C. M. and White, T. (2007) 'Macroscopic effects of microscopic forces between agents in crowd models', *Physica A*, 373, 694–712.

Hoogendoorn, S. and Bovy, P. H. L. (2003) 'Simulation of pedestrian flows by optimal control and differential games', *Optimal Control: Applications and Methods*, 24, 153–172.

Lerner, A., Chrysanthou, Y. and Lischinski, D. (2007) 'Crowds by example', *Eurographics*, 26, 655–664.

Milazzo, J. S., Rouphail, N. M., Hummer, J. E. and Allen, D. P. (1998) 'The effect of pedestrians on the capacity of signalized intersections', *Transportation Research Record: Journal of the Transportation Research Board*, 1646, 37–46.

Parisi, D. R. and Dorso, C. O. (2007) 'Morphological and dynamical aspects of the room evacuation process', *Physica A*, 385, 343–355.

Pelechano, N. and Badler, N. I. (2006) 'Modeling crowd and trained leader behavior during building evacuation', *IEEE Computer Graphics and Applications*, 26, 80–86.

Pelechano, N. and Malkawi, A. (2008) 'Evacuation simulation models: Challenges in modeling high rise building evacuation with cellular automata approaches', *Automation in Construction*, 17, 377–385. 1162_New Vol 2.

Reynolds, C. (1987) 'Flocks, herds, and schools: A distributed behavioral model', *Computer Graphics*, 21, 25–34. Saiwaki, N., Komatsu, T. and Nishida, S. (1999) 'Automatic generation of moving crowds in the virtual environment', *Advanced Multimedia Content Processing*, 1554, 422–432.

Reynolds, C. (1999) *Steering behaviors for autonomous characters*. Game Developers Conference, 763–782.

Santos, G. and Aguirre, B. E. (2004) *A critical review of emergency evacuation simulations models*. preliminary paper 339. University of Delaware Disaster Research Center.

Sime, J. D. (1993) *Crowd psychology and engineering: Designing for people or ball-bearings*. International Conference on Engineering for Crowd Safety, March 1993, London, UK.

Sime, J. D. (1999) 'Crowd facilities, management and communications in disasters', *Facilities*, 17, 313–324.

Stanton, R. J. C. and Wanless, G. K. (1995) 'Pedestrian movement', *Safety Science*, 18, 291–300.

Still, G. K. (2000). *Crowd Dynamics*. PhD Thesis, University of Warwick, UK.

Still, G. K. (2012) *Crowd Modelling: Crowd Safety in the Complex and Built Environment*. Cumbria. UK: Crowd Modelling Ltd.

Treuille, A., Cooper, S. and Popovic, Z. (2006) 'Continuum crowds', *ACM Transactions on Graphics*, 25, 1160–1168.

Wong, K. H. L. and Luo, M. (2005) 'Computational tool in infrastructure emergency total evacuation analysis', *Intelligence and Security Informatics, Proceedings*, 3495, 536–542.

Chapter 5

Space and flow in public areas

Chapter objectives

This chapter examines:

- Principles and theory of crowd flow
- Crowd processing and monitoring methods
- Crowd communication practices

Crowd management and control involves ensuring that crowds do not block entrances, exits or pedestrian flows, and organising how the crowd is going to be distributed inside the venue. This means taking preventive measures to avoid injuries by establishing processes to ensure that the venue will not be overcrowded, controlling access points, and procedures for the admittance, seating and dispersal of crowds of spectators.

John Fruin provides both a practical and theoretical basis for understanding crowding and its relationship to venue management and the design of places of public assembly. Fruin's analysis shows that there are four interacting elements in every crowd situation: *energy*, *time*, *space*, and *information*. Event site designers can use Fruin's insights to develop control strategies to prevent the occurrence of critical crowd forces.

From his analyses of major crowd incidents and an engineer's knowledge of the basic principles of traffic flow, Fruin (1985, 1993) proposes four primary factors which can raise the probability of crowd disasters occurring:

1 **Increased force**: i.e., the pushing forces and pressures within a crowd, such as those produced by a crowd crush. The greater the forces, the greater the likelihood of crushing occurring and, consequently, the greater the risk of disaster.
2 **Lack of information**: i.e., insufficient provision of information (e.g., communications, signs or actions of personnel) to inform individuals in the crowd to act or react.
3 **Space** is the size and configuration of the area occupied, i.e., the extent to which the layout and/or amount of space (e.g., standing and seating areas, stairs, doors or escalators) which comprise an event location are able to accommodate safe crowd movement.
4 **Time** is simply the period during which the crowding occurs, i.e., lack of consideration given to how crowd flow and density can be successfully managed by controlling timings, e.g., mass crowd arrival leads to high densities as opposed to safer, staggered entry which results in gradual density increases.

Fruin's observations are supported by other researchers. Dickie (1995) claimed a flaw or hazard in the facility was a key factor found in the majority of crowd disasters. Sime (1999) proposed that excessive numbers concentrated around an entrance or exit point, where flow rate is naturally reduced, resulted in overcrowding and increased crowd forces, ultimately leading to trampling and crushing. Langston et al. report that "Poor venue design and crowd management as a result of inadequate research into crowd behaviour has led to many disasters resulting in wider scale loss of life and injury" (Langston et al. 2006: 396).

The safety of the public in event environments is largely determined by the interaction of the venue or site's architectural design and efficient crowd management. Therefore it is essential that event managers obtain an understanding of crowd dynamics and the theory of crowding in relationship to site/venue design and management. Key texts providing practical and theoretical basis for understanding crowd management are Berlonghi's *Understanding and planning for different spectator crowds* (1995), and Fruin's *Crowd dynamics and auditorium management* (1984), and *Crowd dynamics and the design and management of public places* (1985).

Space

This element is considered in two ways when analysing crowd effects. The first is the critical density or average area per person that occurs in uncontrolled crowds. When average densities in a crowd reach the approximate area of the human body, – about 0.19 square metres per person, individual control of movement becomes impossible, and phenomena such as shockwaves will be propagated through the crowd mass and cause the sudden uncontrolled surges that unleash the crowd's destructive force. Fruin claims the primary crowd management objective is the avoidance of critical crowd densities (1985).

The second is the particular architectural configuration or type of pedestrian facility involved. Architectural features that typically are implicated in dangerous crowding incidents are those that rigidly confine people within an inadequate space, or are not properly designed for crowd pressures and efficient mass movement. Minor design deficiencies that present no apparent problems under normal traffic conditions can be accentuated in crowds, potentially triggering more dangerous, 'domino effect' accidents.

Density and movement

In the various definitions of crowds provided in Chapter 3, specific figures were deliberately not given in relation to crowd density. This was because the huge variety of different types of crowds and events make the inclusion of numerical data unsuitable. Official UK guidelines concerning safe crowd densities and levels, i.e., the *Guide to Safety at Sports Grounds* (Department for Culture, Media and Sport, 2008) recommend a maximum of 47 people per 10 square metres when standing, and a maximum of 40 people per 10 square metres if moving. Alternatively, older guidelines concerning safe crowd densities at festivals, such as Glastonbury, i.e. *Event Safety Guide: A Guide to Health, Safety and Welfare at Music and Similar Events* (HSE, 1999) recommend only 20 people per 10 square metres.

But of course, both the type of event and movement of the crowd influence the density at an event. In general, it is suggested that people in close proximity over a given area can constitute a safe density distribution, but people should not be so densely packed as to cause crushing, i.e., the density must be safe. Crowds do not fill a space evenly, but rather cluster, exploit short-cuts and exhibit herding behaviour (Still 2000).

The different crowd density levels given above are similar to how Fruin's (1971) six levels of pedestrian flow rate – from level A to level F – are defined. These levels of flow indicate varying levels of walking speed, flow of movement and restrictions in passing, crossing or reverse movements, are:

Level A

- Flow rate of less than 23 people per metre per minute.
- Virtually unrestricted choice of walking speed.
- Minimum manoeuvring needed to pass fellow pedestrians.
- Unrestricted crossing and reverse movements.

Level B

- Flow rate of between 23 and 33 people per metre per minute.
- Normal walking speeds, restricted only occasionally.
- Occasional interference in passing fellow pedestrians.
- Occasional interference in crossing and reverse movements.

Level C

- Flow rate of between 33 and 49 people per metre per minute.
- Partially restricted walking speeds.
- Restricted passing movements, but possible with manoeuvring.
- Restricted crossing and reverse movements, with significant manoeuvring needed to avoid conflict.
- Reasonably fluid flow.

Level D

- Flow rate of between 49 and 66 people per metre per minute.
- Restricted and reduced walking speeds.
- Passing fellow pedestrians rarely possible without conflict.
- Severely restricted crossing and reverse movements, with multiple conflicts.
- Momentary flow stoppages possible when critical densities are intermittently reached.

Level E

- Flow rate of between 66 and 82 people per metre per minute.
- Restricted walking speeds, occasionally reduced to shuffling.
- Passing fellow pedestrians impossible without conflict.
- Severely restricted crossing and reverse movements, with unavoidable conflicts.
- Flow achieves maximum capacity under pressure, but with frequent interruptions and stoppages.

Level F

- Flow rate variable.
- Walking speed reduced to shuffling.
- Passing movements are impossible.
- Crossing and reverse movements are impossible.
- Frequent and unavoidable physical contact.
- Sporadic flow, on the verge of complete breakdown and stoppage.

It is important to note that there are different levels of flow specific to walkways, queuing areas and stairways. And it should be recognised that crowds, in general, do not distribute evenly, but tend to cluster in particular areas, such as areas with a good view or near to concessions stands. Therefore, while the average density over the whole event area might be acceptable, it is crucial to be aware that particular areas will be very dense while others will be relatively unused and action may be needed to redistribute density more evenly.

Crowd flow

According to Hughes (2003) the speed at which individuals walk is determined by the ground on which they walk, the density of surrounding individuals and the behavioural characteristics of those individuals. In unfamiliar surroundings or unfamiliar circumstances, people will behave differently; for instance, stopping and starting more frequently, moving more slowly, and relying heavily on signage and ushering.

Individuals seek to minimise their estimated travel time towards a particular goal, while simultaneously attempting to avoid extreme crowd densities. They prefer not to take detours or to move in the opposing direction to the main crowd flow, even if the direct route they subsequently choose is crowded (Helbing et al. 2001). They typically move according to the principle of 'least effort', usually preferring the fastest route. If alternative routes are of the same length, individuals choose to take the one which offers the straightest route, that with the least changes in direction, for as long as possible, provided that the alternatives are not more attractive (e.g., in terms of being better lit, less noisy or a more attractive environment). Goffman (1971) terms this the 'law of minimal change'.

Provided there is sufficient time to reach their destination, people prefer to walk at an individually desired speed, corresponding to their most comfortable – i.e., least energy-consuming – walking speed. In order to avoid collisions, they try to keep a certain distance from other people and from environmental borders, such as walls or obstacles. This distance decreases if the individual is in a hurry or if crowd density increases, for instance, around a particularly attractive place, such as a food outlet. As crowd members turn corners, they tend to slow down and move further into them, becoming more densely packed and appearing to 'hug' the corner. People will often turn sideways when trying to move quickly through a crowd, as reducing the leading surface area of their body while trying to navigate through the crowd helps to lessen congestion (Fukamachi and Nagatani 2007).

When individual walking speed is maximised

> [I]ndividuals will usually not take complicated decisions between various possible alternative behaviours, but apply an optimized behavioural strategy, which has been learned over time by trial and error. Hence a pedestrian will react to obstacles, other pedestrians, etc. in a somewhat automatic way.
>
> (Helbing et al., 2001: 364)

Family groups and groups of friends prefer to move together as a unit. For example, people who arrive at an event together prefer to move around the event, and to leave together. If group members become separated, they are likely to try to reform their group before exiting. However, this may produce movements contrary to the main flow of the crowd, which can hinder the flow as a whole. Hierarchically organised groups – e.g., parents with children – are likely to behave differently to groups who are not organised according to a hierarchy – e.g. groups of friends (Pan et al. 2006).

Recent important studies of crowd flow at mass events have been made by Dirk Helbing and his research team. The following observations are from Helbing's reports and provide the basis for understanding crucial crowd behaviours.

Crowd jams occur when densely packed crowds push forward towards a narrow door, gate or alleyway (a bottleneck). The faster people wish to move, due to impatience, the more densely packed they become and the slower they can actually move.

As individuals compete with other crowd members to move through a narrow space it becomes clogged and the crowd forms an arch-shape, radiating outwards. This often is an uneven process as one entrance or exit may become clogged while another is underused, as the crowd prefer to use the route with which they are familiar.

Bottlenecks should be eliminated in the site design, but some are unavoidable – box offices and ticket inspection points, for instance, where organised ushering and queuing control will be required to maximise the crowd flow. However, sometimes at uncontrolled bottlenecks, crowd self-organisation occurs. Seeing their progress is obstructed by other crowd members, individuals may initiate a queue or join an existing queue. Thus, a more effective transition is often achieved, as a result of crowd members leaving in an orderly and single-file manner rather than exhibiting competitive behaviour. Nevertheless, this behaviour cannot be expected and planning should not rely on it occurring.

When a crowd is in counter-flow, approaching the opening from opposing sides and where, due to the narrowness of the opening, crowd members are only able to pass through in one direction at a time, the direction of movement through the bottleneck alternates between right-to-left and left-to-right. This oscillation is due to the movement of the crowd from one side of the bottleneck, e.g., moving right-to-left, being continually halted by mounting pressure from the crowd wanting to move in the opposite direction, e.g., moving left-to-right. Thus, the opposing crowd flows take turns to pass through the bottleneck, resulting in oscillating crowd movements.

When congestion occurs, people typically follow the person in front of them, thereby creating flow patterns. Lane formation is a common form of crowd self-organisation

Figure 5.1 Bag check and wrist-banding entrance.

that occurs when people are moving in opposite directions. They self-organise to create distinct lanes, one for each direction of movement. This helps to reduce collisions and increase speed and, therefore, is considered a form of optimal self-organisation. Such lane formation may begin as small channels of people moving in opposite directions, but these channels then merge to create larger lanes. However, in high density crowds, nervous crowds or large disturbances, lanes formed may break down due to continuous overtaking manoeuvres (Helbing et al. 2005).

Crowd processing

The objective of Front of House crowd control strategies is to prevent the build-up of large accumulations of patrons in short periods of time. A significant problem occurs at 'early arrival' events, where a large accumulation of patrons may build up prior to gate opening, and the mass exodus that occurs immediately after the performance.

A review of crowd disasters shows that typically they occur in short periods of time when the critical capacity of a venue has been temporarily exceeded but intensive pressure to use the facility continues. Usually, the crowd continues to press ahead because it has no knowledge of what conditions are at the bottleneck. Those at the bottleneck find it impossible to resist the crowd pressures from behind.

Front of House managers need a good sense of the patron capacities and processing rates of all the Front of House facilities and pedestrian spaces for which they are responsible. They should not allow admissions to exceed the rate of crowd dispersal inside the venue. A common control is to estimate the entry rates and take measures to prevent an excessive build-up of people outside the venue. Short counts, using a stopwatch and hand counter, can be made of ticket takers, stairs, doors, escalators, checkrooms and so on, to develop an understanding of the flow of the crowd. Processing rates will vary according to the type of event and the patrons.

Early opening and delayed closing

A common practice is to use time based strategies to overcome crowd build up. Early opening of a venue to extend the time period during which the crowd can enter, entertainment after the event or other strategies to lengthen the time over which the crowd can leave, reduces crowding within the venue and traffic pressures on external transit, road and parking facilities.

A ticketing system could be put in place so that the venue will not be overcrowded or people turned away. Tickets can be a useful tool to control the crowd flow even when an event is free. They can also be used to inform attendees of arrival times and gate numbers. Staggering arrivals could lessen the likelihood of crowd congestion at entrances. Ticketing may also help reduce the likelihood of people waiting at the event overnight in the hope of obtaining entrance.

Tickets are an important crowd management information factor. Reserved section and seat tickets determine specific area occupancy, and routes of entry and exit. Tickets also provide a means of instructing patrons on rules of conduct expected and on items that are prohibited within the venue.

Ticketing

A key issue for crowd and site management is the use of tickets for access to venues. Checking of tickets to ensure authenticity, correct dates and seating, requires attention to detail and systems. Different types of ticketing – paper tickets, plastic wrist bands, wrist stamping, laminated cards on lanyards around the neck – all require immense attention to detail in terms of ease of entry and exit, verifying, collection and monitoring. The tasks required to process tickets and seat patrons for a performance or event include the monitoring of patron movements in and out of the auditorium and assisting with any special seating requirements, and to provide general information on ticket categories, prices and availability.

The processing time for the various methods for selling and checking of tickets should be considered in terms of rapid movement of people. The quickest method of all is for customers to simply throw money into a number of boxes as they pass through a gate, in the manner of old time cash toll booths on highways and bridges. This relies on the customer having the correct change. Also it creates an easy opportunity for theft. The usual means of cash purchasing of tickets is at a box office, where delays occur in giving change, ensuring discounts are correct, and often time spent in providing other information about the event, such as finishing times, or programme detail. Pre-booked tickets or E-tickets issued from a different pick up point, save some transaction time, but only if the customer has a hard copy print. If the ticket is a digital ticket on a phone, delays occur from verification requirements that can be exacerbated by poor reception coverage. In general, E-ticketing merely moves the delays from one queue to another.

Figure 5.2 Temporary fencing defining different access areas.

The procedures to issue, check and process tickets include checking that all equipment and materials are available and operational before commencing ticket issue. Issue tickets and receipts, if required, in accordance with organisational procedures and ticketing system. On entry to the venue, checking tickets/passes for validity and seating location is required. There is also a need to provide patrons with accurate auditorium information and to advise them of any special restrictions or requirements that may apply.

Queueing theory

There will need to be preventive measures to avoid crushing at public entrances. Queueing requires consideration in the way in which it can be dealt with effectively. And there is a need to be mindful of the exit arrangements where queueing can also occur. A primary tool for studying the problem of crowd congestion is **Queueing theory**.

Any system in which arrivals place a demand upon a finite capacity, a limited space or limited resources may be termed a queueing system. Queueing theory is a branch of statistics which deals with arrival times of people (or transport) and service rates (time taken for ticket purchase, or buying food or souvenirs, ticket checking, wrist banding, etc.). Queueing theory is useful in crowd safety management, turnstile design, entry and exit systems, concession planning and crowd flow assessment, venue ticket sales, queueing race design and transport loading (to and from a venue), density and emergency egress analysis, traffic control and planning, and for determining the sequence of production operations.

The basic principles are that queues have an arrival rate, a service rate, and a discipline. The accepted method of defining a queue uses the following:

● expected number of arrivals per time period (mean arrival rate)
● expected number of services possible per time period (mean service rate).

Formulae are used for calculating the average number of people in the queue, and the average time a person spends waiting in the queue. From this the density of the crowd in the queue is calculated and management decisions can be made regarding the number of entrances, staff and ticketing processes to be used.

Flow charts

An event manager needs to 'walk the event', using the perspective of the attendee, to create a flow chart showing how the audience will physically experience the site or venue. This process will need an understanding of audience behaviour – which way will they want to walk or turn and how will they respond to the site layout? – and understanding of the needs of service suppliers to the event, and the requirements of emergency services.

Flow charts show, in a diagrammatic form, the shape of the event and the sequence of activities that will take place. This is useful in three respects:

1 It makes the operations manager think through all that is intended to happen.
2 It acts as a communication tool for all the other personnel and suppliers who are involved.
3 It identifies any bottlenecks or possible problems.

A flow chart will show the complexity of the event and how many activities will be running in parallel with each other, and can identify where blockages may occur. The flow chart can be discussed with other staff to see if they can consider any alternatives and solutions to bottlenecks, separation issues and timing of activities, where necessary.

Flow charts anticipate the sequence of choices and encounters as suppliers and audience enter a site or venue. It attempts to anticipate and then control the choices people will make as they enter, for example:

- Which way will they turn?
- Where is the point of entry into the event?
- What is the first point of contact with a member of the event team?
- What is the shortest or most efficient route around the venue/site between attractions?

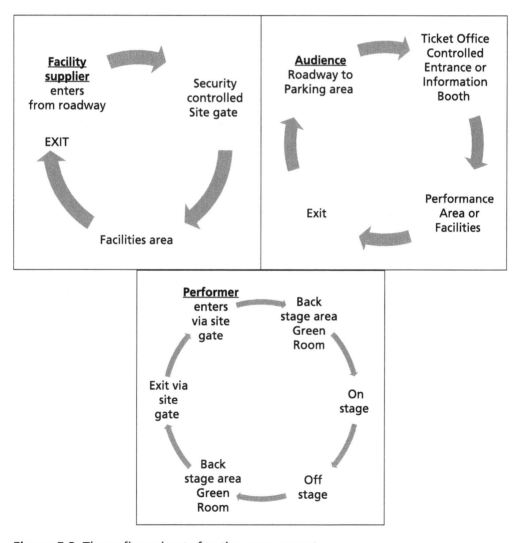

Figure 5.3 Three flow charts for the same event.

- Where is the information desk?
- Where are the toilets and the refreshments?
- Where is the meeting place for friends?

Different times of an event will have different flows and will require charts for those periods (Figure 5.3).

In the three charts shown in Figure 5.3, three different flows of supplier, performers and audience all occur at the same 3-hour time period on the same site. The charts should be overlaid on each other and on the site map (see Chapter 6) to assess where potential bottlenecks and separation issues may occur.

Crowd monitoring and control

Crowd management, i.e., the facilitation of crowd movement and activities, is preferable to crowd control, i.e., the actions taken to control the crowd once behaviours become undesirable. A key element of managing audiences is to monitor and report on crowd movements throughout the festival site or venue, the arrival flow rates, how the queues build up, areas of high crowd density and different types of crowd behaviour.

Factors which can influence crowd behaviours and, therefore, must be considered when preparing for monitoring include:

- Size of the crowd.
- Demographics of the crowd, e.g., age, gender.
- Location and lay-out of the event.
- Type of event.
- Density of crowd in different areas of the event.
- Timetable of event activities.
- Weather conditions.

By continually observing and monitoring the crowd, signs of potential problems or trouble, or any indications that disorder is imminent can be quickly acted on. Crowd dynamics, whether density accumulation or aggression, can be seen to evolve in the build up to an event, with typical indications of trouble including crowding at entrances, people congregating in key areas, for example, near concession stands or in areas with the best view, leading to rising crowd pressures, pushing and shoving. There should very rarely be a need to intervene at the last minute if observations and monitoring are sufficient and efficient; early intervention should be possible.

Monitoring crowd behaviour is an essential aspect of any crowd management system because it indicates whether the processes in place are working, and enables detection of potential problems at an early stage. When planning monitoring requirements consider the following:

- How quickly crowding could develop to a dangerous level in various areas inside the venue.
- How quick the response could be to crowding problems, such as by preventing more people coming in or by dispersing people from overcrowded areas.
- If a crowding incident occurred, how quickly it would be known about and acted upon to prevent any escalation.

The likelihood and consequences of any sudden crowd movements need to be established. Instances of this behaviour could include invasions of the stage or an auditorium, mobbing of celebrities or running between various stages.

Monitoring information should be managed proactively rather than reactively – i.e., if footfall counts indicate that more individuals than expected are arriving at the event early, act accordingly to prevent problems before they arise. Use should be made of information available from the multiple agencies involved in organising the event. For instance, use knowledge regarding the departure and arrival times of park-and-ride buses to give an indication of when more people are likely to arrive at and leave the event.

Procedures are needed for recognising the early stages of undesirable behaviour, pinpointing potential problem areas and identifying undesirable/disruptive elements in the crowd. This duty is usually undertaken by managerial Front of House personnel and excludes the specialist security activities performed by licensed security staff. It requires the establishment of:

- venue security and monitoring procedures
- various formats for identification worn by those associated with the performance of specific tasks for the event – e.g. Traffic Control, Security, Backstage Crew, etc.
- restricted items and associated policies
- observation points at the venue (including fire and safety exits, entrance doors/gates) for possession of alcoholic beverages and weapons, abnormal or suspicious behaviour and intoxication.

It is essential to use multiple forms of crowd monitoring during an event, in order to assess the crowd and their behaviour from multiple perspectives. These include:

- staff on the ground, to listen and feel how the crowd is acting
- undercover officers in the crowd
- stewards, marshals and ushers
- CCTV
- helicopters (or drones) to give an overall view of the event
- commanders overseeing from the command centre.

Planning issues to consider are:

- whether there are enough staff within the venue to monitor all the areas where there are potential crowding problems
- if there are enough good vantage points for staff to monitor all the areas effectively
- if information from different areas of the venue can be communicated to a central location quickly.

Crowd characteristics

To successfully manage a crowd at an event it will be necessary to distinguish different types of crowd action and behaviour by monitoring. Generalised or random management procedures based on an oversimplification of a 'crowd' may result in inappropriate crowd management which, ultimately, could have disastrous consequences. Crowd hazards can be categorised by observable characteristics:

- **volatility**: to what degree the crowd has reached an unpredictable situation
- **degree of lawlessness**: how much criminal behaviour is taking place
- **level of violence**: can be assessed as potential or occurring
- **level of property damage**: how much is likely to occur and where – for example, parking area, toilets, walk-ways etc.
- **likelihood of accidental injury or death**: emergencies.

Berlonghi (1995) argues that it is important to consider or anticipate the different crowd types when planning an event, so that appropriate interventions and timely responses can be prepared in reaction to each of the different types, should they emerge during the event. For instance, the successful management of an event involving a spectator crowd – gathered to watch a particular event of interest – is likely to involve very different preparation and management to an event involving a crowd participating in an activity. Whereas more forceful action may be needed to effectively manage the participatory crowd, a less intrusive style may be more appropriate for a crowd peacefully observing an event such as a concert or book reading.

Moreover, those involved with crowd management and control must be able to differentiate these individual crowd types within the larger mass, in order to act or react appropriately towards each (Adang and Stott, 2004). The way in which authorities, such as security staff and the police, react towards and treat a crowd will impact on how the crowd behaves. Distinct groups within the crowd should be differentiated and treated appropriately. For example, rather than considering all crowd members to be troublesome and acting accordingly, running the risk of alienating the whole crowd, authorities should differentiate, and target, only those groups known (or thought likely) to be unruly.

Definition box 5.1

Berlonghi (1995) provides a categorisation of crowds by behaviour and actions and identifies 11 different types:

1 **Ambulatory crowd**: A crowd calmly entering or exiting a venue, walking to or from car parks, or around the venue to use the facilities.
2 **Disability or limited movement crowd**: A crowd in which people are limited or restricted in their mobility to some extent, for example, limited by their inability to walk, see, hear or speak fully.
3 **Cohesive or spectator crowd**: A crowd watching an event that they have come to the location to see, or that they happen to discover once there.
4 **Expressive or revellous crowd**: A crowd engaged in some form of emotional release, for example, singing, cheering, chanting, celebrating or moving together.
5 **Participatory crowd**: A crowd participating in the actual activities at an event, for instance, in community fun runs or in a parade.
6 **Aggressive or hostile crowd**: A crowd which becomes abusive, threatening, boisterous, potentially unlawful and disregards instructions from officials.

---

7 **Demonstrator crowd**: A crowd, often with a recognised leader, organised for a specific reason or event, to picket, demonstrate, march or chant.

8 **Escaping or trampling crowd**: A crowd attempting to escape from real or perceived danger or life-threatening situations, including people involved in organised evacuations, or chaotic pushing and shoving by a panicking mob.

9 **Dense or suffocating crowd**: A crowd in which people's physical movement rapidly decreases – to the point of impossibility due to high crowd density, with people being swept along and compressed, resulting in serious injuries and fatalities from suffocation.

10 **Rushing or looting crowd**: A crowd whose main aim is to obtain, acquire or steal something – for example, rushing to get the best seats, autographs or even to commit theft – which often causes damage to property, serious injuries or fatalities.

11 **Violent crowd**: A crowd attacking, terrorising or rioting with no consideration for the law or the rights of other people.

One crowd may exhibit all or part of the above types, planning must therefore consider each or at the least, the most likely categories. Fruin (1993) also categorised crowds by observable characteristics:

● **Emotional intensity**: depends on the event and/or special effects taking place.
● **Limited movement**: the crowd has limited or restricted movement.
● **Excessive movement**: the crowd has unlimited movement in an uncontrolled area.
● **Individual behaviour**: depends on how much individual control and responsibility is being exercised. The more this is evident, the more restrained the crowd.
● **Group behaviour**: depends to what degree individuals are dominated by the group. The more this is evident, the closer to 'mob mentality'.

Crowd control staff

A security command and control structure, following a logical strategy, should be in place for the event, with a central control point responsible for the overall event security management across multiple locations. A Site Administration and Communication Centre and its embedded Emergency Operation Centre is the logical location. The CCTV monitoring room would ideally also share the location.

The security control of an event should be given to key operational personnel with plentiful experience of crowd events. The command structure should be clear and easily understood and include all staff concerned with crowd control, including security contractors, with all roles and responsibilities clearly defined. The structure should allow control to be exercised over all areas of the site/venue to coordinate action where required. Too many levels of command should be avoided, because in an emergency information needs to be passed on quickly. All parties should be thoroughly briefed, so as to understand:

- their own roles and responsibilities
- the roles and responsibilities of others
- how actions by one party can impact on actions by another party
- who is in command of the operation overall
- the boundaries of operational control – i.e., when control of the event could shift from the event organisers to the police.

It will be necessary to establish precise job descriptions, expectations and authority of all personnel working on crowd management and inform them of all the rules, regulations and emergency procedures.

The person in charge of security should be supportive and intrusive in the appropriate measure. Often, they will be required to make a judgement call regarding how to react to an incident. This should involve an assessment of the benefits and drawbacks of implementing a specific contingency plan in order to execute the event safely while also meeting the expectations of the crowd. For example, would cancelling an event halfway through to alleviate overcrowding cause more problems, in terms of the crowd being disappointed, than permitting the event to continue, with the possibility that a few crowd members may be injured, in order to allow the crowd to see the event they expected to see? More difficulties and more disorder could be created by overreacting to a situation that's not there, or is very unlikely to happen.

Assessing required staff numbers

There will need to be adequate staff with the necessary skills to carry out crowd control duties during both normal and emergency situations. There are various factors to consider when deciding how many staff will be required:

- the size and layout of the venue
- duty-of-care responsibilities for staff security and comfort
- the total number of crowd control tasks and other duties that need to be carried out, such as managing traffic, checking tickets, monitoring the crowd, etc.
- how demanding each task is
- the likely size and behaviour of the crowd, using previous events held to give an estimate
- the distance people have to travel – people travelling a long distance, such as for an international event, are not likely to be familiar with the venue and may need more assistance
- any expected problems, such as people arriving without tickets
- seasonal factors, time of day, weather – more staff will probably be needed at high season or peak hours
- the experience of the staff
- extra staffing that may be needed to cover rest breaks and absences due to illness and leave
- insurance and legal liability coverage for volunteers and staff.

The working conditions for staff and volunteers, such as rosters, hours worked and any exposure to health risks, particularly stress and vulnerability to possible aggressive or violent behaviour, must be taken into account when planning the staffing for an event.

Figure 5.4 Security guard at vulnerable border fencing.

It's easy to change the numbers or makeup of the security staff based on the size and needs of a specific event when using contractors. Many contract security firms provide staffing for every security-related area, providing added convenience and flexibility.

Stewarding and ushering

The crowd control task of stewards and ushers is crucial as they are often the first point of contact for crowd members. They direct the audience to event locations and to seats, ensuring safe entry and exit. Stewards and ushers are responsible for a controlled entry to a performance space to prevent stage rushing by excited patrons. They will also clear the auditorium of patrons at the conclusion of the performance/session/event in accordance with safety requirements and regulations. Problems that can occur include:

- crowds rushing to obtain best vantage places close to the stage – deaths have occurred from this
- patrons sitting in incorrect seats
- patrons moving onto seats to which they are not entitled
- complaints about field of view
- complaints about other patrons' behaviour
- broken or missing seats

- rushing at exits to attend other performances in other venues, this has also been a major cause of serious injury.

Stewards should also have good knowledge of the local area, in order to efficiently divert traffic, give directions or suggest the best areas from which to observe the event. Key tasks are to:

- prevent overcrowding by making sure the number of patrons does not exceed the venue's legal crowd limits in the various parts of the venue
- assist in the diversion of patrons to other parts of the venue, including the closing of turnstiles, when the capacity for any area is about to be reached.

At large events where popular performers attract young audiences, additional crowd control measures need to be taken:

- patrons must be prohibited from the stage unless arrangements are made with the authorities prior to the event
- at least one security staff member per metre of stage, including the length of side extensions of the main stage must be provided; their principal duties are to prevent patrons climbing onto the stage and to remove injured or distressed patrons from the crowd
- patrons must be prohibited from climbing onto any structures within the venue
- stage barriers of suitable design must be provided
- exits from the audience area must be provided at either end of the stage
- additional staff may be required for backstage, perimeter and for performer security.

It is also important to consider the context of the event when deciding how problematic an issue may be and, consequently, what control measures need to be taken. For example, at a rock/pop concert with a predominantly young audience, a reasonable amount of 'crowd surfing' is expected and, therefore, providing the appropriate safety measures are in place to cope with these individuals, it should not be considered a high risk. However, at a concert with a predominantly older audience, crowd surfing would not be anticipated and, therefore, if a few individuals engaged in the behaviour, it could be indicative of a problem.

Incidents of sexual molestation in mosh pit areas are common, and careful crowd monitoring is required to identify and apprehend perpetrators. Action should be immediately taken to apprehend the assailant and report to the police. It is important to ensure the victim is protected in a sensitive manner, and enable police to carry out their duties in the quickest and most effective manner to contain the incident. Police Inspector Steve Burk urges security staff not to dismiss the crime due to a belief that inappropriate touching is 'par for the course' in the mosh pit. "It's quite clear that the general belief of a lot of young people is that being inappropriately touched by someone else is what happens in the mosh pit" he said. "My view is if you're not comfortable treating women like that in the middle of the mall you don't treat them like that in the middle of the mosh pit either" (Stephens 2017: 1).

Actions by performers such as late cancellation, walking off stage, encouraging fans to move closer, offensive language or gestures, throwing souvenirs to the audience, have precipitated inappropriate or hazardous group reactions. Auditorium staff should monitor crowd reaction to these actions and alert management to potential problems.

Prior to a performance entertainers should be fully informed of their responsibilities for maintaining order, and the problems associated with inciting potentially dangerous group behaviour. Performers should provide advance notice of cancellation, before patrons begin entering the venue. If that is not possible, communication with the crowd should not be delayed if cancellation occurs after they have entered the venue. Announcements should clearly establish refund policies, exit routes and the need for orderly movement.

Crowd monitoring tasks

Position staff in the crowd so that they can:

- sense atmospheres, tensions and moods
- look out for signs of distress
- respond quickly to incidents and accidents
- address, and discourage, any dangerous behaviour quickly before it spreads, such as jumping on seats or climbing up scaffolding for a better view
- help people and deal with queries.

Where crowding problems are likely to develop slowly at particular points within the venue, staff may be given specific areas to check by patrol at regular intervals.

The tedium created by waiting and/or the perception that other gates are being opened first, or later arrivals are being admitted first can create problems. Such things as appropriate music, use of humour, food and beverage services moving through the group, cheerful security staff moving through the group and good communication including a public address system, can help defuse the situation.

Monitoring points

Monitoring a crowd involves positioning staff in locations where they are able to identify undesirable/disruptive elements in the crowd. This requires an understanding of how to identify potential problem areas, and establishing procedures for dealing with undesirable behaviour. It also requires staff to observe and screen people for possession of alcoholic beverages and weapons, abnormal or suspicious behaviour and intoxication. Venue areas to be monitored may include:

- approach roads, street entrance and footpaths outside the venue
- entries and queueing areas
- Stage and auditorium within the venue
- Food stalls, bars, toilets
- barriers, gates and fences.

There should be at least one member of staff at each exit point from the venue. Their principal duty is to ensure that the gates are open when required and that both sides are free from obstructions. Where an exit point also serves as an entry there must be at least two members of staff.

Hand counters, for use at entrances to assess crowd numbers and flow, have the disadvantage of tying monitors to the task. Turnstiles can record numbers automatically and computerised systems linked to sensors at entrances can provide information on how quickly people are entering and when an area is expected to become full. Pressure detectors are sophisticated monitoring systems available for monitoring crowd pressure against fixed barriers or fences.

Watching crowds from a fixed point can be carried out as a specific task or, where staff are few in number, at the same time as other duties such as checking tickets. For monitoring the auditorium or performance spaces, good vantage points are needed. Crowd monitoring processes at entrances to the event are used to:

- check all accesses to the venue before arrival of audience to ensure functionality
- identify the maximum number of customers the area can accommodate
- monitor the crowd size and ensure that the maximum number is not exceeded
- ensure that queues are controlled firmly and courteously
- monitor crowd behaviour and promptly report any problems to the appropriate personnel or security personnel
- undertake crowd surveillance to ensure the security of individual patrons, removal of anti-social behaviour, control of drinking behaviour
- enforce conditions of entry – refusing entry due to intoxication, etc.
- request that customers surrender restricted items and confiscate, if necessary, according to the event policy. Restricted items to be surrendered or confiscated may include: portable seating, umbrellas, alcohol, dangerous or illegal items, e.g. drugs, weapons, items that are potential weapons.

There may be some internal site areas where crowds are likely to build up and monitoring is required. Problem areas might include:

- areas where people queue, such as pay desks, ordering and information points
- popular stalls, attractions or exhibits
- refreshment areas
- auditoriums and performance spaces.

Closed circuit television (CCTV)

The discreet and appropriate use of CCTV is recommended particularly for crowd monitoring and surveillance. It may be possible and advantageous to set up a CCTV system bespoke to the event, or use a permanent system in the venue or area being used for the event. This may range from a few fixed cameras at key locations to the use of a large number of remote-control cameras with zoom lenses. CCTV allows an overview of key site or venue areas such as entrances, departure routes and problem areas to be relayed to a central control point. For street events there are usually some crime prevention cameras that can be used for event monitoring.

CCTV is commonly used to monitor crowd movement and behaviour, deter crime, detect offenders and delay their actions. Camera operators can focus on the activities of particular people either by controlling or directing cameras to an individual's activities. Such surveillance may deter or detect the sale of drugs, sexual assaults and aggression both inside and outside the venue, although care must be taken to minimise the discomfort that the presence of CCTV can present to the vast majority of customers who are neither selling drugs nor causing a disturbance. Using CCTV can help clarify whether an emergency or security alert is real, but is only effective if it is properly monitored, maintained and can provide an active response. It is important that appropriate lighting complements the system during daytime and darkness hours.

Customers should be informed, by signage, that CCTV surveillance is in operation.

It is important to be aware that CCTV may portray a false image. For instance, CCTV pictures may show an area to be very densely populated, whereas in reality, the density is fine. Therefore, a range of measures should be used in parallel, to assess issues such as density. For example, in addition to CCTV, observations by on-ground staff of how freely people are able to move through a crowd can be used to indicate density.

Ensure there are sufficient qualified staff to continue to monitor the CCTV system during an incident, evacuation or search. Give consideration to the number of camera images a single CCTV operator can effectively monitor at any one time. In the UK, contract CCTV operators must carry an SIA CCTV (Public Space Surveillance) licence. The event security contractor should be aware of this and should ensure that only licensed staff are conduct monitoring.

Post-event dispersal of the crowd

One of the most dangerous periods for crowd and traffic control is after the event concludes. Site layout should ensure that there are multiple routes through which the crowd can disperse, rather than limiting the number of exit points. Sufficient staff should be available to direct pedestrians and traffic in all the event perimeter areas.

Duty of Care requires a plan to safely disperse the crowd from the event site. The duty is to both patrons of the event and the surrounding communities. Some strategies to consider are:

- Notifying neighbouring councils and appropriate authorities likely to be affected by a dispersing crowd, especially if it is likely to disrupt residential community traffic, pedestrians or businesses.
- Identifying potential areas of convergence and bottlenecks such as narrow bridges and walkways and planning strategies to address these, which could include the deployment of staff or closing roads to incoming traffic for a period of time.
- Notifying patrons before and during the event of any dispersal strategies or procedures to be followed.
- Staging the dispersal of attendees using sequential departures, such as Car Park 1 then 2 or Camping area 1 then area 2.
- Placing of appropriate signage indicating drink-drive or other penalties in force.
- Use of non-antagonistic crowd dispersing strategies such as use of a street sweeper at an appropriate hour if the crowd needs to be dispersed by a certain time.
- Courtesy buses and shuttle buses to move people from the area as quickly and safely as possible.
- Specially designated pick-up zones where parents and friends can collect patrons.
- Reminding patrons to take care when leaving, such as observing litter or noise restraints and if necessary, use the breathalyser testing booth.

Staff crowd management training

The organiser of the event is responsible for ensuring that all staff and volunteers are adequately trained and are familiar with the procedures and layout of the venue. Staff and volunteer training is an important element because:

- untrained staff and volunteers are often unaware of the importance of crowd control
- they need to learn how to identify potentially dangerous situations at an early stage and how to react quickly and effectively to prevent an incident
- they need to know exactly what their duties are in both normal and emergency situations, and how their duties relate to the overall crowd management structure
- some skills, such as communicating and controlling crowds, can only be obtained through training and 'on the job' experience
- the morale and self-confidence of staff and volunteers is improved by training.

Utilising personnel who have plentiful experience in planning for and managing crowd events is a must. Knowledge of crowds and their likely behaviours, and of varying types of crowds and their likely compositions, develops from years of experience of dealing with crowds and managing crowd events on a regular basis.

Consider the amount of training each member of staff or volunteer requires. In particular, their level of seniority or experience. Junior staff may require only induction training to do their job safely, whereas senior staff may need to be trained in a variety of roles to supervise the actions of others. Training could include:

- instructions on the basics of normal and emergency crowd movement and assembly
- initial handling of accident victims, altercations and other crowd incidents
- communications procedures and use of communications equipment
- avoidance of actions that would incite or trigger dangerous crowd behaviours
- conduct, responsibilities and demeanour during an emergency
- first aid
- general health and safety, such as fire precautions
- training in awareness of risk of crime, for example, closing down an event is a high-risk time for theft
- responsibilities for contacting and liaising with the emergency services.

Consider obtaining feedback from staff and volunteers on the training they have received and establishing a central training register. The register could be used to keep a record of the training courses attended, qualifications individual members of staff and volunteers have obtained, and any results and assessment reports from supervisory staff.

Communicating with the crowd

"Disasters are characterised by poor communications prior to, during and in the aftermath of an incident, in which it is very often the victims, rather than the designers and managers of crowd settings who are blamed" (Sime 1995: 2). Communicating with, and providing information to, the crowd is vital for a successful event. Information communicated to, or withheld from, the crowd can influence their behaviour. Hence, communicating with the crowd is essential in maintaining order and managing behaviour.

Pauls (1984) noted that people at the back of a crowd or queue are often unaware of what is occurring, most typically a crush, at the front of the crowd or queue and, therefore, unknowingly contribute to the forces causing that crush. "Crowd incidents often exhibit what can be termed a failure of front-to-back communication" (Pauls 1984: 31). People in a crowd do not have a broad view of what is happening around them, and unless authoritative information is received from a reliable source, may act on the speculations of others nearby. If there is a perception of danger, the human flight response can cause the sudden type of movement that unleashes the massed energy of the crowd. The opposite of the flight response can also occur when there is a competitive scramble to attain some intensely desired or valued objective.

Managing the crowd's expectations is important in terms of managing their behaviour more effectively. This can be achieved by:

- providing the crowd with information about, for example, the reasons why they are having to queue or are being asked to act in a certain way
- communicating with the whole crowd when appropriate
- listening to the crowd and trying to facilitate their needs and solve any problems wherever possible.

Bear in mind that expectations are likely to be higher if the event is paid entry, since crowd members attend with certain expectations about what they want to see in return for their money.

Pre-event communication

As much information as possible should be provided to prospective crowd members prior to the event, to influence their behaviour on arrival. This information can be communicated via media advertising and announcements, literature and programmes distributed with event tickets, or a website, for instance. It should inform crowd members:

- how they can arrive at the event – e.g., directions, public transport available
- where they are going to go when they get to the venue – e.g., parking facilities, park-and-ride facilities, directions to the event entrance
- what they will want to do when they get inside the event – e.g., toilets, phone charging, first aid posts
- what they will not be allowed to take into the event – e.g., potential hazards such as glass bottles, umbrellas, picnic chairs, alcohol, etc.
- emergency and evacuation procedures.

Be aware that English will not be the first language for all crowd members, particularly at very large international events. Therefore, try to provide signs in multiple languages or make use of pictograms, as a universal language, e.g., ticks and crosses next to pictures to indicate what behaviours are and are not allowed. On-site visual information notice boards, centrally controlled electronic display monitors and other directional or information signs should supplement and reiterate pre-event communication.

During the event

During the event full communication with the entire crowd will be essential. The whole crowd, not just those in auditoriums or in closest proximity, should be provided with accurate, comprehensive and timely information, both audio and visual. This is particularly important in queueing situations, whether entering or exiting. Pushing and shoving from the rear of a crowd, where people are unaware of what is happening at the front of the crowd, should be prevented by ensuring communication is adequate, with information visible to all crowd members and not just those at the front (Pan et al. 2006).

Communication messages

The public need to know what to expect and must have sufficient time to plan their actions. Failure to provide the required information at an early enough stage may lead to confusion and aggression.

When planning what information, advice, warnings and instructions need to be provided for the public, think about:

- what people need to know so that they can respond appropriately
- what sorts of assistance people require in order to respond appropriately, for example, detailed instructions, or straightforward direction.

In planning where and when relevant information should be given, consider:

- who the visitors are and what they already know about the place and the event
- the layout of the venue and what assistance people will require to find their way about
- what directions, advice, warnings or other general information people will need
- at what stage of the visit, and where, people will need the information
- in what form the information should be presented
- what languages other than English should be used.

Site administration office – communications centre

There needs to be an administration office at festival sites, provided with a variety of communication systems, computer records of essential planning documents and contracts, contact lists for essential personnel and staff authorized to make informed decisions as required.

This office should be the contact location for all sub-contractor enquires, media liaison and operational management processes. Its function is as a facility for control of operations and coordination of resources. In an emergency situation it can also function as an Emergency Operations Centre (EOC) as the location for the emergency response and recovery structure.

It should be located near the service entrance gates and be clearly visible and signposted. All crowd and staff communications should be controlled from this office.

On-site communication systems

Ideally, multiple systems should be established to enable messages to be directed at different sections of the crowd including crowds massed outside the venue. As public announcements are an important element of the safety plan for an event, consideration should be given to the style and content of announcements:

- What volume is required for announcements to be heard over spectator noise?
- Will announcements be easily understood by the audience?
- Are multiple language announcements required?
- What wording will lend credibility to the instructions?

A simple means of communication is individual communication by staff or volunteer crowd stewards, and is often the most effective and most well received, as crowd members perceive stewards to be most similar to themselves, as opposed to police or other authority figures (i.e. 'us' versus 'them' mindset). In particular, communications when problems are imminent, or have already arisen, should be appropriate for the crowd profile. Thus, a more gentle, human approach is often more effective at changing crowd behaviours than more aggressive, heavy-handed actions.

Summary

- The safety of the public in event environments is largely determined by the interaction of the venue or site's architectural design and efficient crowd management. An understanding of crowd dynamics and the theory of crowding in relationship to site/venue design and management is essential.
- Poor venue design and crowd management as a result of inadequate research into crowd behaviour has led to many disasters resulting in wider scale loss of life and injury.
- The primary crowd management objective is the avoidance of critical crowd densities. When average densities in a crowd reach the approximate area of the human body, individual control of movement becomes impossible, and phenomena such as turbulence or shockwaves through the crowd mass cause the sudden uncontrolled surges that lead to crushes.
- Architectural features that typically are implicated in dangerous crowding incidents are those that rigidly confine people within an inadequate space, or are not properly designed for crowd pressures and efficient mass movement.
- Crowd disasters typically occur in short periods of time when the critical capacity of a venue has been temporarily exceeded but intensive pressure to use the facility continues.
- The faster people wish to move, due to impatience, the more densely packed they become and the slower they can actually move. Usually, the crowd continues to press ahead because it has no knowledge of what conditions are at the bottleneck. Those at the bottleneck find it impossible to resist the crowd pressures from behind.
- The objective of Front of House crowd control strategies is to prevent the build-up of large accumulations of patrons in short periods of time. Time-based strategies can overcome crowd build up.

- Queueing theory is useful in crowd safety management, turnstile design, entry and exit systems, concession planning and crowd flow assessment, venue ticket sales, queueing race design and transport loading (to and from a venue), density and emergency egress analysis, traffic control and planning, and determining the sequence of production operations.
- Flow charts show the complexity of the event and how many activities will be running in parallel with each other and can identify where blockages may occur. Flow charts anticipate the sequence of choices and encounters.
- A key element of managing audiences is to monitor and report on crowd movements throughout the festival site or venue, the arrival flow rates, how the queues build up, areas of high crowd density and different types of crowd behaviour.
- Monitoring procedures are needed for recognising the early stages of undesirable behaviour, pinpointing potential problem areas, and identifying undesirable/disruptive elements in the crowd.
- There will need to be adequate staff with the necessary skills to carry out crowd control duties during both normal and emergency situations.
- The crowd control task of stewards and ushers is crucial as they are often the first point of contact for crowd members.
- Monitoring a crowd involves positioning staff in locations where they are able to identify undesirable/disruptive elements in the crowd. This requires and understanding of how to identify potential problem areas and establishing procedures for dealing with undesirable behaviour.
- The discreet and appropriate use of CCTV is recommended, particularly for crowd monitoring and surveillance.
- One of the most dangerous periods for crowd and traffic control is after the event concludes. There should be multiple exit points. Sufficient staff should be available to direct pedestrians and traffic in all the event perimeter areas.
- Communicating with the crowd is essential in maintaining order and managing behaviour. People in a crowd do not have a broad view of what is happening around them, and unless authoritative information is received from a reliable source, may act on the speculations of others nearby. If there is a perception of danger, the human flight response can cause the sudden type of movement that unleashes the massed energy of the crowd.
- As much information as possible should be provided to prospective crowd members prior to the event, to influence their behaviour on arrival.
- Multiple communication systems should be established to enable messages to be directed at different sections of the crowd.

Bibliography

Adang, O. M. J. and Stott, C. (2004) *Preparing for Euro 2004: Policing international football matches in Portugal*. Unpublished report for the Portuguese Public Security Police. (In Challenger 2013)

Berlonghi, A. E. (1995) 'Understanding and planning for different spectator crowds', *Safety Science*, 18, 239–247.

Challenger, R. (2013) *Understanding Crowd Behaviours*. Leeds: The Stationery Office (TSO).

Department for Culture, Media and Sport (2008) *Guide to Safety at Sports Grounds*.

Online. Available HTTP: <http://www.safetyatsportsgrounds.org.uk/sites/default/files/publications/green-guide.pdf>

Dickie, J. F. (1995) 'Major crowd catastrophes', *Safety Science*, 18, 309–320.

Health and Safety Executive (HSE) (1999) *The Event Safety Guide: A Guide to Health, Safety and Welfare at Music and Similar Events*. Norwich: HSE Books.

Fruin, J. J. (1971) 'Designing for pedestrians: A level of service concept', *Highway Research Record*, 355, 1–15.

Fruin, J. J. (1984) 'Crowd dynamics and auditorium management', *Auditorium News*, May 1984. International Association of Auditorium Managers.

Fruin, J. J. (1985) Crowd dynamics and the design and management of public places. In J. Pauls (Ed.) *International Conference on Building Use and Safety Technology*. Washington: National Institute of Building Sciences, pp. 110–113.

Fruin, J. J. (1993) The causes and prevention of crowd disaster. In R. A. Smith and J. F. Dickie (Eds) *Engineering for Crowd Safety*. Amsterdam: Elsevier, pp. 99–108.

Fuckamachi, M. and Nagatani, T. (2007) 'Side effect on pedestrian counter flow', *Physica A*, 377, 269–278.

Goffman, E. (1971) *Relations in Public: Microstudies of the Public Order*. New York: Basic books.

Helbing, D., Buzna, L., Johansson, A. and Werner, T. (2005) 'Self-organized pedestrian crowd dynamics: Experiments, simulations, and design solutions', *Transportation Science*, 39, 1–24.

Helbing, D., Molnar, P., Farkas, I. J. and Bolay, K. (2001) 'Self-organizing pedestrian movement', *Environment and Planning B: Planning and Design*, 28, 361–383.

Hughes, R. L. (2003) 'The flow of human crowds', *Annual Review of Fluid Mechanics*, 35, 169–182.

Langston, P. A., Masling, R. and Asmar, B. N. (2006) 'Crowd dynamics discrete element multi-circle model', *Safety Science*, 44, 395–417.

Pan, X., Han, C. S. and Law, K. H. (2006) 'A multi-agent based simulation framework for the study of human and social behavior in egress analysis', *Proceedings of the ASCE International Conference on Computing in Civil Engineering*, 92.

Pauls, J. (1984) 'The movement of people in buildings and design solutions for means of egress', *Fire Technology*, 20, 27–47.

Sime, J. D. (1995) 'Crowd psychology and engineering', *Safety Science*, 21, 1–14.

Sime, J. D. (1999) 'Crowd facilities, management and communications in disasters', *Facilities*, 17, 313–324.

Stephens. K. (2017) 'Five women sexually assaulted at Tasmania's Falls Festival'. Online. Available HTTP: <www.news.com.au/entertainment/music/music-festivals/January 2017>.

Still, G. K. (2000) *Crowd Dynamics*. PhD Thesis, University of Warwick, UK.

Still, G. K. (2012) *Crowd Modelling: Crowd Safety in the Complex and Built Environment*. Cumbria, UK: Crowd Modelling Ltd.

Chapter 6

Safe site design

Chapter objectives

This chapter describes the planning detail required for:

- Site inspection
- Site layout designing
- Site map making
- Positioning of facilities and services

Site design is concerned with the arrangement of activities and fixed facilities at an event. It aims to safely optimise movement, reduce congestion and maximise the use of space. The designers of workplaces (and an event location is a workplace) are required to ensure that hazards and risk that may be inherent in the design of a workplace are eliminated or, at the very least, reduced at the design stage.

A common factor in many crowd crush disasters is the crowd being constrained within a passageway without any means of lateral escape to the side, in a tunnel at the Love Parade, Duisburg 2010, on the Koh Pich Bridge at the Water Festival Cambodia 2010, and the lack of a fire escape at the Kiss Nightclub, Santa Maria Brazil 2013. The case studies in the appendix describe these tragedies which exemplify the observation by Langston, Masling and Asmar that "Poor venue design and crowd management as a result of inadequate research into crowd behaviour has led to many disasters resulting in wider scale loss of life and injury" (2006: 396).

Safe site design is about making decisions at the beginning of the event process that will have a positive impact on safety, eliminate hazards and control risks to health and safety. The particular site hazard control planning issues are site/venue precinct traffic and pedestrian control, and crowd and operations movement within the event site.

A safe design approach begins in the conceptual and planning phases and defines options about the site or venue design, methods of construction and work practices that enhance safety. Consultation is critical at all stages of the process, particularly with staff, contractors and suppliers, and there is a need to establish effective ongoing consultation mechanisms to identify existing and potential hazards. For each event, this must involve an evaluation of how the crowd, service suppliers, and staff are likely to move around the event, and the most appropriate form of control interventions to manage site hazards.

The specific site design issues are precinct control and operations movement within the event site. This will involve the design of traffic areas, increased lighting and traffic separation. Clear, comprehensive signposting at venue approaches will be required, with all entrances and exits clearly marked. Careful consideration should be given to the location of crowd facilities and amenities, to make them as accessible as possible. For instance, in relation to where queues are going to form – particularly when entering the event itself – it is important to think about what facilities the crowd have access to – i.e., Have they got toilets? Have they got shelter? Have they got stands to buy food and drinks from? Access to facilities such as these while queuing, may help to alleviate the crowd's discomfort.

Estimates of audience numbers

Accurate estimations of audience numbers will be vital when preparing the site plan and set-up of an event. This will ensure that there is enough space for the amount of spectators and also include safe entrances and exits to prevent overcrowding. For large multi-day, multi-activity festivals it is important for both the event operations team and the event sub-contractors that the anticipated audience attendance number is accurately estimated. Accurate audience number estimations are needed in order to determine how many staff are required to man the parking, control traffic and for both security and first aid facilities and staff.

The consequences of underestimated attendance can severely impact the event management team's ability to provide safe facilities and services. For example, a lack of parking available for the patrons may cause illegal parking and frustration/anger directed towards staff by both attendees and local residents.

For a significant portion of an audience, public transport is used to get to and from an event. For a major event it is crucial that the public transport services flow through the event's perimeter to the front of house without any disruption. It is of course absolutely crucial that sufficient numbers of buses are provided. It is always preferable to overestimate requirements than to have delays and overcrowding that can lead to people finding their own way on foot through traffic areas.

Front of House (FoH) management involves ensuring that crowds do not block entrances, exits or pedestrian flows, and organising how the crowd is going to be distributed inside the venue. Accordingly capacity management must be considered. The estimated attendance is vital for setting a maximum limit on the number of spectators to be admitted in accordance with identified hazards and venue capacities, and to identify the number and type of staff required for managing spectators.

Ticketing is the most appropriate way to monitor the expected amount of attendees and cater for those numbers. For a venue and event with restricted space this is a simple matter, limit the number of tickets to be sold to the capacity of the venue. Pre-selling tickets will provide organisers with accurate information about expected numbers. However, limiting numbers can be more difficult to organise for open (free) events or events without presales (walk-up sales only). To deal with the possibility of excess arrivals, consider making the event ticketed, even if it there is no entry charge.

In regards to the staging of performances incidents could occur due to incorrect audience number estimations. If there are too many unexpected people, there could be issues with the audience not being able to see the performance due to the auditorium (stages) set up incorrectly for the amount of spectators.

Planners should consider the consequences of incorrect audience number estimations causing queuing frustration due to not enough food stalls/sellers and water. Or the fenced alcoholic beverage area being too small, or not enough staff hired for drink sales. Lengthy queues for too few toilets can cause impatience, frustration, anger and possibly outbursts of violence. If there is a long wait for the toilets, some people (mostly males) may be inclined to urinate publicly. Worse, there is a possibility of toilets becoming 'out of order' due to overuse, or because there is not enough staff hired for cleaning purposes. In addition, if there aren't enough waste management facilities, people are more inclined to throw their rubbish on the ground/floor.

Site and venue safety evaluation

Following the choice of site or venue for an event, an immediate task is to assess the hazards the venue or site may have, its estimated audience, and the production equipment and process its programme will require. It is not possible to accurately plan for the safety of an event site or venue without knowing all of the programme elements and their staging and audience requirements.

It is essential to identify hazards associated with the venue or site in order to plan effective safety measures. A site inspection by a competent person should identify specific hazards of the site. Remember that hazard identification does not only involve identifying the hazards themselves but should also include identification of contributory factors – the type of event, the type of crowd expected and environmental considerations.

Event organisers must address issues associated with the location of the proposed event. The idiosyncrasies of the venue site must be attended to. Access, placement of amenities, entrances to the event site, parking for cars and buses, walking paths, distances between performance spaces, attractions and amenities, and disability access are all important considerations. Appropriate shade, shelter and seating with good sight lines, are all significant concerns. As is the need for sufficient toilets, first aid facilities, food and beverage outlets, waste management, etc. An evaluation should also address methods of crowd control, evacuation and emergency procedures. To assess the safety of a particular site or venue the following must be evaluated:

- accessibility of location for customers, suppliers and emergency agencies, staff and performers
- existing features of venue or site
- storage considerations
- logistics of setting up
- capacity of the location, spatial considerations and likely obstructions, and versatility
- suitability for a safe flow of audience within the site, services, suppliers, performers, participants and visitors
- traffic control and parking
- crowd monitoring and control infrastructure
- legal considerations and possible constraints on the event.

The questions to be asked include: Does the proposed venue provide the space, capacity, access and facilities required? What are the emergency safety aspects of the venue? What are the safety requirements of the venue or site contracts and regulations?

To answer will require an evaluation of the operational structures within the venue including relevant on-site personnel, sub-contacted suppliers and concessions; on-site safety services and facilities available, or the cost of bringing those to the site; and, importantly, the professionalism of the venue management.

Pre-event inspection

The event site should be visited prior to the event to thoroughly assess the geography of the location and its capacities, and to determine where potential hazards and areas of trouble, such as crowd congestion and reduced rates of flow, could be. It is important to work with the geography of the location and make use of physical street furniture wherever possible.

Think about people who may be harmed and how. These could include:

- anyone in the crowd
- anyone exposed to overcrowded conditions for a prolonged period of time; children, young people, people with special needs and the elderly are particularly vulnerable
- staff and contractors.

Photographs should be taken of the site in order to record important data and to enable planning consideration. Evaluate distances, sight lines and obtain, or create, venue building floor plans or a site map. Obtain, or create, lists of facilities and equipment included in the hire.

A venue inspection should:

- check that there is adequate access for arrivals and departures by whatever means of transport are to be used that ensures avoidance of collisions with vehicles due to pedestrians and vehicles sharing the same route
- check that there are adequate stairs, gangways and walkways within the venue for pedestrians and any planned traffic
- ensure that all emergency equipment is properly maintained and in good working order and, where appropriate, test it; examples of such equipment include fire-fighting equipment, fire alarms, smoke alarms, public address and other communication systems
- check the emergency exits; check that escape routes are unobstructed; check that the emergency lighting is working and that all direction and information signs are in place and are legible.

For this undertaking, site documentation is vital. Detailed information of all aspects of the site must be collected in order to record important data and to enable planning consideration to take place with the clients, technical contractors and facility suppliers. For detailed and efficient planning, venue building floor plans or a site map, and lists of facilities and equipment included in the hire, must be obtained. It is essential for the event manager to walk through the premises in order to evaluate distances, sight lines and any possible safety hazards.

One of the primary considerations in evaluating the safety of a venue should be how the potential venue is designed and whether certain characteristics are likely to add to or detract from the occurrence of risk. In particular that it provides the required space, access and facilities. It will be necessary to check:

- Are approvals for the use of the site for public performances and the number of patrons expected for the event required, or if current approvals are adequate for what is planned?
- Does the site allow for adequate crowd management, with existing regimented seating areas and flow barriers?
- Are there spectator overflow areas to avoid congestion should spectator turnout significantly exceed expectations (a common phenomenon in rock concerts)?
- Are there nearby areas for overflow parking, if anticipated spectator parking areas are filled, and are shuttle buses desirable, feasible or necessary?
- In the event of a mass casualty situation, is space available for an on-site triage area to permit stabilising medical treatment before removal of critical patients?
- Can the streets adjacent on all four sides of the venue be closed to all vehicles other than emergency, service and residents, to permit a perimeter for access as well as a buffer zone?

Environmental hazards

In outdoor settings, control of rodents, snakes, spiders, mosquitoes and insects of significance to public health must be addressed. If particular hazardous species are known to inhabit the area, or if vectors of particular diseases are endemic in the area, the attending first aid and medical personnel should be alerted. Medical and first aid personnel will need alerting to the presence of potentially poisonous and noxious plants and trees. Consideration needs to be given to the potential effect of the event on nearby domestic or farm animals and native fauna.

Swimming and water areas

Purpose-built swimming areas must comply with national or state requirements for water quality and other requirements such as fencing. Other water courses in the vicinity of the venue which may be used for water recreation or washing should be assessed for suitability against guidelines where available. Where these water courses are considered unsuitable for recreational use they should be fenced off and warning signs should be erected.

Water quality must be addressed in both designated swimming areas and water that could be utilised for swimming in hot weather. Experience has shown that where audiences attend an outdoor concert in hot weather, particularly in overnight situations without washing facilities, any nearby water area will be employed as a makeshift swimming/bathing/washing area.

Some form of trained supervision should be considered for:

- families with small children
- spectator groups for which alcohol consumption, with subsequent judgment impairment, is anticipated
- water that has additional hazards such as steep, slippery sides, submerged snags or unusually variable depths.

Appropriate life-saving and resuscitation equipment should be on hand for use by trained staff.

Site layout and design

If the venue for an event is one that is purpose built for public entertainment, and the event programme contains normal performances and standard presentation styles, the event design usually falls into routine formats adjusted for crowd variations. However, if it is a greenfield festival site (a site with little or no infrastructure where all facilities, equipment and services will need to be brought onto the site) or adapted purpose buildings, or a street event, a considerable amount of safety planning is required for the event site design.

It will take careful and comprehensive site lay-out planning to minimise and, if possible, eliminate hazards before they occur rather than attempting to deal with them after arrival at the event location. The design of the site layout of facilities should be organised with the overall objective of facilitating efficient operations that are as free from risk as possible. Designing out hazard risks, whether with machinery, substances, buildings or systems of work, is planning at its best. It is also cost-effective to eliminate as much risk as possible at the event design stage, rather than have to manage it later, especially after an accident has occurred.

Major considerations are the provision of adequate parking arrangements and parking restrictions, audience arriving by private vehicle and public transport to and from the event. Bus drop-off, pick-up points and parking places are positioned away from the area immediately around the entrance(s), to reduce the risk of congestion. This will involve the design of public traffic areas, increased lighting and traffic separation. Clear, comprehensive signposting at venue approaches, will be required, with all entrances and exits clearly marked.

It is important to note that any issues relating to the pedestrian planning and design may involve a range of agencies (police, civil defence, architects, medical, waste management, security forces, etc.) and that the presentation of plans/suggestions be clearly understood by all parties.

Separation issues

A key site planning consideration is to ensure there is a clear separation between the movement of the audience and the suppliers of event services. Therefore attention must be given to the provision of separated entrances and parking arrangements for suppliers, staff and performers isolated from those used by the audience. Access points may include: backstage gates/doors, emergency gates/doors, sub-contractor gates/doors. Controls will be necessary at these restricted access points to prevent entry of any unwanted persons.

Ideally there should be four distinct and well separated entrances and exits.

1 **Public:** the roadways, parking and gates into and out of the event enclosure.
2 **Service:** entrances and exit in constant use throughout the event by service providers, contractors and stall holders. This gate will allow access to the restricted areas behind stalls, to waste collection points, toilets and equipment locations such as generators.
3 **Backstage:** access for staff, security, performers and VIPs to the backstage and green room area.
4 **Emergency:** clear unimpeded roadways for the rapid ingress and egress of emergency vehicles to emergency service locations on the site: first aid stations, evacuation points, emergency control centre, power and mains water supply controls.

Crowd/traffic-related issues

Virtually all events will require space separation for the arrival and the departure of the guests, participants and performers, suppliers and volunteers. The varying requirements of each of these groups must be considered, as they pass through the event, creating potential bottlenecks, and a potentially hazardous mixing of vehicles and foot traffic. Getz (1997) suggests an excellent checklist for event managers to prevent crowd/traffic-related problems:

● provide ample space at access and egress points
● avoid dead ends and bottlenecks that will lead to congestion or movement against the flow
● provide adequate and appropriately orientated signage
● screen and block off no-go areas where risks may be high
● separate vehicle and pedestrian movements where possible
● trial run the event site if possible
● use lighting to avoid hazards and maximise security
● segregate ingress and egress traffic flows
● provide, test and adequately sign emergency exits and procedures.

Access entry

Access for staff and participants to all parts of the event site are required for a variety of modes of transport. Marshals are required to ensure the smooth flow for participant parking. There needs to be adequate space and assistance for unloading at points for dispersal of goods and personnel, emergency entries and exits. These need to be well patrolled and adequately lit.

There will need to be preventive measures to avoid crushing at public entrances. Queuing requires consideration on ways in which it can be dealt with effectively. And there is a need to be mindful of the exit arrangements where queuing can also occur.

The entrance to an event should be large, spacious and well signed. Space is required for ticketing, bag check and security assessment. To prevent crowding and facilitate pedestrian movement, venues should provide several dispersed entrances and exits rather than centralised ones.

Access for staff, sub-contractors, stall holders, performers, first aid and emergency personnel, waste disposal and performers to all parts of the event site are required for a variety of modes of transport. The space and assistance for unloading at points for dispersal of goods and personnel, emergency entries and exits need to be well patrolled and adequately lit. There needs to be supervised separation if these traffic movements intersect with public access areas. Handling equipment for the unloading trucks and vans in the backstage area include trollies, barrows, and for large items, forklifts.

Emergency services access

The needs of emergency services for access to, and egress from, the venue, as well as movement around and within the site, and access to all sub-sections of the venue, including performance, spectator and parking areas, must be taken into account in planning for the event. A separate parking area should also be made available for attending health and emergency services personnel and vehicles. On-site, provide sufficient room for marshalling, manoeuvring, repositioning or redeployment of emergency vehicles.

The site design must also include:

- an incident control centre (EOC) which should have back up power and lighting
- meeting points for emergency services
- triage and ambulance loading areas
- emergency access and egress routes and the security of these routes.

Dedicated perimeter roads may be required for emergency services. In order to provide access and a buffer zone, adjacent streets on all sides of a venue may need to be closed, and parking banned, with access restricted to emergency service and residents' vehicles. Roadways and access routes should be clearly distinguished, signposted and kept clear. Ensure departing vehicles cannot be prevented from leaving by congestion produced by other vehicles arriving.

Consider adequate access and marshalling areas for large numbers of emergency vehicles should a major incident occur. Provide a suitable site for aeromedical evacuation. Consider that in the event of a mass casualty situation, the venue layout may need to provide space for an on-site triage area to permit treatment prior to removal of patients.

First aid posts should be dispersed strategically throughout the venue and staffed by trained personnel. On-site first aid medical care posts should be located in as quiet a place as possible, with direct transport access. Medical aid posts should be clearly sign-posted from all directions and be clearly marked on site maps.

Sites suitable as evacuation assembly areas must be selected or created. The most efficient evacuation routes to the evacuation assembly areas from different areas of the site or venue must be determined. The assembly areas and routes must be distinct and easily recognised on site maps. The placement of prominent signage to direct the crowd for an evacuation is necessary.

Street and unconfined events

For events held in unconfined spaces, such as parades on public streets, complete coop-eration between all public safety agencies and the event organiser is vital. A street carnival or fun run or parade has particular problems for crowd control where attendee number control and monitoring become very difficult tasks. Ample advance prepara-tion and attention to even the tiniest details can help keep things safe, sound and sane at events where borders are either transient or non-existent. Where the event is a moving one, such as a parade, procession, or a fun run, it is preferable to choose a route which will minimise possible trouble, and not place additional demands on police and security resources.

Such events have recently become a preferred terrorism target due to their ease of access. The types of security 'hardening' measures that can be implemented at venues such as stadiums, purpose built venues and even temporary greenfield festival sites, are very difficult to install where entrances and boundaries to the location can be porous. Considerable resources and pre-planning will be necessary.

Other particular problems for crowd control at a street event or parade may be the practical difficulties in getting visitors and residents to and from the area because of the limited capacity of public transport, the absence or suspension of parking facilities, together with road closures and diversions.

It will be essential to conduct detailed discussions at a very early stage of planning with police, emergency services, residents' and business representatives, local authori-ties and any other interested parties. The plans will need to include arrangements for security, effective monitoring of overcrowding at the site and at associated areas such as approach roads and bus/train stations. Planning will need to include procedures for managing crowd behaviour, and incidents such as accidents and injuries, petty crime, and larger emergencies.

Where the event is a parade, procession, or a fun run, and requires the closure of any public roads it will be a requirement to submit a transport management plan. The local government authorities must be contacted to seek permission from traffic authorities for the closure of any public roads. There may be a legal requirement that residents affected by road closures are given notice by advertising the closures in local and/or metropolitan newspapers as directed by the traffic authorities and council (this will depend on the impact of the event).

While street events present a number of unique challenges depending on their location, there are common elements and processes to all other special events. There must be control of the points of entry and exit for attendees, vendors and equipment handlers. There need to be good sight lines for the crowd to prevent rushing or surging for the best view, facilities for performers, toilets, first aid facilities, child minding, food and beverage outlets, and stalls and concessions.

Detailed planning should clearly outline the location of activity, layout of amenities, routes for processions and street performance, and processes to guide the 'flow' of traffic efficiently. The planning should also address methods of crowd control, evacuation strategies and emergency procedures. There should be a contingency plan for adverse weather or emergencies affecting outside events. This might mean moving a large crowd into the most protected areas available in a quick, efficient and non-alarming manner. This contingency plan must be communicated to all key event and facilities personnel.

Emergency vehicles are usually positioned on the perimeter of the event, with ambulances at the beginning and end of a parade or fun run route, or at key points that allow an easy rapid exit from the area. Emergency and first-aid personnel are stationed in the volunteer check-in area, and police and private security located and patrolling throughout the event location. A comprehensive public address system is required that can give messages to the entire crowd or a particular crowd location. Where access to certain streets is controlled, residents could be encouraged to carry some form of identification to allow them into the area.

Site maps

Site maps are used to visually demonstrate how resources are to be distributed during the event. They are used to plan control of traffic flow through the site or venue clearly outlining the location of activities, positioning of facilities and amenities, roads, barriers and fences. The site map also acts as a communication tool indicating the proposed use of space to all the different stakeholders.

The site map is sent to all interested parties. It is essential for suppliers and subcontractors, who may need to know distances between fixed positions, electrical or water supplies, or the dimensions of entrances for ease of access. Suppliers will look on the plan for the storage areas and drop-off points for their goods. Maps are often provided on programmes or tickets to assist the audience with the layout of the event site, showing the location of (among other things) the exits and evacuation routes.

A site map will almost certainly be required by other agencies, such as the health and safety authorities and emergency services (fire, ambulance and police) to ensure that all their regulations have been taken into account and that the event will be able to function safely. Although many revisions may take place, the final draft of the site map should be sent to all interested parties.

Creating the site map

The three basic features of such maps include scale, projection and key symbols for staff, volunteers and suppliers. For large events, an accurate, scaled map will enable a visual understanding of space. The need for detail and accuracy in site maps increases in direct relationship to the size and complexity of an event. No matter the size of the event, all site maps should include all the features and constraints of the site, such as doors and gates, walls and fences, electrical connections and the amount of power available, cleaning and drinking water, waste outlets, posts and pillars, and access roads etc.

The map should indicate where everything connected to the event will be placed, and how the attendees and the service suppliers will circulate. It should not just include the actual dimensions of structures but also crowd and traffic movement.

A site map can be created by computer or drafted by hand. The event manager should use an accurate, scaled map, and the northerly direction should always be indicated. Having a universally accepted direction on the map is a sound risk strategy, so that when suppliers or other groups come onto site, there can be no misunderstandings. Visual aids are an important element of layout planning. These comprise representations, including drawings, templates, three-dimensional models, movement patterns and cartoon maps.

Any symbols that are used on the map should be explained. There is now a common visual symbol language, and this must be used at all times so that people from different countries can 'read' the map. All entrances and exits and parking facilities must be clearly marked. First aid and emergency access must also be clearly shown, so that these areas are kept free of obstructions, and emergency vehicles should be able to access all areas.

Not all items need to be on one single map, since it can then appear too complex and again lead to misunderstandings. Consideration should be taken of those who will be reading the plans. Not all event attendees are 'map literate', or will have the inclination to spend time trying to sort out the various intricacies of a complex map.

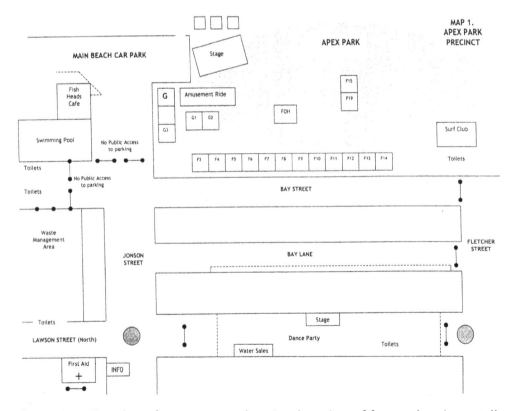

Figure 6.1 Site plan of street event showing location of fences, barriers, stalls, stage and amenities.

It may be necessary to create several versions of the map, one for the audience, one for suppliers, another showing the provision of power services and water facilities for the contractors, and even other versions for particular groups of people with different information needs. For example, performers will want to know the location of the green room and where they can wait and relax during the event, stall holders will need to know the exact location of the space they have been allocated, first aid teams will want to evaluate the positioning of first aid posts.

Site maps can be designed to be displayed on the internet, and they should be appropriately simple and yet offer good communication. By indicating lost-children points, information booths, cash withdrawal facilities and mobile recharge facilities on the plans, the event manager is demonstrating that the event and the management are child and people friendly. An aerial orientation may be suitable for this purpose. The site map may also be used for a seating chart at a concert, or within a festival programme to show where the different entertainments and facilities are sited.

Computer Aided Design (CAD)

Layout design planning of a large complex event where many different activities are occurring is a time-consuming process. The industry is now using computer-based approaches transferred from other industries, such as building and construction, to assist in this process. The benefits of these approaches are as follows:

1 Alternative layouts can be quickly generated for comparisons and evaluation.
2 Interactive processes between the positioning of equipment/stands and the flow of customers can assist in visualising the reality of movement of customers in the finished design.
3 The computer software can be linked with other software packages to quantify resource needs and to develop site maps showing full details and part details for different groups of people.
4 Costs can be predicted for different configurations.

There are a huge range of software platforms available. The best to use are those that provide 3D perspectives, and automatic resource allocation and calculation. Commonly used software in the events industry are – AutoCAD, Sketch Up and Vectorworks.

Vehicle traffic management

A vital task of site management is the control of traffic in the streets and roads areas surrounding the event location. The hazards of mixing of excited crowds and vehicles is self-evident. For events held in established entertainment venues traffic control is usually a minor matter. However, for events held on sites usually used for other purposes, e.g. parks, streets, other public areas, traffic control becomes a serious responsibility for the event management and liaison with a range of authorities and compliance with a variety of regulations is mandatory. The supervision of an approved Traffic Management Plan will be required and qualified staff will be needed to implement the plan. Emergency services need to be informed of any traffic alterations from the norm, such as the blocking off of public streets.

Traffic control has to occur for five distinct spheres:

1 public transport
2 private vehicles
3 pedestrians
4 service vehicles – contractors, performers, staff, VIP
5 emergency vehicles.

Each must be kept separate from each other, in both external (outside the event's boundaries, but in the immediate vicinity) areas and internal (including service, restricted access and public) areas.

Crowd/traffic-separation related issues

The basic principle is to keep all vehicles at a safe distance from pedestrians. Service providers requiring essential access should be identified in advance and checked before being allowed through. There should be access control, careful landscaping, traffic-calming measures and robust, well-lit barriers or bollards. Ideally, non-essential vehicles should be kept at the maximum possible distance, at least 30 metres from the event entrances.

A traffic management plan will be required and qualified staff will be needed to implement the plan. The example box outlines the regulation system in New South Wales and the process for compliance.

Example: New South Wales events traffic control regulations

In New South Wales, the government has categorised events that require traffic control into four classes.

Class 1 Event (e.g. New Year's Eve, bicycle ride/fun run on major road network, Sydney COD march)
- Impacts major traffic and transport systems
- Disrupts non-event community over wide area
- Requires police, one or more councils and road traffic authority (RTA) involvement
- Requires detailed traffic management plan (TMP) including traffic control processes (TCP) with traffic control devices approved by RTA or council and widespread advertising

Class 2 Event (e.g. event blocks off main street in local community)
- Impacts local traffic and transport systems
- Disrupts non-event community over local area

- Requires police, council and RTA involvement
- Requires detailed TMP including TCPs with traffic control devices approved by RTA or council and local advertising

Class 3 Event (e.g. on-street neighbourhood party)
- Class determined by council in consultation with police
- Does not impact local or major traffic and transport system
- Disrupts non-event community in immediate area only
- Requires local council, police and, when on an unclassified metropolitan road, RTA consent.
- TMP including TCP/s required and local advertising is necessary when a road closure is required

Class 4 Event (e.g. small ANZAC Day march, demonstration or parade under police escort)
- Class determined by council in consultation with police
- Requires police consent only Schedule 1, Summary Offences Act.
- No TMP required, no advertising required

Role of major agencies in traffic control

Local council (first point of contact) – lead agency for special events

Sets initial event class in consultation with other agencies (at local traffic committee) on classified and unclassified roads then council, following advice of LTC, issues conditions. If any condition results in a metropolitan council (or a classified road event for a regional council) exercising a 'delegated function' an RTA-approved TMP must be obtained.

Police-only agency involved in all four event classes

Police approval required for every event (Schedule 1, Summary Offences Act 1988); will not approve event that carries risk to life/property; will cancel any event in an emergency (e.g. adverse weather); with agencies are developing conditions of approval for 'bicycle races'.

RTA – involved in events that impact major traffic and transport systems

Manages Special Event Clearways/Variable Message Signs (ads/towing operations); approves council's proposed regulation of traffic (Roads Act Sec 116) for all classified roads and metropolitan unclassified roads via TMP on classified roads; RTA updates Road Occupancy Database (in Metro Sydney Councils/Police/RTA) recommend that:

- A qualified person (Work Site Traffic Controller) creates TMP (including Traffic Control Plans)
- Traffic Control Devices must be properly approved (no tape and wheelie bins)
- Traffic Control Devices installed under direction of qualified person

Responsibilities of the event organiser

The event organiser is responsible for:

1 Public liability insurance (indemnifying the police, council and the RTA);
2 Preparation of the Transport Management Plan and Traffic Control Plans, that are directly linked to, and required by NSW WorkCover Authority to address the event organiser's risk liabilities in 1. above;
3 Mandatory advertising (managed by RTA) of road closures and, if required Special Event Clearways as a direct result of the event to advise motorists of alternative routes;
4 Major and minor signposting for the Special Event Clearways, if required, (including large advanced notice warning boards) and tow truck operations to ensure the event space is available;
5 Traffic management equipment and staff which includes, but is not limited to:

   a supply and erection of pedestrian/crowd barricades, if required
   b supply and erection of road closure barrier boards
   c Certified Traffic Controllers, as required to execute the Traffic Control Plans mentioned in 2. above;
   d Portable variable message signs.

Parking

If existing public parking facilities at the event location are inadequate, consider nearby parking facilities. If it is needed to set up additional parking areas, certified traffic marshals may be required.

Parking areas and vehicle entrances and exits should be indicated on the site plan and car parking instructions communicated to patrons before the event or as they arrive. It may be a requirement to submit a parking plan as part of the transport management plan. Some key considerations are:

- adequate lighting for the car park and the surrounding area
- obstruction free entrance and exit area
- clearly marked parking spots
- a separate entrance and exit to encourage a directional flow of traffic
- drivers encouraged to reverse into parking spaces if possible
- controlled, signposted and marked walkways for pedestrians in the car park

- shrubs and trees trimmed to minimise risk of physical injury and ensure maximum visibility
- a separate parking area for staff, performers, media, stall holders and VIPs
- surfaces well maintained and free of water, mud, oil
- signage visible and able to be seen at night
- allocated spaces for the disabled.

Marshals are required to ensure the smooth flow for participant parking. It will help to avoid congestion and aggression if staff are available to direct drivers to parking spaces or alternative parking areas. It will also assist traffic control if drivers are forewarned by advance publicity about any limitations on parking space and about parking arrangements in general parking areas are signposted well before the venue. Staff directing traffic should wear distinctive (Hi-Vis) tabards or other clothing to distinguish them as event traffic control personnel.

Secure parking

It is important to provide sufficient parking for people attending and working at the event. It is sensible to provide a designated parking area for staff, contractors, stall holders, service providers, performers and media, separate from the public parking. If site layout permits, it may be possible to locate this area within the event enclosure. VIP parking should always be in an on-site restricted secure area.

Ambulances, police vans and fire service vehicles should be provided with their own dedicated parking spaces on-site. Power supply to these parking areas is usual. Provision of on-site spaces should be made for medical staff. These parking areas should have directly unimpeded access to the emergency exits and entrances.

Traffic and parking controls

Pedestrian routes from car parks must be separated from all other vehicle routes as far as possible. Marshalls equipped with stop/go signs should control any location where pedestrians cross roadways. Any areas where parking is potentially dangerous should be physically cordoned off and the penalties for illegal parking prominently signposted and enforced.

Public transport

For a significant portion of an audience public transport is used to get to and from an event. For a major event it is crucial that the public transport services flow through the events perimeter to the front of house without any disruption. It is of course absolutely crucial that sufficient numbers of buses or taxis are provided. It is always preferable to overestimate requirements than to have delays and overcrowding that can lead to people finding their own way on foot through traffic areas.

An event that is serviced by public transport has the advantages of requiring fewer parking spaces and a reduction in congestion on roads around the event.

A designated area for people to get off and on buses should be provided as close to the entry and exit gates as possible. This area should be out of any other traffic streams.

It should be well lit and marshals should be provided to control queues and give directions. Private vehicles should be prohibited from the area.

A separate taxi rank and drop off area could be provided. If Uber drivers intend to use the designated area they should be obliged to apply for a special pass to be displayed on their windscreen without which they will be prohibited from the area.

If the event is not accessible by scheduled public transport it may be necessary to provide hired shuttle bus services and/or additional parking spaces. A drop-off and pick-up area for private vehicles could also be provided. This is particularly necessary if the audience includes the elderly, the very young and the infirm or incapacitated. This area could also be used by taxis. This area should be separate from all other transport areas and parking should not be permitted. It should not be used as an Uber pick-up area.

Event signage

A key safety element is the use of signage to communicate information and instruction to both the event attendees and staff. Signs are required to provide essential information at 'decision points' – locations where attendees make choices or require direction. This is particularly important for traffic and crowd control, and for emergency procedures. Clear, comprehensive signposting at venue approaches, entrances and exits, and around and throughout the venue is vital. The location of each sign and its content should be included on the site map and listed in the safety plan.

There are seven types of signage used at an event:

1   External to the venue, giving directions and parking areas for different sorts of vehicles and purposes, this signage should be easily read from a moving vehicle.
2   Internal directional and identification signs – 'tickets this way', 'you are here' boards, toilets, restaurant, children's play area.
3   Statutory emergency signage, e.g. fire exits. Note that emergency signage must be powered independently of the site or venue power supply.
4   Hazard warning signs – with international symbols – flammable liquids, slippery floor, 'now wash your hands' notices, evacuation and emergency procedures, first aid facilities.
5   Information signs – ticket prices, prohibited behaviour and items, restricted access areas, programme changes.
6   Sponsorship and advertising signs.
7   General signs, e.g. 'thank you for coming and have a safe journey home'.

Signs within the venues and leading to the venue need to be clear, direct, uncluttered and easily visible. It is probable there are regulations and restrictions regarding where signs can be located and fixed, and this should be investigated before placement. Care should be taken with regard to their durability and how they are fixed, in case of rain or high wind.

Thought should be given to their size and legibility from a distance, and where they should be sited, bearing in mind that once the customers have arrived their bodies may obscure the signs.

It is useful if the height and sites for placing can be consistent so that the attendee becomes used to looking at a particular height and in a particular direction for information.

Particularly useful are self powered variable electronic message signs with automatic adjusting LED displays that allow remote modem message changes. They are easily positioned and the wide view angle LEDs are highly visible at acute angles. These devices are also available with CCTV surveillance cameras that can transmit to the communications control room for both traffic and crowd monitoring.

On the schedule of work for the event it should be noted when, and by whom, signs are going to be put up, checked regularly for vandalism, damage or loss; and removal at the end of the event. Often these are the first and last on-site tasks.

It is important to locate directional signs appropriately and to orientate them correctly to features on the ground at events, fixed maps are usually vertical and orientated for architectural convenience, perhaps on a wall or in a prominent position along the edge of a road or pavement.

A vertical map should be located so that buildings on the left of the map are to the left on the ground, and buildings on the right of the map are to the right on the ground. Things at the top of the map will then be behind the map board, and things at the bottom of the map will be in front of the board. This is the most readily understood orientation, and should be used whenever possible. Any other orientations require the user to revolve the map in their head, causing difficulty in recognising the correct direction.

Compare the orientation of map boards with the signs used on main roads. When approaching a road roundabout, there is usually a sign indicating the exits from the roundabout. This always shows the driver entering from the bottom of the map, so that points straight ahead are at the top of the sign, while the left of the sign indicates a left turn and the right of the sign indicates a right turn. It is rare to see a roundabout sign where the driver enters from the right, the left or the top.

Signage must be thoroughly thought through in advance and installed correctly. It must not be unsuitable, inadequate and illegible, or look hurried and temporary. Signs should have a corporate feel about them, and be made to look similar and professional. Uniformity in their design enables the customers to recognise at a glance what is being said. Different colours could be used to denote different types of signs – for example, a certain colour could be used for directional signs and another colour to denote room and space identification. Care should be taken with certain colours, because of colour blindness. Providing key information in languages other than the primary language of the attendees can eliminate confusion and the use of internationally recognised symbols is essential for emergency and hazard signage.

Presenting too much information can be as dangerous as presenting too little (O'Toole and Mikolaitis 2002). Signs are meant to communicate, and if too much information is given and causes confusion then it has failed in its purpose. Acronyms and symbols should only be used when it is expected that all attendees will understand them.

Similarly, it is important to check the signs for error or poor wording. Do not rely on an external supplier to spot grammatical errors; there are far too many examples of stupid mistakes with wording – e.g. 'Service entrance – do not enter'; 'Yield to Peds'; 'Disabled Door'; 'Don't Do That'.

Entrances and perimeters

For crowd control purposes an event site with secure boundaries is greatly superior to open access. It enables the organisers to regulate who is in the event site and control behaviour. Controls will be necessary at access points to prevent illegal entry to the venue, gatecrashers or unwelcome persons, and the entry of undesirable items.

The style and quality of perimeter security will depend on the risks and vulnerabilities identified in the event's security assessment. If any searching of persons or vehicles has taken place then a robust perimeter must be maintained in order to have full confidence in the security regime applied. Where possible, use existing structures to contain an event area.

Temporary fencing will require supporting processes such as patrol, CCTV coverage and alarms to ensure reduction in risk. Equally, any temporary fencing must adhere to health and safety legislation, and fire regulations, remembering safety must always have priority over security.

Careful consideration should also be given to the location of barriers, to ensure that they assist event personnel – i.e., the authorities and stewards – with crowd management and control, rather than acting as hazards or obstructions.

Barriers and fences

Water-filled barriers are polyethylene composition containers that are light and easy to move into position, but when filled with water are able to withstand low speed vehicle impacts. Pin connectors allow the barriers to be installed straight or curved.

Temporary chain mesh fence panels on rubber post feet are the most commonly used temporary fencing for outdoor events to provide secure site compounds. Supplied in standard 2.1m × 2.6m or 2.1m × 3m panels, installation by experienced crews is a rapid procedure. The modular construction means that gates for access at any section are easily inserted. A major advantage of this form of fencing is that it can be used to create secure crowd funnels and walkways that can be quickly widened by staff or in an emergency pushed over to release crowd crush situations. Care must be taken to inspect fence components during erection. The wire mesh often breaks away at connection points creating a jagged projection into walkways that can cause nasty cuts or damage clothing.

Fences are often covered with opaque plastic or cloth to give an impression of solidity. The notion is that by creating an illusion of being confined between walls and not being able to see options on the other side of the fences, the crowd will be docile and obey instruction. It also prevents the taking of short cuts and enables security staff to easily see occurrences of fence jumping.

External lighting provides an obvious means of deterrence as well as detection, but take into account the impact of additional lighting on the neighbours. If it is carefully designed and used, external lighting will help security staff and improve the capabilities of CCTV systems.

Entrances and exits

All events will require space for the arrival and departure of the audience, participants and performers, suppliers and volunteers. The varying movements of each of these groups must be controlled as they pass through the event, to eliminate bottlenecks, overcrowding and hazardous situations. Excessive numbers concentrated around an entrance or exit point, where flow rate is naturally reduced, can easily result in over-crowding and increased crowd forces, ultimately leading to trampling and crushing (Sime 1995).

The box office entry gates/doors will need monitoring to ensure easy control of queues and the selling and checking of tickets. Security controls will be necessary to prevent gatecrashers or unwelcome persons, and the entry of undesirable items.

The entrance to an event should be large, spacious and well signed. Space is required for ticketing, bag check and security assessment. To prevent crowding and facilitate pedestrian movement, venues should provide several dispersed entrances and exits rather than one central access. Pauls (1984) suggests the key factors which must be addressed for safe crowd ingress are:

- location and number of entrances
- separation of ticketing and admission areas
- risk of excessive crowd concentration
- design of doors to allow maximum ingress and egress
- a separate door for entry and exit should be used to separate opposing crowd flows
- exits should be wide enough to accommodate groups of people, so as to prevent the group having to disperse upon exiting and, subsequently, having to wait for all group members before leaving.

Fruin states "dispersed and equally balanced ingress and egress points are preferred over a single centralised location. The influence of external facilities on the volume and direction of movement must be considered" (1984: 4). He recommends a balanced ingress (or egress) system in which the entry and exit points are distributed around a site and not focused on one shared system.

The exits should allow people to leave a venue easily and quickly. Because of the shorter time span at the end of the performance, pedestrian facilities are taxed to the maximum, and dense crowding often occurs. The site design must ensure that they can pass through the system at the same speed throughout its length. Potential obstructions and routes that have limited space must be eliminated.

Internal site movement control

Once they have entered an event, there may be a constant physical flow of people and materials around the site. To ensure crowds do not block entrances, exits or pedestrian flows, significant planning is required to organise how the crowd is going to be distributed inside the venue to include preventive measures to avoid injuries and systems to ensure that the venue will not be overcrowded. Well-designed auditoriums and festival sites characteristically have direct lines of patron flow and clear lines of sight. Circuitous and narrow passageways, 'dogleg' routes, obscured doorways and stairs, and ambiguous pathways create confusion, and in an emergency flight response situation, have the potential for disaster. In such emergencies 'the-line-of-sight' becomes 'the-line-of-flight'.

As Fruin (1984) noted, spatial features that are typically implicated in dangerous crowding incidents are those that rigidly confine people within an inadequate space, or are not properly designed for crowd pressures and efficient mass movement. This includes corridors and stairs of inadequate width, insufficient numbers of doors or gates, escalators and protective guardrails that are either too low or not provided at all. Minor design deficiencies that present no apparent problems under normal traffic conditions can be accentuated in crowds, potentially triggering more dangerous, 'chain reaction' or 'ripple effect' accidents.

Stairways, gangways and ramps

Significant planning is required to organise how the crowd is going to be distributed inside the venue and not block entrances, exits or pedestrian flows. Stairways, gangways and ramps should be designed to ensure a steady flow along their length. Fruin states "arrangements that result in unbalanced use of egress or ingress routes, dead ends, or similar confusing and irregular pathway choices, are not acceptable" (1984: 3).

Crowd movement is eased by roundabouts and strategically placed obstacles, such as railings, trees or columns, all of which are flexible but have the same psychological effect as a wall, used as wave breakers, preventing large crowd pressures building up, and encouraging lane formation (Helbing et al. 2005). Corners in corridors should be rounded, rather than angular, and obstacles smoothly contoured. Line-of-sight paths should be made as long as possible, allowing individuals to see their destination and, thereby, more likely to choose the most direct route and to move quickly.

Site design must consider gradients, escalators, approaches to stairways, segregation of conflicting flows of people, widths, hand rails, lighting and the length of flights of stairs. Gradients are particularly problematic, movement down an incline poses risks where stumbling, pushing and congestion may cause sudden, uncontrolled surges downwards.

Differences in the traffic characteristics of pedestrian facilities should be carefully noted. Stairs have less capacity than corridors or ramps, and backups will develop where the two intersect. A stair that has the same overall width as an escalator has about the same pedestrian traffic capacity, but the escalator has the more dangerous mechanical delivery characteristic. For this reason, the entrance and exit approaches of escalators must be kept free of obstructions or conflicts with other traffic flows.

Space should be allowed for crowds observing a particular event or gatherings around a particular point of interest – such as a street busker – where ring structures result, emanating outwards from the point of interest.

Auditorium

For auditorium control the crucial consideration is of course the audience size, and if they are sitting or standing. Sightlines are of major importance. Jostling for a view is a major cause of crowd disturbance and crush. Each member of the audience should be able to see what is happening on the stage or performance area.

If the audience is standing, punter barriers will be required to restrict access to the stage and to protect the audience in the case of crowd surges. Additional infrastructure and equipment requirements may include crowd barrier protection for lighting, audio and vision mixing positions power supply equipment, platforms, gantries and lighting towers.

To prevent overcrowding in a particular auditorium or big top within a multi-venue event site, entry control can be a solution. Means of restricting entry could be by security staff or ushers simply stopping entry after capacity has been reached, or a limited number of tickets to the performance space are issued. This of course relies on the entrance to the space able to be closed.

There must be obstruction-free space around emergency exits. The emergency (crash) doors must never be locked and the exterior area of the doors must be clear of any impediments, well lit, and have appropriate signage.

Seating

The type of seating required is dependent, to a large extent, on the type of event being organised. As a guide it is recommended that:

- individual movable chair seating should not be used in enclosed and restricted facilities at events for more than 2,000 people
- individual movable chair seating can be used in unconfined, outdoor areas
- general admission seating can be used for events that are expected to attract a disciplined and orderly audience
- reserved seating should be the only seating allowed for those events that attract excitable and competitive crowds
- special facilities should be provided for handicapped patrons
- the legal capacity level of each area should be prominently displayed for public viewing and enforced.

There must be enough space between rows of seats to enable people to move freely without disturbing others. To reduce the evacuation time in an emergency situation, adequate aisles between seats and down the walls of the auditorium is essential.

Location of stages

The safe location of stages or other performance areas in multi-venue festival sites is dependent on crowd flow through the site between stages and backstage ingress and egress from restricted access perimeter service roads. If several attractions may be taking place at the same time, avoid placing popular attractions close together, or near entrances and exits, and where traffic will slow down. The other stage location considerations of noise spill, closeness to amenities, etc. must be secondary to crowd safety concerns.

Accommodating special needs

There may be people attending who have difficulty with the written word, have vision or hearing or speech impairment, have mobility difficulties, or are from other cultures. For those with difficulties with movement, all entrances and routes should be kept free of obstructions, and ramps, stair lifts and kerb lifts provided. The idea is to provide a 'continuous pathway' of uninterrupted travel to or within a venue that provides access to all required facilities for non-ambulatory people. These pathways should be clearly indicated on the site map and signage erected. This concept is extended by 'access precincts' to incorporate those areas linking public and commercial service providers to allow a precinct to be used as independently as possible within the limits of a person's disability.

A useful aide memoire for an event manager when considering special needs includes the following:

- use large-print signage and/or braille, site signs positioned at the right height for wheelchair users to provide information about the services provided
- consider different types of fire alarm systems for those who are hard of hearing
- provide special communication devices for use during the event
- where possible, remove physical barriers to ensure access to all buildings and elements of the event
- provide special seating or viewing areas
- consider the width of the aisles, the gradients to be covered, the dimensions of gates and doors to be passed through, and their ease of opening
- install accessible toilets and washing facilities
- add handicapped parking places with easy access to the site
- discuss with a range of people with difficulties what they feel would be useful to make their visit to the event more comfortable and enjoyable.

Facilities and stalls

Certain elements of the event should be next to each other, and their relationships should be considered carefully – for example, the closeness of catering to waste facilities, or auditorium and toilets.

Concession stalls should be located so that people have to pass by the stalls many times as they go from one attraction or venue to another but without impeding the crowd flow. Food stalls will require water for cleaning, waste collection, and power for lighting, cooking, refrigeration, etc. These services must be supplied and installed by qualified and licensed contractors. The setting up of all stalls, particularly food stalls, must be supervised to ensure compliance with health regulations. The prime risk for attendees is food poisoning, but spills of hot cooking oils, or other liquids, cuts from broken glass, and slips on fallen food or rubbish are other potential hazards.

Stall holders will need a secure back area behind their stall for storage and parking. Ideally there should be a restricted access service road running behind the stalls which has its entry separated from the public entry. Service access is used constantly during a festival and requires monitoring and control.

Restricted areas

There should be clear demarcation between public and restricted areas of the event site, with appropriate access control measures into and out of the restricted areas. These areas could include:

- stage, backstage and green room
- audio and visual control/mixing desks
- box office
- administration communications office
- emergency operations centre
- staff rooms and toilets
- media room
- equipment storage
- generators
- support scaffolding for temporary structures
- first aid and medical posts
- stall holders' rear access
- waste exchange area
- emergency access
- emergency parking
- staff, performer and VIP parking
- if alcohol is being sold, the sale and consumption must be in an age restricted fenced area with clear signage showing where and under what restrictions alcohol can and can't be served.

It will be necessary to allow only authorised personnel to enter restricted access to the event support facilities and performance areas. Fencing, barriers, signage and security staff may be required to make sure the boundary between public and private areas of the event is secure. Security may involve lighting, human resources, dogs or other techniques.

Access points to restricted areas should be kept to a minimum and clearly sign posted access points may include backstage gates/doors, emergency gates/doors, sub-contractor gates/doors. Ensure there are appropriately trained and briefed security personnel to manage access control points or alternatively invest in good quality access control systems, especially in VIP or restricted access areas.

Entry and exit procedures should allow legitimate users to pass without undue effort and delay. Ideally, adopt a photo ID card access control system which varies in appearance for the different levels of access across the site. Security staff should be instructed what to examine when checking passes and this should be quality assured through testing. Ensure staff are fully aware of the role and operation of the restricted access control system. The installer of an electronic system should provide adequate system training.

Backstage

The backstage area must be a secure restricted area fenced off from the general public areas of the site with its own supervised and security controlled gates, parking and security checkpoints. Performers, stage crews, staging sub-contractors, VIP and media will access the event through these gates.

The backstage area is where staging equipment and props are unloaded from transport and stored when not in use. Often power generators for the stage are located in this area. Unloading and equipment handling areas will need to be well lit, have level hard surfaces, be free from obstruction, be separated from working areas and walkways, and have adequate materials handling equipment. Adequate facilities need to be available for storage and loading resources which need to be distributed during the

Figure 6.2 Side stage access control fencing – note covering to prevent public view of backstage.

run of the event. Items need to be secure, particularly if the event is in an open space, subject to pressure from people or vulnerable to weather changes.

Only staff with tasks in the area should have access. An access pass applied for in advance of the event should be issued to performers, performers support technicians and accompanying persons, VIPs, media, etc. who will normally enter the event via the backstage gates. It is good practice that sign-on sheets are used to record the ingress and egress of everyone using the backstage gates. At the worst, a sign-on sheet can be used as evidence in contract disputes, at the best it gives the stage manager quick information about who is on site and who is missing.

The backstage area is usually the responsibility of the stage manager who will often delegate artist liaison staff to make contact with the performers on arrival, give them the appropriate run sheets, introduce relevant crew members and look after their needs while on site.

Green room

It is usual to have a dedicated backstage space for performers so that they can prepare and rest between performances. This is usually called the green room. There are often several, sometimes with different levels of comfort and facilities. In general, the room will be lockable, with toilet and washing facilities, make-up mirrors, clothing racks, and food-serving benches. If possible air conditioning and a fridge should be provided. The green room is also for the provision of hospitality to the artists – i.e. food and drink. It can also provide a place for storage of performer's equipment and personal belongings. The quality of a room and the length of time a performer will occupy a room will be items in their contract and will depend on their status. Often a VIP will be allocated a green room for their use while attending the event.

Green rooms are often carelessly managed, with food left uncovered and unrefrigerated, alcohol and illicit drug use common, and there is the possibility of slips from wet floors and overloaded power sockets. Many performers travel with an entourage that can include, personal assistants, publicists, stylists and bodyguards. It is important to establish the numbers, roles and identity of these persons as they will be occupying the green room and backstage area.

The green room area will need to be a secure restricted area within the already limited access backstage area sealed off from the general public areas of the site. It will need its own security controlled gates or checkpoints with access only given to those on a pre-submitted list of names. Only performers and their entourage, key members of stage crews, senior event management and media will access the green rooms.

Stage

The performance area, arena or stage is one of the most hazardous and strictly controlled environments at an event. Access to the stage, and the immediate side and rear stage areas, must be stringently limited to the stage crew and performers and rigorously enforced. Even the famous triple A – Access All Areas pass should not allow right of entry to a stage. Permission can only be granted by the stage manager, who should also have the authority to remove anyone, even a celebrity performer, VIP or senior staff member from the stage if that person is regarded as causing a hazard or nuisance. At some events, VIPs and performers' entourages are permitted to view performance from a special area side-stage.

It should not be possible to gain access to the stage from the auditorium. Security staff should be placed on the auditorium floor at the stage apron behind stage barriers. The number of security staff and the type of stage barrier required will depend on the volatility of the crowd and the style of performance. At the most extreme events, one guard every 3 metres, and 2-metre high punter barriers, are common.

On-site facilities and services

The placement of facilities in the event site should be assessed not just for convenience of construction, but by identifying and evaluating risk hazards that could lead to an injury.

Site lighting and power requirements

If the event is to be held at night or in a dark venue, it is essential to ensure there is enough light to see walkways and exits. Back-up generators are needed to provide adequate lighting in case of blackout. It is advisable to have the services of a qualified electrician on site in case problems arise with lighting equipment. Even in venues darkened for the performance, lighting should always be adequate to identify exits as well as corridors and aisles leading to them. Auxiliary battery power or generators should be installed to provide light in a power outage and to power the public address system. The latter may permit directions to be given to spectators in a power failure, thereby alleviating panic.

As many concerts are performed with only stage lighting, access to the main lighting or house lights is essential in case of an emergency. The location of the controls for these lights, and the operation of the controls, must be known and easily accessible for those on site who are responsible for emergencies.

Areas of the site that will need lighting include secluded areas that might be used for urination, settling arguments by fights, sexual predation, drug deals and other offensive acts. Parking areas and public transport waiting areas also need lighting.

Power supply

One of the most hazardous items of equipment commonly located in areas of the event accessed by the public are those that supply power to the site.

Mains grid power is provided to the event by distribution boards connected to the grid by 3 phase transformers. The hazards arise from poorly connected leads, overloading (a constant problem caused by stall holders) faulty and unearthed devices plugged into the board, and faults in the boards themselves. The risks of electrocution and fire is high.

Most outdoor events usually rely on truck-mounted mobile generators (gensets) that can power their entire operation and can provide their rated output 24 hours a day. These large gensets are exceptionally complex pieces of equipment. They may include sophisticated transforming and computer-controlled switching equipment, natural gas pressurization compressors, extensive sound insulation and muffler baffles and a wide array of other seemingly ancillary equipment. The large diesel engines that power many gensets – both mobile and permanent – typically feature oil and water-heating and circulation systems so that they are ready for instant start up at any time. Testing and maintenance of gensets is a significant consideration. Maintenance and testing are typically done by equipment vendors.

Large generators need to be refuelled a couple of times a day, and the greater the load they are under, the bigger the volume of fuel they consume. In the case of diesel-fuelled generators, this means refuelling trucks need to have ready access to wherever the generator is located. So, added to the risks of electrocution is the presence of highly flammable liquids which will require secure flameproof storage.

Stages, platforms and other performance facilities

One of the factors determining stage configuration will be the expected behaviour of the crowd. While classical music and ballet performances usually attract a mature and reserved audience, teenage and sub-teen fans at rock concerts have been known to storm the stage in order to touch their idols. Such incidents, apart from being disruptive, have caused injuries. It is therefore necessary for event planners to understand the audience that a particular performance will attract.

Stages are usually elevated above the floor or ground, to provide a better view of the performance, especially for spectators farther back. This, in itself, impedes those who would rush the stage in an attempt to touch a performer. However, a stage or a platform alone is usually insufficient to deter determined and agile spectators, and an additional physical deterrent is needed.

For live music concerts with a standing audience an effective practice is to erect a 'V' shaped barrier in front of the stage to deflect patrons to the outside of the stage should any surge come from behind. It also provides an additional barrier to prevent spectators from reaching the stage. Security staff can be positioned in this spectator-free zone, or should be able to gain access to it quickly at either end if necessary.

A punter barrier is an L shaped metre and a half high fence mounted on a 3 metre long foot that extends towards the audience. The audience weight on the foot – the horizontal part of the L – prevents the fence – the upright part of the L – from being pushed over. Often there is a raised walkway on the stage side of the barrier that gives security staff a height advantage over the audience.

Barriers and fences used for indoor concerts can be utilised in an outdoor setting. However, opaque board fences are often erected instead. Board fences have the added benefit of providing a walk space on the spectator side of the fence as well as behind. As most outdoor concerts do not have seating, spectators in the front rows seated on the ground have to take a position several metres back from the fence, to allow for a sight-line over the top of the fence to the stage. This area permits emergency access to the front rows of spectators.

Any stage protection barrier must be capable of a certain amount of flex in order to prevent the crushing of spectators in the front by a crowd surge from behind. At the same time it must be sufficiently solid to prevent collapse and the associated injuries. Fences installed often fail to address this two-fold requirement. Barrier posts must be securely anchored to the floor, not merely mounted to freestanding bases. They should also have some padded protection.

The front skirt around the base of a stage can be constructed so as to breakaway under the pressure of a crowd surge, thus allowing spectators to be pushed under the stage rather than being crushed against its base. It is important to note that this idea is not practical where there is less than 2 metres clearance beneath the stage, due to the potential for head injuries should a spectator collide with the stage. It should be stressed that use of a break-away stage skirt does not remove the requirement for a barrier in front of the stage, and should be seen only as a backup should the barriers fail.

Temporary structures

Due to their transitory nature, many events require easily-constructed temporary structures. This includes the stage platform itself, as well as towers to house speakers and floodlights, temporary seating (bleachers), dance platforms, roofs, towers and masts, viewing platforms, marquees and large tents, and artistic or appearance items such as archways, overhead signage and even sideshows.

It is essential that all such temporary structures be designed and erected with a margin for safety and a view to potential hazards. This should be done under the supervision of a local government inspector, and must conform to local government building and/or engineering specifications.

Temporary structures are often hurriedly erected as access to the venue may only be permitted a short time before opening, and they are usually designed for rapid removal at the conclusion of the event. In addition, these temporary structures are frequently neither designed nor erected to withstand other than intended use, therefore little or no safety margin is incorporated. High wind or spectators climbing for a better vantage point can overstress the structure. A number of accidents have occurred in the past when such structures have been poorly designed or constructed.

Temporary structures should also be inspected periodically during events of longer duration. Any that may be used for other than their intended purpose should be signposted and/or secured to prevent inappropriate use or access.

Doors and windows

If using a temporary building structure as a location for an event, a survey of the existing doors, windows and build materials could be made to identify any safety and security deficiencies. External doors should be strong, well-lit and fitted with good quality locks where possible. Due to the temporary nature of these structures extra security staff or other appropriate security measures may be required. Doors that are not often used should be internally secured ensuring compliance with relevant fire safety regulations and their security monitored with an alarm system. As a minimum accessible windows should be secured with good quality key operated locks.

Seating

Seating in a theatre, arena or similar location often combines the standard fixed seating, with additional foldable or stackable seating on the central floor, whereas temporary seats are often not secured to the floor or to one another. While this may not present any problems with sedate audiences, more enthusiastic spectators may pose difficulties. Persons standing on the seats for a better view are susceptible to injury if balance is lost or they are jostled. In such instances, other spectators can be affected, sometimes caused by a 'domino effect' in closely spaced chairs with potential for a significant number of injuries. If an audience becomes hostile, portable chairs can be used as dangerous missiles.

Portable, folding or stacking chairs should be secured to the floor and to one another. Where this is not possible, attachment of the legs of each row of chairs to two long planks, one running under the front legs, and one running under the back, is an alternative solution.

Loading

The collapse of temporary scaffolded raked seating caused by poor construction or inferior materials has caused severe injuries and deaths on many occasions. There is a limit to the load capacity of any structure, and precautions should be in place to prevent overloading. Any viewing platform or vantage point, such as a building veranda or balcony, can be the source of a major incident if spectator numbers are not properly controlled.

The bases of temporary scaffolded structures must be protected from damage by vehicular traffic or have buffer zones designated around them. Restrictions must be enforced to prevent persons climbing them from the sides or rear, and access to underneath the scaffolds must be forbidden and prevented by fencing.

Toilet facilities

It is essential that there are sufficient toilet facilities at the event for the number of expected attendees. If alcohol is being sold, this could increase demand. If there are not enough permanent toilet facilities at the site there will be a need to provide portable toilets. Discussion should be held with a reputable supplier about the number and placement of toilets, and arrangements for emptying during the course of the event, as required. A visit by the supplier to the site before the event would help them to assess the requirements. Toilet locations should be:

Figure 6.3 Portaloos and restricted service areas.

Safe site design

- well-signposted
- well-lit (including surrounding area) if night usage is expected
- serviced (including pump-out of portables) on a 24-hour basis during the event (vehicle access is obviously necessary)
- located away from food storage and food service areas.

In determining the number of toilets to be provided for particular events, the following criteria should be considered:

- the duration of the event
- the type of crowd
- whether the event is pre-ticketed and numbers known or un-ticketed with no crowd estimates
- peak times at the end of programme items, consider staggering finishing times where there are multi programmes
- whether alcohol will be consumed.

Calculating the number of toilets required for an event is a matter for conjecture and there is no uniform standard. Where local laws or regulations do exist these must be applied. The following tables should only be taken as a guide.

Toilet facilities where alcohol is not available

Number of male patrons	WCs	Urinals	Hand Basins
Up to 250	1	2	2
Up to 500	2	4	4
Up to 1000	4	8	6
Up to 1500	6	15	10
Up to 2500	8	25	17

Number of female patrons	WCs	Hand Basins
Up to 250	6	2
Up to 500	9	4
Up to 1000	12	6
Up to 1500	18	10
Up to 2500	30	17

Toilets for disabled patrons
At least one unisex toilet for disabled people is required per 500 patrons

Toilet facilities where alcohol is available

Number of male patrons	WCs	Urinals	Hand Basins
Up to 250	3	8	2
Up to 500	5	10	4
Up to 1000	9	15	7
Up to 1500	10	20	14
Up to 2500	12	30	20

Number of female patrons	WCs	Hand Basins
Up to 250	13	2
Up to 500	16	4
Up to 1000	18	7
Up to 1500	22	14
Up to 2500	40	20

These figures are for events of 8 hours duration or longer. The figures may be reduced for shorter duration events as follows:

● Duration of event: 6 to 8 hrs – reduce the toilet requirement listed above by 20 per cent
● Duration of event: 4 to 6 hrs – reduce the toilet requirement by 25 per cent
● Duration of event: less than 4 hrs – reduce the toilet requirement by 30 per cent

In an outdoor setting, it is a relatively simple matter to provide additional toilets by hiring temporary, portable toilets. This solution may not be suitable for indoor settings, for which provision of additional toilets may be more difficult. One possible solution is to convert some men's washrooms to women's for events where a predominantly female audience is anticipated or vice versa. As a means to overcome long line-ups, particularly at female toilets, some organisers provide additional, unisex toilets to be used by either males or females.

Food vendors and staff toilets

Separate toilets and hand washing facilities should be made available for food handlers and staff in an area off limits to the public. Toilet facilities will also be required backstage.

Maintenance

Organisers should ensure that adequate cleaning supplies are available for cleaning staff. Cleaning schedule for toilets and hand-basins should ensure:

● an adequate supply of toilet paper and soap;
● cleaning of toilets to a suitable timetable;

Figure 6.4 Toilet queue – ideally the wait should be no more than 10 minutes.

- provision for disposal and removal of sanitary napkins; and
- availability of plumber or appropriate maintenance person to repair or remove blockages.

Pumping out should be conducted on a regular schedule via a restricted access service road running behind the line of toilets. If necessary pumping facilities should be provided and maintained for the ongoing storage and disposal of sewage.

It is good practice to have an attendant in the toilet area to manage unacceptable queues, and report maintenance and first aid problems. Security staff should be present to discourage the selling and use of drugs in this area. Where no attendant is present, toilets should be regularly patrolled.

Campgrounds

Facilities provided in campgrounds should be adequate for the number of people present. They should be adequately lit at night and kept clean. Access to the facilities should be maintained and the pathways kept clear. In addition to the provision of showers and toilets, adequate signage, litter bins and litter clearance must be arranged. There should be constant patrols by security staff throughout the period the campsite is occupied. Instances of theft, intrusions on privacy, constant disturbance of other campers, should result in warnings or expulsion.

There may also be a fire risk at campground settings in country and bushland districts. Provision must be made to ensure fires are restricted or banned altogether during periods of high fire risk.

At events where the duration is overnight or longer, hygienic washing facilities should be provided. Suggested minimum requirements for facilities for camp grounds based on 2–3 nights camping are as follows:

Sex	WC	Urinal	Hand basins	Shower
Male	1 per 50	1 per 100	1 per 75	1 per 100
Female	1 per 25	N/A	1 per 75	1 per 100

Water

It is vital that free drinking is water available to attendees, participants, staff, volunteers, contractors, performers, etc. at the event particularly if:

- large crowds are expected
- the weather is likely to be hot
- participants are required to walk a long distance e.g. in a parade
- there is the chance participants will overheat (e.g. if there is a mosh pit, vigorous sport)
- possibility of dehydration from alcohol and drugs.

It is a legal requirement that there is free drinking water readily available when selling alcohol.

It is also important that sufficient water supply, under pressure, is available for food concession stalls for food preparation and cleaning, for toilets, for dust control, and, for emergency services in case of fire.

Waste management

Even small events can generate large amounts of waste. It is probable that there is a requirement to submit to the local council a waste management plan as part of the event approval application. Some aspects for consideration are:

- waste receptacles – type, quantity and placement
- emptying of receptacles – frequency, operational issues (e.g. how will waste trucks access necessary pick up areas)
- managing waste which has not been placed in receptacles (litter)
- types of waste – food, paper, plastic, glass and cans
- basic recycling bins
- types of packaging used in order to minimise waste.

Food waste should be deposited in covered containers placed strategically around the venue. Covers are essential, especially in outdoor settings or if high temperatures are expected. Spectator density may prohibit access by garbage removal vehicles, so to prevent containers from overflowing, containers should be emptied regularly, and waste moved to a temporary, properly prepared holding area, until bulk removal at designated times or after the event.

Arrangements should be made for the appropriate storage or disposal of empty containers from backstage and stall holder areas. Special arrangements must be in place for the collection and disposal of various forms of hazardous waste, including waste from food preparation areas, 'sharps' and other hazardous materials. Where possible, specific containers for recyclable materials should be installed.

Avoid the use of litter bins around critical/vulnerable areas of the event i.e. do not place litter bins next to or near areas of crowd density, support structures. Review the use and security of compactors, wheelie bins and metal bins to store rubbish within service areas, goods entrances and near areas where crowds congregate.

All event sites should have in place an agreed procedure for the management of contractors, their vehicles and waste collection services. The vehicle registration of each vehicle and its occupants, should be known to the event security or management in advance.

Litter management

Litter, especially broken glass, can cause major problems at events. Not only is it unhygienic to leave litter lying around but serious injuries can occur from broken glass and it may even be used as a weapon or missile. In order to minimise these problems it is important that:

Figure 6.5 Industrial waste bins.

- adequate litter receptacles are provided
- a 'no glass' policy is considered
- a container is provided specifically for the disposal of glass and sharp objects
- a separate syringe disposal unit is considered
- litter is collected regularly throughout the event.

A major consideration is a provision for the safe disposal of needles, syringes and other sharps away from the reach of children.

On-site first aid – emergency medical aid

At most events there will need to be sufficient emergency medical staff, facilities and equipment to handle routine accidents and crowd incidents. Lives have been unnecessarily lost at events by the lack of simple equipment such as stretchers and oxygen. Preventable deaths have occurred because of lack of knowledge of treatment for overdoses, heart attacks, falls and burns. There is an obligation to provide treatment for non-life threatening but distressing injuries suffered by attendees, staff and service providers. Experience from events has shown that most casualties are from:

- heatstroke, dehydration, respiratory distress
- age-related illness
- illicit drug and alcohol abuse
- cuts from broken glass and drink can ring pulls
- injuries from missiles, usually bottles and cans
- fainting and exhaustion from a combination of hysteria, heat and alcohol
- and at concerts, often at or near the stage barrier: trampling or crushing from crowd pressure; crowd surfing and stage diving; epilepsy attacks brought about from strobe lighting.

Planning for medical aid services begins with establishing what level of on-site medical care, if any, is expected to be needed given the nature of the event; and, what mix of medical personnel will be required on-site, for example, first aiders, paramedics, nurses, doctors. The extent of the on-site medical facilities required is dependent on:

- the number of people likely to come
- the temperature and weather
- the density of the crowd
- the length of the programme
- the type and level of audience participation
- the proximity to local services (doctors, hospital, ambulance).

The crucial factor is the type of audience expected. They might be disabled or elderly and therefore not in the best of health. Young audiences bring their own problems in that they may be excitable and vulnerable to dehydration, hyperventilation and crushing.

Medical teams

When considering the size and type of medical teams required the questions are:

- How many teams are needed? For example, is one ambulance per 10,000 people and 1–2 doctors per 50,000 too much or not enough?
- Who can see, treat and discharge patients?
- Will there be peak periods or special circumstances requiring additional staff?

At small events, at the very least, a trained, certificated first aid officer should be on site at all times, including the production periods of site set-up and bump out.

It is important to communicate with local emergency medical services, to establish their response times and whether they can handle a mass crowd disaster.

First aid facilities

First aid posts should be dispersed strategically throughout the venue and staffed by trained personnel. These posts need to be kept in a hygienic condition and contain adequate medical equipment and supplies, hot and cold or sterile water and a supply of drinking water. It is essential they have communication links to the communications control room, and their own allocated team communications channel. Facilities should include first aid kits of different sorts, including travelling kits, first aid rooms (or rest rooms, sick bays) and welfare and drug counsellors. At large events, a medical centre should be equipped to provide skilled response to cardiac, drug overdose, spinal injury cases and other emergencies. For big venues, a large room or marquee might be used as a casualty station.

At some venues, first aid personnel are located under the stage or immediately back stage to accept injuries suffered at the front of the spectator area.

Important considerations in the establishment of on-site medical aid posts are:

- they should be within 5 minutes of all sections of crowd, but located in as quiet a place as possible
- there should be a mode of transport to the aid post from all areas of the site
- medical aid posts should be clearly sign-posted from all directions, clearly identified with illuminated signage, marked on site maps
- the location should be known by all security and other event personnel
- they should be stocked and staffed for the duration of the event and for spectator arrival and departure periods
- facilities should be provided for injured or sick patients to lie down; with privacy in clinical areas
- there must be a means of communication with the primary medical control point, mobile medical teams in the venue, event organisers, security and other support staff
- there must be a means of communication available for attending medical personnel to communicate with off-site medical staff and ambulance services
- provision for the storage, collection and disposal of clinical waste is required.

Other considerations are:

- how will medical staff be fed, watered, rested and protected from the elements
- work safety for the medical team including standard occupational health and safety provisions, and protection from violence

- medical teams should be provided with maps of the venue
- arrangements for easy movement of medical teams onto and off the site
- medical team members' attire should make them easily identifiable
- first aid kits need to be checked regularly to see if the medicines, dressings or equipment are current, in the case of medicines, sufficient and appropriate.

Coordination questions are:

- Will medical staff operate in a facility to which the injured must make their way, or will clearly identified medical teams patrol spectator areas?
- How will medical staff be notified of or summoned to spectators requiring assistance in widespread spectator areas?
- How will medical supplies be transported, including secure on-site storage of drugs?
- Will there be vehicles to transport spectators to the on-site medical facility?

First aid officers should always record treatment in a register. Normally, this would include the injured person's name and occupation; the date, time and place of the accident; how the accident occurred and what the injured person was doing at the time. The record will also include the nature of the injury, a brief description of the treatment given and the name of the person who gave it.

Figure 6.6 First aid post.

It may be the case that an injury has occurred and been treated without the knowledge of the person's family or friends who may be on site at the event. Medical staff will need to contact them to obtain knowledge of any outstanding medical conditions, to tell them about the treatment applied, to take the person home or to their own doctor, or if the person has been sent off site to a hospital.

Use of the sound system used by the performers may appear to serve the internal requirement, however, there have been occasions when those responsible for it have refused to allow its use except during the change of performers. This has resulted in the delay of public announcements such as requests for next of kin of injured spectators. A social media message system or use of electronic signage could be established instead.

Ambulance services

The relevant ambulance service must be consulted to determine ambulance requirements for the event. Some considerations are:

- Will ambulances be pre-positioned on-site, or will they have to be called to the venue on an as-required basis?
- If ambulances are on-site for participants, (for example at sporting events) are these ambulances exclusively for participants, or will they be available for injured spectators?
- Are the medical vehicles appropriate to the terrain? For example, regular ambulances for road networks, 4-wheel-drive vehicles for off-road areas, golf carts or similar vehicles for densely packed or widespread spectator areas.

Summary

- Site design is essential to control hazards in traffic and pedestrian control, and operations movement within the event site. It involves the design of traffic areas, and separation of vehicles and pedestrians, and the location of crowd facilities and amenities.
- Consultation is critical at all stages of the process, particularly with staff, contractors and suppliers.
- Accurate estimations of audience numbers will be vital when preparing the site plan and set-up of an event.
- A site inspection is essential to identify hazards associated with the venue or site in order to plan effective safety measures.
- Attention must be given to the provision of separated entrances and parking arrangements for suppliers, staff and performers isolated from those used by the audience.
- Controls will be necessary at restricted area access points to prevent entry of any unwanted persons.
- There will need to be preventive measures to avoid crushing at public entrances. Queuing requires consideration on ways in which it can be dealt with effectively.
- The needs of emergency services for access to, and egress from, the venue, as well as movement around and within the site.
- Sites suitable as evacuation assembly areas must be selected or created. The most efficient evacuation routes to the evacuation assembly areas from different areas of the site or venue must be determined.

- The placement of prominent signage to direct the crowd for an evacuation is necessary.
- For events held in unconfined spaces, such as parades on public streets, complete cooperation between all public safety agencies and the event organiser is vital.
- Site maps are communication tools that stakeholders the traffic flow through the site, the location of activities, positioning of facilities and amenities, roads, barriers, doors and gates, walls and fences, electrical connections and the amount of power available, cleaning and drinking water, waste outlets, posts and pillars, and access roads etc.
- The site map should indicate where everything connected to the event will be placed, and how the attendees and the service suppliers will circulate through the site.
- A traffic management plan for the control of traffic in the streets and roads areas surrounding the event location will be required and qualified staff will be needed to implement the plan.
- Public transport services should flow through the events perimeter to entrances without any disruption.
- A designated area for people to get off and on buses should be provided as close to the entry and exit gates as possible.
- Signs are required to provide essential information at 'decision points' – for traffic and crowd control and for emergency procedures.
- Clear, comprehensive signposting at venue approaches, entrances and exits, and around and throughout the venue is vital.
- Secure boundaries enable the organisers to regulate who is in the event site and control behaviour. Controls will be necessary at access points to prevent illegal entry to the venue, gatecrashers or unwelcome persons, and the entry of undesirable items.
- The box office entry gates/doors will need monitoring to ensure easy control of queues and the selling and checking of tickets.
- The entrance to an event should be large, spacious and well signed. Space is required for ticketing, bag check and security assessment.
- To prevent crowding and facilitate pedestrian movement, venues should provide several dispersed entrances and exits rather than one central access.
- Spatial features that typically are implicated in dangerous crowding incidents are those that rigidly confine people within an inadequate space, or are not properly designed for crowd pressures and efficient mass movement.
- Planning and lay-out design is required to organise how the crowd is going to be distributed inside the venue to include preventive measures to avoid injuries and systems to ensure that the venue will not be overcrowded and crowds do not block entrances, exits or pedestrian flows.
- The placement of facilities in the event site should be assessed not just for convenience of construction, but by identifying and evaluating risk hazards that could lead to an injury.
- Certain elements of the event should be next to each other, and their relationships should be considered carefully – for example, the closeness of catering to waste facilities, or auditorium and toilets.
- There should be clear demarcation between public and restricted areas of the event site, with appropriate access control measures into and out of the restricted areas.
- The backstage area must be a secure restricted area fenced off from the general public areas of the site with its own supervised and security controlled gates, parking and security checkpoints.

- It should not be possible to gain access to the stage from the auditorium.
- Any stage protection barrier must be flexible in order to prevent the crushing of spectators, but sufficiently solid to prevent collapse.
- It is essential that there are sufficient toilet facilities at the event for the number of expected attendees.
- If the event is to be held at night or in a dark venue, it is essential to ensure there is enough light to see walkways and exits.
- Back-up generators are needed to provide adequate lighting in case of blackout.
- Facilities provided in campgrounds should be adequate for the number of people present. They should be adequately lit at night and kept clean.
- It is vital that free drinking water is available to attendees, participants and staff.
- All event sites should have in place an agreed procedure for the management of waste collection services.
- At most events there will need to be sufficient emergency medical staff, facilities and equipment to handle routine accidents and crowd incident.
- First aid posts should be dispersed strategically throughout the venue and staffed by trained personnel.

Bibliography

Emergency Management Australia (1999) *Safe and Healthy Mass Gatherings* (Australian Emergency Manuals Series: Manual No. 12). Australia: Commonwealth of Australia.

Fruin, J. (1984) 'Crowd dynamics and auditorium management', *Auditorium News*, May. International Association of Auditorium Managers.

Getz. D. (1997) *Event Management and Event Tourism*. New York: Cognizant Communications.

Glenn. B. (2007) *Beyond Borders*. Coppell, TX: International Association of Assembly Managers.

Health and Safety Executive (HSE) (2015) *The Event Safety Guide: A Guide to Health, Safety and Welfare at Music and Similar Events, The "Purple Guide"*, 2nd edn. Norwich: HSE Books.

Langston, P. A., Masling, R. and Asmar, B. N. (2006) 'Crowd dynamics discrete element multi-circle model', *Safety Science*, 44, 395–417.

Mellor. N and Veno. A (1998) *Public Events: Safety and Security Strategies*. Victoria: Centre for Police and Justice Studies, Monash University.

O'Toole, W. and Mikolaitis, P. (2002) *Corporate Event Project Management*. London: Wiley.

Pauls, J. (1984) 'The movement of people in buildings and design solutions for means of egress', *Fire Technology*, 20, 27–47.

SETON (2007) *Solutions for a Safe, Secure Workplace*. Regents Park, NSW: Seton Australia.

Sime, J. D. (1995) 'Crowd psychology and engineering', *Safety Science*, 21, 1–14.

Tarlow. P. (2002) *Event Risk Management and Safety*. New York: John Wiley & Sons.

Worksafe Victoria (2006) *Advice for Managing Major Events Safely*. 1st edn. Victoria: Government of Victoria.

Chapter 7

Site management
Production and operational work practice hazards

Chapter objectives

This chapter examines event work practice hazards in event production and operations phases, in particular:

- Site construction
- Communication systems
- Staff stress and vulnerability
- Ergonomics and protective clothing
- Hazardous machinery and equipment.

The implementation of an event plan is conducted in three distinct phases, each phase has its own distinctive set of hazards:

1 **Production:** the setting up of the event equipment and facilities involving technical staff and contractors on a site or venue closed to the public.
2 **Operations:** the conducting of the event involving performances and activities with the public on-site or in the venue.
3 **Shut Down:** the closing of the event, dismantling of the site, return of equipment and clearing and cleaning the event location.

A crucial factor in assessing hazards is the event environment itself, not just the individual hazards. A site or venue may be inherently hazardous through a combination of elements that in themselves may not be individually hazardous. It may be that a particular task or piece of equipment may be safe in one location and dangerous in another, or is safe in daylight, but hazardous on a dark and stormy night.

Work practices are a major safety issue. A task may be safely performed if the worker has the appropriate protective clothing, equipment and training, but perilous if these are absent. Consider, for instance, traffic controlling. In a safe environment staff directing traffic should be wearing hi-vis vests, communications headsets, hats and boots, have glow stick directional wands, and operate in a well-lit area that has signage, cones and barriers. Yet it is common to see the task performed by people in ordinary day clothing standing in the middle of a road simply waving a torch, with no signage, no lighting and no safety.

Production – overseeing and coordinating the site/venue set-up

The site production phase of an event is the construction of the festival site or the movement of equipment into a venue (bump-in) and organising appropriate storage and handling of physical elements where required. This phase requires the managing of an efficient and safe receipt and distribution of resources throughout the event site. Facilities and equipment must be correctly arranged in correct working order and in accordance with production plans and sub-contractor agreements. This in turn requires control of resource deliveries, arrivals and departures of service suppliers.

A key task is to monitor safety issues, at regular intervals through ongoing liaison with contractors and other stakeholders to ensure that work is carried out in accordance with instructions, and identifying the need for adjustments and organising appropriate changes to maintain the integrity and quality of the event production procedures.

This will require the monitoring of the construction of temporary structures or installation of equipment to check that all sub-contractors meet their obligations to make certain that all safety issues have been addressed in accordance with relevant legislation and organisational procedures.

Although the following list is not comprehensive, and not applicable to all events, it gives an idea of what should be considered when site managing a location for an event:

● on-site services and facilities
● sub-contractor personnel on the site
● storage considerations

Site management

- technical facilities
- logistics of setting up
- capacity of the location, spatial considerations and likely obstructions, and versatility
- safe flow of movements within the site, services, suppliers, performers and participants, and audience
- traffic control and parking issues
- legal regulations and constraints on the event.

Consultation with sub-contractors and suppliers is critical for safety at all stages of the process, and there is a need to establish effective ongoing consultation mechanisms to identify existing and potential hazards. The site (or production) manager will liaise with all site construction or venue bump-in staff to brief them on communication and hazard control mechanisms. This will involve providing clear instructions to appropriate personnel regarding the movement of physical elements to ensure safety and avoid damage to equipment, the planning and organisational requirements for the bump-in/bump-out process, the roles of key personnel, and the expected and typical issues and problems to be encountered.

Site construction scheduling

An event construction site combines a number of hazardous situations into a constricted time and space. The site needs to be secured, infrastructure built and installed, equipment and facilities positioned, and staff familiarised with tasks. All within a very short time span. Most event staff accidents are due to a combination of cramped spaces, lack of time and interference by other workers.

Consider the risks of having boxes of staging equipment left on site while fences and marquees are being erected, or preparing food while roads and walkways are being levelled and surfaced. Or putting up signage while the electrical supply is being tested. Even tasks that are closely related have a sequence that ensures safety, for instance, sound equipment is not placed on a stage until the riggers hanging and setting lighting have finished.

Vital for the safe coordination of the set-up of an event, task and resource delivery scheduling is an overall operational sequence of the various production tasks from arrival on site, through set-up, testing and rehearsals, audience influx, performance, site break-down and final departure.

Production scheduling

There are four basic steps to scheduling tasks:

1 Develop a network diagram that shows each production task and its dependencies – the resources and workforce personnel required.
2 Create the workflow time-lines for each task – the order in which they must occur.
3 Estimate the duration of each task.
4 Allocate delivery times for the resources for each task.

In effect, this amounts to putting all the tasks, resources and workers into a timetable matrix. Performance indicator milestones are used for monitoring actions and can point out problems or clashes. Priorities, the essential tasks for which subsequent tasks require prior completion, can be indicated.

The process commences with making a list of the ideal work personnel numbers, skills required and supervision needs. In particular, noting whether the task is subcontracted, outsourced or under direct control. Which tasks require paid staff and which can be undertaken by volunteers is crucial information. List the tasks in detail and then check the task list with as many people as possible. A missed task results in additional effort and could cause the project to fall behind schedule.

Critical Path Analysis and Gantt charts assist the site manager in identifying the activities to be undertaken for the event and which activities are reliant upon other activities before they can be completed. Software such as Microsoft Project can make this task easier. The Gantt chart provides an overview of the project and how individual tasks combine to complete the production. It also illustrates how one work team interacts with another and can show a team member the importance of completing their part of the work on time. It allows for a breakdown of tasks and personnel allocated over time for their effective completion. Of course, some tasks where there is no overlap of space, can be scheduled simultaneously.

Schedule of resource supply

Concurrently with the task schedule, it will be necessary to compile, adjust and finalise a resource delivery schedule, including adequate contingency plans.

The delivery of resources should be on a 'just in time' (JIT) schedule. JIT schedules increase efficiency and decrease wastes of time by receiving equipment and goods, only when they are needed in the production process. This means that the storing and movement of materials and components can be kept to a minimum, which saves workforce time; there is also less likelihood of accident, damage or theft. Supplies are delivered right to the event production site only when they are needed to the location where they are needed within a very narrow time slot.

It also applies to workers, it means that staff and volunteers arrive when they are wanted and are not sitting about waiting for their job to start.

The main disadvantage of JIT is that there is little room for mistakes. Event production is very time reliant, and if resources are not delivered on time, the whole production schedule can be delayed. Also JIT means that there is little time for replacement of faulty equipment or unexpected incidents.

The process requires close contact with the nominated contractor personnel to determine and then verify appropriate times for on-site delivery of resources in accordance with agreed procedures.

Site construction

Precinct control

Securing the site is the very first action. It is dangerous to allow the public to be able to walk (or worse, drive) through an event construction site. Not only can people be injured by contact with hazardous equipment and processes, workers are also put at risk by being forced to take avoidance actions, by people interfering with equipment and safety control guards. An open site is also an attractive target for thieves and the loss of small easily stolen tools and consumable materials can cause both delays and disputes. To secure a site three measures are required – fencing, restricted access and surveillance.

If the site is unfenced, temporary fencing will be needed and the erection of the fences is usually the first (and after the event ends, the last) construction task. However, internal fences, i.e. those used to isolate restricted areas (stages, alcohol service, audio visual desks, etc.) are erected after the main infrastructure is in place. It is usual to have some form of security and first aid service on site during this period.

There will need to be a centrally located administration office on site to liaise with sub-contractors, staff, volunteers and the public. It should have communications, resources, reserve finance and personnel able to make informed decisions in accordance with strategies to deal with potential problems. The administration office is the first building on site. Drop-in temporary buildings are ideal.

Sub-contractor management

In conjunction with the various contractors, a site production manager will interpret technical production requirements to determine temporary facilities and stage rigging requirements and their impact on other aspects of work. The task is to liaise with and supervise licensed riggers and sound and light technician sub-contractors to ensure a smooth flow of work and efficient set up in accordance with safety and licensing regulations. Rigging requirements may relate to one or more of the following:

● lighting, audio and vision mixing positions
● stage, backstage
● art installations
● signage
● platforms, raked seating, lighting and speaker towers.

Other sub-contractors will require accurate briefings or specifications on precise site facilities placement – water, toilets, storage, fencing and barriers, box office, security and emergency services areas. Liaison may be required during set-up with other specialists, e.g. acousticians, pyro-technicians and special effects technicians.

The event site manager will liaise with local authorities to ensure statutory requirements are integrated into the planning process. Licensing requirements and regulations may relate to:

● builders and building work
● electricians and electrical work
● plumbers
● caterers
● event precinct traffic control
● handling of hazardous materials
● forklift operations
● special effects

Safety monitoring

The event site manager will provide clear instructions to appropriate personnel regarding the monitoring of vehicle access and movement, the movement of physical elements to ensure safety and avoid harm. This will include:

- monitoring the bump-in/bump-out process to ensure that work is carried out in accordance with instructions
- organising appropriate storage and security of physical elements where required, including valuable items and any hazardous materials
- monitoring construction or installation to ensure that it meets design specifications, budgetary constraints and timelines
- ensuring that all parties meet their obligations, adhere to safety standards and work within project requirements
- monitoring all work to ensure that it is completed to specifications and any changes required are negotiated, agreed with the appropriate personnel and implemented
- monitoring the set-up to ensure that all occupational health and safety issues have been addressed in accordance with relevant legislation and organisational procedures
- checking that all aspects of the venue space used and any equipment has been set up to allow for easy access, and to avoid risk of injury to audience, participants, performers and staff
- ensuring that all signage is content accurate and placed correctly.

Weather impacts

The impact of weather on the event will depend on the activities being coordinated. It is very important to carefully consider potential weather impacts and to include them in the hazard assessment. It is advisable to monitor weather forecasts in the lead-up to the event to enable planning for the predicted weather conditions. The Bureau of Meteorology can provide long and short-range forecasts. Contingency Planning should be made to deal with conditions such as:

- **heat:** provision of shelter, water, first aid, sun cream, insect repellent
- **wind:** provision of shelter, and ensuring structures and dangerous items are secure
- **rain:** provision of shelter, and protecting leads and wiring
- **hail:** provision of shelter
- **cold:** provision of shelter and warmth.

In the case of extreme weather it may be necessary to cancel or postpone the event to ensure the safety and security of those present. Establish before the event:

- conditions for cancellation/postponement
- who is responsible for deciding to cancel/postpone
- when should a decision about cancelling/postponing an event be made
- how to advise staff, volunteers, performers and people planning to attend the event of the cancellation/postponement
- contingency plans if the event is still able to go ahead.

On-site operations and facility control

Safe site operations management establishes and implements processes that will have a positive impact on safety, eliminate hazards, and control risks to health and safety. It involves the coordination of all aspects of the on-site operation at the time of performance. All systems, procedures and logistics for on-site management require safety/hazard management controls and protocols associated with the movement of people and equipment at event venues.

The site manager is responsible for the overall control of the event site and will liaise with the appropriate personnel and check that all required services have been arranged. It is the site manager (or on large events, the safety officer) who has the responsibility to check that all aspects of the event set-up, facilities and equipment allows for safe patron access and minimises the risk of injury to patrons. And if there are any deficiencies, including staff shortages, take prompt action to rectify the situation. Key requirements for this set of tasks are an in depth knowledge of:

- occupational health and safety requirements that affect the allocation of work and the movement of physical elements
- key areas of event staging and the standards that relate to typical event operations
- roles and responsibilities of organisations involved in staging of outdoor events including government agencies and other authorities.

Site operations

Operations management commences with a reconfirmation of all safety requirements and a briefing with all operational staff and contractors to clarify roles and responsibilities and agreed procedures for the event. The briefing may include:

- details of the event in an event manual
- communication procedures and protocols
- emergency protocols and evacuation procedures
- event policies and procedures
- opening and closing procedures for each functional area
- security and conflict resolution techniques
- staff responsibilities and reporting mechanisms
- incident report documentation.

Immediate pre-opening activities

The site or operations manager and the event manager will communicate with appropriate personnel to ensure that all technical pre-show checks are completed within the required timeframe, that required technical elements are operating, and check that all required services have been arranged.

They will then, in conjunction with the stage manager(s), Front of House manager and safety officer, check that all aspects of the venue space used and any equipment has been set up to allow for easy access, especially for those with disabilities, and to avoid risk of injury to attendees, performers and event staff. In particular the team will check that:

- the auditorium is correctly configured
- all emergency evacuation areas are clear and that safety equipment is operational
- the venue and site is clean and tidy
- there is adequate access for arrivals and egress for departures by whatever means of transport are to be used
- there are adequate stairs, gangways and walkways within the venue for pedestrians and any planned traffic
- all emergency equipment is properly maintained and in good working order and, where appropriate, test it; examples of such equipment include fire-fighting equipment, fire alarms, smoke alarms, public address and other communication systems
- all event emergency systems have an uninterrupted power supply (UPS) available which is tested.

They will identify any deficiencies, including staff shortages, and take prompt action to rectify the situation. Checking all aspects of the set-up of the venue, facilities and equipment may include:

- toilet facilities
- box office (FoH)
- food and beverage outlets
- merchandising stores/stands
- stages
- signage
- fences
- traffic control
- emergency services positioning.

The process is to identify any deficiencies and discrepancies and take prompt action to rectify the situation. Deficiencies and problems may include:

- incorrect set ups
- incorrect staging
- faulty or non-availability of technical equipment
- lack of equipment to manage displays and signage
- shortage of food and beverages
- inappropriate or lack of space at entries and exits.

Supervision of the event operation and venue services

The constant task throughout the event is to supervise and monitor the provision of services in order to identify any problems as they arise and take prompt action to resolve hazardous situations. A reporting system from the leader of the staff team responsible for each function area of activities should be established.

Pre-event checks can only show if the event site has been constructed according to the design plan. However, the design may contain flaws and may be unable to cope with unforeseen issues. Therefore it will be necessary to monitor throughout the event that:

- the site allows for adequate crowd management, with sufficient flow, seating areas and facilities

- that traffic control, parking and public transport areas are operating smoothly for access for arrivals and egress for departures
- stairs, gangways and walkways within the venue for pedestrians are clear and adequate
- the emergency exits and evacuation routes are unobstructed and free from hazardous and combustible materials
- all direction and information signs are in place and are legible
- all floors, stairs and other areas which people use are well-maintained and do not present tripping or slipping hazards
- refuse and combustible materials have been removed to safe storage or disposed of
- equipment storage areas, restricted areas, and any other potential hazards are inaccessible to unauthorised persons.

Compliance

To ensure compliance with public health requirements, a public health audit should be carried out prior to the commencement of the event. Subsequent periodic surveillance should be undertaken at appropriate times during the event. These are particularly important for outdoor events in hot weather with transient food vendors who may not have sufficient sanitary or refrigeration mechanisms available.

It is preferable that environmental health officers should have access to resources to assist in overcoming any problem noted (for example, toilet servicing, unsafe areas, fencing repairs, water testing) rather than simply using their powers to stop the event or particular operation.

Figure 7.1 Water filled barriers used to define emergency access road.

On-site staff communications

Communication is a critical issue when organising any kind of event. Essential information needs to flow unhindered between all staff both during normal operations and in emergencies, and key communication control personnel need skills and experience in dealing with stressful situations.

The communication system technology needs to be top grade, be multi-modal and not rely on one single system, and have its own backup power supply. Staff and security services communication on large events is usually via headset or handheld radios with channels assigned to the event's various function and facilities components, each with a coordinator that oversees that component. When a problem arises, staff use the specific radio channel to discuss the problem. This allows conversation about lost children, medical incidents, weather changes and concerns, etc. to be private.

Communications within the venue

General staff and volunteers need to be kept informed about problems and emergencies within the venue. If it is not feasible to supply all staff with radios, it could be done by the use of coded public address messages. These alert staff to contact the control room. All staff, including volunteers and temporary staff, should be provided with a set of protocols for contacting management, first aid and security staff.

Sample of a specific protocol for communications:

Example: Communications at the All Green Festival

All key staff, security, emergency service and waste management personnel will have two-way radio units (walkie talkie). Site manager Trent Roden will be in charge of handling two-way radios, ensuring batteries are charged and all units functional. WT will be used for all confirmations i.e. between FOH and stage manager to confirm artist is in green room or side of stage.

Primary: Two way radio (WT).
Secondary: Mobile phone; as mobile phone communications can be intermittent due to high usage among patrons WT should be used first.

WT CHANNELS

1 Security
2 General communications (event manager/FoH/BoH/stage and site managers, catering)
3 Emergency services (police, ambulance)
4 Waste management

NAME	TITLE	Radio Channel	Mobile
Anthony Mcfadden	Event manager	WT(all)	0xxx 334 756
Samantha Hickey	Production manager	WT(2)	0xxx 764 456
Luke Hutchins	Stage manager (main)	WT(2 & 5)	0xxx 786 345
Trent Roden	Site manager	WT(2 & 5)	0xxx 234 908
James Browning	FoH manager	WT(6)	0xxx 567 890
Ami Watts	BOX manager	WT(6)	0xxx 667 856
Mike Bambach	Finance		0xxx 567 098
Kasey Cascade	Cascade Towers bar manager	WT (2)	
John St John	Ambulance	WT(3)	
Kenny Rotten	Waste management	WT(4)	
Ron McDonald	Catering	WT(2)	
Bobby Hammer	Security	WT(1)	
Sgt Hugh Asper	Police	WT(3)	

Two-way radios will be restricted to the following key personnel i.e. event manager, expo coordinator, stage manager, site manager, security and traffic attendants.

All communications between additional event staff will be maintained via mobile phone. A contact list will be issued to all staff members prior to the event date, complete with all event staff names, company details, position and numbers.

This contact list will be tailored for individual staff groups i.e. a less detailed contact list will be issued to volunteers (with key contacts), while the event manager's contact list might be quite detailed i.e. trade and expo vendors details and performers, etc.

Whatever methods of communication are used, the system should be designed to give accurate, up-to-date and relevant information. In considering the best way of communicating with staff, think about:

- who needs to communicate with whom
- when and how frequently the communications take place
- where staff are located
- the speed with which a person is required to respond to information or commands
- how many people need to be involved in the same communication at the same time
- other relevant factors, such as the resources and equipment available.

All communication needs are dependent primarily on the nature of the event – what works for one venue may be totally inadequate for another. For instance, methods of communication which will be most effective in the staging of an orchestral performance are not likely to be much good when hosting a football match. How the communication strategy is managed ultimately depends on the integration of various factors, as no single solution exists which will work for all events.

Liaison with outside bodies may be useful in communications planning. Consider liaising with the local police force, local government services and public transport operators. For example, the local police may be responsible for monitoring traffic flows to and from the venue and a means of communication between them and the event's traffic management team will enable an efficient traffic flow and response to accidents, breakdowns or other incidents. Similarly, if there are special public transport arrangements, communication channels need to be maintained to schedule arrivals and departures, especially if there have been cancellations or delays.

Overseeing of the event breakdown

At the end of the event the site manager is required to oversee the breakdown of the event to ensure it is completed in accordance with safety requirements; coordinate the packing and removal of all materials and equipment in accordance with pre-arranged details; and to close and secure the venue. To assist in these tasks, a site manager will rely on the ESMS and checklists that have identified hazards and the controls for those hazards. The site manager will also depend on crowd monitoring procedures, a security team and first aid services.

The post-event task of cleaning up the site, returning hired or borrowed equipment and restoring the site to a reasonable condition takes as much planning as other elements of the event's production. The disposal of waste, the lack of litter, the repair of damage to existing equipment, the removal of signage, posters etc. all need to be addressed. It is essential to complete the event with a careful acquittal of all contractual obligations relating to the site, the provision of services and use of equipment. The processes are:

- close and secure venue as required in accordance with organisational procedures
- oversee the breakdown of the event to ensure it is completed in accordance with sub-contractor agreements
- coordinate the packing and removal of all materials and equipment in accordance with pre-arranged details
- check the venue to ensure items and belongings are not left behind
- check and sign accounts in accordance with contractor agreements. Note any outstanding items requiring post-event action
- debrief personnel as required and use feedback constructively to enhance the safety of future events
- debrief with contractors if it is necessary to discuss any difficulties or suggestions for future improvements.

The procedure for the dismantlement of a site is often the exact reverse of the bump-in process. The last facility set-up on a site is usually the first to be removed. Normally this would be the concession staff holders as they are numerous and quickly packed up. Frequently this occurs even as the final performances are happening. Left on site they would create a hindrance for the movement of larger infrastructure. All smaller infrastructure and delicate equipment is next off site. Internal fences and barriers are removed. Deconstruction of stages and scaffolding is followed by disconnection of power, and finally the perimeter fences are removed. Greenfield or street sites will need rubbish removal, cleaning and perhaps environment rehabilitation or regeneration.

Safe work practices and equipment use

A particular challenge for event managers is the common use of large numbers of volunteers performing a range of tasks that involve both physical and physiological hazards. Often these volunteers are untrained in the tasks required of them. A safe workplace for volunteers and employed staff requires an understanding of how physical and physiological hazards present at events and how those risks are controlled.

Event sites and venues can create combinations of hazard conditions such as:

- noise, vibration
- light, heat radiation
- fibres, dust, and fumes
- heat, humidity
- biological agents such as insects, mites and bacteria
- electricity
- aggression/violence.

The characteristics of each hazard need to be identified and will include:

- how it occurs
- how it affects specific parts of the body, such as the extent of damage to tissue and long-term effects
- factors relating to concentration and time.

For staff working on an event the principal hazards are workplace violence, stress and injury from hazardous equipment.

Violence

There's a potential risk in most events for some form of violence to occur and often risk assessment is necessary. Attention must be given to the vulnerability of workers in certain locations or when performing certain tasks that expose them to conditions of possible harm from violence or aggression, and security expertise may be required to assess the operating conditions.

Workplace violence can be defined generally as incidents in which workers are abused, harassed, threatened or assaulted in the course of their work. Many event organisers are caught unprepared when ugly incidents occur. Situations with a risk of confrontation and attack are those which involve contact with the public, and working with valuables and cash handling. The event occupational groups worst affected by workplace violence are:

- guards and security officers
- first aid attendants and police
- traffic control and parking officials
- sales people (includes ticket sellers, bar attendants, waiters and waitresses)
- stewards and ushers.

Attackers can be angry customers or random assailants who have snapped for one reason or another. Attacks can arise from aggressiveness caused by poor crowd control issues, performance cancellations, or from intoxication or drug-influenced behaviour. Also, aggression or overt violence can come from fellow workers, both up and down the organisational chain.

(AIC Research)

Assessing the risk

The two primary safety controls for workplace violence are the structural aspects of the workplace, and protocols and methods of dealing with the public; and co-worker and supervisory support and team culture. To consider both types of controls, questions such as the following need to be asked:

- What are the risk factors?
- How many staff are exposed?
- When are they exposed?
- What existing controls are in place?
- How effective are they?
- How likely are violent incidents?
- What are the potential injuries?

Controlling the risk

As with other workplace hazards, the hierarchy of controls should be used. For example, to control cash-handling risk:

- eliminate the hazard entirely – no cash on premises
- substitute less hazardous procedures – use drop safe or limited cash float
- put in engineering controls – widen counters, install screens
- use administrative controls – alarms, staff rotation through vulnerable zones
- provide training – train staff in dealing with hold-ups.

In the case of external or client-initiated violence, there are many techniques available, including careful design and location of facilities, that will reduce the opportunity for perpetrators. Some of these techniques go under the heading of 'target hardening', making it more difficult to commit acts of violence. More subtle strategies include increased visibility in contact areas, used together with closed circuit television, and appropriate furniture and fittings, that is, those that are not potential weapons.

If there is a prior history of drug or alcohol influenced attacks, a ban on selling alcohol and a policy of denial of entry to alcohol and drug affected people may be appropriate.

Above all, a clear policy of zero tolerance towards any violence needs to be implemented together with procedures based on the risk assessment. The policy and procedures need to be made clear to attendees, as do the sanctions if the policy and procedures are violated. If incidents are likely, staff need to be trained in how to spot them and deal with them. Any incidents or breaches must be reported.

Response to violent incidents

The response to an act of violence is a real test of the system. The aim is to have an effective immediate response that controls and defuses the situation and reduces the risk of long-term psychological harm for employees.

Everyone should know who has the authority to take charge of the situation. That person should be trained to coordinate the response, including taking care of employees who may be injured, in shock or are otherwise affected by the incident. At this point, the workplace must be made safe, first aid and medical assistance arranged and immediate support provided.

The area of the event site (or even the whole site) may be in disarray as a result of the incident. To enable the event to return to normal as quickly as possible after the disruptive incident, previously agreed plans should be implemented as quickly and efficiently as possible. The following actions should be included:

- provide clear information regarding the situation to all staff
- allow staff time to recover, but encourage early return to work
- provide advice on legal matters and workers' compensation arrangements
- investigate the incident and review management procedures.

Stress

In general, negative stress is the psychological and physical reactions experienced when someone is faced with disproportionate demands they are unable to satisfy. Often referred to as psychological injury, occupational stress is defined as the negative response to workplace demands that go beyond an ability to enjoy or cope with them. Typical stressful tasks at events are crowd and traffic control, ticketing and ushering, particularly when performed by under-trained and inadequately supported volunteers working excessive shifts in heat, cold, dust or rain.

Workplace demands come from both outside the organisation from the public, and from inside the event organisation, for example, from supervisors, managers, co-workers and sub-contractors. Individuals will respond differently to the same type of workplace demands, depending on factors such as individual perceptions, personality, skill levels, knowledge and health, the level of control or decision-making allowed to deal with the demand, and importantly, the social and technical support received from the workplace, and training. These factors are said to mediate or affect a response to the same type of demands.

Some people successfully cope with and even enjoy stressful demands and the freedom to impose their solutions to control a situation. For others, factors such as a lack of control, direction and support can be causes of stress or stressors in their own right. It is this combination of workplace demand and mediating factor that determines whether the workplace demand is a stressor. Effects can be quite severe and lessen a person's ability to respond to simple demands, in turn making things even worse.

Negative stress within a workplace can be explained in terms of combinations of demands and control. Negative stressful work is characterised by high psychological demand, low job control, low organisational support and high job uncertainty. Stress-related consequences are related to the organisation of work activity and not just its demands and/or person-based characteristics.

Identifying stress

Indicators of workplace stress are symptoms such as:

- changes in a person's mood or behaviour, such as deteriorating relationships, irritability, indecisiveness, absenteeism, reduced performance or increased mistakes
- evidence of substance abuse – being drunk or stoned on duty
- health complaints, such as frequent headaches, lack of sleep or nausea
- complaints of stress
- claims for psychological injury.

Stress is often a symptom of poor employment relations and can seriously affect productivity and service quality. A preventative approach would not wait for such symptoms or complaints to occur, but would involve regular discussions with staff on matters such as appropriate workload, training, support and future changes to avert any stress occurring in the first place. Event organisations who talk regularly with their employees and have sound systems and procedures in place for dealing with issues like absence and discipline are much more likely to avoid work-related stress and be able to deal with potentially stressful situations when they arise. However, few event organisations provide means for the effective management of volunteer stress problems.

Assessing the risk

Assessing the risk of stress requires gathering information on the demands and the workplace mediating factors that moderate or contribute to that stress. Assuming that workplace stress already exists, questions to be asked, include the following:

- Who is affected?
- How are they affected, that is, what are the risk factors – demands and mediating factors – and how do they operate to produce stress?
- When does the stress occur? Is it continuous or concentrated at certain times?
- What controls exist? Are there procedures to deal with stress? Are they used?
- What are the effects on health, morale, operations?

Controlling the risk

Depending on the evaluation, a number of controls are available. The preferred option is the removal of the stressors entirely; however, this may not be practical, in which case, controls are needed to minimise risk. The Health and Safety Executive in the UK has drawn up a number of management standards to address workplace stress, which are as follows.

DEMANDS	Workload, work patterns and the work environment	*The standard is that* – employees indicate that they are able to cope with the demands of their jobs; systems are in place locally to respond to any individual concerns.
CONTROL	How much say the person has in the way they do their work	*The standard is that* – employees indicate that they are able to have a say about the way they do their work; systems are in place locally to respond to any individual concerns.
SUPPORT	Encouragement and resources provided by the organisation management	*The standard is that* – employees indicate that they receive adequate information and support from their colleagues and superiors; systems are in place locally to respond to any individual concerns.
RELATIONSHIPS	Promoting positive working to avoid conflict and dealing with unacceptable behaviour.	*The standard is that* – employees indicate that they are not subjected to unacceptable behaviours, for example, bullying at work; systems are in place locally to respond to any individual concerns.
ROLE	People understand their role within the organisation and the organisation ensures that the person does not have conflicting roles	*The standard is that* – employees indicate that they understand their role and responsibilities; systems are in place locally to respond to any individual concerns.
CHANGE	Managing organisational change (large or small)	*The standard is that* – employees indicate that the organisation engages them frequently when undergoing an organisational change; systems are in place to respond to any individual concerns.

Ergonomics

Ergonomics looks at the degree of match between the people and those activities or processes, including the equipment, the environment and the systems of work involved. Where there is not a match that meets the worker's physical and psychological needs, there is usually a potential hazard. Ergonomics is able to help identify potential hazards and either design out risk altogether or to minimise it.

Biomechanics applies the physical laws of mechanics to the body to estimate the stress exerted on muscles and joints when a person adopts certain postures or carries out certain movements. Biomechanics principles are:

- keep joints in a neutral position; do not stretch the muscles and ligaments spanning the joints
- keep work close to the body
- avoid bending forward from the waist
- avoid twisting the trunk.

Figure 7.2 Wrist-banding – note worker's poor posture.

Because event sites are temporary workplaces, these principles can be, and often are, ignored or worse, deliberately violated, increasing the danger of injury.

Physiology measuring estimates the energy demands on the heart and lungs from muscular effort during movements. There is a limit to the amount of energy that the heart and lungs can normally supply to the muscles when performing movements or adopting postures before experiencing general fatigue.

This is not just true of heavy physical labour, but also for simple tasks performed over a lengthy period, such as inspecting or collecting tickets over a 3 or 4-hour period without a break; a common volunteer working experience.

Knowing what that level is for particular tasks helps in the design of work. The limits on the rate of work, length of work period and the right equipment need to be established in order to optimise output that will not cause any damage to the body. It can also help to identify the frequency and length of any rest breaks that might be required.

Prolonged posture in the same position can result in injuries. This applies to sitting, standing and hand and arm postures, for example, bent wrists and unsupported, raised arms. Combine poor posture with the application of force and repetition and the chance of injury referred to as occupational overuse syndrome (OOS) increases. Here, the need for a sympathetic design of workstations and equipment is clear.

Occupational overuse syndrome, previously known as repetitive strain injury (RSI), is a collective term for a range of conditions characterised by discomfort or persistent pain in muscles, tendons and other soft tissues or without physical manifestations. It is usually associated with tasks that involve repetitive or forceful movement or both, and/or maintenance of constrained or awkward postures.

The investigating of manual tasks using ergonomic principles can identify the hazards, eliminate them or, failing that, control them.

Identifying and managing ergonomic hazards

Potential hazards are identified after having first identified the context for investigation, usually, a workplace or function, and then listing the main activities or processes found there.

> site → processes → hazards → potential injury → severity → probability → risk → control → implement → monitor and evaluate or review

Note that various factors – work organisation, skills and experience, age, gender and special needs, will qualify the task ergonomics. A fit and strong 25-year-old female will be less distressed by stacking chairs all day in an auditorium than a male septuagenarian.

The data collected will then need to be analysed in order to provide an understanding of the potential risk. A manager must know the hazards, the potential injuries, the likelihood of them occurring and their severity, as well as priorities for action. The next step is to eliminate or control that risk by developing a preferred solution. In this context, ergonomists talk of optimising the match between people and their work.

To optimise the match between people and their work, the following control options are possible –

- job redesign, which includes

  - modifying the object handled
  - modifying the workplace layout
  - rearranging the flow of materials
  - using different actions, movements or forces
  - modifying the task with mechanical assistance
  - modifying the task with team lifting involved
  - mechanical handling equipment
  - training
  - shorter shifts
  - more frequent breaks
  - rotating staff through different tasks.

Personal protective clothing and equipment

Personal protective equipment (PPE) is anything used or worn by a person to minimise risk to the person's health or safety and includes a wide range of clothing and safety equipment. PPE includes boots, face masks, hard hats, ear plugs, respirators, gloves, safety harnesses, high visibility vests, torches, litter pick-up (grabber) sticks, communication headsets. For example: traffic control staff need two-way radios, safety vests, day and night reflective 'stop' and 'slow' batons, safety tapes, night wands, hard hats and brims. They should also have access to witches hats, bollards, barricade boards and a full range of signs.

Personal protective equipment is one of the least effective ways of controlling risks to work health and safety and should only be used:

- when there are no other practical control measures available (as a last resort)
- as an interim measure until a more effective way of controlling the risk can be used
- to supplement higher level control measures (as a back-up).

Other clothing used for protection from weather, sun, cold, rain, etc, should be worn by outdoor workers according to the environmental conditions.

If PPE is required, the person who is directing the work must provide PPE to workers at the workplace. This will usually be the event site or operations manager, but could also be, for example, a contractor at the workplace. The worker should not be charged for clothing or equipment. If the worker already has their own PPE it must meet the minimum standards required by work health and safety laws. PPE must be maintained, repaired or replaced so it continues to minimise the risk to the worker who uses it. This includes ensuring the equipment is clean and hygienic, and in good working order.

Event management usually does not pay for shoes or clothing that is generally considered not to be PPE. This includes workers' regular clothing such as pants or jeans. However, if a uniform, such as an event tee shirt or cap is required these should be supplied at no cost.

Personal protective clothing and equipment used at a workplace must be:

- selected to minimise risk to work health and safety
- suitable for the nature of the work and any hazard associated with the work
- a suitable size and fit and reasonably comfortable for the person wearing it
- maintained, repaired or replaced so it continues to minimise the worker's health and safety risk
- used or worn by the worker, so far as is reasonably practicable.

A worker who is provided with PPE must use or wear it in accordance with any information, training or instruction from the event site manager, so far as they are reasonably able, even if that worker is an employee of a contractor. If a worker refuses to wear or use the PPE, the event site manager should remove the worker from duties that require the wearing of protective clothing and equipment.

Selection processes for choosing the right PPE must involve consultation with workers which should also include:

- a detailed evaluation of the risk and performance requirements for the PPE
- compatibility of PPE items where more than one type of PPE is required (for example ear muffs with a hard hat)
- consultation with the supplier to ensure PPE is suitable for the work and workplace conditions, and complies with the relevant standards.

The event site manager or contractor should ensure:

- PPE is used properly in accordance with the manufacturer's instructions
- PPE fits correctly and is reasonably comfortable for the worker who is to use or wear it

- PPE does not interfere with any medical conditions of the worker using the PPE
- workers are instructed and trained in how to use, maintain and store the PPE
- appropriate signs are used to remind workers where PPE must be worn
- periodic assessments are carried out to ensure PPE is used properly and is effective.

There are problems with using PPE. Wearing some items may adversely affect the performance of tasks being undertaken, for example restricting vision or mobility, or it may be uncomfortable to wear and some workers may not be able to wear it, for example, workers who are allergic to latex cannot wear rubber gloves. Also the PPE may create new hazards, for example, some items of PPE can hinder the body's natural cooling mechanisms by preventing evaporation of perspiration. If the PPE is uncomfortable or does not fit properly, the worker should consult with their manager.

Performance area and stage safety

The performance area, arena or stage is one of the most hazardous working environments at an event. To focus audience attention onto the performance, the immediate side and rear stage areas are darkened as much as possible during a performance. Yet these are the spaces where the stage crew congregate; performers wait their turn to go on stage; and instruments, spare and reserve sound equipment, and props and stage furniture are accumulated ready for use in very confined space. It is also the place from which VIPs and performers' entourages view the performance. During a music performance the area usually experiences very loud sound from stage mounted speakers. During vocal recitals, plays or speeches, the side stage area must operate with maximum quiet.

A performance stage is a very busy working environment with stage crews working with tight time pressure to ensure the 'flow' of a programme. Adding to the conditions are nervous and anxious performers, especially novices. The most common incidents of injury are falls, trips, electrocution and a range of other injuries that can arise from working in a dark, noisy, busy, confined space filled with equipment and people. Safety measures for the stage include:

Pre performance set up (working stage)

- stage crew to wear hi vis vests, gloves and hard capped boots and hard hats if rigging above is in progress
- bright stage lights on a separate system to the performance lighting
- all lighting stands and gantries to be securely fixed to prevent them being pushed over
- all leads to be taped down to the floor and either covered with cable protectors or conduit ramps if crossing a walkway, or raised 2 metres or more above a walkway
- performers to be prohibited from the stage for rehearsal or sound checks until all equipment is correctly installed.

Performance stage

- stage crew to use communications headsets and be issued with torches
- on-stage power supply boxes located out of performers' movement areas, and drink and instrument storage location

- riser edges, stage edges and walkways delineated with light reflecting safety tape
- side stage working and waiting areas clear of equipment and instrument storage cases, stools, etc., and lit with low light
- access to the stage by side, rear stairs only
- public access to the stage for awards, performer interaction, etc., should be from within the auditorium directly to the stage not via the side stage
- stairs to have handrails and steps to be edged with non-slip, hi-vis edging tape
- evacuation route to backstage lit by illuminated emergency signage.

The management of the physical staging of the programme of an event is the responsibility of the stage manager. It involves tasks to organise the performance area prior to performance to ensure that it is set in accordance with the performer's requirements. The stage manager is responsible for the presentation of all the staged elements during a live production. As such, it requires the skills and knowledge to safely operate a range of staging equipment plus a sound knowledge of stagecraft, the types of issues that may arise during performance and how these affect staging personnel. This requires a broad understanding of artistic and technical elements of the production/event such as staging, lighting and sound elements and the typical problems and responses involved.

The stage manager will have full control of the stage and backstage areas, working alongside technical specialists. If the event has multiple stages, each stage will have its own stage manager. Each will be independently responsible to the site operations manager. The stage manager will be responsible for:

- effective communication, team leading and delegation in relation to the stage management of a production
- problem solving and decision-making processes and their application in an immediate production/event environment
- relevant occupational health and safety legislation and regulations as they apply to maintaining a safe backstage environment.

He/she is in direct control over audio, visual and lighting production and crew and has autonomy to make relevant decisions relating to the safe and efficient functioning of the area. The stage manager is the immediate point of contact for all technical, backstage, lighting, audio-visual and staffing issues associated with performances.

The stage manager will conduct technical rehearsals in consultation with relevant colleagues. The purpose of the technical rehearsal (also known as a run through) is to test and modify the physical staging elements in accordance with the programme design documents. Sound levels for fold back monitoring, room equalization, and auditorium levels will be conducted by the sound engineer. The lighting technician will aim and focus lights on the stage areas and artists according to the stage plot, and run through the various lighting changes. A key task is to ensure all relevant safety procedures are followed, with particular reference to control requirements for any potentially hazardous sequences

Before the commencement of the programme, the stage manager will provide briefings and documentation to the staging personnel to reiterate staging elements, safety procedure and policies. This will include:

- running appropriate checks on all stage elements and equipment to ensure that they are in working order

- checking all transient staging elements to ensure they meet operational standards, and to avoid any accidents or performance complications. This includes amplifiers, cabling, props, instruments etc.
- communicating with contractor personnel in a clear and concise manner to ensure efficient, safe and disciplined production practices. This will include all sub-contracted technicians, e.g., sound, lighting and performers' stage crew
- inform Front of House that pre-staging in complete and the audience can enter the auditorium.

Performer misbehaviour

Actions by performers such as late cancellation, walking off stage, drunkenness, poor performance, running over time, encouraging fans to move closer, offensive language or gestures, throwing souvenirs to the audience, have precipitated inappropriate or hazardous crowd reactions. Entertainers should be fully informed of their responsibilities for maintaining order, and the problems associated with inciting potentially dangerous crowd behaviour. The stage manager has the task of monitoring performances to ensure that offensive behaviour is brought to a halt, even if this requires drastic action such as removing a performer from the stage, or turning off the sound and lights. Usually a hastily arranged technical hitch can be used as a cover for the stage manager to give the performer a warning message. If a performance is cancelled, the audience should be told without delay. Illness can always be used as a reason. Announcements should clearly establish refund policies, exit routes and the need for orderly movement.

Hazardous equipment

'Equipment' covers a wide range of appliances, machinery and tools. On an event site there will be machinery and equipment usually employed on a building site such as cranes, scaffolding, temporary power connections, earth moving and road construction machines, scaffolding and fencing. There will be warehouse lifting and loading machines such as forklifts and trollies. Specialist stage equipment for sound reinforcement and lighting, amplifiers, generators and scissor lifts. Food stalls will have portable ovens, generators, gas cylinders, stoves and grillers. Emergency services will have firefighting, first aid and rescue equipment: a huge agglomeration of paraphernalia all brought together in a temporary location shared with thousands of attendees. Every item is potentially hazardous and as a result, the risks are wide-ranging and include electrical shock, fire and explosion, burns, slips, trips and falls and crushing of fingers and toes.

There are lengthy and detailed duties of event organisers with respect to machinery and equipment. They include:

- consultation
- hazard identification
- risk assessment
- training, information, instruction and supervision
- record keeping.

And particularly the control of risk during:

- installation, erection and commissioning of machinery and equipment
- use of machinery and equipment
- maintenance and repair
- dismantling, storage and disposal.

Registration, licensing, certification, permit to work

Most equipment must be registered and operators of equipment must be certified by a recognised certifying authority. The regulations provide details. Permit to work procedures or certification are defined as a written authority document that may include:

- approval to undertake work and activities including tests, measurements and monitoring
- authorisation by a responsible or designated person directly in control of the equipment
- appropriate precautions and controls to be followed
- incorporate checklists, conditions and actions such as the frequency and duration of the work and tests
- follow recognised industry standard recording practices as required to assist in ensuring a safe working environment.

Hazard identification and assessment process

The hazard identification and assessment process looks at the work processes or activities to identify the exposure to equipment hazards. Site plans would normally be required. A hazard register is created by identifying the processes and the hazards associated with the equipment used in each of the processes. Another method would be to list all the equipment used and, by identifying the associated processes, identify the hazards. In particular, hazards may be posed by the layout and condition of the event site or venue work environment and any reasonably foreseeable abnormal conditions such as power failures, breakdowns or, in the case of outdoor events, changes to the weather.

Preferably, identification of hazards should be done before and during the introduction of equipment into the workplace, before and during any alteration or change to the system of work associated with the equipment, and whenever new or additional health and safety information becomes available.

The next step is assessing what risk there is of injury occurring (given the effectiveness of existing controls) by identifying the risk factors – the factors that could lead to an injury, the likelihood of an injury occurring, and the severity of any injury. Those closely involved with production, together with any specialists, would be able to help, as would information from manufacturers and suppliers.

Overseeing equipment use work processes

When identifying hazards associated with machinery and equipment, systems of work should be considered as containing potential hazards as much as the physical machinery or equipment itself. The machine may be safe in itself, but not the system of work in which it is used. This requires looking at:

- policy and procedures for purchasing/hiring equipment
- instruction and supervision
- work organisation
- skills and experience of the employees
- work practices and procedures
- emergency procedures.

A hierarchy of controls is then used to assess whether any existing controls can be improved on in order to further minimise the risk. The key questions will be:

a   What are the common types of controls associated with specific machinery and equipment?
b   Are the control measures eliminating or reducing the risk?
c   Is the process of monitoring and evaluating the controls working effectively?

Controls associated with machinery and equipment often require consideration of access and special attention needs to be paid where there is the potential for contact by members of the public.

To assess site and venue workplace environmental conditions and develop a monitoring strategy, the hazard identification and assessment should include:

- location
- physical features of equipment
- environmental variability
- area or space available
- tasks and activities being undertaken
- the number of people occupying the area
- the movements of people and equipment
- the way in which the hazard or condition is being generated
- the rate of generation.

Common types of controls associated with equipment

Special attention needs to be paid to dangerous parts of equipment where there is the potential for contact or entrapment. *Guarding controls* typically include:

- permanently fixed physical barriers where no access of any part of a person is required
- interlocking physical barriers where access to dangerous areas is required during operation
- physical barriers securely fixed by means of fasteners or devices
- presence-sensing safeguarding systems.

Operational controls are used to control hazards associated with equipment. They must be:

- suitability identified, with their nature and function clearly indicated
- readily and conveniently located
- guarded to prevented unintentional activation

> ### Definition box 7.1
>
> Guarding must so far as is practicable prevent access to the danger point or area of the machine.
>
> Guarding is a permanently fixed physical barrier, if access to the area of the machine requiring guarding is not necessary during operation, maintenance or cleaning of the machine.
>
> Guarding is an interlocked physical barrier which allows access to the area being guarded at times when that does not present a risk and prevents access to that area at any other time, if access to the area of the machine requiring guarding is necessary during operation, maintenance or cleaning of the machine.
>
> Guarding is a physical barrier which can only be altered or removed by the use of tools, if using either a permanently fixed physical barrier or an interlocked physical barrier is not practicable.
>
> Guarding is a presence-sensing system that eliminates the risk arising from the area of the machine requiring guarding while a person or any part of a person is in the area being guarded; if none of the above types of guarding is practicable.
>
> Any guarding needs to be as difficult as is reasonably possible to by-pass or disable, whether deliberately or by accident.
>
> Any guarding must not cause a health and safety risk in itself.
>
> If the machine to be guarded contains moving parts and those parts may break or cause workpieces to be ejected from the machine, the guarding to be used must control any health and safety risk from those ejected parts and workpieces.

- capable of locking in the OFF position to enable disconnection of all motive power and forces
- be of failsafe type.

Operational controls can include emergency stops and warning devices. They need to be prominent and clearly and durably marked, that is:

- coloured red (push buttons, bars or handles)
- unable to be affected by electrical or electronic circuit malfunction.

Locking switches that require keys to open the lock could be used in conjunction with a danger tag system that promotes greater safety consciousness among the workforce for all situations in which danger to people could arise from:

- the operation of machinery or equipment
- the flow of steam, electricity, gases or liquids
- the use of faulty or unsafe equipment.

Danger tags could include multiple locking systems and would require written authorisation by a competent person for them to be opened. Such systems would be implemented and monitored in liaison with relevant key personnel.

Lock out/Tag out protocols

Placing an out of service tag on faulty equipment to alert others it is unavailable for use. Once you have placed a tag on the faulty equipment you should tell your supervisor and arrange for it to be repaired. This includes any electrical equipment, chairs, desks, doors, etc.

For employees who perform repairs or maintenance work this will also involve isolating and tagging machinery or equipment during repairs, service or maintenance work to alert others that the equipment is being worked on and must not be operated.

No person is to work on electrical or mechanical components, such as electricity, hydraulics, steam, compressed air etc., unless a properly completed 'Danger Tag' and, if available, a lock has been attached to the appropriate controls. This is to prevent the individual or others being injured from its activation.

Stop work

Should an accident occur, the equipment must be stopped and access to equipment be controlled using measures such as:

- lockout or isolation devices
- danger tags
- permit to work systems.

If the equipment cannot be stopped, operational controls that permit controlled movement of the equipment must be fitted and safe systems of work be used

Key information transfer and feedback

When purchasing equipment or entering into sub-contractual arrangements, the event manager will need to ensure that hazards are not being introduced as a result. For example, if instituting a work process using hazardous equipment, people who will work with the item should be made aware of the risks involved in its use, the control measures and any specific training requirements. Key information required to control risks should be recorded and transferred from the manufacturer to all users.

It is important to note that if a piece of equipment, machinery or tool, is modified in some way by the operator or by the employer, that person is then regarded as liable for any injury arising from its use. For example, silencing the reverse beeper on a forklift so that it can be used without its sound intruding during a concert may lead to a collision. The person who made the modification is liable. This also applies to modifications in the layout of a venue – blocking emergency exits with temporary storage, for example. It is common on event sites to see 'make do' modifications and inappropriate use of

Figure 7.3 Phase 3 to 2 phase power supply box.

equipment – lighting trees and trusses are often employed as load bearing supports or bracing.

Items intended for other purposes should not be used as substitutes, for example pool chlorine can be used to clean concrete surfaces, but can release toxic chlorine gas if it is mixed with certain other cleaning agents. Inhalation of chlorine gas can cause difficulty breathing, chest pains, cough, eye irritation, increased heartbeat, rapid breathing and death.

Staging equipment

Damaged or faulty staging equipment is the most frequent cause of injury and death on performance stages. Electrocution or falls are regularly suffered by stage crew and occasionally by performers.

The equipment most susceptible to interference or damage from the environment on an outdoor event is usually power cabling, power supply racks and power amplifiers for loudspeaker systems.

For external events contractors should provide high-voltage equipment that cannot be affected by rain or water, and they should always ensure safety is the first priority under any conditions. It is entirely practical to install enormous LED screens, concert sized PA systems and a full lighting rig that can operate happily in all but the most adverse of weather conditions. Video, sound and lighting equipment rated for outdoor use will be quite indistinguishable from its indoor equivalents, both visually and in terms of performance.

Manufacturers of AV equipment have weatherproof equipment that is exactly the same as the indoor product with added design innovations that close any gaps or holes, cover any electrical contacts and seal in any point where cables connect. The internationally recognised standard for weather and waterproofing of electrical equipment is an IP Rating. IP stands for 'International Protection', and an IP rating on a piece of AV equipment, such as a loudspeaker will feature the letters 'IP' followed by two digits, e.g. IP65. The numbers refer to two tables of standards regarding the level of protection afforded against solids (first digit) and liquids (second digit). In the example of IP65, which is one of the most common ratings for AV equipment suitable for outdoor use, 6 is the highest level rated for solids, meaning 'No ingress of dust; complete protection against contact'. The 5 indicates that 'Water projected by a nozzle (6.3 mm) against enclosure from any direction shall have no harmful effects'. The liquids rating goes all the way to 8, which indicates the equipment is certified to be permanently immersed in water up to one metre deep.

Hazardous substances and dangerous goods

Hazardous substances and dangerous goods are classified according to different criteria. A substance may be classified as both. Hazardous substances are classified only on the basis of the health effects – both medium and long-term – that may result from exposure to them. Dangerous goods are classified on the basis of the immediate physical or chemical effects that may have an impact on people, property or the environment, such as classes of substances or articles that are, for example, explosive, flammable or radioactive.

To determine whether produced substances are hazardous, the event organiser will need to check the hazardous substance regulations or the OHS authority. If there are any products or other materials being used that are hazardous, they should be listed in a hazardous substances register. The Hazardous Substances Information System, an internet database, provides information on hazardous substances and exposure standard information. It is used to support the hazardous substances regulatory framework for the various jurisdictions.

Those using hazardous substances will need to know about:

- the hazard's chemical and physical properties
- the routes of exposure
- the health effects
- the recommended controls.

The online database, and the labels on containers should, together, provide that information. Warning signage should be placed on the storeroom or locker and the substances should always be kept under lock and key.

Control

The details of the hazard and the controls have to be inserted in any information, instruction and training for anyone likely to be exposed to a hazardous substance. In particular, employees should be able to demonstrate an understanding of:

- labelling of hazardous substances
- hazards they are likely to be exposed to
- safe work practices
- risk controls
- emergency procedures
- first aid and incident reporting
- atmospheric monitoring
- health surveillance.

Information, instruction, training and supervision need to be regularly reviewed in order to be kept up to date and for their effectiveness to be evaluated.

Fireworks and flares

If there is to be a fireworks display, check on the storage and set-up, and the types of fireworks and the safety distances for operating. The pyro-technician will need to obtain the necessary permit from the appropriate regulatory authority, police and fire brigade. Permits generally stipulate that the fire brigade must be informed that a fireworks display is being held, and ideally a firefighter should be in attendance whenever fireworks are being let off. The fire brigade must receive a list of fireworks beforehand so that they know what precautions are required.

Fireworks have to be set up at the ground itself as it is illegal to transport fireworks in a trailer when they are fused. Once the fireworks are at the venue:

- make sure that fireworks arrive and are stored away prior to the public arriving on site
- before the fireworks are set up they need to be locked away for safety
- establish a security cordon to prevent people from coming into the area where the fireworks are stored and where they are to be set up
- check that everyone knows what to do in the case of an accidental fireworks explosion
- check if there is anything combustible in the area where the fireworks are to be kept prior to the show, such as gas cylinders
- place metal buckets filled with sand at regular intervals around the venue in case of fire.

Fire safety

The risk of fires starting can be minimised by enforcing the fire regulations applicable to the venue and/or site. Most new venues will conform to current safety requirements. However, temporary structures will need constant monitoring by trained fire marshals. These staff can be off-duty fire officers or specially trained security personnel. Locations for appropriate fire control equipment should be planned with the local fire authorities.

Management should ensure that fire extinguishers are appropriately marked and authorised for the locations they will be kept. Regular checks should be made to ensure that they have not been interfered with or replaced.

The local fire authority should monitor fire prevention and preparedness measures to ensure relevant standards are met. Organisers and health personnel should consider potential fire hazards in the planning process and discuss any concerns they may have with the fire authority. Particular attention will be required to monitor fires lit by attendees in camping areas, food stalls, rubbish bins and dry grass or woodland areas.

Summary

- A site or venue may be inherently hazardous through a combination of elements that in themselves may not be individually hazardous.
- Work practices are a major safety issue. A task may be safely performed if the worker has the appropriate protective clothing, equipment and training, but perilous if these are absent.
- An event construction site combines a number of hazardous situations into a constricted time and space.
- Monitoring of the construction of temporary structures or installation of equipment by sub-contractors is necessary to make certain that all safety issues have been addressed in accordance with relevant legislation and organisational procedures.
- Consultation with sub-contractors and suppliers is critical for safety at all stages of the production process.
- Most event worker accidents are due to a combination of cramped spaces, lack of time and interference by other workers.
- For the safe coordination of an event, task and resource delivery scheduling is vital.
- It is very important to carefully consider potential weather impacts and to include them in the hazard assessment.
- A constant task throughout the event operational phase is to supervise and monitor the provision of services, in order to identify any problems as they arise and take prompt action to resolve hazardous situations.
- A reporting system from the leader of the staff team responsible for each function area of activities should be established.
- A public health and safety audit should be carried out prior to the commencement of the event.
- Subsequent periodic surveillance should be undertaken at appropriate times during the event.
- On-site communication is a critical issue. Essential information needs to flow unhindered between all staff, both during normal operations and in emergencies.
- Key communication control personnel need skills and experience in dealing with stressful situations.
- The communication system technology needs to be top grade, be multi-modal and not rely on one single system, and have its own backup power supply.
- It is common at events for large numbers of volunteers to perform a range of tasks that involve physical and physiological hazards. Often these volunteers are untrained in the tasks required of them.
- For staff working on an event the principal hazards are workplace violence, stress, and injury from hazardous equipment.
- Attention must be given to the vulnerability of workers in certain locations or when performing certain tasks that expose them to conditions of possible harm from violence or aggression.

- Typical stressful tasks at events are crowd and traffic control, ticketing and ushering, particularly when performed by under-trained and inadequately supported volunteers working excessive shifts in heat, cold, dust or rain.
- Ergonomic hazards arise from a mismatch between workers' physical and psychological needs and work practices or processes, including equipment, environment and the systems of work involved.
- Personal protective equipment is anything used or worn by a person to minimise risk to the person's health or safety and includes a wide range of clothing and safety equipment. It is one of the least effective ways of controlling risks to work health and safety.
- The performance area, arena or stage is one of the most hazardous working environments at an event. Damaged or faulty staging equipment is the most frequent cause of injury and death on performance stages.
- On an event site there will be a wide range of appliances, machinery and tools. When identifying hazards associated with equipment, systems of work should be considered as containing potential hazards as much as the physical machinery or equipment itself. The machine may be safe in itself, but not the system of work in which it is used.
- Controls associated with machinery and equipment often require consideration of access, and special attention needs to be paid where there is the potential for contact by members of the public.

Bibliography

Atkinson, W. (2000) 'The everyday face of workplace violence', *Risk Management*. 47(2), 12.

Bajaj, B. (2003) Risk Management. In R. Best, C. Langston and G. Valence (Eds) *Workplace Strategies and Facilities Management: Building in Value*. Oxford: Elsevier Butterworth-Heinemann.

Borger. H. (2009) 'Bullying one and all', *National Safety*, 77(2).

Capra, M., Earl, C. and Parker, E. (2005) 'Planning and management for public health impacts at outdoor music festivals: An international study', *Environmental Health*, 5(1), 50–61.

Emergency Management Australia (1999) *Safe and Healthy Mass Gatherings. Manual Number 12*. Commonwealth of Australia: Australian Emergency Manuals Series.

Getz, D. (1997) *Event Management and Event Tourism*. New York: Cognizant Communications.

Ketonen, A. (2003) *Facility Management at Events. School Of Tourism and Services Management*. Jyväskylä Polytechnic.

Kroemar, K. and Grandjean, E. (1997) *Fitting the Task to the Human*. 5th edn. London: Taylor & Francis.

Mayhew, C. (2000) *Preventing Violence Within Organisations: A Practical Handbook*. AIC Research and Public Policy Series No. 29. Canberra: Australian Institute of Criminology.

Safework Australia (2015) *Personal Protective Equipment (PPE)*. Online. Available HTTP: <http://www.safeworkaustralia.gov.au>.

Seton (2007) *Solutions for a Safe, Secure Workplace*. Regents Park, NSW: Seton Australia. Health and Safety Executive (HSE) (2003) *Working Together to Reduce Stress at Work: A Guide for Employees*. Norwich: HSE Books.

Thompson, W. and Marks, F. (2001) *Understanding New South Wales Occupational Health and Safety Legislation*, 3rd edn. Sydney: CCH Australia.

Toohey, J. (1995) Managing the stress phenomenon at work. In P. Cotton (Ed.) *Psychological Health in the Workplace: Understanding and Managing Occupational Stress*. Melbourne: Australian Psychological Society.

Toohey, J., Borthwick, K. and Archer, R. (2005) *OH&S in Australia*. Melbourne: Thomson.

Underwood. R, (2003) Managing plant safely: An overview. In *The Master OHS and Environmental Guide*. Sydney: CCH Australia.

Worksafe Victoria. (2006) *Advice for Managing Major Events Safely*. 1st edn. Victoria: Government of Victoria.

Chapter 8

Food, alcohol and drugs

Chapter objectives

This chapter provides:

- detailed guidelines on the hygienic serving of food
- responsible serving of alcohol
- a discussion about illegal drug use and sex offences

Food

Food safety is a vital aspect of public health planning for public events. Unless proper sanitary measures are applied to food storage, preparation and distribution at mass gatherings, food may become contaminated and present a danger to public health. Special one-off outdoor events in warm weather pose additional risks as they tend to have less than ideal circumstances for food handling, transport and storage.

All food should be prepared in sanitary conditions, with handwashing facilities provided. Hot food should be served and kept at the temperatures required by legislation. All uncooked food should be stored in cold rooms at the temperatures required by legislation. Licences and permits are needed for certain event activities such as sale of alcohol and handling of food. As with other regulations, the onus of responsibility is upon the event organiser to gain appropriate licences and permits. However, the site operations manager must have immediate access to the relevant documents as they will be the person directly dealing with the various authorities. A decision may need to be made about the control of domestic animals if they are to be permitted into the event site.

To ensure adequate standards are met, an environmental health officer should initially assess food service proposals, including the proper authorisation of vendors, as part of the pre-event planning. An assessment should be based on current food hygiene legislation and food safety codes. This assessment should be followed up with a pre-event audit as well as periodical monitoring of food safety throughout the event.

This assessment should form part of an overall food safety plan for the event including:

- quantities and types of food
- lines of supply
- premises
- preparation techniques
- means of distribution
- licensing/permit process and authorisation of vendors.

Appropriate licensing and registration requirements of the responsible health authority must be met, including an 'off-premises' food catering licence as appropriate. During the event, on-site environmental health officers must have the authority to close down any vendor who is contravening food hygiene legislation and public health requirements. In some cases, such as open site street festivals, this may be the responsibility of the local council authority.

Event organisers should consider selecting food vendors that provide nutritious food varieties.

Food vans or stalls

The fit out and construction of all food selling premises, whether it is a food van purpose built for festivals and events, or a temporary stall inside a venue or tent, must be in accordance with local health regulations and codes of practice. The premises or area to be used for food storage, preparation and service must be easily cleaned and not allow the harbouring of rodents and insects nor the build-up of dirt and food particles.

Figure 8.1 Food stalls – public area.

Food preparation and cooking equipment must be in a safe working order and easily cleaned.

The safety of both staff and the public is an important consideration, and occupational health and safety standards must be met. Some of the hazards to be avoided include loose power leads, trip hazards, inadequate refuse disposal, inappropriate positioning of equipment (especially hot equipment), poor ventilation and extreme temperature in the work environment, badly stacked supplies and unguarded equipment.

Refuse disposal

A regular disposal system should be put in place. Putrescible refuse, in particular, can cause problems from odour, insects, rodents or other animals. Adequate disposal facilities must be easily accessible to food handlers as well as waste removal contractors. A separate refuse collection should be organised for food premises and should be continually monitored to ensure the frequency of collection is appropriate. Where possible the separation of refuse into dry, wet and hazardous disposal units should be encouraged. There should be separate containers for food scraps, containers and papers, and used oil waste.

Hand washing

Hand washing facilities for the exclusive use of food handlers must be provided. Potable water must be used for hand washing, the water must be running and, where possible, hot water should be available. Soap and disposable handtowels should be provided in the hand washing area. Potable water must be supplied to all sink areas. Hot water should be used where possible. An appropriate detergent and sanitiser should be used to adequately clean all sinks and hand basins.

Food supplies

It is important that foods used are only sourced from registered outlets and are not prepared in domestic kitchens. Food proprietors must ensure that food supplies have been prepared and transported in accordance with relevant standards. The length of time food is transported should be kept to a minimum. Temperature requirements should be maintained and the food should be protected from contamination at all times. Food transport vehicles should be clearly identified and subject to surveillance and monitoring.

Food handling

Every effort should be made to minimise the risk of cross contamination during the food handling process. Food utensils and surfaces used for the preparation of raw and ready to eat food should be clearly distinguished. In cramped circumstances this becomes more difficult. Adequate cleaning and sanitising between uses play an important role. Gloves should be worn and changed frequently. There is a temptation to continue to wear the same gloves even though the work being undertaken has changed. Frequent hand washing should be encouraged.

Appropriate food storage is critical to ensure there is no contamination between raw and cooked or ready to eat foods. The less than ideal conditions that confront food handlers working in temporary facilities may lead to a compromise in food-handling. Space is often a major problem. Ensure that, at a minimum, raw and cooked or ready-to-eat foods are stored appropriately. Food handling staff must be aware of the requirements for strict hand washing and cleaning and sanitising of equipment between handling raw and ready to eat foods. Equipment must be adequately cleaned and sanitised between each separate process. This is particularly critical where equipment is used for preparing different food types.

Thawing, cooking, heating and cooling

The goal in temperature control is to minimise the time potentially hazardous foods are in the danger zone of 5°C to 60°C. Key points to remember are as follows:

- Thaw food under refrigeration or cold running water.
- Cook food thoroughly to achieve a core temperature of 70°C.
- Reheating of food should be minimised. Where reheating is required the food should be heated thoroughly and stored above 60°C.
- Cooling of food should be carried out quickly under refrigeration.

Cleaning and sanitising

Regardless of the type of facility in which the food is prepared, all food contact surfaces must be regularly cleaned and sanitised using an appropriate sanitiser (sodium hypochlorite (100–200 ppm) is considered to be appropriate). All other surfaces should be cleaned to minimise the risk of contamination to food products, pest infestation and occupational hazards such as slippery floors.

Chemical storage

Chemicals must be stored in separate areas to foods and all chemical storage containers must be clearly marked as to their contents. Food containers must never be used for the storage of chemicals.

Food storage – temperature control

Storage facilities that are of adequate size and appropriate for the purpose must be provided. Both refrigerated and heated storage areas require continuous power supply. Refrigeration can become a problem in particularly hot weather when refrigeration units struggle to cope. Potentially hazardous food must be stored at temperatures below 5°C or above 60°C at all times. All proprietors should indicate alternative refrigeration suppliers or the organiser or authority could identify alternative suppliers in the public health emergency management plan in case of refrigeration failure.

Raw foods should be stored separately if possible, or at a minimum, stored below cooked or ready to eat foods. There should be sufficient storage conditions available to ensure adequate protection of food from the elements and pests. Exposed food available on display must be protected from insect pests, dust and human contact.

Food handling staff considerations

Proprietors should be encouraged to select staff with food handling training to work in temporary facilities. Selection of staff should include issues such as high personal hygiene standards. Food proprietors should ensure a non-smoking policy is implemented in the workplace. Food handlers dress should be appropriate to the task they are performing, and include some form of hair covering.

Food handlers should not work while they are in an acute stage of any gastrointestinal illness or cold. Food handlers who have open wounds should ensure all wounds are appropriately dressed with a waterproof dressing and the dressing should be changed regularly. Separate toilet facilities should be provided for food handlers.

Gas cylinders

At many food stalls, portable pressurised gas cylinders provide cooking fuel. These cylinders must be securely connected to stoves and burners and pipes and regulators checked for leaking gas by a licensed plumber. The cylinder and its gas lines must be kept at a safe distance from any open flame. The burners and stoves must be in a well-ventilated space.

If such cylinders fall over and the cylinder neck or valve is cracked, the uncontrolled release of the stored pressurised gas can turn the cylinder into a deadly projectile. For this reason, all portable gas cylinders must be secured both top and bottom, by ropes or chains to a structural post, wall or similar anchor point.

At some street events portable pressurised gas cylinders provide gas used to inflate children's balloons, and to carbonate beverages. Frequently, such cylinders are not secured, or are merely fastened to a two-wheeled hand trolley used to move them, which itself is not independently secured. As is the case with cooking gas cylinders, a fallen or broken cylinder is a major hazard.

Other stall holders

If the event incorporates stalls selling clothing, memorabilia, performers' merchandise, etc, run by independent operators they must comply with the appropriate health and safety regulations. Power cables and leads should be safely installed, and guy ropes, pegs, flags and signage should be fixed and located in a manner that does not impede pedestrian movement.

Tattooing and body piercing

Due to the popularity of tattoos, body piercing and branding, mobile operators have begun to appear at many events. Checks should be made as to the need for proper licensing or registration of such service providers and their compliance with any health legislation. Due to the potential of cross-infection, particularly of blood-borne diseases, any such operations should be inspected to ensure (as a minimum):

- disposable, single-use items are utilised;
- proper sterilisation equipment and techniques are employed; and
- clinical sharps containers are utilised for used needle disposal, and these containers are located safely away from children.

No skin penetration procedures should be allowed to occur if the minimum infection control procedures are not followed.

Alcohol and drug use at festivals

Alcohol intoxication and illicit drug use at events can be a catalyst for, and can exacerbate, unruly behaviour and hooliganism, and also be the cause of severe life threatening incidents that will require specialist medical attention.

Management decisions regarding the policy and attitude towards both alcohol and drug consumption at an event should be based on best hazard and risk minimisation practice, rather than morality. People at festivals will engage in risky behaviour. We live in a drugtaking society, and regardless of how many police or security staff are at an event, it's inevitable some people will choose to consume drugs and/or alcohol.

Safe partying

An event organisation can choose from many forms of control, ranging from outright prohibition at one end of the spectrum, to complete liberty at the other. Many public health experts (but few police officials and politicians) claim that the most successful harm minimisation strategies involve 'judgement free' attempts to ameliorate the adverse health consequences of mood altering substances without necessarily relying on a reduction of consumption of these substances, but as much as possible controlling that consumption. An event policy of 'safe partying' aims to reduce health risks for all patrons.

Safe partying consists of a range of measures that control behaviour in a way that's non-confrontational and non-judgmental. Most importantly, operating this under this concept of harm minimisation enables health workers to provide immediate and informed assistance to festival patrons suffering from effects of intoxication or adverse drug reaction. Patrons in distress shouldn't hesitate to seek help because of a fear of being disciplined, first aid staff and volunteers are there to treat people, not judge them. Whereas under a prohibition policy, police, security and first aid teams are shunned and avoided by casualties and their friends, and expert assistance is too often sought too late, or not at all, resulting in hospitalisation or death.

Alcohol

Alcohol has become an integral part of modern society and its use is common and is an expected part of festivals and events. It is unfortunately a fact that misuse of alcohol is a significant factor in crowd disturbance and unsocial behaviour. Excessive alcohol consumption creates many of the problems experienced at festivals such as lacerations and cuts to people treading or falling on broken glass, antisocial, argumentative and aggressive behaviour, sexual assaults, urinating in public places (although this may be an outcome of a lack of available and accessible public conveniences).

Accordingly, managing the sale, service and consumption of alcohol is an important aspect of event management. If alcohol is to be available at an event, it is important

Figure 8.2 Easily undermined method of restricting alcohol by selling tickets limited by age and amount.

that the organisers have clear policies relating to the serving of alcohol and ensure that the policies are enforced. Ensuring the responsible service of alcohol and putting in place strategies to prevent (and, if necessary, manage) intoxication among guests to negate the likelihood of undesirable and detrimental consequences.

Adverse health and social effects

Alcohol is an intoxicating substance often mistaken as a stimulant drug. This is because its consumption may initially cause the drinker to feel relaxed or even excited, depending on the social situation they are in. It is the most commonly used. However, alcohol is actually a depressant drug. When consumed, it depresses the actions of the central nervous system, including heart rate and breathing rate. Concentration, coordination, balance and judgement are also adversely impacted. After initial consumption, it only takes a few minutes for alcohol to reach the brain. Eating food before or while drinking will slow the absorption of alcohol, it will not prevent a person from becoming intoxicated.

The elimination of alcohol from the body takes time. Engaging in such behaviours as dancing, exercise, drinking coffee, eating greasy foods or vomiting will not speed up this process. Short-term effects include:

- relaxation
- reduced concentration and coordination
- increased confidence and a lowering of inhibitions
- blurred vision and slurred speech
- mood changes, including aggression or depression
- headaches, nausea and vomiting
- sleepiness
- coma and even death.

Consuming alcohol in tandem with other drugs (including illicit drugs, prescription medications or over-the-counter medicines) is not safe. Combining alcohol with other depressant drugs can make it more difficult for a person to control their actions and react to dangerous situations. Also, the central nervous system is further depressed, which may result in cardiac or respiratory arrest. Combining alcohol with stimulant drugs (including caffeine) can make it more difficult for a person to know when they are intoxicated.

Binge drinking occurs when a person drinks a large quantity of alcohol over a short period of time. The health risks include: damage to the bowel; depression of the central nervous system; hangovers, which include headaches, nausea, shakiness and vomiting; and an increased risk of harm from dangerous situations, such as drink driving, violence and coercive and/or unprotected sex. Binge drinking may also result in alcohol poisoning. When a person's blood alcohol concentration rises to a dangerous level, they may have a seizure, lose consciousness and fall into a coma. Death may result. Emergency medical assistance should be sought if any of the following signs and symptoms are present:

- the person is unconscious and cannot be awakened by pinching, prodding or shouting
- the person's skin is cold and clammy, pale or bluish in colour

- the person is breathing very slowly
- the person has been vomiting but is not waking up.

Implementing strategies to assist guests to drink responsibly

There are a number of harm minimisation strategies that event managers can put in place to encourage guests to drink responsibly and avoid intoxication. To provide an environment that is enjoyable and to ensure the health and safety of guests and the community, and to prevent intoxication that may result in antisocial behaviour and injury, it is essential that the responsible service of alcohol is practised. There are five key components to the responsible service of alcohol that event managers must consider:

- selling and serving alcohol responsibly
- implementing strategies to assist guests to drink responsibly
- monitoring guests for intoxication
- refusing to serve alcohol to intoxicated guests
- ensuring the safety of all guests.

Ensuring that appropriate strategies are developed and implemented to prevent alcohol-related harm will lessen the chance of the event being soured by injuries and antisocial behaviour. A comprehensive alcohol risk management plan will give the event manager a greater chance of being able to relax and enjoy the event, while also being able to act quickly upon incidents should they occur.

Harm minimisation benefits

An event that is organised, well-structured and effectively manages alcohol can provide a number of benefits.

- The risk of sexual violence attributed to alcohol during or immediately after the event is reduced.
- Risks can be effectively and efficiently managed. Adequate planning prior to the event will ensure that risks are identified and controls are put in place to manage any incident that does arise.
- Guests are more likely to enjoy the event without concern over the effects that excessive alcohol consumption may occur.
- Legal requirements will be met, which reduces the risk of insurance claims and financial penalties.
- Alcohol becomes an adjunct to the event, rather than the primary focus. This enables the true purpose of the event to be identified, engaged in and celebrated.
- The risk of financial loss is minimised. Events at which alcohol has not been well managed may incur a financial loss due to property damage that results in clean-up and repair costs.
- There is a greater chance of obtaining permission to run the event, or similar events, again. Events that are adversely impacted by alcohol are less likely to be granted permission to be conducted at a later date.
- The likelihood of obtaining sponsorship to deliver future events will not be adversely impacted.

Responsible service of alcohol

In most jurisdictions the provision of alcohol in a responsible and controlled manner is a legislative requirement. Event managers and anyone involved in the provision of alcohol at an event may be liable should it be proven that alcohol served irresponsibly resulted in harm.

Police will require the necessary approvals and licences to be acquired and will check to make certain the event is meeting licensing requirements, such as for example, that non-drinking areas are cordoned off from drinking areas and that service is denied to underage people. It is commonly a requirement that staff serving alcohol must have been trained in the responsible serving of alcohol.

Legislation and regulations in many jurisdictions require event managers that are responsible for events at which alcohol will be sold, served and consumed to:

- complete and submit a Liquor Permit Form
- obtain an Occasional Liquor Licence
- liaise with relevant authorities (including police and health personnel)
- closely monitor the event and take appropriate action if a guest becomes intoxicated
- ensure that relevant laws are adhered to, including in relation to the responsible service and consumption of alcohol.

Responsible alcohol service can assist in positively changing the binge drinking culture common to many events, while promoting harm minimisation strategies. It should be made prohibited on the event site to:

- sell or supply alcohol to an intoxicated person
- permit the sale or service of alcohol to someone who is intoxicated
- allow someone who is intoxicated to consume alcohol
- obtain or attempt to obtain alcohol for someone who is intoxicated
- assist an intoxicated person to obtain or drink alcohol.

If there is non-compliance, the event manager, and anyone involved in running the event, may be faced with a serious incident at the event, which results in harm to those in attendance and the community. Those involved in running the event may also face large financial penalties.

Staff

In most jurisdictions, there are mandatory training requirements in relation to the responsible service of alcohol. The licensee, approved manager (i.e. the person who will be in charge of the function) and any person engaged in the sale or service of liquor must have completed a training course in the responsible service of alcohol. At least one event manager must be nominated. This person must attend the event from start to finish and must not be impaired by alcohol during the event. The event manager, as the event licensee, must comply with all relevant legislative provisions, including those relating to the responsible service of alcohol.

There should be an adequate number of event staff on hand to undertake the required duties, including selling and serving beverages and food, monitoring the behaviour of guests and cleaning up rubbish. Staff who are selling or serving alcohol are not permitted to consume alcohol immediately before or during the event.

When event staff are trained, confident in carrying out their duties and are supported by alcohol-related policies and procedures, they will be more likely to serve alcohol responsibly. The event manager should brief all staff and volunteers on what their roles and responsibilities will be before, during and after the event, including in relation to alcohol provision.

Event staff should be equipped with sufficient knowledge to provide guests with information about the alcoholic beverages available at the event. This information should include the type of drinks available, the strength of each drink and standard drink details.

Event staff should monitor the alcohol consumption levels and drinking patterns of guests for early signs of intoxication. Appropriate action should be taken if intoxication is detected, including the provision of free drinking water and non-alcoholic beverages, offering food, and assisting the affected guest to safely leave the premise with at least one friend. Event managers and their staff/volunteers should avoid letting a guest get into a taxi alone.

It is essential that event managers consider security arrangements. It is standard practice to employ one licensed crowd controller for every 50 guests present in a designated alcohol drinking area (minimum of two). Note that it is an offence for an unlicensed person (excluding a licensee or an approved manager) to perform crowd control functions. Only licensed security contractors should interact with intoxicated persons.

Alcohol-free events

The most extreme control measure is to prohibit of the sale of alcoholic beverages at events where unruly audiences are expected, or where a significant number of the patrons will be under the legal drinking age. It is commonly believed that alcohol is needed for an event to be enjoyable and successful. However, alcohol-free events can be extremely successful as:

- underage guests can attend and feel a part of the event
- guests who choose not to drink are more likely to attend the event and feel welcome
- the event becomes more culturally inclusive
- the event will not be soured by alcohol-related antisocial behaviour
- health and safety are actively promoted.

Consider running the event as alcohol-free. Alcohol-free events can be just as much fun and result in even greater successes than events that are marred by the adverse effects of alcohol consumption.

Selling alcohol

Event managers are encouraged to monitor the drinking behaviour of guests and follow-up on inappropriate methods of consumption in a timely and polite manner. If alcohol will be a part of the event, the type of alcohol being sold or served should be considered. Offering and promoting the availability of low and mid-strength beer alternatives is one way to reduce the alcohol intake and corresponding blood alcohol level of guests. Alcoholic punches that contain wine or spirits are not permitted as maintaining consistency of the mix and determining standard drink measures is very difficult.

The amount of alcohol that will be sold or served at the event should be carefully considered. When applying for an occasional liquor licence there will be a requirement to indicate how much alcohol will be available at the event and how many people will be expected to attend.

The way in which alcohol is served should be considered. It is recommended that plastic cups be used to serve alcohol, rather than glasses or glass bottles. As well as being a catalyst for injury, broken glass could be used as a weapon if aggressive behaviour transpires among the guests.

All alcohol sold at each bar should be opened by bar staff at the point of sale. Sales could be limited to four drinks at any one time. This number will be monitored by the licensee throughout the day and will be adjusted as required.

Activities that encourage heavy and rapid consumption should not be permitted. An example of a rapid alcohol consumption method is a funnel (also commonly referred to as a 'beer bong'). Vouchers, drink cards or any other mechanism that will promote rapid alcohol consumption should be prohibited.

The price of alcoholic beverages should not be so low as to encourage heavy and rapid consumption. Non-alcoholic beverages must be offered, and these should be at a comparable price to alcoholic drinks. Non-alcoholic beverages such as water and soft-drinks enable guests to space their alcohol and also provides options to guests that are underage or do not drink alcohol. Provide water, free of charge, from jugs at the bar counter or in water coolers throughout the venue.

Time

The time period in which alcohol is available can be adjusted depending on the nature of the event. Place restrictions on the availability of alcoholic beverages at certain times, for example opening the bar at an all-day event in the late afternoon and clos-ing before the commencement of the final act would be a suitable strategy for a dance music festival attended by teenagers, but would not be acceptable for a mature age audience at a jazz festival. The bar should close prior to the event finishing time to provide guests with time to drink water or non-alcoholic beverages and leave the event in an orderly manner. The selling and serving of alcohol must conclude early enough to allow the orderly exit of guests and for the clean-up to begin.

Designated area

Designated drinking areas must be established, which will make it easier for staff to check for valid identification and for alcohol consumption to be controlled in a particular area. The risk of injury will also be minimised. Alcohol should be sold, served and consumed in designated, licensed areas only. This makes the role of the event manager, event staff and security personnel simpler when having to monitor the alcohol consumption and drink-ing behaviour of guests. Also, guests that are under the legal drinking age or choose not to drink alcohol can relax and socialise in an environment free from alcohol.

The areas in which alcohol is sold, served and consumed should be assessed prior to the event, as part of the risk management process. The area should be free from as many risks as possible, including bodies of water and major roads, which can increase the risk of injury to guests who are drinking alcohol. The area should be well lit and patrolled. Security should be watchful for public urination, settling arguments by fights, sexual predation, drug deals and other offensive acts.

Figure 8.3 Age restricted alcohol drinking area.

If an external area is to be used, it must be fenced or cordoned off so that access cannot be obtained without the authority of event security staff.

Age

Alcohol must not be served to anyone less than the legal age for drinking. Apart from the obvious dangers arising from inexperienced intoxicated teenagers to themselves and others, serving alcohol to an underage person may result in penalties under the legislation. Underage drinking can be prevented by event and security staff requesting valid photographic identification (e.g. a current driver's licence, a current passport or a proof-of-age card) from guests who wish to enter the designated drinking areas and consume alcohol. Some events issue different wristbands for underage people and prohibit their entry into designated areas.

Wristbanding

Wristbands can be attached to patrons who provide satisfactory evidence of age identification (photo ID only) and who meet responsible service of alcohol requirements (e.g. are not displaying evidence of intoxication) at separate wristbanding outlets. These outlets could be located in close proximity to the points of entry to the event. Consumption of alcohol is restricted to persons wearing a wristband. All security and bar staff should continually monitor wristbands to patrons to ensure compliance with regulations. Procedures should be implemented in response to evidence of tampering/ transfer of wristbands and for persons refused service of alcohol. In such cases wristbands are removed by security staff and the person escorted from the bar area. They will then be required to revisit the wristbanding outlet.

Food

If alcohol is being sold or served event managers are strongly encouraged to provide food throughout the entire period of the event, (time periods may need to be specified in contracts with food vendors). Eating while drinking slows the absorption of alcohol in the body. Also, guests may drink less if food is available. Foods that are high in salt should be avoided, as these foods increase the thirst reflex and could encourage more alcohol consumption.

Signage

Signs indicating that the area is licensed must be displayed. The signs must also indicate that underage guests will not be admitted into the area. Posters about the responsible service of alcohol should be displayed at the venue. Event managers can ensure that all advertising materials for the event and signage displayed at the event specifies that alcohol will not be served to persons less than the legal age for drinking.

There are a number of guidelines that must be considered when developing advertising materials for events. Advertising for events should:

- not emphasise the availability of alcohol;
- not refer to the amount of alcohol available;
- not encourage the excessive consumption of alcohol;
- not encourage attendance at an event by advertising alcohol at discounted prices; and
- make equal reference to the availability of non-alcoholic beverages.

It is unacceptable to:

- advertise free drinks on arrival;
- undertake advertising and promotion that encourage guests to consume alcohol in excess; or
- offer complimentary drinks (unless as part of a package that includes food).

Event advertising that does not focus specifically on alcohol may increase the likelihood of a broader range of guests participating in the event.

To assist in fostering an event that considers and promotes the safety and health of all guests and the community, event managers may consider using the following messages when designing advertising materials:

- alcohol will not be served to anyone under the age of 18 years;
- guests should pre-arrange transport from the event so they do not drink and drive;
- arrange for a friend or colleague to be the designated driver who will not consume alcohol during the event;
- eat before and during the event;

- try and space your alcoholic drinks with water or soft drinks; and
- be careful and keep an eye out for your friends during the event.

Monitoring guests for intoxication

A person is 'drunk' (intoxicated) if their speech, coordination, balance or behaviour appears to be impaired; and there is enough reason to believe that this impairment is attributed to alcohol consumption. In assessing intoxication, the following signs should be observed and monitored.

Noticeable changes in behaviour:

- becoming loud or disorderly
- arguing with staff or other guests
- suddenly using bad language
- becoming aggressive
- drinking faster

A lack of judgement:

- being careless with money
- annoying other guests
- slurring or mistakes in speech

Clumsiness:

- spilling drinks
- trouble removing items from a wallet or purse

Loss of coordination:

- swaying and staggering
- difficulty walking straight
- bumping into furniture and other guests

Decreased alertness:

- drowsiness
- delays in responding to questions
- falling asleep

Strong smell of alcohol combined with some of the above behaviours.

The following strategies can assist event managers and staff in identifying intoxicated guests:

- monitoring guests for the signs of intoxication listed above, including their physical and emotional state;
- monitoring noise at the venue;
- being vigilant for early signs of antisocial and aggressive behaviour among guests; and
- monitoring drink orders.

Refusing to serve alcohol to intoxicated guests

Intoxicated people can reduce the enjoyment gained from the event among the other guests and can cause problems for event staff. Common issues attributed to intoxication include aggressive and violent behaviour, sexual violence and damage to property (including at the venue and in the community).

In most jurisdictions it is against the law to sell or serve alcohol to an intoxicated person, or even to assist an intoxicated person to obtain alcohol. The following points are designed to assist event managers and event staff in refusing service to an intoxicated guest:

- politely refuse the sale or service of alcohol
- be sure to provide the reason for refusing to serve the guest
- if necessary, refer the guest to signage that states intoxicated persons will not be sold or served alcohol
- offer the guest water or a soft drink, or food
- offer to help the guest arrange transport to safely leave the venue.

When the sale or service of alcohol is refused, the intoxicated guest may become agitated and angry. Using clear and affirmative language and applying conflict resolution skills can help to dissolve the situation. If a guest begins to exhibit aggressive behaviour, they should be given a verbal warning to leave the premise. If the verbal warning is not heeded and the guest becomes increasingly aggressive towards staff and other guests, the event security officers should offer assistance. The safety of the guest (and other guests) must be considered, and if necessary, security staff should escort the guest out of the venue, while ensuring they have safe transport home.

Removal of patrons from licensed premises

If a patron is intoxicated or disorderly, annoying or endangering other patrons, personnel or established property, the security officer will contact the security supervisor and advise of the location and nature of incident. The security officer will then approach the patron politely, but firmly and explain the licensing policy pertaining to the event and request they leave the licensed premises. If the patron refuses a request to leave the premises the security supervisor will assess the situation and may consider physically removing the patron.

Assisted removals

At all stages of the assisted removal the amount of force used must be reasonable and necessary and the following procedure will be followed:

- security officer notifies security command of location and nature of incident
- a security supervisor should attend the process of removing intoxicated/disorderly patron(s)
- once removed from the licensed area security patrolling the outer grounds will be notified so that they can monitor his or her progress
- should the situation warrant further action, security staff should detain the person(s) and contact police for appropriate further action
- a full record of any such event will be entered into the incident report book.

Multiple assisted removals

Multiple physical removals are to be approached exactly as the removing of one patron. The security supervisor is to take control and direct officers to form pyramids around the patrons they intend to remove. When all the persons are effectively contained the controller(s) will guide the patrons outside the closest entry/exit control point. Should the situation warrant further action, security staff should detain the person(s) and contact police for appropriate further action.

Other considerations

In relation to harm minimisation at events involving alcohol, event managers should consider a number of other factors including:

- reviewing the venue for physical safety hazards
- enforcing a policy of denial of entry to alcohol and drug affected people
- ensuring the event is not attended by unwelcome or uninvited persons (event staff and/or security officers should monitor entry and exit points)
- ensuring that alcohol is not brought into the event
- having an adequate number of bathrooms available
- ensuring signage is erected to direct guests to toilets, transport and medical care
- providing enough seating for guests in the designated drinking area
- ensuring the area is regularly cleaned to prevent injury and a large clean-up following the event
- providing rubbish bins
- monitoring the crowd for behaviour that poses a threat to the safety or security of guests, including damage to property, theft, sexual violence and physical violence
- considering transport for guests following the closure of the event.

While transport is not the sole responsibility of an event manager, it is recommended that some consideration be given to how guests will safely get home from the event, particularly if they have been drinking alcohol. Strategies could include: having an information stand with public transport information and a telephone for guests to call a taxi; or hiring a mini bus (depending on the size and nature of the event). If guests are likely to walk home or catch a taxi to another venue following the event, they should be encouraged to do so in groups.

On-site breathalysers

Public breathalysers have become a popular method for consumers to test themselves at the source of alcohol consumption. They are now often found in almost all licensed businesses and event organisers are setting up breathalyser booths at festival exit points to enable attendees to check their sobriety before driving home.

Breath analysers do not directly measure blood alcohol content or concentration, which requires the analysis of a blood sample. Instead, they estimate blood alcohol content indirectly by measuring the amount of alcohol in the breath. Two breathalyser technologies are most prevalent. Desktop analysers generally use infrared spectrophotometer technology, electrochemical fuel cell technology, or a combination of the two. Hand-held field testing devices are generally based on electrochemical platinum fuel cell analysis. The presence of a breathalyser testing booth on an event site promotes a safer working environment, protects valuable people and equipment. It also can assist in reducing liability and complying with laws surrounding the responsible service of alcohol.

Illicit drugs

There are two main problems with drug use at festivals and events. The first is the erratic, violent or dangerous behaviour of a person influenced by drugs. The same methods of controlling the individual used for alcohol intoxication can be used by security and medical teams. Isolate, then restrain the individual, remove them from the crowd, calm them down, and provide appropriate medical treatment. These actions should only be performed by trained security and first aid staff, not by ordinary staff or volunteers.

The second problem is death or severe reactions to ingested drugs. The growth in new psychoactive substances and the ever-evolving chemical composition of drugs, means that the person taking the drug often has no idea what they are taking or what effect it will have on them, and if there is an adverse harmful reaction, first aid teams have no way of knowing what substance antidotes can be used. Ecstasy pills, for example, are often adulterated with particularly harmful substances like PMA or 4-MTA.

Taking illicit drugs, especially ecstasy, at festivals is not particularly unusual. A July 2011 report by Australian Institute of Health and Welfare found more than 11 per cent of 20- to 29-year-olds and 7 per cent of 18- to 19-year-olds had taken the drug in the previous 12 months. According to annual research among 1,000 ecstasy users, 70 per cent of these pills are taken at clubs, festivals and dance parties.

The effects of illegal drugs will always be unpredictable. Generally, when mixed with alcohol they are exaggerated in some way, which can result in anything from nausea to heart failure. Festival goers also get into distress through intoxication and by mixing illicit substances, and by exhaustion from lack of food or dehydration.

Mixing alcohol and drugs

A person under the influence of drugs is less likely to make considered decisions about how much alcohol to drink. The following information about individual drugs and what can happen when mixed with alcohol is provided by the Australian National Drug and Alcohol Research Centre.

Alcohol and marijuana (cannabis)

The results, both physical and psychological, of using cannabis and alcohol together, can be unpredictable. Having alcohol in the blood stream can potentially cause the body to absorb the active ingredient tetrahydrocannabinol (THC) faster. This can lead to the cannabis having a much stronger effect than it would normally have. The physical effects can be dizziness, nausea and vomiting. Psychological effects include panic, anxiety or paranoia. Stronger types of cannabis can pose even greater risks, because it may contain three times as much THC.

Alcohol and cocaine

A common but particularly dangerous partnership, alcohol and cocaine together increase the risk of heart attacks and fits and even sudden death. The two drugs interact to produce a highly toxic substance in the liver called cocaethylene. It can increase the depressive effects of alcohol, making reactions to the cocaine stronger. People are more likely to be aggressive with cocaethylene in their system. Cocaethylene takes longer to expel from a system than either the alcohol or the cocaine, subjecting the heart and liver to a longer period of stress. Mixing alcohol and cocaine can be fatal up to 12 hours after taken.

Alcohol and ecstasy (MDMA)

It's possible that alcohol will deaden the 'high' experienced from ecstasy while the drugs are in a person's system. However, combining these drugs can be deadly. Ecstasy dehydrates, but so does alcohol, increasing the risk of overheating and dehydration when combined. Alcohol is involved in most ecstasy-related deaths, many of which are from heatstroke after people have danced for long periods of time without drinking water to replacing the fluids they've lost. As alcohol is a diuretic, which means it makes drinkers urinate excessively and sweat more, it's even harder to retain enough fluids when consuming alcohol while on ecstasy. There's also a greater strain on their liver and kidneys when combining the two drugs. And, as with many other combinations, users are likely to experience nausea and vomiting.

Alcohol and amphetamines

The effects of amphetamines, often called 'speed', are very much like an adrenalin rush. When taken, breathing, blood pressure and heart rate speed up. Like ecstasy, speed can also increase body temperature and cause dehydration – which is heightened when alcohol is added. As speed already puts pressure on the heart, that pressure can be fatal. Alcohol can intensify emotions and suppress inhibitions. Under the influence of speed users may feel more confident or energised, but can easily become anxious, paranoid or aggressive, particularly when alcohol is also used. As the full effects of alcohol are not felt until the speed has worn off, mixing the two means users can drink dangerous amounts without realising.

Alcohol and heroin

Alcohol with heroin is one of the most dangerous combinations of drugs. 'Downers' like heroin slow down heart rate and breathing. When combined with another 'downer' such as alcohol the risk of overdosing is doubled. Even small amounts of alcohol seem to lower the amount of heroin needed to fatally overdose. Around three quarters of people who die from heroin overdoses have drunk alcohol at the same time.

Alcohol and 'legal highs'

Previously known as 'legal highs', drugs such as 'meow meow' actually became illegal in 2010 when they were classified as class B drugs. Powerful stimulants, drugs such as meow meow are part of the cathinone family, a group of drugs that are closely related to the amphetamines. They're derived from the plant khat, commonly used as a stimulant in East Africa, and have similar effects to ecstasy and speed. These drugs can over-stimulate circulation, damaging the heart, speeding up the nervous system and causing fits. They can also cause anxiousness and paranoia. As with any drug that gives a 'high', combining them with alcohol can create a risk of everything from nausea and vomiting to coma and death.

Alcohol and tobacco

A serious long-term risk to health. Tobacco and alcohol work together to damage the cells of the body, multiplying the damage. Alcohol makes it easier for the mouth and throat to absorb the cancer-causing chemicals in tobacco.

Overdoses

Drug overdoses can be accidental or on purpose. The amount of a certain drug needed to cause an overdose varies with the type of drug and the person taking it. Overdoses from prescription or over-the-counter (OTC) medicines, 'street' drugs, and/or alcohol can be life-threatening. Know, too, that mixing certain medications or street drugs with alcohol can also kill.

Physical symptoms of a drug overdose vary with the type of drug(s) taken. They include:

- abnormal breathing
- slurred speech
- lack of coordination
- slow or rapid pulse
- low or elevated body temperature
- enlarged or small eye pupils
- reddish face
- heavy sweating
- drowsiness
- delusions and/or hallucinations
- unconsciousness which may lead to coma.

Staff should be aware of the behaviour and physical signs that indicate a person has taken an overdose of drugs. This can include:

- hallucinating
- confusion
- convulsions
- breathing slow and shallow and/or slurring their words
- a person's personality suddenly becomes hostile, violent and aggressive.

Staff must use caution and protect themselves. They should not turn their back to the victim or move suddenly in front of him or her. If possible using mild restraint without touching the person to ensure the victim does not cause harm to any other person or himself or herself. Security and first aid teams must be called for assistance. In potentially dangerous situations the police should be called and the staff and other patrons should leave the area until the police arrive.

If the person is semi- or fully unconscious, staff should call for emergency services and lie the victim down on his or her left side and check airway, breathing and pulse. If qualified, a staff member can give first aid applying CPR or rescue breathing as needed. If possible staff should ask the person or the person's friends:

- the person's name
- the name of the drug taken
- the amount of the drug taken, if known, e.g. the number of pills or amount of liquid ingested
- when the medication or drug was taken
- how the person is feeling and reacting
- any medical problems the person has.

Pill testing

With no quality control in the world of illegal drugs, users can never be 100 per cent sure of exactly what's in the substance they are taking. It could be cut with other cheaper drugs such as tranquilisers or even toxic substances such as drain cleaner.

Deaths at music festivals can possibly be avoided with a simple harm-minimisation intervention. Pill testing, or drug checking as it's known in Europe, provides feedback to users on the content of illegal drugs, allowing them to make informed choices. Canberra-based emergency doctor and senior lecturer in medicine at ANU David Caldicott said pill testing at music festivals in parts of Europe had seen fewer people use and mix drugs "and as a consequence, reduce the chance of people overdosing" (Boddy 2016: 2). President of the Australian Drug Law Reform Foundation, Dr Alex Wodak, supports the introduction of pill testing in night clubs and at festivals and raves. "The principle is simple, every drug death of a young, fit, healthy Australian could largely if not totally be prevented" (Wodak 2016: 1).

Pill-testing kits or booths at venues where pills are known to be consumed could inform users about the content of illicit drugs. As the equipment can test drugs in real time, people intending to take them could have them checked beforehand. Provision at an event of professionally manned analytical drug testing facilities that allow festival-goers to check the content of their pills and change consumption habits accordingly. This can vary from informal marquis testing kits to advanced pharmacological analysis facilities.

Marquis kits are easy to obtain by individuals in countries where they are legal and use reagents to detect if a compound is present in a pill. Personal sales of kits have increased significantly showing a desire on the part of drug takers to inform themselves about the substances they are ingesting. The reagents they contain have been used as a presumptive test by law enforcement for decades to give a preliminary idea of what drugs are present, but are a crude tool if they are being used to decide whether or not to consume a product.

Drug testing is about testing drugs, not potential users. The analytical testing being proposed by medical advocates is to conduct pill testing in the broad light of day by professionals with knowledge of the subtleties of the results. A far better scenario than the festival attendee surreptitiously testing their drugs under torch light in a tent with a dubious kit. It means individuals can take samples of their drugs to a team of medics and chemists and check if the chemicals have caused problems in the past or are risky to use. Dr David Caldicott says "When people are given information about their health, not about being naughty, it changes two-thirds of their behaviour. It is good practice to suggest that we never tell them that the drug is good or safe, merely tell them what's in their drug and contextualise it for their consumption" (Boddy 2016: 1).

Support for testing

Professor Alison Ritter (2011) argues that there are good reasons why an event should introduce on-site pill testing to help avoid the needless loss of young lives. Pill testing has been shown to change the black market. Products identified as particularly dangerous that subsequently became the subject of warning campaigns were found to leave the market. Research also shows the ingredients of tested pills started to correspond to the expected components over time. This suggests pill testing might be able to change the black market in positive ways.

Research shows young people are highly supportive of pill testing. More than 82 per cent of the 2,300 young Australians aged between 16 and 25 years surveyed in 2013 for the Australian National Council on Drugs supported its introduction. The finding is consistent with young people's overall views about drugs, they want better information in order to make informed choices (Ritter 2011). A major review in Europe found that two-thirds of drug users wouldn't consume contaminated drugs and would warn friends of any harmful results. Thus, drug testing provides a significant opportunity to reduce drug-related harm and consumption, as well as engaging festival attendees in counselling about their drug-taking behaviour.

Pill testing is not a radical idea. As a harm-reduction intervention provided by community and local governments, it's available in several European countries including the Netherlands, Switzerland, Austria, Belgium, Germany, Spain and France. But the legal status of the service is unclear and there is no formal government endorsement of the measure. In Europe, political support has enabled drug testing to exist in a grey area of the law; ad-hoc local arrangements and special agreements with police help circumvent the need for complex legal reform. Ritter claims pill testing changes behaviour: research from Austria shows 50 per cent of those who had their drugs tested said the results affected their consumption choices. Two-thirds said they wouldn't consume the drug and would warn friends in cases of negative results.

Visits to pill-testing booths create an important opportunity for providing support and information over and above the testing itself. They enable drug services to contact a population that is otherwise difficult to reach because these people are not experiencing acute drug problems. Indeed, the intervention has been used to establish contact and as the basis for follow-up work with members of not-yet-problematic, but nevertheless high-risk, groups of recreational drug users. An advantage for first aid teams is that if a drug-checking team is onsite information is thereby available about what drugs are being used, potency and possible contaminating substances, enabling swift and accurate on site treatment.

The European experiment has demonstrated that a common-sense harm-reduction strategy is achievable with collaboration between health professionals, law enforcement officers and festival organisers. A drug-testing strategy rather than waiting to treat young people in emergency departments is a safe, cost-effective and ethical way to achieve this outcome. Individuals can already buy cheap testing kits themselves on the internet. Such kits are better than nothing. But it is preferable that if an individual is going to test the drugs she or he is proposing to take, that testing is as safe and reliable as possible and administered by a professional.

Arguments against testing

A harm-reduction approach to drugs is always a balance between benefits and risks: the availability of pill testing reduces harm, but it may increase risks for some. Not everyone will use the service and some may ignore the results and risk being subjected to potentially harmful drugs. It may also lend the appearance of safety when, in reality, the pills remain illegal and potentially harmful. Particularly if it is not always possible to ensure that pill-testing kit results are accurate.

There is a belief among senior police that pill testing would actually increase drug use. For instance, a spokesperson for NSW Police said that no test could guarantee the safety of an illegal drug or its effect on an individual. "The NSW Government will not facilitate or sanction the testing of illegal drugs, creating the dangerous fiction that they are then safe to consume" (Boddy 2016: 1).

There is some veracity in this position. Testing has to answer three questions: Which drugs are in the pill? What quantity of the drugs is in the pill? And are there any dangerous contaminants in the pill? Not all testing answers all three questions. The reagent kits that can be bought from specialist shops give a qualitative test that tells what drugs are in the pill, but cannot tell how much, or what other dangerous contaminants are in it.

The number of drugs now available to a consumer has grown rapidly in recent times, particularly synthetic psychoactive compounds. Many are resistant to analysis by anything other than a sophisticated testing system used by an analytical chemist. The gap between the utility of simple reagent test and laboratory analysis is growing. For instance, reagent testing would struggle to identify high purity MDMA (more than 200mg in a tablet, which could be fatal).

University of Queensland Alcohol and Drug Research and Education Centre director Professor Jake Najman sounds a warning about confidence of on-site testing. He claims that in 2015, 75 new synthetic drugs came onto the market, the impacts of which on the human body are largely unknown and potentially risky. He believes pill-testing facilities would be unable to detect these new substances because criminal chemists change recipes too quickly for detection. "The problem is a legal system which encourages chemists to develop products to escape detection and some of these products are going to be potentially lethal" (Gregory 2017).

Paul Dillon, Director of Drug and Alcohol Research and Training Australia warns that the pill testing concept is based on the false assumption that if a drug user knows what they are taking, then it is actually safe:

> As far as ecstasy is concerned, the substance users are looking for is MDMA. Test a pill and find out that it contains MDMA and many believe that this means that the pill is 'safe'. MDMA is not a safe drug and many of the deaths that have occurred across Europe this year have actually been due to MDMA overdose. Pill testing for adulterants would not necessarily have assisted in preventing those deaths.
> (Dillon 2015: 2)

The problem is that the only pill testing that is effective requires expensive equipment and highly trained technicians, and it is not instantaneous. So, instead of attempting to provide professional testing, many politicians and some police endorse a deterrence-based approach to drug use at music festivals, with a strong police presence and drug sniffer dogs to catch offenders. And arguments that the testing cost should be carried by the event organisers, quickly run into a range of economic excuses.

Although such deterrence methods are undoubtedly well-intentioned, evidence suggests that they are ineffective at protecting festival attendees from the harmful effects of contaminated substances. In fact, some evidence shows that drug dogs may actually increase harm, as frightened festival-goers hastily consume large quantities of drugs to avoid detection. Very few drugs are deposited in amnesty bins, instead binging, or pre-loading outside the festival site occurs.

Water

Many alcohol/drug related issues are exacerbated by heat and a lack of water, as attendees get caught up in the day's excitement and forget to rehydrate. An adequate supply of safe drinking water must be available to all attendees in all parts of the festival site. An appropriate means of access to drinking water for spectators must be considered in a street or outdoor venue or events such as 'raves' where the activity produces an extreme heat environment. Event duration and location and the expected ambient temperature should be considered in deciding the quantity of drinking water required. Water pressure must be adequate to provide for all uses and peak demands. Alternate water supplies should be available should existing supplies fail to meet demand or be rendered unsafe or unusable.

Where possible, drinks sold at the venue should be in plastic containers or in plastic or paper cups, rather than in cans or bottles. It is preferable that water is available for no cost, and if the only type of water available is in pre-packaged bottles, it should be as low cost as possible. Sponsorship should be considered in such cases. While the provision of water and soft drinks is essential, event managers may like to incorporate other non-alcoholic beverages that are popular in different cultures into the event (e.g. herbal teas and yoghurt drinks).

Chill-out space

A valuable harm minimisation practice is to provide a special area offering patrons time out from the crowd and heat. A 'chill-out space' is a safe, non-judgmental area where patrons can relax and recover that provides free water and activities for groups of people who need a break.

Health promotion

In addition to alcohol and drug information, it is important to consider the opportunities to promote health messages at public events. Examples include:

- Sunsmart: encourage provision and use of shade areas. Encourage the use of sunscreen creams, hats etc. and make them available for purchase by spectators.
- Safe sex: promotion of safe sex messages can be conveyed and provision of free condoms should be considered.
- Hearing protection: consider providing advice about hearing protection, and possibly free ear plugs, to spectators and participants. This is applicable to venues such as rock concerts and car races.

Infection control and personal hygiene issues

Infectious disease transmission through unsafe sexual practices or drug use may be a health risk at some events, particularly those that involve spectators camping at the venue overnight. As a means of reducing these risks, consideration should be given to provision or availability of condoms and a properly licensed needle exchange/disposal mechanism. While these are sensitive and controversial issues, they are nevertheless important public health concerns in contemporary society and must be addressed.

Sexual assault at music festivals

There is an increased risk of experiencing sexual violence in mass gatherings, as well as the prevalence of alcohol and drugs, and it's become evident that music festivals have a rape and sexual assault problem. The instant community feeling of a festival might contribute to lowered barriers or provide the perfect hunting ground for predatory sexual violence. Festival staff are often are ill-equipped to deal with sexual violence and there's a serious lack of training of security staff in properly responding to reports of such incidents (Stephens 2017).

Project SoundCheck, an Ottawa-based organisation, is hoping to prevent sexual assault at mass gatherings with its programme that focuses on bystander intervention and training. The project was started in response to a 2013 study done at the Ottawa hospital emergency room that found one in four new cases of sexual violence happened at or around a mass gathering. Since the programme began in 2015, it has delivered training to a few thousand people at a variety of festivals, and at least 5,000 people have received the group's abbreviated bystander intervention checklist card. The handout includes six steps to help check in and prevent sexual violence, beginning with the basics: "Watch what's going on: is everyone having fun?", to the more specific: "Seems like things #JustGotWeird? Yes? Time to check in!" and "Stick around: say hi, ask what's up, ask the person who may be at risk, 'Do you need help?'"

The project is based on bystander intervention and surveillance by attendees at the festival, and creating a sense of a caring supportive community. The basic act of talking about sexual assault behaviours that won't be tolerated and giving people instructions for how to recognise what is happening and intrude, empowers people to intervene. The project founders say that people want to prevent sexual violence, they just don't know how to talk about it and they don't know what to say. The objective is that everyone attending a festival feels comfortable to intervene and report sexual violence and have the training to use it (Warner 2016).

Ottawa Bluesfest has been one of the earliest proponents of Project SoundCheck and incorporates bystander intervention training by the provision of the Project SoundCheck manual and sexual assault prevention tip sheets in its volunteer induction.

Offensive behaviour

Event managers should be vigilant about sexual violence, and consider strategies to reduce the likelihood of this transpiring during or following an event. Some tips include:

- considering how technology (text messaging, emails and social networking websites) is used to promote an event, as inappropriate promotion can lead to unwelcome guests

- monitoring the use of mobile phone cameras and videos during the event as situations involving sexual violence may later appear on social networking sites and web video channels, which can have legal implications for those involved
- placing signage around the event that address issues such as consent, positive sexual health practices, looking after your mates and watching your drink
- including messages about personal safety, including in relation to sex, on event tickets and advertising
- reminding guests that they should leave the event in groups.

An important issue for event managers to consider is drink spiking. This occurs when a foreign substance has been added to a person's drink without their knowledge. Both alcoholic and non-alcoholic drinks can be spiked. Most people assume that prescription drugs (e.g. valium, rohypnol) or illegal drugs (e.g. ecstasy, ketamine, LSD) are used in drink spiking. However, it is important to note that drink spiking commonly involves extra shots of alcohol being added to a drink.

Event managers and staff should monitor activity at the event for any signs of drink spiking. If a person becomes affected after consuming a drink that has been spiked, they should be taken to a quiet place, an ambulance should be called and a staff member should remain with the affected person. The Australian Federal Police have developed a website dedicated to drink spiking. This can be accessed at www.thesource.gov.au/drinkspiking/default.htm. Should any incident arise at an event that results in injury, it should be immediately reported to both the first aid teams and to security. The event manager may need to complete a confidential incident report form.

Summary

- Licenses and permits are needed for certain event activities such as sale of alcohol and handling of food.
- Food safety is a vital aspect of public health planning for public events. All food should be prepared in sanitary conditions, with handwashing facilities provided.
- During the event, on-site environmental health officers must have the authority to close down any vendor who is contravening food hygiene legislation and public health requirements.
- The fit out and construction of all food selling premises, whether it is a food van purpose built for festivals and events, or a temporary stall inside a venue or tent, must be in accordance with local health regulations and codes of practice.
- Management decisions regarding the policy and attitude towards both alcohol and drug consumption at an event should be based on best hazard and risk minimisation practice, rather than morality.
- An event organisation can choose from many forms of control, ranging from outright prohibition at one end of the spectrum, to complete liberty at the other.
- The most successful harm minimisation strategies involve 'judgement free' attempts to ameliorate the adverse health consequences of mood altering substances.
- Misuse of alcohol is a significant factor in crowd disturbance and unsocial behaviour, and managing the sale, service and consumption of alcohol is an important aspect of event management.
- It is important that the organisers have clear policies relating to the serving of alcohol and ensure that the policies are enforced.

- In most jurisdictions the provision of alcohol in a responsible and controlled manner is a legislative requirement. Event managers and anyone involved in the provision of alcohol at an event may be liable should it be proven that alcohol served irresponsibly resulted in harm.
- In most jurisdictions, there are mandatory training requirements in relation to the Responsible Service of Alcohol.
- Alcohol should be sold, served and consumed in designated, licensed areas only to make it easier for staff to check for valid identification and for alcohol consumption to be controlled.
- Alcohol must not be served to anyone less than the legal age for drinking. Event and security staff must request valid proof of age from guests who wish to enter the designated drinking areas and consume alcohol.
- Signs must be displayed indicating that the area is licensed, underage guests will not be admitted, and about the responsible service of alcohol.
- Taking illicit drugs, especially ecstasy, at festivals is not particularly unusual.
- The two main problems with drug use at festivals and events, the erratic, violent or dangerous behaviour of a person influenced by drugs; and death or severe reactions to ingested drugs.
- The effects of illegal drugs will always be unpredictable. Severe distress is caused through intoxication, by mixing illicit substances, and by exhaustion from lack of food or dehydration.
- Pill-testing kits or booths at venues where pills are known to be consumed could inform users about the content of illicit drugs. As a harm-reduction intervention, it's available in several European countries.
- Some experts and young people support pill testing. The finding is consistent with young people's overall views about drugs, they want better information in order to make informed choices.
- The number of drugs now available has grown rapidly in recent times. Particularly synthetic psychoactive compounds. Many are resistant to analysis by anything other than a sophisticated testing system used by an analytical chemist. Pill-testing facilities would be unable to detect these new substances because criminal chemists change recipes too quickly for detection.
- Many alcohol/drug related issues are exacerbated by heat and a lack of water, as attendees get caught up in the day's excitement and forget to rehydrate. An adequate supply of safe drinking water must be available to all attendees in all parts of the festival site.
- There is a risk of sexual violence in mass gatherings, as well as the prevalence of alcohol and drugs, and music festivals have an increasing rape and sexual assault problem.

Bibliography

Australian Government Department of Veterans' Affairs (No year [cited 2016 Oct]) *Alcohol Dependence. Online.* Available HTTP: <https://www.therightmix.gov.au/assets/factsheets/DVA0007_2_Alcohol_Dependence_v4.pdf>

Boddy. N. (2016) 'Canberra doctor behind push for pill testing trial at music festivals', *The Canberra Times*, February 28.

Department of Health WA (2002) *A Planning Guide for Event Managers: Alcohol, Safety and Event Management*. Perth: Department of Health WA.

Department of Racing, Gaming and Liquor (2008) *Responsible Service*. Online. Available HTTP: <www.rgl.wa.gov.au/Default.aspx?NodeId=94>.

Department of Racing, Gaming and Liquor (2009) *Occasional Licences*. Online. Available HTTP: <www.rgl.wa.gov.au/ResourceFiles/ApplicationKits/Liquor/Occasional_licence. pdf>.

Department of Racing, Gaming and Liquor (2009) *Mandatory Training*. Online. Available HTTP: <www.rgl.wa.gov.au/ResourceFiles/Policies/Mandatory_Training.pdf>.

Dillon. P. (2015) 'Pill testing isn't a silver bullet to prevent drug deaths, but it is part of the solution', *Sydney Morning Herald*, December 2015.

Douglas, B., Wodak. A. and McDonald. D. (2012) *Alternatives to Prohibition of Illicit Drugs: How We Can Stop Killing and Criminalising Young Australians*. Report of the second Australia21 Roundtable on Illicit Drugs, University of Melbourne.

Gregory. K. (2017) *Pill testing at music festivals needed after rave overdose, doctors say*. ABC News, 4 January 2017. Available HTTP: <www.abc.net.au/news/8159864>

Harris. R. L. (2005) *Patty's Industrial Hygiene and Toxicology*, 5th edn. Brisbane: John Wiley.

IAPCO (2004) *Safety and Security at Congresses: A Crucial Area of Risk Management*. London: International Association of Professional Congress Organizers.

Melbourne Convention and Exhibition Centre (2008) *Occupational Health and Safety (Oh&S) Site Induction*. Victoria: MCEC.

Mellor. N. and Veno. A. (1998) *Public Events: Safety and Security Strategies*. Victoria: Centre for Police and Justice Studies, Monash University.

Monash University (2008) *Guidelines for Managing the Impact of Alcohol and Other Drugs*. Melbourne: Monash University.

National Drug and Alcohol Research Centre (n.d.) *NDARC Fact Sheet: Alcohol*. Online. Available HTTP: <http://ndarc.med.unsw. du.au/NDARCWeb.nsf/resources/ Alcohol1/$fi le/ ALCOHOL.pdf>, accessed October 2016.

National Drug and Alcohol Research Centre (n.d.) *NDARC Fact Sheet: Standard Drinks and Safe Drinking Levels*. Online. Available HTTP: <http://ndarc.med.unsw.edu.au/>, accessed October 2016.

National Drug and Alcohol Research Centre (n.d.) *Harmful Effects of Alcohol*. Online. Available HTTP: <http://NDARCWeb.nsf/resources/NDARCFact_Drugs5/$fi le.pdf>.

Ritter. A. (2011) *National Drug Strategy Household Survey Report July 2011*. Australian National Council on Drugs. Australian Institute of Health and Welfare.

Stephens. K. (2017) 'Five women sexually assaulted at Tasmania's Falls Festival'. Online. Available HTTP: <www.news.com.au/entertainment/music/music-festivals/>, January 2017.

University of Western Australia (2007) *University Policy On Alcohol and Other Drugs*. Online. Available HTTP: <www.universitypolicies.uwa.edu.au>.

Warner. A. (2016) *Sexual Assault at Music Festivals: Changing the Conversation*. Online. Available HTTP: <http://www.cbcmusic.ca/posts/14511/sexual-assault-music-festivals-changing-conversation>, accessed April 2017.

Weitzel, A. F. (2007) *Let's Keep it Clean*. Coppell, TX: International Association of Assembly Managers.

Wodak. A. (2016) 'Pill testing trial to begin at Sydney music festivals, vows drug expert', *Sydney Morning Herald*, February 28.

Worksafe Victoria (2006) *Advice for Managing Major Events Safely*. Victoria: Government of Victoria.

Chapter 9

Security and law enforcement on-site

Chapter objectives

This chapter concerns the roles of police and security staff at an event. It includes guidelines for:

- use of passes and searches
- selecting a security contractor
- security screening of staff
- performer and VIP security.

Most people attend an event with the purpose of peacefully enjoying themselves. However, there are sometimes antisocial elements in a crowd such as criminals in search of victims, and people with psychological problems or social agendas.

Physical security is important in protecting against a range of threats and addressing vulnerability. Put in place security measures to remove or reduce risks to as low as reasonably practicable, bearing in mind the need to consider safety as a priority at all times. Security measures must not compromise public safety.

Risk assessment will determine which measures to adopt, but they range from basic – keeping communal areas under surveillance, security staff, CCTV, perimeter fencing and security lighting – to specialist solutions, such as perimeter detection systems equipment.

While events would seem to be vulnerable to violent incidents, it could be anticipated that attendees may not tolerate a high level of security when that security impacts upon the event experience. The event organisation, host community and attendees should all be aware of the risks and preventative measures required to prevent security breaches or terrorist activities. It is important to anticipate and resolve problems before they occur, rather than after the event. Different types of events can have their own issues, for example:

- rock concerts can create problems with abuse of alcohol and/or drugs, and in some cases, even the use of weapons
- religious or 'healing' events can attract an inordinate number of ill or infirm, thus increasing the potential for on-site medical or health related emergencies
- certain sports events can attract over-reactive supporters and anti-social behaviour
- events for senior citizens can often increase the number of medical incidents.

The provision of security services is vital in relation to public safety, particularly within the venue. The types of security that can be provided at large public events are:

- police officers in uniform
- private security guards in uniform.

The composition of security services will vary according to the event, with different events better served by one or a combination of the two categories. In many events, uniformed police perform functions such as dealing with traffic and drug violations and crime control, leaving the internal event security to private personnel employed by the organisers. The key security considerations are:

- Will the event organiser/promoter use police officers for on-site security, or will private security officers be engaged?
- If private security officers are to be used, what will their roles and functions be, and how will their services integrate with the police? Are they permitted to work outside the venue?
- Will the police service only public areas outside the event perimeter, or on-site as well?

Police

As soon as a venue is chosen contact police and local government to establish security measures. Develop a security policy, and communicate these requirements to venue security staff. Security aspects of the event need to be planned. Consider the enforcement policies to be exercised for offences on-site, so that discretion will be exercised consistently throughout the event, for example, the definition of disruptive behaviour and how it will be dealt with, and how you will deal with any property damage.

The police must be notified at least 6 weeks before each event. They will require:

- details of the event manager's hotline for complaints
- name of the crowd control/security company
- contact number for the crowd control officer responsible for staff
- the number of security staff
- names of all security staff
- operational procedures
- emergency procedures, including an evacuation plan
- the event manager or promoter to be present at all times during an event and readily contactable by the police.

A policy should be agreed with police about what should happen in the event of disturbances and persons being found possessing or selling drugs.

Figure 9.1 Mobile police station.

General security staff

The roles and function of the security staff are crucial for the prevention of violence and crime at music festivals and dance parties. At these events their major function is crowd control, as the crowd is likely to be made up of mainly younger people and there is no structured seating.

The security staff who will be in direct physical contact with patrons need to be properly licensed and registered, physically fit and over 18 years of age. They need:

- good communication skills
- basic training in fire fighting
- basic training in evacuation procedures
- a basic knowledge of first aid and the ability to recognise distress
- some knowledge of self-defence and how to control violent or unruly behaviour and intoxicated persons
- to know their limitations on removing patrons and refusing entry to patrons
- to know lawful search techniques.

A register should be maintained of the names and identifying numbers of the security staff.

Each security staff member should be given a written summary of all they are expected to know and do, including securing a clear passage for all emergency vehicles and staff. It should be emphasised that if the size of the problem means the security staff cannot prevent it from happening, they should immediately report the matter to the security controller

Security staff members must be issued with unique identification, such as a number on their uniform, so that they can be easily identified by the patrons. It is important that they be issued with some sort of noise protection, have a torch if the event is held at night, and have communication equipment that is effective under noisy concert conditions.

Security staff are expected to:

- assist in identifying patrons who are banned from the venue, such as people who

  - are intoxicated by alcohol and other drugs
  - attempt to sell or distribute drugs
  - are being aggressive or anti-social
  - are underage at an adult dance party
  - do not possess tickets
  - are in possession of forged tickets

- refuse entry or remove from the party persons known to the promoters and security staff to be drug dealers, and notify the police immediately
- check identity documents to keep out minors from adult dance parties and to help stop underage drinking; identity documents include a driver's licence, a passport and, for licensed premises, a proof of age card
- patrol toilet areas (male and female), preferably every 30 minutes
- prevent patrons, as far as possible, from climbing fences and other structures such as light towers, advertising hoardings, speaker columns and mixing towers; make

sure all parking area entrances and emergency exits are kept clear and that vehicles are correctly parked
- make sure that gangways and exits are kept clear
- control all exits including openings in a boundary fence
- guard areas on-site which collect and store significant amounts of money
- secure off-site cash transfer and banking.

Security staff should co-operate with ushering and stewarding staff to:

- identify and investigate any incident, such as violence, among the patrons, and report the findings to the security controller
- know the location of, and be able to operate, the fire-fighting equipment at the venue
- know the location of the first-aid posts
- direct distressed or unwell patrons to first-aid posts
- fully understand any methods or signals used to alert staff that an emergency has occurred
- be capable of recognising potential fire hazards and suspect packages, reporting such findings immediately to the security controller
- immediately follow any instruction given in an emergency by a police officer or the security controller, or in the case of fire, instructions from the commander of the fire brigade
- report to the security controller any damage or defect which is likely to be a threat to patron safety
- assist as required in the evacuation of the venue, in accordance with the evacuation plan
- assist in the prevention of breaches of venue regulations.

Screening and patrolling

Routine searching and patrolling of premises represents another level of vigilance, covering both internal and external areas. Keep patrols regular, though not too pre-dictable (i.e. every hour on the hour). Regular patrols of the surrounding local area are advisable for extra security and to reassure local residents.

Briefing

To enable security personnel to perform their duties effectively, it is vital that they be appropriately briefed prior to the event. This briefing should provide security personnel with:

- details of the venue layout, including entrances, exits, first-aid posts and any potential hazards
- clear direction on the management of unacceptable behaviour
- details of emergency and evacuation plans, such as raising alarms, protocols for requesting assistance and evacuation procedures
- instruction for the operation, deactivation and isolation of any on-site machinery and utility supply in case of emergency.

Figure 9.2 Police assisting members of the public.

The greater the cooperation between security firms, event management, and the police, the better; and the larger the event, the closer the liaison required. The manager must be aware of which staff are on duty on any particular night and this information must be recorded in case individuals need to be interviewed by police for any reason.

Security procedures

Careful consideration should be given to the level of visible security at an event, and to the uniforms they are wearing. Both must be appropriate for the event and crowd profile. Having heavy duty security teams or police tactical teams visible at an event gives the crowd the impression that disorder is expected. It is more acceptable to make use of stewards and police officers in a public relations role, and engage the stronger security measures only when needed. Similarly, if the crowd is expected to be predominantly compliant, it is more appropriate for security personnel to be dressed in their day-to-day uniforms, rather than kitted out in full riot gear.

Judging how a crowd is likely to react to intervention from authority and, subsequently, knowing when it is appropriate to intervene and when to take a step back, also develops from experience of dealing with crowds first hand. Nothing can compare to actually being on the ground and seeing crowds, because they're not like a textbook, they don't behave like a textbook either, and it's only seeing them first hand that you do get the experience and knowledge.

Given their understanding and experience, security professionals can easily foresee the need to administer crowd control and to plan for the mitigation of incidents. They train extensively, working in teams, and practice nonviolent crises intervention and proven restraint techniques. Outcomes are expected to be quick and effective and with the least disruption possible. Training and experience enables them to use measures that are intermediate and most likely to diffuse or de-escalate a situation.

It's also important to make a distinction between individuals who perform straight security functions, like guarding an entrance, versus other types of 'security' staff who have as much, if not more, influence over the safety and comfort of venue guests. During the last decade, an increased emphasis on customer service has led to a 'softer' approach to security in order to create a friendly atmosphere and reduce crowd anxiety. Strategies for minimising security risks have also shifted more emphasis towards predicting and preventing incidents, so security personnel are often less conspicuous these days.

Most security contractors employ the concept of 'early and often' as part of the security process. The duties defined as 'early and often' includes assisting guests, being accessible, answering questions, providing directions and responding to concerns. These duties are not seen as interfering with conflict identification and mitigation responsibilities but are following the training for nonviolent crisis intervention. Early preventive techniques identify and teach useful skills such as appropriate attitude, approach, personal space and body language. The use of force to any degree is the last resort.

The important point is that the process of greeting is twofold. It provides an opportunity for the security personnel to assess individual crowd members, and audience members will be reassured by the presence of a carefully selected and well trained person. Any persons inclined to inappropriate behaviour, for one reason or another, will be put on notice subtlety and in a nuanced way.

Passes

All staff, contractors and service providers should be issued with their own individual pass that should be worn at all times when on the site. The issuing of a pass must be strictly controlled and limited to senior security staff.

A low security pass could be a simple label worn round the neck or pinned to a shirt, or a specially coloured wristband, or even as simple as a tee shirt printed with 'staff', 'crew', or 'volunteer' and the event logo.

At a higher security level, a photo pass is to be worn at all times, either in a pouch or pinned to clothing, and is issued to a particular person who has been screened and is not transferable. The pass should contain secure printing devices to deter duplication or counterfeiting. Electronic ticket checkers that read bar codes and wirelessly communicate with computer databases to quickly and reliably identify invalid passes can increase security.

It may be an advantage to be able to record and track the details of participants quickly, accurately and securely. Radio Frequency Identification (RFID) offers a number of significant advantages over barcode readers which are cumbersome, time consuming and intrusive. The advantages of RFID technology include:

● RFID is faster and can be tuned to specific read ranges. For example, if desired, it could be a 5-foot range to track anyone going by a checkpoint or gateway

- access control – scanners at entrances or within auditoriums or rooms can instantly verify that the person has legitimate access
- CEU tracking – people can be tracked automatically when they enter and exit an area
- VIPs can be tracked so that staff or key security people can be notified when they have come 'within range'.

Staff passes should be issued at four levels:

1 A general pass for all staff that permits movement to all areas of the site except restricted areas. This pass may also be valid for staff parking, staff toilets and amenities or cafeteria.
2 A specific area pass for staff working in a restricted area such as backstage, loading areas, green rooms, Island sites and VIP sterile zones, communication/emergency control/administrative centres, technical booths for audio and lighting, box office, bars and first-aid posts.
3 An Access All Areas pass issued to senior event management and valid as the name suggests for access to all parts of the event.
4 Security staff pass. This pass must identify the wearer with a photo, name and clearly state that the wearer is a security operative.

For service providers, such as a stall holder, or waste remover, depending on the level of security required, passes are provided that are valid only for the general public areas and the service areas of the event site. At a low security level the pass could be transferrable from one person to another with the number of passes limited appropriately.

At a higher security level, photo passes should be worn by all contract and agency staff at all times. Some service contracts will require their staff to wear the company's own identification badges. These should not be used as a substitute for an event issued pass, but as an additional security measure.

The event organisation and the contractor should agree a procedure for providing temporary replacements if a screened contractor is unavailable. A common system used is where the event organisation retains contractors' passes between visits, reissuing them each time the contractor comes on-site after the contractor's identity has been verified. The event organisation will need to decide what additional personnel security measures to implement, for example, restricted or supervised access, when the replacement is on site. All pass arrangements should be included in the contract between the two parties.

Media passes

At popular and large events there are usually a considerable number of requests for media passes. Each will require security assessment. Large media organisations such as television networks, national press or national radio broadcasters, are usually given accreditation as a matter of course. However, the bona fides of individuals should be checked. Claiming to represent a media outlet is a common method of attempting to enter an event for free or for a fan to obtain access to a celebrity. Most events require authorisation from the editor or CEO of the media organisation, and a proof of identification for individuals. Access to performers or areas of the event site may be provided at different levels. For instance, major media may be granted access to the green room area of the event, while lesser media might be limited to access during particular times of the day, or only to public areas of the site.

Temporary passes

Visitors to private or restricted areas should be escorted and should wear clearly marked temporary passes, which must be returned on leaving. Anyone not displaying security passes in private or restricted areas should either be challenged or reported immediately to security or management. Passes should include a photograph of the bearer, and returned against signature.

Searching of persons entering the event

Bag checks

The security of an event relies on having some control over persons entering it. The security will differ on event operational and production periods. All persons entering the event should go through a search regime. Everyone entering the event (including performers and VIP guests) should be subject to a search of bags, or security staff could conduct random bag searches. Experience shows that most visitors not only accept searching, they actually expect to be searched. It instils confidence that an event is a safe environment and an enjoyable experience.

Search queues allow the profiling of visitors by security staff. This allows an opportunity to identify possible problem individuals.

Body searches

At times of a high security risk the search could extend up to full body searches of every person entering the venue. Everyone entering the event (including performers and VIP guests) should be subject to a search of outer clothing, pockets and bags, to be carried out by a security officer of the same sex. Body searches should ideally be complemented by the use of metal detectors to deter the carrying of weapons, and to reassure customers.

Warning notices

You must advise attendees that searches will be carried out, and that they should arrive early and be encouraged not to bring prohibited items into the event. Advance tickets, the event website and display advertising should contain the message that alcohol, drugs, weapons and fireworks will not be permitted into the event, and that purchase of tickets is deemed as consent to a search of persons and property for prohibited material prior to admission. The event policy on non-entry and ejection must also be stated to reduce the likelihood of arguments with staff. Ensure that event regulations include a right to refuse entry unless searched.

Notices must be strategically placed at the entrance to the venue, informing customers that the police will be informed in the event of individuals being found in possession of controlled substances or offensive weapons. Customers should be warned by signage that covert police surveillance may be in operation.

Confiscated items

If it has been decided to confiscate prohibited goods, arrangements for the storage and disposal of these goods are required. Different approaches to seized alcohol have been used. In some cases the alcohol has been opened by security personnel and dumped into large drums in front of the patron. This has created a hostile audience and conflict with security and event management before the event has commenced.

Two strategies that can be applied to all prohibited material (not just alcohol) are giving the attendee the option of returning it to his/her car, with a subsequent loss of place in line, or storing the item tagged with a numbered sticker at the entry gate for return after the event. Such an approach can also be applied to any item if confiscation, for whatever reason, is deemed inappropriate.

Drugs or offensive weapons that are seized must immediately be handed over to the security manager for storage in a secure place until they can be taken by the police.

Staff

Provide sufficient staff to carry out the searches. Consider the fact that visitors often arrive in large groups, close to the event start time. This can impact on the ability of the searchers to achieve their aims. Ensure the searching staff are properly briefed on their powers and what they are searching for.

'Right to search' legislation varies widely from country to country and city to city. However, in general, security guards or other event staff cannot touch any possessions in a bag, but instead ask the owner of the bag to move items in order to have a better look. If the person refuses they can deny entry.

Event staff rarely have the right to insist on performing a body search (although it has become common in the USA, in many cases causing distress and complaints about inappropriate touching). Prior consent must be established. Staff must not perform strip searches under any circumstances. Ensure that temporary staff and volunteers have a clause within their contracts allowing them to be searched. Bag search areas must have sufficient space to prevent crowding. Consider separating queues into those with bags, and those without that can be fast tracked through the search area.

Selecting a security contractor

Engage a security firm that will act as a partner, not just a provider. It helps if the firm specialises in the type of events being planned, although many of them are capable of offering quality services for all types of events. Make sure they offer the range of staff that will suit the event needs and enhance the experience for the audience, and, of course, ask for references. Make sure they're compliant with licensing regulations applying in the location of the event, don't just take their word for it. Also consider the level of insurance and liability the security firm takes on, and understand the limitations of those protections. Although event management is responsible for mistakes or negligence of their own, hiring a contract security force can lessen the burden of certain types of liability, including injuries that lead to workers' compensation claims.

One of the best ways to evaluate a company is to attend an event staffed by them and evaluate if security and customer service is up to par. Talk with the staff or even try to smuggle in a disallowed item (something harmless, of course, like food or a drink),

Figure 9.3 Security guard.

ask for directions, or attempt to walk through a prohibited area during the event. Investigate how the company interviews, hires, and places each individual. What type of background checks and screening are done? Does it meet or exceed legal requirements for drug screening? Be specific with questions about the way the company treats its staff. Ask about their turnover rate and what type and level of benefits they offer. Does it include such perks as tuition reimbursement or free uniforms? What type of shifts are offered to the employees and can they rotate?

Also ask how they determine which specific position an individual is suited for (e.g. security officer versus guard). How extensive and frequent is the training and continuing education provided to their individual staff members, and what specialised training do members of their staff have? For instance, do they have individuals who specialise in dealing with alcohol-related incidents or suspicious packages? Perhaps most importantly, evaluate the management staff carefully. Particularly the qualifications and experience of their management team.

Expect qualified companies to comply with legal requirements for security personnel, to provide background checks and drug screening, to provide ongoing training and to have established relationships with local law enforcement (if they don't have all of the above, they may not be reputable).

Security screening of staff

Event organisations deal regularly with many different types of risk when hiring staff. One of them is the possibility that staff or contractors will exploit their position within the organisation for illegitimate purposes. They could be thieves, stalkers infatuated with a celebrity or star performer, or someone much more sinister. Terrorist attacks are easier to carry out if the terrorist is assisted by an 'insider' or by someone with specialist knowledge or access.

A terrorism infiltrator could be an employee or any contractor staff (e.g. cleaner, caterer, security guard) who has authorised access to the event premises. A staff employee or volunteer, either with the organisation for some time or newly joined, could be using their insider position in order to seek information or exploit their access to breach security.

There is an increasing necessity to apply security screening to volunteers. It is unlikely that a volunteer will be a terrorist seeking to infiltrate an event, but the possibility must be guarded against. It is common for event managers to accept volunteers without a background security check and place them in a position where their easier access to a venue or festival site allows them to either smuggle in offensive weapons, or allow another person to bring them on-site. Volunteer application forms should be routinely forwarded to police, and security bag checking of volunteers when they come onto the event site should be standard practice. Volunteers should never be used for security duties.

Controls

The infiltration risk can be reduced but can never be entirely prevented. Instead, as with many other risks, the organisation should employ a process for ensuring that the risks are managed in a proportionate and cost-effective manner. A personnel security process seeks to ensure that the event organisation employs reliable individuals, minimises the chances of staff becoming unreliable once they have been employed, detects suspicious behaviour, and resolves security concerns once they have become apparent.

Pre-employment screening

This involves a number of screening methods, which are performed as part of the recruitment process, but also on a regular basis for existing staff. The ways in which screening is performed varies, some methods are very simple, and others are more sophisticated. In every case, the aim of the screening is to collect information about potential or existing staff and then to use that information to identify any individuals who present security concerns.

Pre-employment screening seeks to verify the credentials of job applicants and to check that the applicants meet preconditions of employment (e.g. that the individual is legally permitted to take up an offer of employment). In the course of performing these checks it should be established whether the applicant has concealed important information or otherwise misrepresented themselves. To this extent, pre-employment screening may be considered a test of character.

Pre-employment checks

The process starts with the job application, where applicants should be made aware that supplying false information, or failing to disclose relevant information, could be grounds for dismissal and could amount to a criminal offence. Applicants should also be made aware that any offers of employment are subject to the satisfactory completion of pre-employment checks. If an organisation believes there is a fraudulent application involving illegal activity, the police should be informed.

Pre-employment checks may be performed directly by an organisation, or this process may be sub-contracted to a third party. In either case the company needs to have a clear understanding of the thresholds for denying someone employment. For instance, under what circumstances would an application be rejected on the basis of their criminal record, and why?

Therefore a pre-employment screening process will be more effective if they are an integral part of the event's policies, practices and procedures for the recruiting, hiring, and where necessary, training of employees. A personnel security risk assessment will help decide on the levels of screening that are appropriate for different roles and responsibilities. For example, consider the difference between a guard checking security passes and a volunteer serving food.

Identity

Of all the pre-employment checks, identity verification is the most fundamental. Two approaches can be used:

1 A paper-based approach involving the verification of key identification documents and the matching of these documents to the individual.
2 An electronic approach involving searches on databases (e.g. databases of credit agreements or the electoral role) to establish the electronic footprint of the individual. The individual is then asked to answer questions about the footprint which only the actual owner of the identity could answer correctly.

Qualifications and employment history

The verification of qualifications and employment can help identify those applicants attempting to hide negative information such as a prison sentence or dismissal. Unexplained gaps should be explored. When confirming details about an individual's qualifications it is always important to:

- consider whether the post requires a qualifications check
- always request original certificates and take copies
- compare details on certificates etc. with those provided by the applicant
- independently confirm the existence of the establishment and contact them to confirm the details provided by the individual.

Employment checks

For legal reasons it is increasingly difficult to obtain character references, but past employers should be asked to confirm dates of employment. Where employment checks are carried out it is important to:

- check a minimum of 3 but ideally 5 years previous employment
- independently confirm the employer's existence and contact details
- confirm details (dates, position, salary) with the employer's HR department
- where possible, request an employer's reference from the line manager.

Criminal convictions

A criminal conviction is not necessarily a bar to employment. However, there are certain roles and responsibilities where some forms of criminal history will be unacceptable. To obtain criminal record information, the event organisation should request that an applicant either completes a criminal record self-declaration form, or submits a Basic Disclosure certificate. Most police forces have an online criminal record checking service.

In some circumstances you may be unable to check staff or volunteers from overseas satisfactorily (e.g. due to a lack of information from another country). In this case, you may decide to deny employment, or to implement other risk management controls (e.g. additional supervision) to compensate for the lack of assurance.

Security checks for contractor staff

Event organisations employ a wide variety of contract staff, such as security staff, traffic controllers, waste management contractors and various infrastructure construction companies. It is important to ensure that contractors have the same level of pre-employment security screening as the event staff. Contracts should outline the type of checks required for each post and requirements should be cascaded to any sub-contractors. Where a contractor or screening agency is performing the checks, they should be audited.

Contractors present particular personnel security challenges. For instance, the timescales for employing contractors are often relatively short, and there is greater potential for security arrangements to be confused or overlooked (e.g. due to further sub-contracting).

In managing the insider risks associated with contractors it is important to ensure that pre-employment checks are carried out to the same standard as for permanent employees. Where this is not possible, due to tight deadlines or a lack of information available for background checking, then the resulting risks must be minimised by additional personnel security measures such as continuous supervision.

Performer, celebrity and VIP security

The responsibility for controlling potential threats to VIPs is an increasing challenge for venue safety and security. Protecting high-profile people has expanded beyond high-level politicians. Celebrities now expect a secure environment when they are either working or visiting public events. A combination of public safety agencies, event security managers and private contracted security teams are required to collaborate on executive protection planning to ensure proper coordination.

At every event there are unique safety and security issues surrounding star performers and high-profile VIP guests. The very presence of a megastar likely means that a massive, fervent crowd will be in attendance, creating safety and security challenges. Big-name VIP guests mean that events also must deal with a throng of aggressive paparazzi, and will need to coordinate security efforts with those of the VIPs' staff to keep the celebrities safe from enthusiastic, or sometimes crazed, fans.

These can range from obsessed fans to mentally unstable individuals who have targeted high-profile people simply because they're in the news. In addition to stalkers infatuated with celebrity, star performers and VIPs can potentially attract dangerous attention. High-profile people and events can be larger-risk terrorist targets, especially when media coverage is involved. Sometimes, members of the media covering VIPs can also cause security hazards.

Very popular performers may need to be protected from being mobbed when they arrive, leave, perform or move about the venue. It is essential there are separate performers' entrances. Attention could be diverted from arriving or departing performers by arranging for other attractions to be in progress at the same time.

While stars and high-profile guests – and the ensuing crowds – have always created security challenges for events, recent trends have changed and intensified the risks. One recent, troublesome development is related to the increase in information technology in the hands of the public. Today, information is more attainable than ever with the internet, and information on VIPs, once limited to publications and public announcements, can now be accessed by handheld wireless devices, such as PDAs and mobile phones.

Therefore, care and retention of sensitive information and communications is particularly pertinent when advertising the event. When publicising the event, consider if the VIP attendance at the event is public or private, official or unofficial. The extent of pre-publicity or public knowledge of an event may cause the level of threat and the resultant security planning to change considerably.

Shared responsibilities

In dealing with the challenges, event security must coordinate with numerous other people and organizations charged with different portions of the same job: protecting VIPs. There are a multitude of agencies with executive protection authority. Political figures are notably protected by government security agencies. Police can sometimes be involved, particularly if a motorcade is involved that requires traffic rerouting. When it comes to entertainers and other non-political celebrities, the security is different but no less extensive, including private security firms and bodyguards.

With the current concerns about terrorist activities, when sizable crowds are formed, the government can be relied upon to take an interest. At any place where large numbers of people gather, especially with something that has publicity value, government security is involved.

For the most part, events can work smoothly with other security entities. For instance, when security agencies examine evacuation procedures they have certain emergency protocols and they will make sure the event organiser knows what is required. The common goal is safety and security, and both understand that each other's role is vital in providing the safest and most secure environment possible. Mostly the security agencies or police coordinate timing, travel routes into and out of the venue, travel around the venue and communication.

Celebrity behaviour

Two recurring problems are, however, having high-profile people take risks seriously, and dealing with their bodyguards.

Celebrities, of course, can be demanding of special treatment. VIP seating, special VIP parking and drop-off points close to VIP entrances. They expect security escorts to and from the drop-off point and to and from seating. They want their privacy protected and to be free from any harassment. However, some VIPs find security measures limit their personal freedom, or want to 'connect with their fans'. Resenting restrictions, they demand that there should be no security measures applied to them.

However, this is selfish and thoughtless behaviour that should not be accepted. Their celebrity itself creates a dangerous situation for everyone at an event. Therefore all high-profile people must be subject to the same security procedures. The awareness of security of celebrities requires an effort to educate the celebrities themselves regarding security risks at an event and how important it is to not have an 'it can't happen to me' mentality. Some VIPs travel without escorts, and safety advice should be provided on reducing their own vulnerability when travelling to and from a venue, avoiding predictable routines, not travelling in ostentatious vehicles, and so on.

Liaison with VIP security

Early identification of all organisations involved in the event, and their roles and responsibilities is essential. Planning must include details of the structures of each organisation and links between respective functional levels. In particular, the clarification of the role, powers and capability of any private security staff or stewards either permanent or temporarily contracted for the specific event. This includes any specialist skills required for searching, e.g. operating search equipment, search arches or luggage scanning.

The earlier the planning begins, the better the plan will be likely to be. Last-minute contacts made by visiting VIPs add stress to already very busy event activities prior to events. Mistakes are generally made when there isn't enough time to allow for a sensible, coordinated plan to be developed.

Even when there are no particular misunderstandings or personality conflicts, sometimes stresses between the event and the VIPs' security teams spring from logistics. That's often the case when changes occur shortly before a star's arrival, or when celebrities make surprise appearances that don't allow for much preparation.

The biggest challenge is to make sure both sides are on the same page. Often, travel plans change and last-minute adjustments need to be made. Communicating these changes is critical to be sure that both the event and VIP security staffs are ready and that both teams understand the need for security procedures, and they work together to be sure security procedures are followed and adhered to.

The preferred method is coordination between event security and the VIPs' security service through the event manager who is in direct communication with both to avoid any potential issues lost in transfer of communication.

High profile events

There may be events which, for various reasons, are deemed to be more high profile and therefore more vulnerable to attack. This may involve pre-event publicity of the attendance of a VIP or celebrity, resulting in additional crowd density on the event day and the need for an appropriate security response and increased vigilance.

In certain cases the local police may appoint a police commander with responsibility for the event to act as an adviser and coordinator to ensure that the security response is realistic and proportionate. This will include liaison with event management, identifying all the key individuals, agencies and departments involved in the event, as well as seeking advice from the relevant counter terrorism security on all terrorism related and protective security issues.

Enhanced security provision at high profile events

During high profile events there may be extra threats, not only from terrorism, but criminal activity, politically disruptive groups, fixated persons, self-publicists and lone adventurers.

Enhanced measures may be required in order to provide static protection or in order to eliminate or reduce the opportunity for attack by placing defensive perimeters between any protected person and a potential attacker. Depending on the nature of the threat and the outcome of the risk management process, consideration should be given to a range of physical, technical and procedural protective security options that may, on their own, be sufficient to exclude, deter, detect or disrupt the threat.

Extra measures to be considered

While celebrities create issues with personal privacy and protection wherever they go, the challenges are especially acute at public assembly venues. Event venues and facilities are not all the same. Different structural and functional challenges exist with each event and venue. The large size of many venues and the large numbers of people who attend events featuring VIPs add up to a large problem.

For major events an 'Island site' is commonly created to provide a sterile zone, with secure perimeter access which is rigorously controlled by static protection measures. Within this general zone, further security zones segregate VIPs from invited guests, the general public and the media. Physical and technical security measures may include:

- Physical protection measures such as extra doors, locks, lighting and target hardening.
- Technical measures including enhanced or extended CCTV and alarms if required.
- Arrangement of secured parking for VIP vehicles and consideration of parking restrictions adjacent to the venue if a VBIED threat is identified.

A 'green room' or place of safety where a VIP could shelter in the event of an incident must be provided. Planning must also incorporate the circumstances under which a venue will be evacuated and VIPs removed. This will include identification of safe routes to and from the venue, as well as safe evacuation/escape routes.

VIP area passes

The size and location of the venue and event means that securing areas is only part of the safety solution for these events. If somebody wants to gain access to a celebrity, they're not going to go through the VIP entry gate and walk by the police. They're going to try to sneak through the fence, or forge or steal credentials or passes. That's where the biggest vulnerabilities lie in terms of VIP security.

The situation is made worse by the fact that an event manager must rely on the trustworthiness of all the people he/she works with. That includes vendors, delivery drivers and service people, and even the event's own staff.

A list of people incorporating invited and confirmed guests to be issued with passes into the 'Island site' should be scrutinised and inspected by all the security agencies involved. The circulation of this list along with other key information such as chronology of events, copies of invitations, car passes and any other relevant materials, such as plans, maps and contact lists, specimen copies of any accreditation passes and badges allowing access to the various security zones, etc., should be restricted to security operatives and partners only.

Security passes

If a staff pass system is in place, insist that staff wear their passes at all times and that the issuing is strictly controlled and regularly reviewed. Visitors to private or restricted areas should be escorted and should wear clearly marked temporary passes, which must be returned on leaving. Anyone not displaying security passes in private or restricted areas should either be challenged or reported immediately to security or management. Passes should include a photograph of the bearer, and be returned against signature.

Summary

- Physical security is important in protecting against a range of threats such as antisocial elements in a crowd, criminals in search of victims, and people with psychological problems or social agendas.
- Security measures range from basic – keeping communal areas under surveillance, and security staff, CCTV, perimeter fencing, security lighting – to specialist solutions such as perimeter detection systems equipment.
- The composition of security services will vary according to the event. In many events, uniformed police perform functions such as traffic and drug violations and crime control, leaving internal event security to private personnel employed by the organisers.
- The greater the cooperation between security firms, event management, and the police, the better; and the larger the event the closer the liaison required.
- All staff, contractors and service providers should be issued with their own individual pass that should be worn at all times when on the site.
- The issuing of a pass must be strictly controlled and limited to senior security staff.
- All persons entering the event should go through a search regime. Everyone entering the event (including performers and VIP guests) should be subject to a bag search or security staff could conduct random bag searches.
- There is an increasing necessity to apply security screening to volunteers. Identity verification is the most basic level.
- Contract staff, such as security staff, traffic controllers, waste management contractors, stall holders and various infrastructure construction companies, present particular personnel security challenges as there is potential for security arrangements to be

confused or overlooked. Contractors must have the same level of security screening as the event staff.

● The responsibility for controlling potential threats to VIPs is an increasing challenge for venue safety and security.

Bibliography

Bellavita, C. (2007) 'Changing homeland security: A strategic logic of special event security', *Homeland Security Affairs* Vol. 3, No. 3, 1–23.

Emergency Management Australia (1999) *Safe and Healthy Mass Gatherings*. Manual Number 12. Australian Emergency Manuals Series. Commonwealth of Australia.

Emergency Management Australia (2004) *Multi-Agency Incident Management*. Manual Number 17. Australian Emergency Manuals Series. Commonwealth of Australia.

Erickson, L. (2008) *Spotting the Angry Attendee*. Coppell, TX: International Association of Assembly Managers.

Henricks, M. (2008) *Star Treatment*. Coppell, TX: International Association of Assembly Managers.

IAPCO (2004) *Safety and Security at Congresses: A Crucial Area of Risk Management*. London: International Association of Professional Congress Organizers.

Mellor, N. and Veno, A. (1998) *Public Events: Safety and Security Strategies*. Victoria: Centre for Police and Justice Studies, Monash University.

NaCTSO (2009) (Partial review: 2014) *Counter Terrorism Protective Security Advice for Major Events.* London: Association of Chief Police Officers of England and Wales and Northern Ireland (now National Police Chief Council).

Paternoster. J. (2010) *Blending Customer Service and Security*. Coppell, TX: International Association of Assembly Managers.

Price. C. L. (2007) *Choosing and Using Contract Security*. Coppell, TX: International Association of Assembly Managers.

Chapter 10

Counter terrorism protective security

Chapter objectives

This chapter provides guidelines for prevention measures and responses to terrorism attack.

Recent horrific terrorist incidents indicate that terrorists are targeting crowded places, and attacks on festivals and events are a real and serious danger. Terrorists generally select targets where they can cause most damage, inflict mass casualties or attract widespread publicity. Terrorism also includes threats or hoaxes designed to frighten and intimidate. Any event could be the target of a terrorist incident. This might include having to deal with a bomb threat or with suspect items left in or around the event area. In the worst case scenario staff and attendees could be killed or injured, and the venue destroyed or damaged in a 'no warning', multiple and coordinated terrorist attack.

At all events there may be a risk of a terrorist attack either because of the nature of the event or the number or nature of the people who host or attend it. The threat exists irrespective of size and capacity of an event and is not specific to any particular type of event. Smaller events in locations with limited protective security measures are possibly at higher risk than well protected mega events such as the Olympic Games. An attack on a food fair held in a town square is easier to accomplish than an attack on a football final in a stadium, and holds the same potential for mass fatalities and casualties.

Attacks by international terrorists are more likely to involve the use of improvised explosive devices, of which the three main types are, person-borne (suicide devices on the person or bag carried device), vehicle-borne (which may be suicide or non-suicide devices), hand delivered or placed devices (non-suicide devices initiated typically by timer or remote control). When suicide tactics are employed they allow terrorists to deploy their device (person or vehicle-borne) at the optimum time and place to maximise the impact in locations where a non-suicide device might be discovered. But terrorists are innovative and their methodology can be expected to change over time. Other means of terrorist attack (such as chemical, biological, radiological, or firearms) are also possible and protective security measures can help make a difference.

Terrorism risk is seen as uncontrollable (Sheppard 2011) which may add to the level of fear experienced. Terrorism implies intentionality, vulnerability and psychological impact (Goldstein 2005) and also includes a threat of further activity. Therefore it creates more fear and anxiety than other emergencies that may have similar actual consequences. Fear and misconceptions may lead people to place themselves in greater danger than that posed by the original incident itself (Gray and Ropeik 2002).

Counter terrorism protective security advice for major events

Prevention of, and responding to, terrorism emergencies is complex and challenging. They are low probability but high risk incidents. They often have no clear boundaries in time and no clear zones of danger and safety. Attacks can be difficult to identify at an early preventable stage, and may call for a large scale response and high capacity from multiple response organisations. And often there are large gaps between advised and real behaviour in terrorism emergencies (Rodgers et al. 2007). It is essential that protective security is undertaken in partnership with the police and other authorities. Preparation and mitigation calls for high level co-operation between expert agencies and experts and the event's security team.

The National Police Chief Council (NPCC) is a UK counter terrorism organisation that can call on the experience of many decades in counter terrorism and protective security by UK police that began with the bombing campaign by the IRA in the 1960s and continues today with attacks from al Qaeda and ISIS. Its advice and guidance to public organisation is provided through the National Counter-Terrorism Security Office (NaCTSO) website. On the site can be found current threat levels and constantly updated advice on all terrorism matters. The bulk of the material in this chapter is from the NaCTSO 2009/2014 publication *Counter Terrorism Protective Security Advice*

Definition box 10.1: Glossary of terms

Active shooter: A person armed with a firearm who is actively engaged in killing or attempting to cause serious harm to multiple people in a populated location.

Emergency management: The plans, structures and arrangements that are established to bring together government, voluntary and private agencies in a coordinated way to deal with emergency needs, including prevention, response and recovery.

Evacuation: The process of relocating people from dangerous or potentially dangerous areas to safer areas. The purpose of an evacuation is to use distance to separate people from the danger created by the emergency.

Mitigation: Measures taken before, during or after a disaster (emergency) to decrease or eliminate its impact on society (people) and the environment (places).

Places of mass gathering (PMG): Are characterised by having a large concentration of people on a predictable basis, and include a diverse range of facilities and sites such as sporting venues, shopping/business precincts, public transport hubs and tourism/entertainment venues.

Police first responder: The general-duties, uniformed police that often provide the initial policing response to calls for police assistance.

Police Tactical Group (PTG): A highly trained police unit that tactically manages and resolves high-risk incidents, including terrorist incidents.

Rapid deployment: The swift and immediate deployment of emergency services personnel to an ongoing situation where delayed deployment could result in serious injury or death.

Situational awareness: The ability to quickly recognise and interpret an event, make sound decisions based on those interpretations, and establish early, effective and continuous lines of communication between the incident site and the controlling agency in order to provide ongoing accurate information about the situation to responders.

Terrorist act: An act or threat committed with the intention of advancing a political, ideological or religious cause, and which is intended to coerce or intimidate an Australian government, a foreign government, or sections of the public, which causes serious physical harm or death to a person, endangers a person's life, causes serious damage to property, creates a serious risk to the health and safety of the public, or seriously interferes with, seriously disrupts, or destroys, an electronic system.

Australia–New Zealand Counter-Terrorism Committee (2015).

for Major Events. Some of the newer material is from 'Recognising the terrorist threat' downloaded from the gov.uk website (NaCTSO/gov.uk 2017). Other material is from publications by the Australia–New Zealand Counter-Terrorism Committee, and the US Department of Homeland Security.

Managing the terrorism risks

Not all risks or emergencies can be prevented, so the concept of prevention needs to have a much broader meaning, and should encompass activities that may reduce the severity or impact of the emergency. General prevention related activities can include gathering and analysing intelligence, developing strategies to reduce the impact on life/property and identifying or eliminating vulnerabilities at potential target event sites.

Events differ in many ways including size, location, layout and operation. Not all will share the same risk profile or have similar vulnerabilities, so the principle of 'proportionality' should generally be applied to any prevention-related activities. This means that protective security measures not only need to be proportionate to the level of assessed risk, but should also try to strike a balance between the threat to public safety and the expectations of the community. However, when measuring proportionality it should be recognised that prevention and mitigation measures for countering terrorism will also help against other threats, such as theft and criminal damage.

At some events there will be an expectation from the general public that security measures will be in place. Equally, an event may take place at a location or in premises where access control and elevated security are an unexpected and unusual (and initially unwelcome) feature. This does not negate responsibility to ensure appropriate security measures are in place.

Of course there is a need to make events as accessible as possible and to ensure there is a welcoming atmosphere within event arenas. The guidance in this chapter is not intended to create a 'fortress mentality'. There is however a balance to be achieved and there are robust protective security measures available to mitigate against the threat of terrorism which should integrate wherever possible with existing security.

Protective measures

Managing the risk of terrorism is a part of an event manager's responsibility when preparing contingency plans in response to any incident in or near an event. In regard to protective security, the best way to manage the hazards and risks to an event is to start by understanding and identifying the threats to it, and its vulnerability to those threats. This will help to decide what type of security and contingency plans need developing.

For some organised events, simple good practice – coupled with vigilance and well exercised contingency arrangements – may be all that is needed. If, however, if there is an assessment that the event is vulnerable to attack, appropriate protective security measures should be applied to reduce the risk to as low as reasonably practicable.

Step one: identify the threats

Understanding the terrorists' intentions and capabilities – what they might do and how they might do it – is crucial to assessing threat. Seek advice from the local police

Counter Terrorism Security Advisor (CTSA) on the threat and on defensive measures. Ask the following questions:

- What can be learnt from the government and media about the current security climate, or about recent terrorist activities?
- Is there anything about the location of the event, its attendees, sponsors, contractors, and staff, or particular activities that would particularly attract a terrorist attack?
- Is there an association with high profile individuals or organisations which might be terrorist targets?
- Are procedures in place and available for deployment on occasions when VIPs attend the event?
- Could collateral damage occur from an attack on, or other incident to a high risk neighbour?
- What information is available from the local police service about crime and other problems in the area of the event?

If the pre-event consultation suggests the event is at risk of attack, perhaps because of the nature or location of the event, then consider what others could find out about its vulnerabilities, such as information that is publicly available, e.g. on the internet or in public documents that identifies installations or services vital to the continuation of the event. Take into consideration any prestige targets that may be attractive to terrorists, regardless of whether their loss would result in event collapse or event cancellation.

Step two: protecting and identifying vulnerabilities

Priorities for protection should fall under the following categories: people (staff, attendees, concessionaires, contractors, general public affected by the presence of the event) and physical assets (buildings, contents, equipment).

There will be a need to develop bespoke plans for each location in a multi-venue event. There should already be plans in place for dealing with fire and crime, procedures for assessing the integrity of those employed or who provide contracting, and measures to secure the event site. There should also be measures in place to limit access into service or back of house areas, and control vehicle access into goods and service areas.

As with step one, consider whether there is an aspect of the event or activities that terrorists might want to exploit. How stringent are the checks on the staff and volunteers, or on your contract personnel? Are the staff security conscious? It is important that event staff can identify and know how to report suspicious activity.

Step three: identify measures to reduce risk

An integrated approach to security is essential. This involves thinking about physical security, information security and personnel security (i.e. good recruitment and employment practices). There is little point investing in costly security measures if they can be easily undermined by a disaffected member of staff or by a lax recruitment process. Before investing in additional security measures, review what is already in place, including known weaknesses such as blind spots in any CCTV system. Many of the security precautions typically used to deter criminals are also effective against terrorists. So before investing in additional security measures, review what is already in place. There may already be a good security regime that only needs strengthening.

Step four: review security measures and rehearse and review security and contingency plans

Rehearsals and exercises should, wherever possible, be conducted in conjunction with all partners, emergency services and local authorities.

Make sure that all staff understand and accept the need for security measures and that security is seen as part of everyone's responsibility, not merely something for security experts or professionals. Make it easy for people to raise concerns or report observations.

Threat levels

Globally, most countries have a government public access website that provides current information about the national terrorism threat level. For example In the UK it is the MI5 – Security Service Home Office and UK Intelligence Community websites. In the US the Department of Homeland Security provides the same service.

Terrorism threat levels are designed to give a broad indication of the likelihood of a terrorist attack (Table 10.1). They are based on the assessment of a range of factors including current intelligence, recent events and what is known about terrorist intentions and capabilities. This information may well be incomplete and decisions about the appropriate security response should be made with this in mind.

'Substantial' and 'Imminently severe' both indicate a high level of threat and that an attack might well come without warning.

Response levels

Response levels provide a broad indication of the protective security measures that should be applied at any particular time. They are informed by the threat level but also take into account specific assessments of vulnerability and risk.

Response levels tend to relate to sites, whereas threat levels usually relate to broad areas of activity. There are a variety of site specific security measures that can be applied within response levels, although the same measures will not be found at every location. The security measures deployed at different response levels should not be made public, to avoid informing terrorists about what we know and what we are doing about it.

Table 10.1 UK threat level definitions

Critical	An attack is expected
Imminently severe	An attack is highly likely
Substantial	An attack is a strong possibility
Moderate	An attack is possible but not likely
Low	An attack is unlikely

There are three levels of response which broadly equate to threat levels as shown below:

- **'Critical exceptional':** Maximum protective security measures to meet specific threats and to minimise vulnerability and risk.
- **'Severe substantial' to 'heightened':** Additional and sustainable protective security measures reflecting the broad nature of the threat combined with specific business and geographical vulnerabilities and judgements on acceptable risk.
- **'Moderate low' to 'normal':** Routine baseline protective security measures, appropriate to the event and location.

The counter measures to be implemented at each response level are a matter for individual event organisations and will differ according to a range of circumstances. All protective security measures should be identified in advance of any change in threat and response levels and should be clearly notified to those staff who are responsible for ensuring compliance.

Protective security planning

The following advice is generic for most events, but recognises that every event is built and operates differently. In the UK, advice and guidance on searching should be available through the local police security coordinator (SecCo), CTSA or police search adviser (PolSA).

It is recognised that for many larger organised events responsibility for the implementation of protective security measures following a vulnerability and risk assessment will fall on a security manager within the organisation team, who must have sufficient authority to direct the action taken in response to a security threat. Depending on the size of the event this role may be performed by more than one person and could be referred to in different job titles.

The security manager must be involved in the planning of the event's perimeter security, access control, contingency plans etc., so that the terrorist dimension is taken into account. The security manager must similarly be consulted over any temporary construction for the event and/or liaise with security personnel for any building used for the event so that counter terrorism recommendations, e.g. concerning surveillance, physical barriers can be factored in, taking into account any planning and safety regulations covered in police guides as well as any appropriate fire safety regulations.

The security manager at most organised events should already have responsibility for most if not all of the following key areas:

- the production of the security plan based on the risk assessment
- the formulation and maintenance of a search plan
- the formulation and maintenance of other contingency plans dealing with bomb threats, suspect packages, protected spaces and evacuation
- liaising with the police, other emergency services and local authorities
- arranging staff training, including his/her own deputies and conducting briefings/ debriefings
- conducting regular reviews of the plans.

For independent and impartial counter terrorism advice and guidance that is site specific, the security manager should establish contact with the local police counter terrorism security adviser (CTSA) to assess the threat, both generally and specifically. A counter terrorism security adviser can assist with undertaking a risk and vulnerability assessment that is specific to the event, and identify a range of practical protective security measures appropriate for each of the response levels.

Contact a counter terrorism security advisor (CTSA) through the local police force at the start of the process. As well as advising on physical security, they can provide information about professional bodies that regulate and oversee reputable suppliers. Local police security coordinators (SecCo) may be allocated to give security advice to large events, liaising with CTSAs for specialist advice on physical security measures.

It is important to obtain advice on physical security equipment being planned for use at the event and its particular application to the methods used by terrorists. The CTSA will be able to comment on its effectiveness as a deterrent, as protection and as an aid to post-incident investigation.

The CTSA will also:

- facilitate contact with emergency services and local authority planners to develop appropriate response and contingency plans
- identify appropriate trade firms for the supply and installation of security equipment
- offer advice on search plans
- assist contacting a police security coordinator (SecCo) for advice if appropriate.

Creating the security plan

When creating the security plan, consider the following:

- details of all the protective security measures to be implemented, covering physical, information and personnel security
- instructions on briefing content to security staff including type of behaviour to look for and methods of reporting
- instructions on how to respond to a threat (e.g. telephone bomb threat)
- instructions on how to respond to the discovery of a suspicious item or event
- evacuation response to a major incident
- event continuity plan – i.e. when to call off the event
- a communications and media strategy which includes handling enquiries from concerned family and friends.

Effective security plans are simple, clear and flexible, but must be compatible with any existing plans for premises/locations used for events, e.g. evacuation plans and fire safety strategies. Everyone must be clear about what they need to do in a particular incident. Once made, the plans must be followed. Successful security measures require:

- the support of senior management
- staff awareness of the measures and their responsibility in making them work
- a senior, identified person within the organisation having responsibility for security.

All necessary regulations will need to be met, such as local authority permissions, health and safety and fire prevention requirements. While it is important not to delay the introduction of necessary equipment or procedures, costs may be reduced if the premises or location to be used already has the necessary security which can be easily integrated within the event security plan.

Staff security awareness

The vigilance of staff (including concessionaire, cleaning, maintenance and contract staff) is essential for protective measures. They will know their own work areas very well and should be encouraged to be alert to unusual behaviour or items out of place. They must have the confidence to report any suspicions, knowing that reports, including false alarms, will be taken seriously and regarded as a contribution to the safe running of the event.

Training is therefore particularly important. Staff should be briefed to look out for packages, bags or other items in odd places, carefully placed (rather than dropped) items in rubbish bins and unusual interest shown by strangers in less accessible places. Review plans for protecting staff and visitors in the event of a terrorist threat or attack.

Any lack of vigilance around pedestrian and vehicle entrances to the event and queues forming outside the main event area affords anonymity to a potential terrorist. Security staff deployed externally should adopt a 'see and be seen' approach and where possible supervise queuing outside the event. The queue should be orderly, monitored by CCTV operators if available and communication between attendees and staff established. This is especially important if large numbers of persons are expected to queue to enter an event. Consider staging the queuing process to ensure security staff are given the opportunity to scrutinise every attendee as they enter the event site. Staff must be briefed on what to look for and how to deal with it.

Improvised explosive devices

Improvised explosive devices (IEDs) range in size from person-borne small containers, rucksacks and suitcases to larger devices, such as those that are vehicle-borne. The latter may be borne by a variety of vehicles, ranging from bicycles and motorcycles through to large goods vehicles (LGVs).

Once assembled, the bomb can be delivered at a time of the terrorist's choosing and with reasonable precision, depending on defences. It can be detonated from a safe distance using a timer or remote control, or can be detonated on the spot by a suicide bomber. Building a bomb requires a significant investment of time, resources and expertise. Because of this, terrorists will seek to obtain the maximum impact for their investment.

Explosive effects of a bomb

A homemade bomb can cause havoc in large crowd, primary and secondary devices can be devastating not just in terms of immediate damage but driving the crowd to narrow confined spaces. When an explosion occurs at ground level there are several effects created that cause damage and injury. The effects will depend on the power, quality, quantity and location of the explosive material deployed. The six basic effects of an explosion are:

- Blast wave: the blast wave is a very fast moving high pressure wave created by the rapidly expanding gas of the explosion. The pressure gradually diminishes with distance but can reflect and diffract around structures.
- Fire ball: the fire ball is created as part of the explosion process and is local to the seat of the explosion. It is generally associated with high explosives.
- Brisance: this is the shattering effect, is very local to the seat of the explosion and is generally associated with high explosives.
- Primary fragments: these are parts of the device or its container (including the vehicle if vehicle-borne) which have been shattered by the brisance effect and are propelled at high velocity over great distances.
- Secondary fragments: these are fragments that have been created by the blast wave. Typical secondary fragments include glass, roof slates, loose gravel, timber and metal. These can travel considerable distances.
- Ground shock: this is produced by the brisance effect of the explosion shattering the ground local to the seat of the explosion, i.e. creating a crater. The shock wave resulting from the crater's creation then continues through the ground.

Causes of fatalities, injuries and damage from blasts

The main causes of fatalities, injuries and damage as a result of an IED are:

- direct weapon effects including primary fragments, lung blast damage, thermal burns and ear drum rupture; secondary fragments such as glass, spall (flakes of material that are broken off a larger solid body) and other objects thrown by the blast
- structure collapse causing crush injuries
- post-event falling debris (including glazing, façade, internal walls etc.), damaged equipment and damaged infrastructure, which can hinder the speedy evacuation of buildings.

Controls

By identifying the areas that would be the most vulnerable, and therefore the most dangerous, security specialists can highlight where additional countermeasures, surveillance and management can be best deployed.

Ensure that all staff are trained in bomb threat handling procedures or at least have ready access to instructions and know where these are kept. Train and rehearse your staff in identifying suspect vehicles, and in receiving and acting upon bomb threats. Key information and telephone numbers should be prominently displayed and readily available.

Protocols applicable to most incidents

- Do not touch suspicious items.
- Move everyone away to a safe distance.
- Prevent others from approaching.
- Communicate safely to staff, business visitors and the public.
- Use hand-held radios or mobile phones away from the immediate vicinity of a suspect item, remaining out of line of sight and behind hard cover.

- Notify the police.
- Ensure that whoever found the item or witnessed the incident remains on hand to brief the police.

Site search

Searches of the event area for suspicious items should be conducted as part of a daily good housekeeping routine. They should also be conducted in response to a specific threat and when there is a heightened response level. As previously mentioned under Security Planning, it is recognised that for the majority of events responsibility for the implementation of any search planning, following a vulnerability and risk assessment, will fall upon the security manager.

Search plans

Search plans should be prepared in advance and staff should be trained in them. The overall objective is to make sure that the entire area, including grounds, are searched in a systematic and thorough manner so that no part is left unchecked. After an evacuation of the event in response to an incident or threat, there will be a need to search the event site in order to ensure it is safe for re-occupancy.

The police will not normally search events. They are not familiar with the layout and will not be aware of what should be there and what is out of place. They cannot, therefore, search as quickly or as thoroughly as a member of staff or on-site security personnel. The members of staff nominated to carry out the search do not need to have expertise in explosives or other types of device. But they must be familiar with the place they are searching. They are looking for any items that should not be there, that cannot be accounted for and items that are out of place. Vehicles, packages, luggage left unattended.

Ideally, searchers should search in pairs to ensure searching is systematic and thorough. The searchers need to get a feel for the logical progression through their designated area and the length of time this will take. They also need to be able to search without unduly alarming any person on site. The search plan should have a written checklist, signed when completed, for the information of the event security manager.

For the search, divide the event site into sectors of manageable size. A site is usually organised into entrance and walkways, auditoriums, stage and back stage areas, and service areas. Each should be identified as separate search sectors. Include any stairs, fire escapes, corridors, toilets and lifts in the search plan, as well as car parks, service yards and other areas outside, including evacuation assembly areas. Temporary information stands, concessionaires and kiosks should be searched before and after use and secured or moved when unattended. Waste bins require particular attention.

Following the search, staff should lock unoccupied offices, rooms and store cupboards; and place tamper-proof plastic seals on maintenance hatches.

Bomb threat

The vast majority of bomb threats are hoaxes designed to cause alarm and disruption. As well as the rare instances of valid bomb threats, terrorists may also make hoax bomb threat calls to intimidate the public, businesses and communities, to draw attention to their cause and to mislead police. While many bomb threats involve a person-to-person phone call, an increasing number are sent electronically using email or social media applications (e.g. Twitter or Facebook). A threat may be communicated via a third-party, i.e. a person or organisation unrelated to the intended victim and identified only to pass the message.

No matter how ridiculous or implausible the threat may seem, all such communications are a crime and should be reported to the police. Event organisation should have a protocol on how the threat information is recorded, acted upon and passed to police.

Suicide bomb attacks

The use of suicide bombers is a very effective method of delivering an explosive device to a specific location. Suicide bombers may use a lorry, plane or other kind of vehicle as a bomb or may carry or conceal explosives on their persons. Suicide attacks are generally perpetrated without warning.

Vehicle-borne improvised explosive devices (VBIEDs) are one of the most effective weapons in the terrorist's arsenal. They are capable of delivering a large quantity of explosives to a target and can cause a great deal of damage. It is not just the effects of a direct bomb blast that can be lethal, flying debris such as glass can present a hazard many metres away from the seat of the explosion.

Controls

When considering protective measures against suicide bombers, think in terms of:

- Using physical barriers to prevent a hostile vehicle from driving into the event through main entrances, goods/service entrances, pedestrian entrances or open land.
- Denying access to any vehicle that arrives at goods/service entrances without prior notice and holding vehicles at access control points into the event until it is established that they are genuine.
- Do not allow unchecked vehicles to park within the event areas or next to public areas where there will be large numbers of people or where there is a risk of structural collapse. Wherever possible, establishing the vehicle access control points at a distance from the event site, setting up regular patrols and briefing staff to look out for anyone behaving suspiciously.

Many bomb attacks are preceded by reconnaissance or trial runs. Ensure that no one visits the event site without proper authority and confirmed identity during the production phase.

A key strategy for minimising the effect of an attack is to prevent the attacker from reaching the areas of the event where they can do the most harm – where the crowd is at its most dense. The method being employed at several venues is to have the first contact with the security personnel as far as possible from the core areas by setting a perimeter crowd intercept fence with multiple bag and pass check gates as far as possible from the actual venue entrance queues. Surveillance is made easier by the thinner crowds in the open space between the perimeter fence and the venue where monitoring by CCTV and foot patrols. It is probable that a suicide bomber will detonate his/her explosives when challenged or detected at the check gates or in the open space, and this explosion, while devastating to those in the immediate vicinity, will not cause the mass casualties that would ensue if they had reached the core areas of the event.

Effective CCTV systems, especially those with an active monitoring and response, may deter a terrorist attack or even identify planning activity. Good quality images can provide crucial evidence in court. There is no definitive physical profile for a suicide bomber, so monitoring staff must be vigilant and report anyone suspicious to the police.

Firearm attacks

Terrorist use of firearms has become frequent, and it is important to consider this method of attack and be prepared to cope with such an incident. Most attacks are made using small arms. Such attacks are popular with terrorist groups, because they are relatively easy to plan and carry out, can cause a high number of casualties, and effectively spread terror throughout the population.

Known terrorist groups are not the only potential source of threat. Any extremist ideology can give rise to a lone actor, while some individuals may not be motivated by any ideology at all. The deadliest mass casualty shooting to occur in Australia, the Port Arthur massacre in 1996, was perpetrated by an individual with no links to an extremist ideology. The Anders Breivik terrorist attack in Norway in July 2011 demonstrates that attacks can occur without forewarning and security services cannot guarantee alert notice of all terrorist attack planning. It is a reminder that attacks may also be inspired by many forms of ideology and driven by local issues.

The typical attacker, in police terminology an active shooter, will attempt to kill and injure as many people as possible within a short period of time. This is why they generally target places where they can achieve the greatest impact – i.e. crowded places. An active shooter incident does not generally include a hostage situation, but can potentially transition into one, particularly during the police resolution phase.

Most incidents can vary greatly from one attack to another. However, there are some common elements for the majority of active shooter incidents; namely:

- Incidents often occur in crowded places where the attacker can access a large number of potential victims.
- Most incidents will evolve rapidly and are often over within 10–15 minutes.
- Many active shooters will continue to attempt to harm victims until confronted by law enforcement personnel or some other type of intervention occurs.
- Most incidents will not be effectively resolved through negotiation or peaceful means.

Controls

In most incidents, active shooters need freedom of movement and ready access to victims in order to achieve their objective. Therefore, minimising the offender's access to potential victims should be the primary objective of any plans or strategies. This is most likely to be achieved through the following activities:

- initiating immediate response activities
- minimising the duration of the incident

- restricting the offender's movements
- moving people from danger
- preventing people from entering the scene
- helping police to locate and contain the shooter.

Shooter's Time + Freedom of Movement = Increased Casualties

For most types of hostile attacks, prevention activities should aim to deter a would-be attacker by providing obvious physical and electronic security measures, coupled with good risk management practices that:

- detect an intrusion – by providing alert and visual detection systems
- delay or limit the intrusion for a sufficient period to allow a response force to attend – by putting in place measures that will potentially limit the movement of the offender.

Prevention-related activities specifically aimed at mitigating or reducing the severity of the incident should also be considered. The main focus of those activities should be on restricting the movement of the offender/s while reducing their access to further victims. How to best achieve this will depend on many variables, such as the physical design and security features of the venue, the movement of the offender and the opportunities for escape/shelter in place.

The US Department of Homeland Security has developed the *Active Shooter: How to Respond* guide that is widely used internationally and outlines three key areas of focus.

1 Escape: Building occupants should consider evacuating the facility if it is safe to do so. They should leave behind most belongings and determine the safest escape route before beginning to move. Maintaining concealment or cover from gunfire while moving is also important.
2 Hide: If safely evacuating the venue is not possible, occupants should seek to hide in a secure area where they can lock the door, lock or blockade the door with heavy furniture, cover windows, turn off lights and remain silent. Mobile phones should also be turned to silent.
3 Take action: If the option of hiding in place is adopted, individuals should continually re-assess the situation and their opportunities to safely evacuate or better secure themselves within the premises. They may also need to consider options to incapacitate the active shooter in the event they are located. This can include using or throwing available objects or using aggressive force when confronted. Such action should only be taken as a last resort and in order to protect the life of the individual or others in that area.

Staff protocols for a firearms/weapons incident

1 Run to a place of safety.

Good cover:
- Substantial brickwork or concrete
- Engine blocks
- Base of large live trees
- Natural ground undulations

Bad cover:
- Internal partition walls
- Car doors
- Wooden fences
- Glazing

2 Hide. Lock the doors if possible and remain quiet. As far as possible, limit access and secure the immediate environment. Encourage people to avoid public areas or access points. Find the best available protection from ballistics. Remember, out of sight does not necessarily mean out of danger.
3 Tell. Immediately contact the police and the control room.
4 Report: exact location of the incident, number of gunmen, type of firearm – are they using a long-barrelled weapon or handgun? Direction of travel – are they moving in any particular direction?

Use all the channels of communication available to inform visitors and staff of the danger.

Police response

Due to the dynamic nature of active shooter incidents, highly trained and equipped police tactical group operators may be unable to respond to a scene in a timely manner. As such, uniformed, general-duties police officers will generally provide the initial response to most active shooter situations and may potentially manage them to their conclusion. While the specific tactics, policies and training of police first responders may vary across jurisdictions, it is expected that the following objectives will guide their initial response activities.

Mission

The main objective of the police first responders in an active shooter incident is to save lives and prevent further loss of life or injuries. This will generally be achieved through a rapid deployment strategy.

The focus of a rapid deployment strategy should be to reduce or suppress the threat posed by the active shooter as quickly as possible. Cordon, manage and negotiate strategies are unlikely to be effective in reducing the time a shooter has to achieve their desired outcomes, or limiting their freedom of movement. The most appropriate response to an active shooter incident will also depend on many other factors, including available police resources, the incident setting and the tactics or weapons involved.

Locate and isolate

Once the decision to rapidly deploy has been made, the focus will generally be on how to reduce the offender's area of operation and access to potential victims. This is best achieved by quickly locating the offender and restricting their movement. To achieve this, first responders may initially need to keep moving past casualties and panicked people to try and reach the offender and contain the threat as quickly as possible.

Command and control

Any response to a major emergency or incident should be managed by an appropriate command, control and coordination structure. In active shooter situations, however, this might not be achievable in the first instance as it may affect any rapid deployment activities. The need to establish effective command and control of the incident, including coordination with venue management, may therefore become a secondary priority that is delegated to subsequent responding units.

Police will conduct some form of major investigation for all active shooter incidents. This could involve criminal and forensic investigations in relation to potential criminal offences (including acts of terrorism), as well as coronial investigations on behalf of the coroner. These investigation processes will need to be extremely thorough and may often be protracted, particularly where the incident has occurred over a broad geographical area, or involves significant forensic challenges.

During the investigation phase the police may also seek assistance from management at the location to help identify potential sources of evidence or witnesses. This could include CCTV footage, and radio, telephone or decision-making logs. Recovery or business continuity plans should identify a suitable liaison officer that can work with the police to help facilitate these types of requests.

Protected spaces

Depending on the layout of the event, in a bomb threat or firearm attack, evacuation may be safer into windowless corridors or basements than outside the building, which is the normal case in emergencies. Protected spaces in permanent structures may offer the best protection against ballistics, bomb blast, flying glass and other fragments. They may also offer the best protection when the location of the active shooter or possible bomb is unknown, or when the threat is near the external evacuation route, or when there is an external attack. Since glass and other fragments may kill or maim at a considerable distance from the centre of a large explosion, moving people into protected spaces is often safer than evacuating them onto the streets. Protected spaces should be located:

- in areas surrounded by full height masonry walls e.g. internal corridors, toilet areas or auditoriums with doors opening inwards
- away from windows and external walls
- away from the area in between the building's perimeter and the first line of supporting columns (known as the 'perimeter structural bay')
- away from stairwells or areas with access to lift shafts where these open at ground level onto the street, because blast can travel up them. If, however, the stair and lift cores are entirely enclosed, they could make good protected spaces
- avoiding ground floor or first floor if possible
- in an area with enough space to contain the occupants.

When choosing a protected space, seek advice from a structural engineer with knowledge of explosive effects and do not neglect the provision of toilet facilities, seating, drinking water and communications. Try to locate vital emergency control systems in part of the event site that offers similar protection to that provided by a protected space.

Open air events

If the event is predominantly in the open with only temporary demountable structures such as marquees, event kiosks or simply an open space, the protected space principle is unlikely to offer any suitable refuge and evacuation may be the only option.

Suspicious deliveries

Events often necessitate receiving a wide variety of deliveries. This offers an attractive route into premises for terrorists. Delivered items, which include letters, parcels, packages and anything delivered by post or courier, has been a commonly used terrorist device. Delivered items may be explosive or incendiary (the two most likely kinds), or chemical, biological or radiological.

Consider the need for a screening process at the delivery handling site, whether at a temporary or permanent structure. Anyone receiving a suspicious delivery is unlikely to know which type it is, so protocols and procedures should cater for every eventuality.

Delivered explosive or chemical devices come in a variety of shapes and sizes; a well-made one will look innocuous but there may be tell-tale signs.

Indicators of suspicious deliveries/mail

- It is unexpected or of unusual origin or from an unfamiliar sender.
- There is no return address or the address cannot be verified.
- It is poorly or inaccurately addressed e.g. incorrect title, spelt wrongly, title but no name, or addressed to an individual no longer with the company.
- The address has been printed unevenly or in an unusual way.
- The writing is in an unfamiliar or unusual style.
- There are unusual postmarks or postage paid marks.
- A Jiffy bag, or similar padded envelope, has been used.
- It seems unusually heavy for its size. Most letters weigh up to about 28g or 1oz, whereas most effective letter bombs weigh 50–100g and are 5mm or more thick.
- It is marked 'personal' or 'confidential'.
- It is oddly shaped or lopsided.
- It has an unusual smell.
- It is tightly taped or tied (however, in some organisations delicate equipment is often well wrapped as standard procedure).

Controls

Although any suspect item should be taken seriously, remember that most will be false alarms, and a few may be hoaxes. Try to ensure that procedures, while effective, are not needlessly disruptive, take the following into account in planning:

- Consider processing all incoming mail and deliveries at one point only. this should ideally be off-site or in a separate building, or at least in an area that can easily be isolated and in which deliveries can be handled without taking them through other parts of the event or site.
- Ensure that all staff who handle deliveries are briefed and trained.
- Make certain that delivery opening areas can be promptly evacuated. Rehearse evacuation procedures and routes.
- Prepare signs for display to staff in the event of a suspected or actual attack.

Chemical, biological or radiological material attacks

Terrorists may seek to place chemical, biological or radiological (CBR) materials into the event site. There have only been a few examples of terrorists using CBR materials. The most notable were the 1995 sarin gas attack on the Tokyo subway and the 2001 anthrax letters in the United States. In 1996 in the US, an Al-Qaeda operative was sentenced for conspiracy to murder for his part in planning attacks using 'dirty bombs', which contained radioactive material.

The impact of a CBR attack would depend heavily on the success of the chosen method and the weather conditions at the time of the attack. The first indicators of a CBR attack may be the sudden appearance of powders, liquids or strange smells within the building, with or without an immediate effect on people.

It is difficult to provide a full list of possible CBR indicators because of the diverse nature of the materials. At present, there are no CBR detectors capable of identifying all hazards reliably. However, some of the more common and obvious are:

● unexpected granular, crystalline or finely powdered material (of any colour and usually with the consistency of coffee, sugar or baking powder), loose or in a container
● unexpected sticky substances, sprays or vapours
● unexpected pieces of metal or plastic, such as discs, rods, small sheets or spheres
● strange smells, e.g. garlic, fish, fruit, mothballs, pepper – however, some CBR materials are odourless and tasteless
● stains or dampness on the packaging.
● sudden onset of illness or irritation of skin, eyes or nose.

CBR devices containing finely ground powder or liquid may be hazardous without being opened.

Controls

The precise nature of the incident (chemical, biological or radiological) may not be readily apparent. Keep the response plans general and wait for expert help from the emergency services. A full site evacuation may not be the best solution. Be guided by the emergency services.

Staff who are responsible for delivery handling should be made aware of the importance of isolation in reducing contamination. Where a hazard can be isolated by leaving the immediate area, do so as quickly as possible, closing doors and windows.

Move those directly affected by an incident to a safe location as close as possible to the scene of the incident, so as to minimise spread of contamination. Separate those directly affected by an incident from those not involved so as to minimise the risk of inadvertent cross-contamination. Provide washing facilities in which contaminated staff could be isolated and treated.

Heavy vehicle attacks

A recent appalling addition to the weapons in the terrorist's arsenal is the simple act of driving a heavy vehicle at speed through a crowd. This type of attack usually occurs at open events conducted on streets or pedestrian malls.

Controls

If there is a plausible threat, institute effective vehicle access controls, particularly at goods entrances and service areas. Insist that contractor delivery vehicles and the identity of the driver and any passengers approaching the goods/service areas are authorised in advance. Consider a vehicle search regime at goods/service entrances that is flexible and can be tailored to a change in threat or response level. Be suspicious of delivery vehicles or other trucks attempting to access the main driveway to the event at the wrong time or outside of normal hours.

Consider using robust physical barriers to keep all but authorised vehicles at a safe distance. Wherever possible, establish the vehicle access control points at a distance from the event site, and brief staff to look out for anyone behaving suspiciously.

Establish roadblocks along the outskirts of the event, which could cause any vehicle attempting to breach security to crash and any other structural measures that prevent access to, or close proximity of, unscreened vehicles to the event space, and that reduce the speed of vehicles, such as bends or chicanes. So-called 'hostile vehicle mitigation' has already seen airport approach roads rerouted away from terminal entrances, installation of concrete bollards on sidewalks and the introduction of checkpoints away from busy terminals.

It should be emphasised that the installation of physical barriers needs to be balanced against the requirements of safety and should not be embarked upon without full consideration of planning regulation and fire safety risk assessment.

A spike strip (also known as traffic spikes, or tire shredders), can be used to impede or stop the movement of wheeled vehicles by puncturing their tyres. Generally, the strip is composed of a collection of long metal barbs, teeth or spikes pointing upward designed to puncture tyres when a vehicle is driven over them. There are two sizes – portable strips that can be quickly positioned by two people are suitable for impeding cars and light vehicles, and heavy duty strips that require installation and are intended to hinder larger vehicles. However, the strips are only a partial control device as vehicles can still be driven on wheel rims, albeit at a lower speed with less steering control.

It is hoped that a relatively simple technology can provide a solution. A British firm has developed a system that can disable the engines of moving targets such as boats or cars by emitting radio frequency pulses that overload the sensors in a vehicle's electronic controls. For as long as it emits the pulses, the engine cannot be restarted. The RF Safe-Stop system created by e2v Technologies uses blasts of electromagnetic pulses to remotely shut off any car engines that are targeted by the device. The transmitter must be mounted beside or above a roadway and can be triggered up to 50 metres distance from the suspicious vehicle.

Hostile reconnaissance

Terrorist operatives may visit potential targets a number of times prior to the attack. Hostile reconnaissance is used on potential targets during the preparatory and operational phases of terrorist operations. It is conducted to obtain a profile of the target location, determine the best method of attack and the optimum time to conduct the attack. Where pro-active security measures are in place, they pay particular attention to any variations in security patterns and the flow of people in and out. Reconnaissance trips may be undertaken as a rehearsal to involve personnel and equipment that will be used in the actual attack.

The ability of the event's security staff to recognise those engaged in hostile recon-naissance could disrupt an attack.

What to look for

- significant interest being taken in the outside of the event site including parking areas, delivery gates, doors and entrances
- groups or individuals taking significant interest in the location of CCTV cameras and controlled areas
- people taking pictures, filming, making notes or sketching of the security measures around events
- strangers walking around the perimeter of the event and being over attentive to surroundings, persons loitering around area for a prolonged amount of time
- vehicles parked outside buildings of other facilities, with one or more people remaining in the vehicle, for longer than would be considered usual
- a person parking, standing or loitering in the same area on numerous occasions with no apparent reasonable explanation
- a person asking unusual questions about number and routine of staff/VIPs visiting the site or event
- individuals asking questions regarding the identity or characteristics of individual visitors, groups of visitors, or the jobs or nationalities of visitors, that attend or may visit the event
- persons asking questions regarding security and evacuation measures
- persons asking questions regarding event staff hangouts
- people attempting to gain entry to the event site during the production phase using suspicious, counterfeit, altered passes or documents etc.
- non-co-operation with police or security personnel.

Those engaged in reconnaissance will often attempt to enter premises to assess the internal layout and in doing so will alter their appearance and provide cover stories. In the past reconnaissance operatives have drawn attention to themselves by ask-ing peculiar and in depth questions of employees or others more familiar with the environment.

Controls

Sightings of suspicious activity should be passed immediately to security management for CCTV monitoring, active response where possible and the event recorded for evi-dential purposes. Suspicious activity that does not require an immediate response, should be immediately reported to the anti-terrorist hotline; for any incident that requires an immediate response call police.

Summary

- Any event could be the target of a terrorist attack. Smaller events in locations with limited protective security measures are possibly at higher risk than well protected mega events such as the Olympic Games.
- Terrorist attacks are low probability but high risk incidents.

- Attacks by international terrorists are more likely to involve the use of improvised explosive devices, firearms or heavy vehicles.
- Attacks can be difficult to identify at an early preventable stage, and may call for a large scale response and high capacity from multiple response organisations.
- Prevention of, and responding to, terrorism emergencies is complex and challenging. They often have no clear boundaries in time and no clear zones of danger and safety.
- It is essential that protective security is undertaken in partnership with the police and other authorities and high level co-operation between expert agencies and experts and the event's security team.
- General prevention related activities can include gathering and analysing intelligence, developing strategies to reduce the impact on life/property and identifying or eliminating vulnerabilities at potential target event sites.
- Most countries have a government public access website that provides current information about the national terrorism threat level.
- For independent and impartial counter terrorism advice and guidance that is site specific, the Security Manager should establish contact with the local police Counter Terrorism Security Advisor (CTSA) to assess the threat, both generally and specifically.
- The vigilance of staff (including concessionaire, cleaning, maintenance and contract staff) is essential for protective measures. Staff should be briefed to look out for packages, bags or other items in odd places, and unusual interest shown by strangers in the site security arrangements.
- Depending on the layout of the event, in a bomb threat or firearm attack, evacuation may be safer into windowless corridors or basements than outside a building, which is the normal case in emergencies.

Bibliography

Australia–New Zealand Counter-Terrorism Committee (2015) *Active Shooter Guidelines for Places of Mass Gathering*. Attorney-General's Department Commonwealth of Australia.

Bellavita. C. (2007) 'Changing Homeland Security: A strategic logic of special event security', *Homeland Security Affairs*, 3(3), 1–23.

Department of Homeland Security (2016) *Active Shooter: How to Respond Guide*. Washington, DC. Online. Available HTTP: <https://www.dhs.gov/xlibrary/assets/active_shooter_booklet.pdf>.

Emergency Management Australia (2004) *Multi-Agency Incident Management* Manual Number 17. Australian Emergency Manuals Series. Commonwealth of Australia.

Emergency Management Australia (2004) *Emergency Planning* Manual Number 43. Australian Emergency Manuals Series. Commonwealth of Australia.

Goldstein, B. D. (2005) 'Advances in risk assessment and communication', *Annual Review of Public Health*, 26(1), 141–163.

Goss, B. D., Jubenville, C. B. and MacBeth, J. L. (2003) *Primary Principles of Post-9/11 Stadium Security in the United States: Transatlantic Implications from British Practices*. Murfreesboro, TN: Middle Tennessee State University. PRTM.

Gray, G. M. and Ropeik, D. P. (2002) 'Dealing with the dangers of fear: The role of risk communication', *Health Affairs*, 21(6), 106–116.

NaCTSO (2009) (Partial review: 2014) *Counter Terrorism Protective Security Advice for Major Events.* London: Association of Chief Police Officers of England and Wales and Northern Ireland (now National Police Chief Council).

NaCTSO/gov.uk (2017) 'Recognising the terrorist threat'. Online. Available HTTP: <https://www.gov.uk/government/publications/recognising-the-terrorist-threat/recognising-the-terrorist-threat>, accessed 10 May 2017.

Rodgers, M. B., Amlot, R., Rubin, G. J., Wessely, S. and Krieger, K. (2007) 'Mediating the social and psycological impacts of terrorist attacks: The role of risk perception and risk communication', *International Review of Psychiatry*, 19(3), 279–288.

Sheppard, B. (2011) 'Mitigating terror and avoidance behavior through the risk perception matrix to augment resilience', *Journal of Homeland Security Emergency Management*, 8(1), 1547–7355.

U.S. Army (2008) *How to Survive an Active Shooter*, Fort A.P. Hill, VA: U.S. Department of Homeland Security.

Chapter 11

Emergency response

Chapter objectives

This chapter concerns responses to emergencies. It provides guidelines on:

- The role of an Emergency Operations Centre
- Emergency communications systems and procedures
- Evacuation procedures and protocols.

Emergency response

An emergency is an event, actual or imminent, which endangers or threatens to endanger life, property or the environment, and which requires a significant, immediate and coordinated response of either, or all, police, ambulance, first aid, fire brigade or disaster management services. An emergency is a situation where the emergency services become actively involved or an urgent evacuation is required. Broadly speaking, they will be situations with the potential for serious injuries requiring immediate and specialist action beyond the capabilities of event operations staff. Emergencies may include:

- fires
- explosions
- terrorism action or threats
- collapse of a structure such as seating, staging or a lighting pylon
- release of hazardous substances such as a gas leak
- unanticipated hostile weather conditions such as flooding or high winds
- excessive or uncontrollable crowd disturbance or rioting.

An emergency incident causes an immediate threat to life, health, property or environment and leads to situations in which important decisions involving threat and opportunity have to be made in a particular short time. An emergency may include multiple incidents at the same time.

Definition box 11.1

Task saturation is when so many things happen at once that, even though each task can be solved in isolation, the combined effect becomes so overwhelming that inaction can result. The challenge of simultaneous small crises requires a strategic method of assessing a mix of threats co-existing in the same time and place.

Emergency situations demand leadership and guidance, initiating crowd evacuation as quickly as possible if required; strategies for communicating with the crowd to provide information; communication with emergency response agencies, and awareness of how individuals are likely to behave during an emergency.

Event operational management procedures must:

- detail arrangements for on-site emergencies not requiring outside help
- specify arrangements to request further police and other emergency services assistance
- specify arrangements to hand over control to police and emergency services as required
- identify personnel who can authorise evacuation
- identify how the event will be interrupted or cancelled.

Included in the emergency procedures are:

- how information should be passed on to the emergency services and by whom
- communication with attendees, staff and outside bodies

- management of the emergency, or dealing with the occurrence itself
- crowd management in an emergency situation
- evacuation procedures
- assistance to the emergency services
- criteria for re-opening the venue and allowing the return of the public.

The other bodies who will be involved in dealing with any emergency situations that may occur at the event are:

- the authorities who enforce the relevant legislation, such as police, the local government authority, fire services and any relevant government departments
- the emergency services, including nearby hospitals and on-site first aid providers
- all those involved in the event operation, such as security firms, sub-contractors and concessionaires operating at the venue
- nearby sites which could be affected by an emergency or subsequent evacuation.

Note: In any major incident, for the purposes of the law, the venue is considered a crime scene and thus under total control of the police.

Cancelling the event

Some potential disasters are foreseeable. The approach of severe weather will require immediate consideration of the safety for attendees and the decision to partially or completely cancel the event. The question of whether the event staff and facilities are prepared for a major storm, inclement weather, bush fire, flood, or other natural safety issues should be the main consideration.

In the event of a foreseeable emergency situation, while calling off an event is clearly a last option, attendees' safety is always of primary focus and concern. Careful risk analysis prior to an event and the subsequent ESMS policy and planning should include cancellation decision making policy and processes.

The key question is when to cancel. Determining when the peak impact of that decision may be on any and all of the event's stakeholders – the performers, service suppliers, sponsors, etc. How can the timing of the cancellation decision strike that delicate balance between those unhappy that the event wasn't cancelled soon enough and those unhappy that the event was cancelled at all?

An argument can be made for several decisions; an early cancellation prior to when many would be travelling to the event, a cancellation on the day just before the event begins, or, just hoping for the best and being prepared for the worst as the event goes on. It is common and understandable to think of the financial repercussions when making cancellation decisions, but the potential impact on attendees must always be the most important consideration.

The late cancellation decision that often seems to be used in the event industry, especially just a few hours before an event begins, is perhaps the worst possible choice. In that situation, attendees are in for an uncertain experience no matter what, and the hesitation to make a decision may have a more dramatic effect than anticipated. Event organisers often see this choice as one that relieves them of the need for a backup plan and covers their own liability, but that is not the case as several successful litigation hearings have ruled.

It is always advisable to seek, and heed, the advice of emergency services about the possible severity and effects of the hazard, and the timing for notices of cancellation or all clear to continue the event.

Suspending or re-scheduling

There is not a clear moment in many events when a decision about cancellation should be made. It may be that the situation can be managed by simply waiting until the storm or emergency has passed. If an event has to be shortened or otherwise adjusted, the question is, what gets cut from the programme? It's crucial to consider the ticketing contract that may require that certain elements be covered. Focus on the must-haves instead of the nice-to-haves, and what items were the most expensive. If the performers have any degree of scheduling flexibility, move their appearances to a time when the majority of attendees will be able to safely attend.

Conversely, some programmes might need to be expanded. The first question is whether the venue or facility is available for another day. Of course, if performers are flying in for an event, changing their plane tickets might also be difficult, so this is an option to consider very carefully.

Cancellation process

If a cancellation must occur, have a clear protocol for how to communicate effectively with attendees prior to the event. Pre-event audience communications should not only be used for event promotion, but also in case important information needs to be relayed. If there is uncertainty about a situation or an unexpected circumstance is unfolding, chances are members of the event audience are also uncertain about their attendance. Have a plan in place to keep them aware of any changes. If possible, provide advance notice of cancellation, before patrons begin entering the venue.

Communication with the crowd should not be delayed if cancellation occurs after entry. Announcements should clearly establish refund policies, exit routes, and need for orderly movement.

There will also be a strong need to be in constant contact with all the event stakeholders – performers, staff, sub-contractors, service providers. Have one central stream of communication run by one person to ensure that all messaging is consistent. In addition to displaying regular updates on the event website, those updates should also reach across all media channels, both mass and social. These don't have to be long updates, they just need to keep everyone informed as the situation develops.

Event cancellation insurance is available through many insurance vendors and is always worth the small amount necessary to cover what may be extensive losses for many parties. Don't hold an event without it. Have procedures for the refunding of ticket sales, and cancellation clauses in contracts with sponsors, performers and service suppliers.

Emergency Operations Centre (EOC)

On any event site there needs to be staff and resources in place to deal with potential problems. An Emergency Operations Centre (EOC) is a facility for control of operations and coordination of resources. It is the focus of the emergency response and recovery structure. The EOC is usually centrally located in the administration centre at festival sites, and provided with open communication, reserve finance and personnel able to make informed decisions as required. Operational and administrative procedures for the EOC are usually covered in the protocols which lay down actions to be followed by staff during operations. These should ensure that:

- response to the signs of an imminent emergency should be immediate
- staff should never underestimate the seriousness of the situation
- a multi-agency approach, with all parties consulted, should be adopted.

Within the EOC at all times there must be staff trained in emergency procedures. A register needs to be made to ensure that this occurs. Often, first aid officers, fire wardens, and security staff are allocated emergency response roles as well. The Australian standard specifies the roles and responsibilities, selection criteria and training requirements for EOC personnel.

Everyone on site needs to know who the EOC staff are. This is usually made clear by colour-coded equipment, such as helmets and Hi-Vis vests that are worn during emergencies.

Documented procedures

The EOC procedures need to be documented and formatted appropriately. They need to:

- state their purpose and scope
- be based on the assessed risk
- address the specifics of the event site
- identify roles and responsibilities
- provide flexibility for the EOC to allow for various circumstances
- take into account the hours when people are on site.

The procedures need to be publicised, accessible and used in training drills.

The EOC has important emergency communication responsibilities. Both internal (to the crowd and event staff) and external (to police, ambulance, fire and rescue services) communications should be coordinated through someone responsible for seeing that messages are made clearly and accurately. It can be extremely stressful and dangerous if, during a serious emergency, misinformation or rumours are spread. This cannot be prevented completely, but can be minimised by having a single source identified as reliable and trusted to whom all staff refer. Before any public announcements are made, facts must be verified and updated in response to enquiries or as further details come to hand and have been clarified. In most cases, the person responsible will be the event safety officer, the event director or the communications officer in the EOC.

Within the EOC should be a secure communications control room that facilitates the provision of vital information by centralised monitoring of relevant radio communications and CCTV surveillance. All emergency communications ought to be channelled through the room which should either be staffed with, or have direct immediate contact with, a representative from each major emergency service agency.

It is essential that the EOC Emergency Communication System for staff, emergency services, and the crowd is an efficient all-service communications system that is simple to activate and operate that:

- provides coverage both within and between organisations
- has compatibility with emergency services' systems
- has a dedicated radio frequency for emergency control and coordination
- has a back-up system in case of primary system failure
- has a back-up power supply.

Communication technology is of great importance and distributing and unifying information is a major issue both in early response and at later stages. For complete communication and effective distribution of information during an emergency, technical infrastructure that is inter-operable and robust for environmental influences is very important. It must also be conceptual and terminological unified to avoid misinterpretations.

Staff

Selecting and briefing the emergency communications team is one of the more difficult tasks. The size of the team will depend on the scale of the issues, but it should include members of management, a team leader, operations coordinators, security and technical experts. Security managers could involve their local police security coordinator when considering holding a significant event.

Security managers should regularly meet with staff to discuss security issues and ensure that staff know their security roles and that they or their deputies are always contactable. All staff, including volunteers and temporary staff, should know how to contact police and security staff. There should also be arrangements for dealing with people who are not employees of the event organisation (e.g. performers, contractors, stall holders).

Transition considerations

Responsibility for implementing and coordinating initial response activities will, in most instances, be assumed by the venue/facility management or security staff in the EOC until emergency agency responders, i.e. police, fire, ambulance, rescue service, are able to take over that responsibility. A critical aspect of managing that response and transitioning responsibility will be the ability to gain 'situational awareness'.

Establishing early, effective and continuous lines of communication from the incident site to the EOC and the responding agency will be critical in order to accurately inform them of the present situation and its subsequent development.

Knowing or understanding the expectations of emergency responders will also enable a faster transition of incident management. Planning and staff capability/training activities should include developing strategies that allow designated staff to safely maintain situational awareness of the incident and relay any new information to first responders. The preferred response when agencies arrive may vary and security staff should consult with local agencies when developing the response plan.

Emergency power

Most event venues rely on the electricity gird infrastructure for power supply. Power failure, caused by storm, excessive power draw leading to an overload cut out, or an on-site accident or grid failure, creates an emergency situation. Backup power supply is essential to provide short-term power to emergency systems, such as all the egress lighting for a minimum of up to 4 hours. Public address systems, security cameras and access control systems may all also be considered essential systems for emergency backup. The duration of an emergency power outage is difficult to predict and causes vary widely. In the wake of major storms, power may come back to some areas almost immediately, or be out for many hours or days. It depends on the damage to the infrastructure.

Providing temporary power in an emergency is a many-faceted issue. Batteries can form an important part of emergency power backup, in the form of uninterruptible power supplies that switch on instantly in the event of a power failure. This keeps essential systems going for a few seconds or minutes, until motorized generators (gensets) can start up and begin contributing power. The EOC should be equipped with small generators to power chargers for batteries to keep emergency radios, cellular phones and flashlights fully charged.

Some permanent venues may have standby gensets that provide short-term power to emergency systems. These usually operate only for a few hours continuously before needing to be shut down. Outdoor events have truck-mounted mobile generators that can power their entire operation independently of the power grid and can provide power 24 hours a day.

The large diesel engines that power many gensets, both mobile and permanent, typically feature oil and water-heating and circulation systems so that they are ready for instant start up at any time. Switches that turn the generator on the moment mains power is cut are common. Testing and maintenance of gensets is a significant consideration and should be conducted prior to and throughout the event by the equipment supplier and the site electrician.

Emergency communications procedures

According to Sime (1995), crowd disasters are characterised by poor communication before, during and after an event. For example, crowds are often given insufficient information about the potential danger or emergency situation and, therefore, have insufficient time to evacuate (Sime 1999).

Informing the public of an emergency

Appropriate arrangements for warning communications to the audience in an emergency should be established before the event. Methods used for disseminating the warning may be audible and/or visual signals. A Standard Emergency Warning Signal (a pulsating wailing siren or beep sound) can draw attention to the fact that an urgent safety message is about to be given.

Warning sirens alone have been shown to be insufficient, i.e., interpreted as meaningless noise (Ramachandran 1990). Rather, specific information is needed by the public and verbal instructions should be broadcast on a public address system or visual warning and instructions given by electronic signs or closed circuit television if available. If public address systems cannot be put in place outside the venue, the public address systems that form part of the electronic siren in most emergency vehicles can be used.

The public address system must be connected to the emergency lighting circuit or other standby power to ensure that communication with patrons is possible during a power failure. If a separate sound system is to be utilised, some means of muting or silencing the stage sound system is required.

Staff communications during an emergency

It is essential to have adequate communications within and between all site and venue staff areas to give staff instructions, such as, to remain where they are, move to another location or evacuate the building. The communication system should be multi-modal and not rely on one single system. Communications may be a combination of public address system (in which case standby power is needed), hand-held radio or other stand-alone systems. Reliance on mobile phones in emergencies is poor planning. Both during and immediately following an emergency, mobile telephone communication is usually unavailable due to excessive demand. Whatever system chosen, it should be tested and available within the communications space.

It is important to decide what to tell staff. They could be told the nature of the emergency, the location of the affected areas, the procedures to follow, and any special information about which escape routes or exits should not be used.

Emergency communications planning

All events need an emergency communication plan that is comprehensive, well-organised, and highlights teamwork and leadership. The objective of an emergency communications plan is to assign responsibilities, set priorities and ensure that issues are dealt with according to an agreed-upon procedure. No single plan can foresee everything that can happen in the event of an emergency. However, by having a plan, there's a greater chance of controlling the emergency, therefore minimising the negative impact.

A worthwhile plan covers three phases: pre-emergency, during-emergency and post-emergency. While the during-emergency plan covers actions taken to contain or minimise the effect of the emergency, the post-emergency plan is aimed at returning the event site and activities to normal operations. Depending on the complexity of an event's operations, preparing an emergency communications plan can sometimes be more difficult than implementing it when an emergency occurs.

An emergency communications plan is essentially a to-do list that will set in motion the responsibilities of the team members: their roles and accessibility; resources and facilities available; procedures; team members' names and positions; important addresses and telephone numbers; and emergency services information and data.

The plan also should include drills and emergency-handling simulations that involve staging a realistic scenario at which an external consultant monitors procedures.

While it goes without saying that the various emergency services (police, health, etc.) must be able to communicate with their own staff, experience has shown that different services must be able to:

- communicate with each other
- communicate between staff outside and inside the venue to get a proper overview of the total situation and
- communicate with senior event organisers, including security, who may be the first to identify an incipient problem.

Interagency communications

To prepare a plan, an event organisation must first look at issues relevant to its event. The variety of people and organisations involved, and the specific types of communications needed for each group. The difficulty is that variables of audience, staff, sub-contractors, performers, equipment, weather, social and economic situations, ensure that each event generates its own unique set of circumstances, even if held in the same location and date year after year. This ever-changing combination of elements creates uncertainty and potential dangers.

Definition box 11.2

Efficient communication is a major challenge for emergency responders during emergency management. Reports show that missing information and information overload are important factors that determine the success of emergency management.

Niels Netten and Maarten van Someren (2011)

In such situations, effective intra- and inter-organisational communication becomes of great importance. Response to an emergency often involves multiple emergency response units of different agencies like the fire department, the police and medical services. During the management of an emergency these 'responders' may operate at different locations but frequently information that becomes available at one location is relevant for responders at other locations. In the case of a relatively confined emergency response operation, the parties involved are able to share relevant information directly by sight and speech. The crucial need for communication arises in situations that involve many different responders who cannot see or hear what is happening, and situations in which the location and activities of other responders may be unknown and responders may well be unaware of who else is active.

In the response phase of emergency management, responders often lack the time to actively seek information that is actually available. For example, if a team is working at one location and is unaware of another team working nearby, they will not search for the other teams' findings or plans. As a result, information is not always available at the right place at the right time. Another possible cause of delay is in communication procedures that involve a number of steps where errors can be made at each step. This lack of information for the emergency responders easily leads to wrong decisions and as a consequence to a less effective collaboration. Chen et al. (2008) give the following list of challenges regarding communication between agencies:

- high uncertainty, sudden and unexpected events
- risk and possible mass casualty
- increased time pressure and urgency
- severe resource shortage
- large-scale impact and damage
- disruption of infrastructure support

- multi-authority and massive people involvement
- conflict of interest
- high demand for timely information.

Studies of disaster management in the Netherlands concluded that information sharing and communication in incident management was worse than expected, leading to errors and less optimal emergency mitigation (Netten and van Someren 2011). In particular, the distribution of crucial information between collaborating responders of different services is often neglected which has had a significant impact on the effectiveness of mitigating the emergency situation.

Accordingly what is required is a communication system that is first of all aimed at meeting the high demand for timely information in a situation with high uncertainty and sudden, unexpected events. One that can be used in small-scale emergencies but also in events that involve many agencies and responders at many locations. In particular, a flexible, non-hierarchical organisation of communication is needed, especially in the early stages of an emergency when relevant information is scarce and communication channels may be damaged. Information distribution is of great importance especially in the early stage of an emergency and communication via informal networks (mobile phone messages by the public to emergency services, for instance) plays a relatively big role. The sharing of information, certainly at the start of the incident response phase, should be through the central communications systems.

However, there is a danger that in situations where multiple responders are involved, the amount of information becomes so large and complicated that information is sometimes withheld by responders or simply forgotten, in spite of its relevance for other emergency services. Sending particular information to all (i.e., broadcast) possibly creates additional processing time for message receivers who already have little time and who often only require part of it for their tasks. Strategic personnel might become confused by reports, requests and irrelevant messages. This leads to information overload. In the context of emergency management broadcasting all information is therefore not the optimal solution for information distribution.

Six different types of probable causes of mistakes made during disaster situations have been categorized by Abbink et al. (2004).

1 Decisions might be made on incomplete information. There may not be enough time or resources to gather all relevant information to support a decision.
2 Information may be contradictory.
3 Incorrect information often occurs due to poor communication or misinterpretation.
4 The use of different protocols, which might happen when multiple organisations are involved that apply different rules or protocols.
5 Exception handling can be the cause of many mistakes because people are not familiar enough with plans of different scenarios.
6 Work overload might also be a cause of errors. For instance, when tasks are not delegated properly, or a party is not aware of the possibility of delegations.

Bruinsma (2010) concludes that mistakes with information are for a large part based on unfamiliarity with protocols, incomplete sharing of information between parties and shortcomings in the manner in which information is sought. Whereby, the role of correct information received in a timely manner is important for the management of an emergency.

Recently, Reddy et al. (2009) analysed the communication and work processes during an emergency exercise. They found several specific causes of communication problems:

- inadequacies of current communication tools: many different types of devices and protocols were used but these were often not connected
- lack of common ground: differences in terminology, work flow and procedures made it difficult to use information between responders, in particular between organisations
- occasional breakdowns in communication: these were caused by technical factors or by the fact that a responder was busy and would not use his communication device.

Use of social media

The widespread use of social media, particularly Twitter, by the public during emergencies has been proposed as a valid communication channel. A study by Helsloot and Groenendaal (2013) showed that in fact the value of Twitter for crisis communication was minor because the tweets from the public contained no new information relevant for emergency management, and that the information and instruction messages from the emergency managers to the public were swamped by the huge number of citizen tweets posted and failed to reach their intended readers. Also the limited number of Twitter followers of emergency services contributed to the messages' invisibility. If an event's emergency processes intend to have a Twitter presence, an extended network with followers is essential to actually stand out during an emergency. Also the information contained must be relevant enough to ensure retweeting.

Protocols for responding to an emergency

The response to an incident must be rapid and authoritative. There needs to be clear and unambiguous information about the emergency and required action. Protocols (policy and procedures) for emergency management are staff instructions and procedures for responding to an emergency situation.

Protocols should provide all personnel with:

- details of the venue layout, including entrances, exits, first-aid points and any potential hazards
- communication guidelines and procedures
- procedures for responding to emergency incidents – accident, fire, first aid, violence, criminal activity, such as first response, raising alarms, requesting assistance
- details of emergency and evacuation plans.

Once an emergency is identified, the police and other relevant emergency services need to be told as soon as possible. It may be helpful if checklists of information are passed on supplied to all staff and displayed on posters. Checklists should include:

- the nature of the emergency/accident/incident and its extent, if known
- the exact official address of the venue
- suggested access routes and meeting points if previously agreed arrangements have to be changed
- relevant information about any hazards.

Note, to avoid false alarms, the local fire or ambulance service may on receiving a call from a member of the public contact the event EOC to verify the emergency in accordance with a pre-arranged procedure.

Emergency Operations Centre communications procedures

- Ascertain the nature of the emergency – severity, urgency, by direct communication with the most senior staff member at the location of the incident.
- Evaluate the response level required.
- Contact the appropriate personnel or service.

Alert

- Alert all staff.
- Ensure that the emergency services have been notified (fire, police or ambulance).
- Communicate with staff.
- Tell staff the nature of the emergency.

Evacuate

- Tell staff which assembly areas are to be used.
- Evacuate staff and visitors in the following order:

    1 Out of immediate danger (for example, out of room)
    2 Out of compartment (for example, in a venue, through the fire doors or smoke doors) or to a clear space a short distance from the emergency
    3 Total evacuation of the venue.

Check

- Instigate a check on all rooms, especially changing rooms and toilets, as well as behind doors, storage areas, and so forth.
- Do a head count of all staff, contractors and visitors.

Report

- Obtain reports, notify emergency services of anyone unaccounted for.

Bomb threat

Bomb threats may come in the form of:

- written threat – avoid unnecessary handling and place in a plastic envelope
- telephone threat – do not hang up and complete the phone threat checklist
- suspect object.

In consultation with police, evaluate the threat as either specific, for example, providing details on the device, motive, location, time of detonation, or non-specific. Every threat needs to be treated seriously unless and until proven otherwise. The evaluation may result in:

- no further action
- a search without any evacuation
- evacuate and search
- evacuate without search.

Search

Security staff should carry out the search for any suspect object. If one is found, it should not be touched, covered or moved. Outside areas, building entrances and exits and public areas within the building should be given priority for checking before looking inside and on the roof. Care should be taken not to use electrical equipment or any other equipment emitting electromagnetic radiation around the suspect object.

Evacuation

Total evacuation needs to be evaluated against risks such as the location of the bomb outside the building, inability to carry out a search, panic and disruption. Partial evacuation may be preferred in the case of specific threats. Evacuation procedures in the case of bomb threats may differ from fire such as opening and not closing windows. In the case of evacuation, people should remove personal belongings, such as briefcases and purses, to facilitate identification of suspect objects.

Emergency grab bags

In an emergency, a 'grab bag' should be available to senior staff which contains essential equipment and information. All relevant contact information, the staff involved, contractors and service suppliers and other site information should be contained in an easily accessible format. Suggested 'grab bag' contents:

- emergency and floor plans (laminated)
- list of contacts (laminated) staff, head office, etc.
- incident log (consider dictaphone), notebook, pens, markers, etc.
- first aid kit (designed for major emergencies): consider large bandages, burn shields or cling film, large sterile strips, cold packs, baby wipes as well as standard equipment
- torch and spare batteries or wind up
- glow sticks
- radio (wind up)
- high visibility jackets for senior EOC staff
- loud hailer and spare batteries

Emergency response

- hazard and cordon tape
- plastic macs/foil blankets/bin liners
- dust/toxic fume masks
- water (plastic container) and chocolate/glucose tablets.

Some extra items to consider:

- spare keys/security codes for locked areas or equipment
- mobile telephone with credit available, plus charger
- disposable/small camera
- hard hats/protective goggles/heavy duty gloves.

Contact lists that may be necessary:

- list of employees with contact details – include home and mobile numbers, next-of-kin contact details
- contact details for emergency glaziers and building contractors
- contact details for utility companies
- event site plan, including location of gas, electricity and water shut-off points
- insurance company details
- local authority contact details.

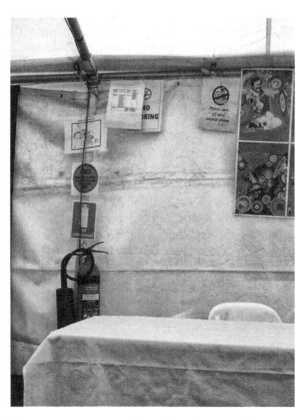

Figure 11.1 Emergency protocols and equipment in a temporary location.

Make sure this pack or packs are stored safely and securely on site or at an accessible emergency location nearby. Ensure items in the pack are checked regularly, are kept up to date, and are working. Remember that cash/credit cards may be needed for emergency expenditure.

There have been incidents that, in hindsight, could have been reduced in severity if only basic forcible entry tools had been available. It is strongly recommended that, at strategic locations in the venue, forcible entry kits are available for the use of emergency personnel. These kits should contain:

- fire axe with prong
- pry or crow bar
- pair of heavy duty bolt cutters.

This list is not exhaustive, and there may be other documents or equipment that should be included.

Evacuation

In the case of an emergency that threatens the crowd, the procedure is to halt all activities and direct the crowd to evacuation assembly areas: safe assembly areas arranged for different types of emergencies. And hold the crowd in these areas until the emergency has passed. The procedures for responding to an emergency that requires an evacuation are:

a   the safe and rapid evacuation of persons from the place of work
b   emergency services communication
c   appropriate medical treatment of injured persons.

The stages of evacuation are:

- decision to evacuate
- warning
- evacuation guidance
- shelter/assembly
- return/recovery.

Planning

Evacuations are difficult operations to conduct. However, difficulties can be minimised if an evacuation plan and protocols are prepared. Event managers must work with local emergency experts and first-responders to create or update the event evacuation plan. Once the plan is created, evacuation instructions must be prepared for clear communications with staff.

Sites suitable as evacuation assembly areas must be selected or created. The most efficient evacuation routes to the evacuation assembly areas from different areas of the site or venue must be determined and rehearsed in drills. The assembly areas and exits must be well defined on site maps. The placement of prominent signage to direct the crowd for an evacuation is necessary. Appropriately trained staff should be appointed to act as both crowd marshals and emergency service contacts. All staff should know their responsibilities for conducting and assisting with the evacuation.

Evacuation procedures must ensure that:

- adequate arrangements are made for the shutting down and evacuation of the event site or venue in the event of an emergency
- details of the arrangements for any such evacuation are kept on display in an appropriate location or locations at the event
- one or more persons are appointed and appropriately trained to oversee any such evacuation and, if appropriate, in the use of onsite fire-fighting equipment
- crowd monitoring is continuous throughout all stages of the evacuation to control crowd flow and density
- stewarding and directing of the crowd is coordinated to avoid overcrowding
- staff are trained in evacuation procedures.

Communication and accessibility of information are vital. Indeed, Drury and Cocking (2007) argue that systems of communication should be prioritised over and above physical features, such as exit widths. In particular, specific information and clear instructions are crucial to start people evacuating. Prior expectations about behaviour can be very dangerous, so experienced personnel are critical for this task.

Professor Still considers the following factors crucial in the assessment of emergency evacuations:

- *Communication method* of alerting the crowd to the danger, e.g. alarms, warning announcements, environmental factors (e.g. increase in temperature), movement of other people, and visual clues. *Timeliness, accuracy, clarity and credibility of communication* will influence the time taken for the crowd to begin to move.
- *Mobility* – the speed at which an individual is capable of moving within a crowd. Mobility differs depending on age, disability, baggage, etc.
- *Social affinity* – the position of an individual within an affinity cluster (i.e., within a family group) impacts on their behaviour during an emergency, e.g. a mother will instinctively put the safety of her child before her own.
- *Alertness* – the speed with which an individual reacts will be affected by his or her state of alertness.
- *Role* – the role of an individual will influence his or her own reaction to an emergency situation, and the reactions and behaviours of others, e.g. the role of police in relation to a crowd will influence the crowd's behaviour.
- *Position* – the physical position of an individual, e.g. whether sitting, standing or lying down, will affect his or her rate of reaction and movement in an emergency.
- *Commitment* – the degree to which an individual feels committed to the environment in which the emergency occurs will influence his or her reactions, e.g. an individual may react more strongly to an emergency in the home compared with an emergency in the office.
- *Focal points* – the visibility of focal points during an emergency evacuation, e.g., emergency exit routes and signs, will influence the speed at which evacuation occurs.

- *Visual access* – the more visible the signage or emergency egress route, the more attractive the route will be to the individual.
- *Familiarity* – the more familiar the individual is with the environment or building, and with the evacuation procedures, the shorter the reaction time and movement time will be.
- *Complexity* – the more complex the environment, the more indecisive individuals will be, and the longer it will take for them to react and move.
- *Enclosure* – individuals instinctively want to reach safe ground in an emergency, and typically want to escape outside. However, it may sometimes be safer to evacuate a crowd inwards, or to a less obvious place of safety.
- *Population density* – the density of the crowd will impact on how quickly they will be able to move and evacuate.

(Taken from Still 2000: 95–97)

Obtain agreement with the evacuation plan in advance with the police and emergency services, the local authority and any neighbours. Ensure that staff with particular responsibilities are trained and that all staff are drilled. Remember, too, to let the police know what actions will be taken during any incident.

Decision to evacuate

The decision to evacuate will normally be taken by the senior event staff. This responsibility often lies with the event safety officer. In exceptional cases the police may insist on evacuation, although they should always do so in consultation with the event security manager. Whatever the circumstances, the police and appropriate emergency services should be advised as soon as possible about the evacuation action.

The first action is to ascertain the size, type and location of the emergency. It could be an incident that requires an immediate evacuation of part of the event area or building, or a full evacuation of the entire site and a halting of all activities. Judgement of the severity of the incident will depend on a consideration of its context. For example, the emergency is small and confined to one location, e.g. a small fire in a rubbish bin in an outside area that is easily cleared of people, will probably not require a full evacuation; whereas the same rubbish bin fire inside a building where toxic fumes will be a health hazard, or in an area close to flammable substances, will initiate an evacuation process.

If an evacuation route takes people near a fire, past a suspect device outside the venue, or through an area believed to be contaminated, alternative routes must quickly be chosen. A very important consideration when planning evacuation routes in response to terrorist attacks is to ensure people are moved away from other potential areas of vulnerability, or areas where a larger secondary device could detonate.

The safest evacuations are those conducted without undue haste or alarm. An early decision to evacuate is a major factor in the efficient movement of people into safety. Evacuations take time, and time is lost by delayed responses by both the audience and by event staff in reaction to the emergency.

Since major emergencies are relatively rare and, therefore, non-routine, individuals are predisposed to deny a serious incident is taking place, preferring instead to believe that an emergency situation is in fact normal for as long as possible and, subsequently, to carry on behaving as normal for as long as possible: "Under normal circumstances it is people's understanding of, and adherence to, the rules of place that allow a place to function. However, in an emergency such rule following may be inappropriate" (Donald and Canter 1992: 205). This failure to initiate some form of evacuation response is often termed 'behavioural inaction' (Muir et al. 1996; Leach 2004).

Evacuation time concerns not only the time taken for individuals to move towards an exit, but also the time taken before movement is initiated (Kimura and Sime 1988; Johnson and Feinberg 1997) i.e., the time taken to recognise there is a danger and to then decide which is the most appropriate course of action (Graat et al. 1999). Therefore, to enhance evacuation efficiency and, in particular, to start people moving, communication and information are vital (Still 2000). "the problem in disasters is not that people tend to panic and act precipitously in response to danger, but that people typically delay or fail to take appropriate evasive action when it is needed" (Mawson 2005: 107).

Example

Analysis of the evacuation of the World Trade Centre on 11 September 2001 by Professor Ed Galea, emphasised just how slow many individuals were to react.

The average time for individuals to abandon their usual activities and begin evacuating was between 5 and 8 minutes, although some people continued their normal behaviours for up to 30 or 40 minutes after the planes hit, sending emails, shutting down their computers, or going to the toilet before leaving the building.

This may be because people were predominantly unaware of what was happening and, consequently, were unsure of the most appropriate form of action. Therefore, they followed their routine place scripts for as long as possible.

Additionally, this lack of immediate response may be due to individuals underestimating the acute need to react and respond quickly in an emergency situation. "Every second can mean the difference between life and death." Professor Ed Galea, University of Greenwich, Speaking on the BBC *Horizon* programme, 10 March, 2009

Source: from Challenger 2013.

It is also important to be aware that when initially responding to an alarm, or the threat of danger, people's responses are heavily dependent on the responses of those around them. For instance, if staff remain where they are, ignoring the alarm, then a person may assume there is no urgency required, or that it is merely a drill of some kind.

Delayed warnings

Delaying warnings, for fear of causing panic, merely delays emergency evacuation and, therefore, increases the risk of causalities. Individuals are predisposed to believe a situation is normal for as long as possible, and so behave as usual, thereby delaying evacuation. Clear information and specific instructions are needed for individuals to override their place script schema and evacuate as appropriate.

Authorities are often reluctant to issue warnings, for fear of causing panic (Sime 1980), yet this delay could actually increase the risk of casualties since individuals then have less time to evacuate (Sime 1999; Mawson 2005). Thus, through actions intended to avoid panic, authorities may actually increase the likelihood of it occurring. "Traditionally managers of public buildings have considered that in the event of an emergency it is better not to tell people the truth if panic is to be avoided. This belief has been translated into safety procedures which in disasters have characteristically withheld information about a threat of a fire from the public beyond the point when escape has been possible. ...The delay is paradoxically a major determinant of flight behaviour, crushing and deaths in major crowd disasters" (Proulx and Sime 1991: 850).

Instructions to the public

Communication and information are vital to initiate movement and enhance the efficiency of an emergency evacuation. Audience warnings must be specific, timely, credible and comprehensible, and in multiple forms as opposed to a single alarm, are highly influential over initiating crowd movement in an evacuation. The public could be informed by recorded or live public address messages, word-of-mouth by staff, including the use of loud hailers and alarms.

Warning interpretation

An issue of concern in the initial stage in the evacuation process is the meanings people attach to warnings issued about emergency situations. The time pressures and stress of an evacuation situation affect the way in which individuals process environmental information and, consequently, the decisions they make (Proulx 1993; Ozel 2001). Therefore, clear information concerning the threat along with clear instructions about how to exit are needed to improve evacuation efficiency.

Even when physical safety standards are satisfied, limited information about a threat makes the whole crowd more vulnerable. Emphasis on the physical aspects of an evacuation means the crowd is treated as "a homogenous mass of bodies or 'ballbearings', rather than . . . a collection of individuals and social groups who need accurate and timely information if they are to remain safe" (Sime 1995: 1).

Providing more, rather than less, information about the nature of the threat or emergency should help the crowd respond more effectively (Wessely 2005). Moreover, provision of information should encourage the crowd to trust authorities, which is crucial for effective evacuation (Cocking and Drury 2008); withholding information simply leads the crowd to mistrust authorities, and to question whether they are providing accurate information as the emergency develops.

Telling people not to panic represents the same lack of trust in the crowd as withholding information and may actually increase anxiety, as crowd members may feel they are expected to panic (Durodie and Wessely 2002).

Information and instruction

A public evacuation warning is intended to bring about an appropriate response to avoid or minimise exposure to danger. Warning messages should give clear and precise instructions to the public:

- provide timely information about the emergency
- state what action should be taken to reduce loss of life, injury and property damage
- state to the public, consequences of not heeding the warning.

The manner of giving instructions will influence the speed of public response. It will help to give short, clear instructions, repeat important information; phrase instructions positively: 'use the green door' not 'do not use the red door'; and be polite, firm and calm. Information to be given to the public include:

- which exits to use and how to get there
- where to assemble, if appropriate
- the reason for the instructions, for example 'to avoid overcrowding in Area A, please use...'.

The warning should cite a credible authority:

- be short, simple and precise
- have a personal context
- contain active verbs
- repeat important information regularly on a known timetable.

In order to be both interpreted accurately and believed, the warning must:

- be specific
- come from a credible source
- convey the nature and extent of the danger
- enable rapid verification
- provide cues to help people prepare for action.

Monitoring staff should provide feedback to operational decision makers on the extent of public compliance with instructions.

It is usually beneficial to keep crowds fully informed about the nature of any emergency, however, this may not always be the situation, for example in the case of terrorism warnings. In situations such as that, there may not be an actual (i.e., it is purely a threat) or immediate (i.e., there is a specific time frame) danger from which to evacuate. Therefore, fully informing the crowd of such a warning, making them aware of a possible terrorist act, rather than simply providing general information about needing to evacuate due to an 'incident', may greatly heighten the crowd's anxiety and serve to create a dangerous situation, with people rushing, pushing and potentially causing crushing, in order to leave. Given their experience in dealing with this particular issue, it is strongly recommended that the police decide on the most appropriate course of action in such circumstances.

Crowd behaviours in emergencies

As detailed in Chapter 3, people develop and, subsequently, follow habitually, scripts or schema for environments with which they are familiar. These schema become ingrained and very hard to break; hence, in an emergency situation individuals will typically act as normal for as long as possible, despite the inappropriateness and danger (Donald and Canter 1992).

Therefore, it is vital that evacuees are provided with clear information and specific instructions, in order to override their schema and break with their familiar behaviours (Donald and Canter 1992). As a result, people in an emergency seldom recognise the urgency and generally do not respond immediately to a hazard. Instead, they try to carry on their behaviours and follow the established rules until the circumstances become urgent.

The physical position of an individual, seated or standing, will also impact on their reaction, as will the extent to which an individual feels committed to the event activities, for example, a participant in a competition or dancing to a band will be more resistant to an interruption than a spectator of the same activity.

Crowd movement and behaviour is also influenced by the actions of fellow evacuees. For example, people typically follow the movement of others during an evacuation (Zhao et al. 2008). More specifically, family members typically exhibit kin behaviour in such situations, wherein they will gather together and wait for each other even backtracking if necessary, before exiting as a group (Yang et al. 2005).

Evacuation guidance

To effectively guide crowds is a challenging issue because emergency events may propagate in uncertain ways and affect the availability of exit routes. Exit route capacities may constrain the speed of crowd movement, and a crowd could be stressed making their behavior different from normal modes.

Factors which may influence evacuation rate include the physical situation of the crowd in the venue – sitting, standing, confined in a venue, etc., the crowds' alertness and density of the crowd; and the complexity of the event site or venue and visibility of exit routes and emergency exit signs.

Proximity of exits is a factor which can influence choice of exit route – a good distribution of emergency exits is needed to minimise the distance to be travelled by each individual. Arrangements will need to be in place to monitor the evacuation closely and ensure that all available exits are used; overcrowding of one or two exits needs to be avoided as far as possible. If the evacuation of the venue is likely to lead to congestion of departure routes or hamper emergency services, make sure that there are sufficient staff to control a phased departure.

If the layout of the venue is complex or the area to be evacuated is particularly large or distant from the exits, it may be more practicable to ask people to gather at various safe points in the venue and then escort them in groups to the exits. Special arrangements will need to be made for coping with the disabled and parents with pushchairs.

All emergency doors must open outwards into a large open area at the same level (sliding or roller shutter type doors should be avoided). Twisting and complex exit systems should also be avoided. Passages leading to emergency exits should never be used as storage areas, and the crash doors must never be locked. Many deaths have been caused by ignoring these simple rules.

Once evacuation action is initiated, choice of escape route is influenced by evacuees' perceptions of their familiarity with the site; for example, people typically prefer to leave same way as they came in, through a normal as opposed to emergency exit (Pelechano and Malkawi 2008). Therefore, they may be reluctant to evacuate via an exit usually prohibited, such as onto a roadway, unless forced to do so (Donald and Canter 1992). More complex environments will typically result in greater indecision with regards to choice of exit evacuation route, although this can be lessened by clearly visible emergency exit routes and signs.

Emergency signs

A key safety element is the use of signage to communicate information and instruction to both the event attendees and staff. Signs are required to provide essential information at 'decision points' – locations where attendees make choices or require direction. This is particularly important for emergency and evacuation procedures. Clear, comprehensive signs directing people to emergency exits are vital. The location of each sign should be included on the site map and listed in the safety plan. All emergency signage must be powered independently of the site or venue power supply.

There is a universal emergency evacuation sign – the green running man sign (although in some countries and in older venues a simple EXIT or 'sortie de secours' sign is common). The evacuation sign is usually mandatory and its size and positioning subject to regulations. It must only be used above exits that lead directly to an evacuation route. Other hazard warning signs with international symbols should be installed where appropriate for fire extinguishers, evacuation routes, emergency procedures and first aid facilities.

Emergency signs within the venues need to be clear, direct, uncluttered and easily visible. It is probable there are regulations and restrictions regarding where signs can be located and fixed, and this should be investigated before placement. Care should be taken with regard to their durability and how they are fixed, in case of rain or high wind. Thought should be given to their size and legibility from a distance, and where they should be sited, bearing in mind that once the customers have arrived their bodies may obscure the signs.

Leadership

Evacuation times can be improved when staff act assertively, both vocally and physically, to guide evacuees. Crowd guidance by staff can improve exit efficiency, occupant survivability, and mitigate or prevent undesirable consequences such as blocking or crushing.

However, this effectiveness depends on the extent of staff understanding of their own roles in the emergency and their corresponding appropriate actions, gained from information and communication before and during the crisis (Turner and Toft 1989). Those trained for an emergency will be able to react and respond more quickly (Donald and Canter 1992), while those who are clearly told what to do are likely to respond in a more timely and appropriate manner, since communication lessens the uncertainty of the situation, thereby enabling people to prepare for action more efficiently (Aube and Shield 2004).

Leader figures, either from the authorities or from within the crowd itself, play an important role preparing crowd members for the evacuation process (Dyer et al. 2008). People in groups do not make decisions by themselves, but rather, wait for orders from a leader (Yoshida 1996). Therefore, careful consideration must be given to the number of individuals within the crowd (whether these are stewards or crowd volunteers) who are aware of the location of emergency exits – i.e., informed individuals – and where these informed individuals should be positioned within the crowd to most effectively act as leaders in an emergency evacuation. The spatial positioning of those leaders is influential over both the speed and accuracy of crowd movement, with leaders positioned in the core, rather than the periphery, of the crowd, i.e., in close proximity to other crowd members, more likely to be influential over crowd movement (Leca et al. 2003; Dyer et al. 2008).

Evacuation assembly areas

A major consideration for an evacuation plan is how to judge where the safest place might be. The evacuation assembly area should be a clear plot of land easily reached by foot from all areas of the event site, large enough to contain all the people at the event, and away from the access points of the emergency services.

The evacuation plan must identify the audience evacuation routes and the evacuation areas for performers, employees and the audience. This involves prior identification of sites suitable as evacuation assembly areas, evacuation routes to the evacuation assembly areas from different areas of the site or venue.

Evacuation and assembly areas

Safe evacuation to assembly areas is vital to an emergency plan and when considering their use:

- ensure that there are enough of them and that they are big enough to accommodate the crowd
- site them away from vulnerable areas such as flammable or chemical stores or car parks in a bomb threat situation
- assembly areas should be a minimum of 200 metres away from any structures. Evacuate in the case of suspected bombs 500 metres from the device
- car parks should not be used as assembly areas. Evacuees must be gathered in locations away from emergency vehicle access routes
- care should be taken that there are no secondary hazards at the assembly point
- designate a location within the assembly area for staff at which information can be shared with emergency personnel
- a PA system for communication with the crowd at the assembly area is vital.

Actions within the assembly area

Staff should gather people into groups in order to identify and register those who have safely been evacuated and account for all staff after the evacuation. This registration will be used by police to inform relatives. They need to be kept together in the one place until the all clear is given. Some will take the opportunity to leave, this should be prevented. People will need to be told how long they will remain in the area and why they must stay in the area. Staff should:

- provide people waiting in assembly areas with updated information on what is happening at regular intervals
- state which authorities are in control of the evacuation

- take police advice on whether or not people really need to be kept there or may be allowed home and, if so, whether names and addresses need to be taken
- not allow anyone, whether injured or not, to leave evacuation areas before the emergency services have given medical advice, assessments or treatment
- arrange meeting point(s) for the friends or relatives who have become separated and advise the crowd of their location.

Also, it is important to recognise that crowd members will want to help during an emergency and efforts should be made to use their resilience and willingness to do so (Glass and Schoch-Spana 2002; Durodie and Wessely 2002).

Post-emergency recovery phase

The Emergency Operations Centre, for simple operational reasons, will need to understand how to cope after an emergency. A phase that is often overlooked in emergency planning is preparation for any recovery. Procedures need to be developed that focus on minimising the consequences to the people involved, to the environment and to the organisation.

The event site may be in disarray as a result of the emergency incident, the recovery phase deals with the actions required to return the site to normal operations as quickly as possible after the disruptive incident. The following actions should be included:

- provide clear information regarding the situation to all employees and attendees
- allow employees time to recover, but encourage early return to tasks
- if the emergency was localised, barricade or fence off the scene, to prevent interference with subsequent investigation and control further hazards
- hold attendees at the assembly/evacuation area until all staff are back in position, then allow attendees to return to the event site
- investigate the incident and record for review.

For people under stress as the result of an emergency, recovery may involve psychological counselling and trauma management. There are professional resources that can assist in developing appropriate procedures for managers to follow in the event of, say, a hold-up. Often people appear to be coping until maybe a week later, when memories of the event may affect staff quite profoundly. It is an area in which experience has helped to develop a number of processes to handle the psychological impact. Counsellors can often provide a session of training to frontline managers and workers who are especially exposed to this risk.

When to re-open the venue

If the venue is physically safe to re-open, consider:

- whether there will be transport to take people home at a time which is later than the original closing time
- whether it is possible to move the number of people back into the venue safely in a short time
- anticipated crowd reaction to closure or re-opening.

If the event is cancelled or postponed it will be necessary to give an assurance that arrangements will be made to compensate or refund, or reschedule the event, and provide information on any transport arrangements that are available (it may be necessary for management to make calls to arrange mass transport at short notice).

Staff training

Because planning and preparation may not be enough, leadership skills during an emergency are vital. The reality is that no organisation can prepare for every single emergency event; this would be an impossible task, and perhaps a misappropriation of financial and human resources. Event management must discover how to work with the leaders in its organisation before an emergency, and how to develop leaders to deal with crises. Management should identify the most effective individuals to lead during an emergency. While planning is important, leadership in a time of emergency, particularly in the immediate aftermath, may exceed any preparation. Emergency management is a test of the quality and character of leadership as much as it is a test of skill. (Aube and Shield 2004; Dyer et al. 2008).

Staff training for emergencies must address procedures for:

- area marshalling
- assisting people with disabilities
- accounting for people.

Training should ensure a complete knowledge of:

- evacuation routes
- assembly areas
- restrictions on vehicular movement
- control and coordination procedures with personnel and emergency services
- communication systems – warnings, alarms, telephones, PA systems
- first-aid personnel and equipment
- emergency response equipment – extinguishers, reels, first-aid kits, breathing apparatus.

Staff training should include a thorough understanding of:

- the vital importance of good communications
- the command and communication structure to be followed
- exactly what staff have to do and why
- how each individual's responsibilities fit into the overall plan
- the relationship with emergency services
- the layout of the venue, locations of emergency equipment, alarm call points, first-aid facilities, emergency exits and access routes for emergency services.

The training process could also identify other more specific individual training needs such as first aid, response to fires, use of communication equipment, and recognition of hazardous situations. Above all, everyone needs to know where the first-aid facilities are located, who their first-aid officer is and their contact details.

Emergency drills

Because of the one off nature of an event and the once only mix of staff, sub-contractors and volunteers, an event site will not have the benefit of emergency procedures that are routine in most workplaces. This means that the event manager must ensure that everyone is aware of and trained in the emergency procedures, with particular emphasis on the emergency protocols.

The importance of evacuation exercises or drills cannot be overstated. External professional advice is valuable for picking up any shortcomings and how these omissions might be addressed. A checklist of all the requirements for a satisfactory exercise, including targets, should be developed and maintained. Prior notice of all drills should be given, with the occupants being briefed beforehand.

After any emergency (or drill) a debriefing should take place with key personnel and, where appropriate, external agencies. The debriefing would focus on reviewing the emergency response and the effectiveness of the recovery procedures.

Equipment testing

A system for regular checks of emergency response equipment should also be instituted. Typically, this includes checking fire-fighting apparatus, but can extend to a wide variety of equipment needs such as emergency communication systems, alarms and the like. It also ensures that all the emergency equipment (e.g. smoke detectors, emergency exists, safety lighting, etc.) at the venue has been identified and is properly maintained.

Summary

- An emergency is an event, actual or imminent, which endangers or threatens to endanger life, property or the environment, and which requires a significant, immediate and coordinated response of either, or all, police, ambulance, first aid, fire brigade or disaster management services. An emergency may include multiple incidents at the same time.
- Emergency situations demand:

  - leadership and guidance, initiating crowd evacuation as quickly as possible if required
  - strategies for communicating with the crowd to provide information
  - communication with emergency response agencies
  - awareness of how individuals are likely to behave during an emergency.

- All staff should know their emergency response roles. Protocols (policy and procedures) for emergency management are staff instructions and procedures for responding to an emergency situation.
- Appropriately trained staff should be appointed to act as both crowd marshals and emergency service contacts for conducting and assisting with the evacuation.
- Evacuation times can be improved when staff act assertively, both vocally and physically, to guide evacuees. Crowd guidance by staff can improve exit efficiency, occupant survivability, and mitigate or prevent undesirable consequences such as blocking or crushing.

- An Emergency Operations Centre (EOC) is a facility for control of operations and coordination of resources. It is the focus of the emergency response and recovery structure.
- The EOC has important emergency communication responsibilities. Both internally, to the crowd and event staff; and externally to police, ambulance, fire and rescue services.
- Establishing early, effective and continuous lines of communication from the incident site to the EOC and the responding agency will be critical.
- Backup power supply is essential to provide short-term power to emergency systems.
- In the case of an emergency that threatens the crowd, the procedure is to halt all activities and direct the crowd to *Evacuation Assembly areas* – safe assembly areas arranged for different types of emergencies. Hold the crowd in these areas until the emergency has passed.
- Communication and information are vital to initiate movement and enhance the efficiency of an emergency evacuation. Audience warnings must be specific, timely, credible and comprehensible, and in multiple forms.
- A public evacuation warning is intended to bring about an appropriate response to avoid or minimise exposure to danger. Appropriate arrangements for emergency and evacuation warning communications to the audience should be established before the event.
- Factors which may influence evacuation rate include the physical situation of the crowd in the venue, the crowd's alertness and the density of the crowd; and the complexity of the event site or venue, and visibility of exit routes and emergency exit signs.
- Clear, comprehensive signs directing people to emergency exits are vital. The location of each sign should be included on the site map and listed in the safety plan. All emergency signage must be powered independently of the site or venue power supply.
- An evacuation assembly area should be a clear plot of land easily reached by foot from all areas of the event site, large enough to contain all the people at the event, and away from the access points of the emergency services.
- The most efficient routes to the evacuation assembly areas from different areas of the site or venue must be determined and rehearsed in drills.
- The assembly areas and exits must be well defined on site maps.
- The placement of prominent signage to direct the crowd for an evacuation is necessary.

Bibliography

Abbink, H., Van Dijk, R., Dobos, T., Hoogendoorn, M., Jonker, C. M. and Konur, S. (2004) *Automated support for adaptive incident management*. First International Workshop on Information Systems for Crisis Response and Management. Royal Flemish Acadamy of Belgium for Science and the Arts. 69–74.

Aguirre, B. E. (2005) 'Emergency evacuations, panic and social psychology', *Psychiatry: Interpersonal and Biological Processes*, 68(2), 121–129.

Aube, F. and Shield, R. (2004) 'Modeling the effect of leadership on crowd flow dynamics', *Cellular Automata, Proceedings*, 3305, 601–611.

Bruinsma. G. (2010) *Adaptive Workflow Simulation of Emergency Response*. PhD Thesis. University of Twente, Netherlands.

Challenger, R. (2013) *Understanding Crowd Behaviours*. Leeds: The Stationery Office (TSO).

Challenger, R., Clegg, C. W. and Robinson, M. A. (2010a) *Understanding Crowd Behaviours, Volume 1: Practical Guidance and Lessons Identified*. Leeds: The Stationery Office (TSO).

Challenger, R., Clegg, C.W. and Robinson, M.A. (2010b) *Understanding Crowd Behaviours, Volume 2: Supporting Theory and Evidence*. Leeds: The Stationery Office (TSO).

Chen, R., Sharman, R., Rao, H. R. and Upadhyaya, S. J. (2008) 'Coordination in emergency response management', *Communications of the ACM*, 51(5), 66–73.

Cocking, C. and Drury, J. (2008) 'The mass psychology of disasters and emergency evacuations: A research report and implications for the Fire and Rescue Service'. *Fire Safety, Technology and Management*, 10, 13–19.

Donald, I. and Canter, D. (1992) *Intentionality and fatality during the King's Cross underground fire*. European Journal of Social Psychology, 22(3), 203–218.

Drury, J. and Cocking, C. (2007) 'The mass psychology of disasters and emergency evacuations: A research report and implications for practice', Brighton: University of Sussex.

Drury, J. and Winter, G. (2004) 'Social identity as a source of strength in mass emergencies and other crowd events', *International Journal of Mental Health (special issue on 'Coping with disasters: The mental health component)'*, 32, 77–93.

Durodie, B. and Wessely, S. (2002) 'Resilience or panic? The public and terrorist attack', *The Lancet*, 360(9349), 1901–1902.

Dyer, J. R. G., Ioannou, C. C., Morrell, L. J., Croft, D. P., Couzin, I. D., Waters, D. A. and Krause, J. (2008) 'Consensus decision making in human crowds', *Animal Behavior*, 75(2), 461–470.

Emergency Management Australia (2004a) *Emergency Planning* Manual Number 43. Australian Emergency Manuals Series. Commonwealth of Australia.

Emergency Management Australia. (2004b) *Multi-Agency Incident Management* Manual Number 17. Australian Emergency Manuals Series. Commonwealth of Australia.

Getz. D. (1997) *Event Management and Event Tourism*. New York: Cognizant Communications.

Glass, T. A. and Schoch-Spana, M. (2002) 'Bioterrorism and the people: How to vaccinate a city against panic', *Clinical Infectious Diseases*, 34(2), 217–223.

Graat, E., Midden, C. and Bockholts, P. (1999) 'Complex evacuation: Effects of motivation level and slope of stairs on emergency egress time in a sports stadium', *Safety Science*, 31(2), 127–141.

Helsloot, I. and Groenendaal, J. (2013) 'Twitter: An underutilized potential during sudden crises?', *Journal of Contingencies and Crisis Management*, 21(3), 178–183.

Johnson, N. R. and Feinberg, W. E. (1997) 'The impact of exit instructions and number of exits in fire emergencies: A computer simulation investigation', *Journal of Environmental Psychology*, 17(2), 123–133.

Kimura, M. and Sime, J. D. (1988) 'Exit choice behaviour during the evacuation of two lecture theatres', *Fire Safety Science*, 2, 541–550.

Leach, J. (2004). 'Why people freeze in an emergency: Temporal and cognitive constraints on survival responses', *Aviation, Space, and Environmental Medicine*, 75(6), 539–542.

Leca, J. B., Gunst, N., Thierry, B. and Petit, O. (2003) 'Distributed leadership in semi-free-ranging capuchin monkeys', *Animal Behaviour*, 66(6), 1045–1052.

Levine, M., Prosser, A., Evans, D. and Reicher, S. (2005) 'Identity and emergency intervention: How social group membership and inclusiveness of group boundaries shape helping behavior', *Personality and Social Psychology Bulletin*, 31(4), 443–453.

Li, H. Y., Sun, X. H. and Zhang, K. (2007) 'Voice alarm system in emergency evacuation', *Engineering Psychology and Cognitive Ergonomics*, 4562, 723–730.

Mawson, A. R. (2005) 'Understanding mass panic and other collective responses to threat and disaster', *Psychiatry*, 68(2), 95–113.

Muir, H. C., Bottomley, D. M. and Marrison, C. (1996) 'Effects of motivation and cabin configuration on emergency aircraft evacuation behavior and rates of egress', *International Journal of Aviation Psychology*, 6(1), 57–77.

NaCTSO (2009) (Partial review: 2014) Counter Terrorism Protective Security Advice for Major Events. London: Association of Chief Police Officers of England and Wales and Northern Ireland (now National Police Chief Council).

Netten, N. and van Someren, M. (2011) 'Improving communication by evaluating the relevance of messages', *Journal of Contingencies and Crisis Management*, 19(2), 75–85.

Ozel, F. (2001) 'Time pressure and stress as a factor during emergency egress', *Safety Science*, 38(2), 95–107.

Pelechano, N. and Malkawi, A. (2008) 'Evacuation simulation models: Challenges in modeling high rise building evacuation with cellular automata approaches', *Automation in Construction*, 17(4), 377–385.

Perry, R. W. (1994) A model of evacuation compliance behavior. In R. R. Dynes and K. J. Tierney (Eds) *Disasters, Collective Behavior, and Social Organization*. Newark, DE: University of Delaware Press, pp. 85–98.

Perry, R. W. (2006) Disasters, definitions and theory construction. In R. W. Perry and E. L. Proulx, G. (1993) 'A stress model for people facing a fire', *Journal of Environmental Psychology*, 13(2), 137–147.

Proulx, G. and Sime, J. D. (1991) To prevent panic in an underground emergency: Why not tell people the truth? In G. Cox and B. Langford (Eds) *Fire Safety Science: Proceedings of the Third International Symposium*. London: Elsevier Applied Science, pp. 843–852.

Quarantelli (Eds) *What is a Disaster? New Answers to Old Questions*. Bloomington, IN: Xlibris Corporation.

Ramachandran, G. (1990) 'Human behavior in fires: A review of research in the United Kingdom', *Fire Technology*, 26(2), 149–155.

Raphael, B. (2005) 'Crowds and other collectives: Complexities of human behaviors in mass emergencies', Psychiatry, 68(2), 115–120.

Reddy, M., Paul, S. A., Abraham. J., McNeese, M., DeFlitch, C. and Yen, J. (2009) 'Challenges to effective crisis management: Using information and communication technologies to coordinate emergency medical services and emergency department teams', *International Journal of Medical Informatics*, 78(4), 259–269.

Sime, J. D. (1980) The concept of panic. In D. Canter (Ed.) *Fires and Human Behaviour*. Chichester: John Wiley & Sons.

Sime, J. D. (1994) Escape behaviour in fires and evacuations. In P. Stollard and L. Johnston (Eds) *Design Against Fire: An Introduction to Fire Safety Engineering Design*. London: Chapman & Hall.

Sime, J. D. (1995) 'Crowd psychology and engineering', Safety Science, 21(1), 1–14.

Sime, J. D. (1999) 'Crowd facilities, management and communications in disasters', *Facilities*, 17(9/10), 313–324.

Still, G. K. (2000) *Crowd Dynamics*. PhD Thesis, University of Warwick, UK.

Still, G. K. (2012) *Crowd Modelling: Crowd Safety in the Complex and Built Environment*. Cumbria, UK: Crowd Modelling Ltd.

Turner, B. A. and Toft, B. (1989) Fire at Summerland Leisure Centre. In U. Rosenthall, M. Charles and P. Hart (Eds) *Coping with Crises: The Management of Disasters, Riots and Terrorism*. Springfield, IL: Charles C. Thomas Publisher.

Wessely, S. (2005) 'Don't panic! Short and long term psychological reactions to the new terrorism: The role of information and authorities', *Journal of Mental Health*, 14(1), 1–6.

Worksafe Victoria (2006) *Advice for Managing Major Events Safely*. 1st edn. Victoria: Government of Victoria.

Yang, L. Z., Zhao, D. L., Li, J. and Fang, T. Y. (2005) 'Simulation of the kin behavior in building occupant evacuation based on cellular automaton', *Building and Environment*, 40(3), 411–415.

Yoshida, Y. (1996) 'A study of evacuation behavior in the World Trade Center explosion', *Fire Technology*, 32(2), 174–189.

Zhao, D. L., Yang, L. Z. and Li, J. (2008) 'Occupants' behavior of going with the crowd based on cellular automata occupant evacuation model', *Physica A*, 387(14), 3708–3718.

Chapter 12

Incident reporting and investigation

Chapter objectives

This chapter covers safety incident investigation, analysis and reporting. It also looks at post event ESMS reporting.

While acknowledging that workplace accidents and deaths are a tragedy, many say that accidents are unavoidable. 'Accidents will happen', they say, and 'It's the nature of the business', or 'Wherever you have people, you will have accidents'. If it is true that all accidents are unavoidable, then, strictly speaking, there is no point in hazard management at all (or in reading this book). But this is irrational.

> [W]e all take steps to reduce risk at work, home and play. If all accidents were inevitable we wouldn't take risk into consideration. We would stop putting lights at intersections, we wouldn't bother with lift maintenance, hospitals wouldn't sterilise equipment and, as a result, we would all live shorter lives.
>
> (Emergency Management Australia 2004: 32)

If some accidents are avoidable, which ones are not? Is it possible that in some accidents nothing could have been done to reduce the likelihood of it occurring? Clearly, some accidents are more avoidable than others, in the sense that some control actions may be difficult, time-consuming or costly, to be implemented. Too often, other motives or agendas intervene, putting staff, attendees and others at risk. It is a question of priorities.

Not one credible accident investigation has ever concluded that it was completely unavoidable. The language used in the investigations into accidents is typical. "The accidents were not inevitable or acts of God – to use that quaint and curious phrase from insurance. They resulted from human activity or, more often, inactivity. They mark a failure to take the right preventive steps". (Toohey et al. 2005: 7).

If an injury-causing incident, accident or near miss occurs at an event, immediate action is needed by the event management to deal with the injury, investigate its cause, and minimise the chance of a recurrence. If the injury or incident is severe, health and safety authorities, police and the event insurance company will investigate its cause and consequences.

In general, incidents are broadly categorised according to their severity.

- **Lost-time injuries:** those occurrences that resulted in a fatality, permanent disability or hospitalisation, or time lost from work of one day/shift or more.
- **No lost-time injuries:** those occurrences which resulted in lesser injuries, for which first aid and/or medical treatment was administered on site.
- **Near misses:** any incidents that occurred that, although not resulting in any injury, had the potential to do so.

(Toohey et al. 2005: 245)

Accident investigations usually uncover a combination of factors that caused the accident to occur: the immediate or technical causes, and the root or underlying causes. On that basis, recommendations are made to deal with the causes and avoid a recurrence.

Incident investigation processes

Incident protocols

Every event needs a simple set of protocols for dealing with incidents. Depending on the event, such protocols could be combined with those covering emergencies. A small, wallet-sized card could be distributed to all staff and sub-contractors containing basic instructions as in this example:

> *In the case of accident or near miss, you should*
>
> *provide for the safety of yourself and others.*
>
> *Notify your manager or first aid officer to arrange any treatment.*
>
> *Leave the site undisturbed unless safety requires otherwise.*
>
> *Complete an incident report form.*
>
> *Assist in any investigation.*

A full set of procedures to be included in the ESMS manual should contain:

- definitions of incident categories
- responsibilities of employees, managers, first-aid officers, medical personnel, authorities
- required activities and timeframes to cover treatment of injuries, notifying and reporting
- investigating and record-keeping.

Records must be kept of any accidents that occur. They must contain as much detail as possible and be kept for reference purposes for at least a year. Similarly, it is good practice to record all incidents that occur on the premises, such as persons ejected from the venue.

Security staff will need to record incidents involving:

- disorder
- violence
- other crime
- ill health
- all other relevant occurrences.

First-aid officers should always record treatment in a register. Normally, this would include:

- the injured person's name and occupation
- the date, time and place of the accident
- how the accident occurred and what the injured person was doing at the time
- the nature of the injury
- a brief description of the treatment given and the name of the person who gave it.

Such recording must be done ethically to take into consideration requirements for privacy, confidentiality and access to personal records. Certain personal information, such as medical and rehabilitation records, must be kept in a secure fashion in order to respect the privacy of those involved.

Investigations

Incidents and accidents occur when hazard controls are ineffective, or don't exist at all, exposing people to danger. Investigations are carried out to prevent a recurrence by finding out why the controls were ineffective and then taking any corrective steps. Investigations therefore focus on the controls that make up the core of the ESMS Plan.

Event organisations need procedures to ensure that all investigations are carried out correctly. Investigations into major incidents require a team that will usually be led by the site manager or safety officer. Such investigations should occur in two time periods – immediately after the incident has happened, to understand why controls broke down and to neutralize the hazard that caused the incident to prevent a recurrence; and after the event has concluded, to enable corrective, preventive and follow-up activity to take place at subsequent events.

Gathering information

The value of an investigation depends on the effectiveness of its recommendations – will they prevent a recurrence? These, in turn, depend on the quality of the analysis – identifying the cause of the incident. Unless the root cause is found and removed, there is the chance of recurrence. Therefore, the quality of the investigation will depend on the information gathered and the logic used – is the information accurate and complete? Does it support the conclusions?

Gathering information for an investigation begins with looking at the accident itself. What happened and what was the course of events immediately leading up to it? At this stage of an investigation the answer to this question should be a simple, factual description, not a causal explanation. The causal explanation occurs after collection of all the relevant information.

The investigation should start promptly in order to best observe conditions as they were at the time of the incident and to locate witnesses. If there has been a death or other notifiable incident, the site should, as far as possible, be left undisturbed, subject to the permission to proceed being granted by police.

Before collecting information, the investigator should gather a quick overview, take steps to preserve evidence and identify witnesses. This would include everyone in the work crew, those who became involved, medical or rescue teams and bystanders.

As physical evidence can change quickly, an early record of the following information is needed, with question such as:

- Where were the injured people when the incident occurred?
- What were the equipment, substances, devices and control measures used?
- Were there danger signs and barriers?
- Were there any damaged, tampered with or removed control measures?
- What was the state of environmental conditions, such as noise, lighting, weather?

The investigator should take photos of the general area and of specific items using everyday items, coins, people, in the photo to indicate comparative size and position. A sketch of the scene should be made and measurement details noted. Any broken equipment, debris and samples of material involved should be removed and stored for further analysis by experts. Notes should identify where these items came from. In cases involving fatalities, these activities must be left to the police.

Witnesses should be interviewed as soon as possible. A small audio recorder is ideal for this purpose. The interviews should be conducted with each individual witness separately rather than in a group, to gather individual perceptions of what happened. The recording should identify the witness, time and location, then allow the witness to talk. The investigator should use simple, positive, open questions; and not interrupt, prompt or ask leading questions. If there is a written record only, the witness should read and sign it to confirm that the record is correct. A general line of questioning would be:

● What happened?
● When did it happen?
● Where were you at the time?
● What were you doing?
● Who was with you?
● What did you see or hear?
● What were the conditions at the time (weather, noise, fumes, light, etc.)?
● What were the injured people doing?
● Why did it happen?
● How might similar incidents be prevented in the future?

The next stage of an investigation is the event organisation's procedures or practices, to determine whether any of these factors exercised any influence on hazard controls. There may also be contributing factors such as organisational pressure, tight schedules, difficult to follow rules, lack of training, long working hours or inadequate rest. This could also include insufficient hazard identification dealing with equipment, maintenance, work processes and lack of safety awareness practices. Past reports of incidents should be obtained. The event SMS policies may have been correct, but implemented inadequately, poorly communicated, or there may have been a lack of clarity about responsibilities at the operational level.

There will be a need to determine if an association between particular workplace hazards and injury can be identified. In particular, trends or hot spots. For that enquiry, performance data need to be gathered and assembled. Data are then keyed onto spreadsheets, where it can be analysed and updated. Many off-the-shelf software programs will be suitable for this activity. After some instruction, spreadsheets are, generally, relatively easy to use and are more adaptable, for example, to particular management reporting formats.

Investigating the incident cause

Once investigators know what happened and how it happened, their next step will be to consider why it happened, why the controls were ineffective. To do that, a causal analysis tree model is often used, that first identifies the incident and then sets out the causes leading up to it. There is typically a need to differentiate between the proximate (immediate) and the distal (underlying) causes of the incident.

A **proximate cause** may be defined as an activity or occurrence which is the most direct, effective or substantial cause of an accident or incident. For example, a volunteer has acted negligently by departing from the safety procedures, or there was an equipment safety guard failure. In contrast, the higher-level ultimate cause or **distal cause**, is the fundamental reason something occurred. This is the larger context in which individuals carry out their actions. For example, an organisation's negligent conduct in failing to train volunteers in safety standards of behaviour, or failing to maintain equipment.

Causal analysis tree model of an investigation

The analysis begins by an investigator asking, 'What caused the incident?' If, say, A is claimed as one factor causing the incident, evidence gathered in the first stage of the investigation is needed to back that claim. The investigator next asks, 'what caused A?' If the answer is B and C, again, evidence for that answer is required. The subsequent question is 'what caused B and C?'

The investigator continues to ask 'what caused that?' until the line of questioning no longer identifies factors that could be demonstrated to have made a significant contribution, directly or indirectly, to the incident occurring. This is the end of the causal chain. As a general rule of thumb, investigators have found you need to ask 'Why?' at least five times before arriving at the root cause.

Example: An example of a Cause Tree

Incident – person electrocuted by touching a metal pole

Cause A – electricity conducted through a non-earthed stage light
Cause B – incorrect cable wiring used to power the light (2 pin instead of 3 pin)
Cause C – the worker who installed light did not know the wiring was incorrect
Cause D – the worker had not been trained and was unregistered
Cause E – the sub-contractor used untrained and unregistered workers to save money
Cause F – the event organisers hired the sub-contractor that offered the lowest quote

Root or distal cause – the event organiser not checking the qualifications of the sub-contractor's staff and accepting the lowest quote

Having identified the causes, it is then a matter of identifying those causes that, had they not been there, would have prevented the incident and its recurrence. These are the root or underlying causes. They are normally contrasted with the direct, immediate or technical causes of the accident (faulty machine guard, repeated lifting of heavy loads).

It is possible in some instances to categorise the causes further – major, minor or contributing. If, for example, there is a manual handling injury, then the investigation should identify the factors that may be applicable in causing injury as described in the code of practice for manual handling, dealing with plant or work in confined spaces.

Incident report

A written report of the investigation should be prepared for consideration by the relevant management, health and safety representatives and others who need to know. This report should include the sequence of events leading up to the occurrence and all relevant information sufficient to explain to third parties what occurred and why.

The report should conclude by identifying any immediate corrective action that can be taken to reduce the hazard and have it implemented urgently. For example, stop all further electrical installation until supervisors can assure management that relevant training has been provided to everyone involved in the process. Generally, the root causes of incidents require more time to address in order to prevent a recurrence. Such preventive recommendations should:

- be clear about what, exactly, needs to be done
- be practical, effective and fit in with operations
- be cost-effective, in that they will represent the best value when compared to any other options
- present a timeframe for implementation
- allocate responsibilities.

Post-event hazard control review and report

One-off events need to be reviewed as soon as possible after they have taken place. As many of the staff are likely to disperse, a rapid debriefing should be carried out as soon as practicable. The information from the review, including any recommendations for improving crowd safety, will be advantageous in planning the next event.

The review needs to assess how far the ESMS safety and security objectives have been met and the performance levels achieved. It might:

- identify any changes to the venue, such as temporary changes due to building work, or changes in the staffing structure
- identify any current or potential problems, including, if possible, the reasons for them
- include liaison with other public safety agencies
- suggest ways of improving the system
- include feedback from staff.

The event manager should decide who should be involved, how the review is to be carried out and what information needs to be collected. Representatives of all crowd control and hazard management agencies involved in the event should be invited to take part in the review. If there is a large number of people involved it might be more manageable to have a number of separate reviews examining particular issues, which can then be combined in a final report.

Recording issues

Performance of safety and security measures can be tested against predetermined standards and the achievement of the objectives in the ESMS. This may be helpful in identifying when and where action is needed to improve performance. There are several types of basic information that can be collected when measuring performance. These include:

Incident reporting and investigation

- the number of people who attended
- the crowd density levels in different areas of the site
- the crowd flows in various areas during the event
- the good and bad features of the venue's design
- the effectiveness of plans and procedures.

It is useful to record problems such as:

- rule violations
- arrests
- injuries to the public and to staff
- sudden crowd movements
- periods of crowd build-up
- difficulties in communications
- complaints from the public.

Problems identified and handled during the event should be highlighted.

When measuring performance, assess all the available information, such as incident report forms, staff observations and injury statistics. One way of conducting the measurement is to compare each aspect of the running of the event with the relevant plans and procedures. If this shows, for example, that the current crowd and traffic separation safety system is not working properly, target dates could be set for designing the necessary improvements.

Debriefing

It is usual that a debrief session takes place after every event, although the size and scale of the event determines the type of debrief. For larger or more unusual events, a more formal, multi-agency debrief usually takes place to examine, for instance, what went wrong, what was successful, and what can be changed for future events. This typically includes communication issues, control structure, tactics, positioning and use of barriers, and stewarding issues.

Each staff team should complete an operational record that includes any debrief points. All actions, decisions and lessons identified should be written down, and kept on file with the planning team or transferred into policy, to be used when planning future events. Everything should be clearly recorded and fully explained, to enable future event organisers to easily understand the resulting policies.

Revising plans and procedures

Once performance has been reviewed, consider what changes to the arrangements are needed for ensuring crowd safety and security in the future. It may be helpful if the conclusions from the review are passed on to everyone involved in ensuring crowd safety in the venue.

The first task is to see if there is any immediate corrective action that can be taken to reduce the risk and have it implemented. For example, if poor hygiene led to attendees hospitalised for food poisoning, rules for food handling, storage and serving will need to be distributed to stall holders and a process for enforcement devised. Generally, the root causes of problems require time to address in order to prevent a recurrence. Such preventive recommendations should:

Figure 12.1 Sub-contractors with the best seat in the house.

- comply with corporate and legal standards
- be clear about what, exactly, needs to be done
- be practical, effective and fit in with operations
- be cost-effective, in that they will represent the best value when compared to any other options
- present a timeframe for implementation
- allocate responsibilities.

Before finalising the recommendations, relevant supervisors and health and safety representatives should have the opportunity to comment on and contribute to them.

A review period should be set for follow-up recommendations and a senior member of staff allocated responsibility to report on the implementation

Summary

- If an injury-causing incident, accident or near miss occurs at an event, immediate action is needed by the event management team to deal with the injury, investigate its cause and minimise the chance of a recurrence.
- If the injury or incident is severe, health and safety authorities, police and the event insurance company will investigate its cause and consequences.
- Accident investigations usually uncover a combination of factors that caused the accident to occur, the immediate or technical causes, and the root or underlying causes. On that basis, recommendations are made to deal with the causes and avoid a recurrence.

- Investigations therefore focus on the controls that make up the core of the ESMS plan.
- Event organisations need procedures to ensure that all investigations are carried out correctly.
- Investigations should occur in two time periods – immediately after the incident has happened, to understand why controls broke down and to neutralize the hazard that caused the incident to prevent a recurrence; and after the event has concluded, to enable corrective, preventive and follow-up activity to take place at subsequent events.
- Records must be kept of any accidents that occur. The quality of the investigation will depend on the information gathered.
- A written report of the investigation should include the sequence of events leading up to the occurrence and all relevant information sufficient to explain to third parties what occurred and why.
- The report should conclude by identifying any immediate corrective action that can be taken to reduce the hazard, and have it implemented urgently.
- Festivals and special events need to be reviewed as soon as possible after they have taken place. A debriefing should be carried out as soon as practicable. The review needs to assess how far the ESMS safety and security objectives have been met. Performance of safety and security measures can be tested against predetermined standards and the objectives in the ESMS.

Bibliography

Bajaj, B. (2003) Risk management. In R. Best, C. Langston and G. Valence (Eds) *Workplace Strategies and Facilities Management: Building in Value*. Oxford: Elsevier Butterworth-Heinemann, pp. 128–145.

Bluff, L. (2009) *The National Review into Model OHS Laws: A Paper Examining the 'Specified Classes' of Duty Holders; Reasonably Practicable and Risk Management; and Access to OHS Advice*. Canberra: National Research Centre for OHS Regulation.

Capra, M., Earl, C. and Parker, E. (2005) 'Planning and management for public health impacts at outdoor music festivals: An international study', *Environmental Health*, 5(1), 50–61.

Emergency Management Australia (2004) *Multi-Agency Incident Management*. Manual Number 17. Australian Emergency Manuals Series. Commonwealth of Australia.

Getz, D. (1997) *Event Management and Event Tourism*. New York: Cognizant Communications.

Mellor, N. and Veno, A. (1998) *Public Events: Safety and Security Strategies*. Centre for Police and Justice Studies, Monash University, Victoria.

Reason. J. (1990) *Human Error*. Cambridge: Cambridge University Press.

Reason. J. (1997) *Managing the Risks of Organisational Accidents*. London: Ashgate.

Tarlow, P. (2002) *Event Risk Management and Safety*. New York: John Wiley & Sons.

Taylor, G., Easter, K. and Hegney, R. (2004) *Embracing Occupational Safety and Health*. Oxford: Elsevier Butterworth-Heinemann.

Thompson, W. and Marks, F. (2001) *Understanding New South Wales Occupational Health and Safety Legislation*, 3rd edition. North Ryde, NSW: CCH Australia.

Toohey, J., Borthwick, K. and Archer, R. (2005) *OH&S in Australia*. Melbourne: Thomson.

Worksafe Victoria. (2006) *Advice for Managing Major Events Safely*. 1st edn. Victoria: Government of Victoria.

Appendix: case studies

Case studies 1 and 2 demonstrate the consequences of faulty venue design and equipment construction.

Case studies 3 and 4 describe crowd crush tragedies in 2010, at the Love Parade, Duisburg, and the Koh Pich Bridge in Phnom Penh, Cambodia, during the 2010 Water Festival. Both examples demonstrate that it is not only the internal event site design, but the approaches and entrances to a large event that can cause major problems.

Case study 1: Indiana State Fair stage collapse

A wind-driven stage collapse killed five people at the Indiana State Fair in August 2011. The Indiana State Fair stage toppled shortly after fair officials advised the crowd of roughly 10,000, gathered for a performance by the country band Sugarland, to take shelter from an approaching storm. Just after officials decided to order the evacuation, a gust of wind ripped through the metal and fabric structure. The National Weather Service estimated that the gust exceeded 60 miles an hour. Along with the five people killed, 40 were sent to hospital.

The investigation into the Indiana incident focused on two critical elements – approval for the design and construction of the stage, and the timing of the evacuation order at the event. This account is based on a report by **Scott Kilman** and **Amy Merrick** **published in** *Rolling Stone*, October 2011.

Stage design

Outdoor stages such as the one that collapsed require engineering compromises. They must be portable and lightweight, yet support the weight of tens of thousands of pounds of equipment. Industry standards for determining safe wind speeds are voluntary, and the building codes in many cities don't provide detailed guidance on temporary structures of this sort. Officials at engineering firms that design outdoor stages said a stage built to industry standards should have withstood such a gust.

One of the worst outdoor stage accidents occurred on 1 August, 2009, when stage scaffolding collapsed during a storm at the Big Valley Jamboree in Camrose, Alberta. A woman was killed and 75 people were injured. Charges were filed in provincial court against festival organisers for failing to ensure worker safety and failing to ensure that equipment could withstand bad weather.

It was unclear which government agency was responsible for inspecting the outdoor stage, and whether any inspection addressed its ability to cope with storm winds. The Indiana Department of Homeland Security, which oversees the state fire marshal and building commission denied responsibility, and Indianapolis officials said the city wasn't allowed to issue permits or conduct inspections on state-owned property such as the fairgrounds.

Weather evacuation warning

During the investigation into the disaster, the question of whether the deadly outcome of the stage collapse was preventable, was brought into sharp focus. The Indiana Governor Mitch Daniels said it did not appear that such a tragedy could have been predicted or how anyone could have foreseen a sudden, highly localised blast of wind. But Mike Smith, senior vice president of AcuWeather Enterprise solutions, argued that the tragedy could have been prevented, if not the stage's collapse. He claims that the event should have had someone responsible for initiating an evacuation of the area when a severe weather warning was issued.

There had been ample prior warning. Weather had created mayhem at other outdoor concerts in the 2011 summer. A Flaming Lips performance in Tulsa, Oklahoma, was cancelled after high winds caused overhead stage rigging to collapse. Wind caused a stage to collapse at Ottawa's Bluesfest while the band Cheap Trick was performing. Eight people were injured. On the same night as the stage collapse in Indiana, organisers cut short the Musikfest festival in Bethlehem, Pennsylvania, because of a lightning storm and flooding.

Paul Wertheimer, founder and head of Crowd Management Strategies, a Los Angeles-based international crowd safety consulting service, claimed many bands and concert promoters are reluctant to cancel events due to weather because of bad publicity and that festival and concert organisers can easily underestimate the danger created by a thunderstorm.

An Indiana State Police timeline of the event showed that fair staff and the National Weather Service were in touch several times on Saturday afternoon and evening. As early as 7 p.m., the National Weather Service advised fair staff that a thunderstorm was expected at the fairgrounds between 9 p.m. and 9:30 p.m. and that it would include, among other things, heavy rain and strong winds. At 8 p.m., weather service officials said the storm would arrive at the fairgrounds at approximately 9:15 p.m. and that it would contain 40 mph winds.

At 8:30 p.m., additional Indiana State Police officers moved to the grandstand to help already-on-site personnel and security workers in the evacuation of concert attendees. At 8:45 p.m., concertgoers were warned that bad weather was on the way. The stage collapsed at 8:49 p.m. after a gust of wind 60 to 70 mph came through the fairgrounds.

Case study 2: Kiss Night Club fire, Santa Maria, Brazil

An almost complete lack of concern for safety within a venue resulted in 234 deaths and long prison sentences for the event and venue operators.

Overcrowding, lack of oversight, poor layout and the use of pyrotechnics are some of the elements that are reported to have contributed to the tragedy at the Kiss nightclub in Santa Maria, Brazil in January 2013. The fire caused a death toll of 234 with 120 people hospitalised for smoke inhalation and burns, and dozens of them in critical condition. Most of the dead were college students 18 to 21 years old. Almost all died from smoke inhalation rather than burns.

The blaze began at around 2:30 a.m. local time, during a performance by a country music band that had made the use of pyrotechnics a trademark of their shows. The club was packed with an estimated 1,200 to 1,300 people. Flames broke out minutes after sparks from a pyrotechnic machine ignited the combustible insulating foam with covered the club's ceiling. The band used a flare meant for outdoor use because they cost a mere $1.25 each, compared with the $35 price tag for an indoor flare.

When the fire started, an attempt was made to quell the flames with a fire extinguisher. But it malfunctioned and the blaze rapidly spread throughout the packed club emitting a thick, toxic smoke. The roof collapsed in several parts of the building, trapping many inside. Because the venue apparently had neither an alarm nor a sprinkler system and only one working exit, the crowd was left to search desperately for a way out. For many, escaping was complicated by the fact that security guards initially stopped people from leaving. Some guards thought at first that it was a fight that happened inside the club and closed the doors so that the people could not leave without paying their bills from the club.

There was only one way out of the club, the same which was used by the public to enter the building, this only exit was a mere 2 metres wide by 2 metres high. The exit was blocked by steel barriers that made it difficult to get out and it was not wide enough for people to leave quickly. Many struggled to find the exit in the dark, as there were no exit signs. It is rare to see such signs in Brazilian clubs.

About 50 of the victims were found in the club's two bathrooms, where the blinding smoke caused them to believe the doors were exits. Police Investigator Arigony said people headed to the bathrooms because the only lights in the dark club were coming from there, and the patrons mistook them for exits. Lots of people couldn't get out and died mainly because of the smoke not the fire (Brooks 2013).

Contributing factors

The club is reported to have had a maximum capacity of 2,000 people, but no-one knows for sure how many people were inside at the time of the fire. However, BBC Brazil spoke to experts who said 1,300 people ought to have been the maximum permitted capacity of the building, based on the club's floor area of 650 square metres (7,000 square feet). The estimate is based on having two people per square metre, and takes into account limits on the number of people in venues like nightclubs, according to ABNT rules.

"If there was really only one emergency exit [in the Kiss nightclub], why was this venue allowed to operate?" said Ivan Ricardo Fernandes, civil engineer and captain of the fire department of Parana, a neighbouring state. Mr Fernandes said that "considering the size and the activity at the venue, two emergency exits would have been required, which together should add up to seven metres wide". "And according to ABNT rules, the maximum distance to be travelled to the emergency exit should be 30 metres," he added (Barrucho 2013).

There was no emergency lighting to show the quickest escape route. Many people thought a door inside the nightclub, which gave access to the toilets, was a possible emergency exit. In an interview with the Folha de Sao Paulo newspaper, Captain Edi Paul Garcia, of the military police, said he had taken some "180 bodies of victims" out of the bathrooms (Brookes 2013).

According to state safety codes in Brazil, clubs should have one fire extinguisher every 1,500 square feet as well as multiple emergency exits. Limits on the number of people admitted are to be strictly respected. None of that appears to have happened at the Santa Maria nightclub.

Licensing and regulation

In the wake of the deadly fire, questions were raised about the club's operating licence. One of the owners of the club is reported to have confirmed that they were in the process of renewing its licence to operate, and that its fire safety certificate had expired last year. According to Col Humberto Viana of the National Civil Defense (the federal emergency authorities), the club did not have a fire safety certificate, which expired in August 2012. However, the venue was allowed to operate until a new inspection was carried out.

The safety certificate is issued by the local fire department, based on an inspection, during which the agency checks that the venue complies with current regulations, and has fire extinguishers, and proper exits and emergency lighting. However, city authorities and the fire departments across the country often do not have enough people to carry out the required inspections, experts say.

"In all those tragedies, the common denominator is that . . . rules are not being followed. The local authorities and firefighters must work together to carry out thorough inspection work," Luiz Antonio Cosenza, president of the Committee for Analysis and Accident Prevention at the Regional Council of Engineering and Agronomy of Rio de Janeiro (RJ-Crea), told BBC Brazil. Inspections help to reduce the number of accidents, said Mr Cosenza. Last year alone, about 90 per cent of all accidents related to construction in Rio de Janeiro were caused by lack of maintenance, he said (Barrucho 2013). Through extensive and passionate debate, the public of Brazil demanded to know whether the failings were those of the club itself or of officials who allowed the club to operate after its licence expired last year. Many hope these questions will lead Brazil to re-evaluate its safety standards and the way they are enforced.

The government of the country's biggest city, Sao Paulo, promised tougher security regulations for nightclubs and other places where many people gather. Since the fire, a Rio de Janeiro consumer complaint hotline has received more than 60 calls denouncing hazardous conditions at night spots, theatres, supermarkets, schools, hospitals and shopping malls around the state. Blocked emergency exits and non-existent fire alarms and extinguishers top the list of most common complaints.

Compiled from reports by Luis Barrucho. BBC Brazil, and,
Bradley Brooks of Brazil nightclub Associated Press

Case Study 3: The Love Parade, Duisburg

At the Love Parade music festival in Germany on 24 July 2010, 21 people were killed and 510 injured on their way into the event.

The Love Parade in Duisburg 2010 was a dance music festival with an estimated attendance of 1 million. The site was a railway yard entered and exited by a single ramp roadway with high brick walls. The ramp meets Karl Lehr Strasse at a right angled T intersection. Karl Lehr Strasse is a two-lane roadway closed for the event for use by pedestrians. It could be entered from either the west or east after a long walk from public transport. The western approach along Karl Lehr Strasse to the entry ramp passes under three bridges, the eastern approach is through a long tunnel under rail lines.

For most of its length the road is walled and there is no possible means of leaving to the side. People can only move forward or backwards. For the 1 million attendees at the event this route was the only way in or out. It was also the same route used by service and emergency vehicles.

The crowd crush occurred when police inexplicably formed cordons by linking arms to create a human barrier to block crowd flow in to the event at the east and west ends of Karl Lehr Strasse. Another cordon was formed at the narrowest point of the entrance and exit ramp blocking preventing people from leaving the event, creating an open space at the T intersection. Crowds massed behind each cordon. When crowd pressure became extreme, the police suddenly dissolved their cordons in Karl Lehr Strasse resulting in a crowd surge that quickly reached the continuing cordon at the ramp entrance and exit to the event site. This incoming crowd mass butted up against a mass of people waiting to exit. This police cordon collapsed and two dense crowds attempted to move in opposite directions – a large crowd attempting to leave and a much larger crowd attempting to enter the event – in the narrowest part of the ramp enclosed by high sheer walls. Movement quickly stopped, but pressure from behind in both directions caused density to rapidly rise to crush level (Loveparade 2010 Videos, 2012).

A portion of the blame for the resulting deaths and injuries must lay with planners and authorities that permitted the faulty design of crowd movement. The funnelling of a crowd into a single confined roadway that is used for both ingress and egress, and by service vehicles, was a clear contravention of crowd management design principles. Add ill-judged police actions, and a tragedy was always likely.

To assist event managers and students to fully understand this tragedy and its consequences, Dirk Helbing and Pratik Mukerji have conducted a comprehensive report, released in 2012, *Crowd Disasters as Systemic Failures: Analysis of the Love Parade Disaster*.

Case Study 4: Koh Pich Bridge in Phnom Penh, Cambodia

One of the worst disasters in recent festival event history occurred in November 2010 at the Cambodian Water Festival. Just like the Love Parade tragedy, the crowd crush on the Koh Pich Bridge is a distressing and shocking instance of faulty crowd management that caused the deaths of over 350 people, with a similar number being injured.

The following account is comprised of edited extracts from a report by the Cambodian Center for Human Rights released in November 2011: *The Koh Pich Tragedy: One Year On, Questions Remain*. The centuries old Water Festival, Bon Om Touk, is the biggest party of the year in Cambodia. Both international and national visitors flock to the capital for the festivities and the boat races, and to give thanks for the end of the rainy season. During the Water Festival in 2010, however, tragedy struck on Monday 22 November, when a crowd of people packed onto the narrow Koh Pich footbridge, which connects Phnom Penh to Koh Pich ('Diamond Island'). The large numbers of people became unable to move and were caught in a crush; this ultimately led to the deaths of over 350 people, with a similar number being injured.

Reports before the 2010 festival anticipated that it would attract record numbers of people, with about 3 million people to visit the city during the festival. The festivities took place over the 3 days of the festival with the main events being boat races on the river. In the evenings, the festivities continued at nine sites throughout the city with carnival rides, traditional arts and music performances, concerts at the Diamond Center (Koh Pich), goods stalls and playgrounds for children, with live broadcasting from all radio stations and television channels.

The last boat race had ended early on the evening of 22 November, the final night of the Water Festival, and it appears that many thousands of people were trying to cross Koh Pich Bridge to attend a free concert on Koh Pich island.

The bridge became overcrowded. At some stage, people began to panic, and to push in all directions in order to try to get out. It seems that as a result, people became stuck and unable to move. People also fell over and were trampled upon. There are reports that at the worst point of the tragedy, people were piled on the floor up to eight deep, as people fell on top of those who had already fallen.

Media and news reports have labelled the tragedy as a 'stampede'. However, CCHR considers that the incident on Koh Pich Bridge is more accurately classified as a 'crush': a crowd of people pressing against one another. Although the people on the bridge appear to have been panicked by something, and may well have pushed to try to escape the bridge, in fact, there was nowhere for anyone to go. There was no 'wild headlong rush' and no 'flight'. Instead, people were trapped together in a confined area and were pressing against each other to the point where they were unable to move.

There is a great deal of uncertainty over the facts about the number of people involved in the crush. Some news articles reported that between 7,000 to 8,000 people were on the bridge at the time, while others estimated the amount to be 5,000. The Main Committee (a government enquiry) that investigated the causes of the incident stated that there were 7,000 to 8,000 people on the bridge, which is 10 to 12 people per metre squared. It is generally accepted that people will start to feel uncomfortable and a crush may occur when there are more than six people per metre squared.

Koh Pich Bridge, which links Phnom Penh to the island, was built between 2009 and 2010, and had only opened just in time for the festival. As it was new, there were no signs of damage at the time of the crush. The bridge is a standard suspension bridge: two arches at either end, with cables supporting the span. The bridge is 101 metres long.

The bridge was supposed to operate a one-way system so that people were travelling in one direction, with a second bridge 200 metres to the south allowing people to travel in the opposite direction. However, it appears that on the night in question, the second bridge was closed, or that the organisers did not enforce the traffic directions and people were walking in both directions over the bridge.

Two Singaporean businessmen, who organised a sound and light show for the festival, said that authorities had closed the second bridge, forcing tens of thousands of people to use a single bridge. There were also reports that concerts had just ended at both ends of the bridge, leading to increased amounts of traffic from both directions.

Susi Tan of the OCIC said that the firm's security team noticed that most visitors were choosing to leave by the northern bridge, and tried to funnel them to the two other bridges. However, she said "the crowd had other ideas". The 20 security guards deployed to stop them failed to do so: "We put up barriers and we tried to block the crowd . . . with a crowd like that, even if you use 100 guards, it would not be enough". A police officer from Phnom Penh that CCHR interviewed said that before the event, police had been assigned to stand at various places in order to enforce the traffic directions and stop motorbikes entering the bridge. However, he said that at the time of the incident, few police officers were standing on guard, and those that were, allowed people to travel in both directions.

There were limited reports in the media about barriers being used on the bridge to stop motorcycles crossing. For example, a vendor near the bridge that night, said barriers were in place to prevent people from walking onto the road, which meant those exiting the bridge were unable to move away quickly: "The rest backed up behind them." One witness stated that 2 days before the crush, he noticed street vendors blocking the way on the bridge.

Of the people CCHR interviewed who were involved in the disaster, 54 per cent said that barriers were in use at the bridge and that they hindered people being able to move away from the scene, and caused people to fall over, increasing the chaos. A police officer from Phnom Penh that CCHR interviewed also said that there were not enough police officers in the area, and instead, a barrier had been left at the entrance. A man from Kandal said that the chains were the size of his wrist. A man from Takeo said: "the barriers and chains were put at both sides of the bridge. I think they were supposed to ban motorcycles from entering, but I could see a motorbike on the bridge and it caused people to fall down. At that time, lots of young people fell over the chains".

It seems clear that the use of barriers on the bridge would have contributed to the scale of the disaster, and indeed to the causes of it. For example, it is likely that the barriers would have meant that people were unable to move away from the crush, which could have contributed to the concentration of people on the bridge, and prevented people from being able to ease the pressure at the centre of the bridge. The barriers are also likely to have been a significant – if not the main – factor in causing people to fall over and be trampled upon.

It also appears that there were well below the number of security guards and police who were reportedly set to be on duty around the bridge, who might have been able to assist if any incident had broken out, as it in fact did.

Both the lack of enforcement of the one-way system, and the barriers on the bridge are likely to have contributed to the scale of the tragedy. These factors also show that the authorities did not appreciate either that such events could take place, or how they could be prevented.

Crowd behaviour

Although the facts of the night of 22 November are unclear, it seems certain that the people on the bridge panicked for some reason. There have been a number of theories as to why people panicked, and what led to the concern of those on the bridge that night. For example, Information Minister Khieu Kanharith said that the crush began when the people became "scared of something".

The bridge was collapsing

One explanation for the panic was that rumours spread that the bridge was collapsing. Shortly after the crush, the RGC explanation of the cause was that the "crush was due to the suspension bridge, and the fact that people from the provinces were not aware that such bridges sway". Similarly, a military police investigator, Sawannara Chendamirie, said it appeared that the panic began when some people began shouting that the bridge was collapsing.

Electrocution and use of water cannons

There were reports that a number of people were afraid when they noticed that some of the lights on the bridge began to spark and people received shocks from the bridge. Thinking they were being electrocuted, people surged forward and tried to escape. For example, one survivor, said, "At first we were frightened of an electric wire. After that I fell and people ran over me. People were stepping on me." Reuters also reported that a scare was set off when several people were electrocuted from an unknown source.

It was reported that the police and military sprayed water onto the bridge to help disperse, calm or cool the crowds. Some reports also stated that this was a "naive attempt to get people moving" or to keep people away from the bridge. However, some of the witnesses said this had the effect of causing electric shocks when the water came into contact with the electric wiring on the bridge. The bridge was illuminated with bright lights, but it was unclear whether water could have triggered any electrocutions. However, even rumours about possible electrocutions, even if none actually took place, may have contributed to the causes of the panic itself.

Fainting

As a result of so many people being so tightly packed together on the bridge, a number of people began to faint. This also caused panic, and people started to push and try to exit the bridge as quickly as possible. For example, a soft drink vendor said that trouble began when about 10 people fell unconscious in the press of the crowd. It was also noted that Information Minister Khieu Kanharith gave a similar account of the cause.

Fight between gangsters

There were some reports that rumours spread of a fight that had broken out between two rival gangs. There were also some reports that pick-pockets, possibly coordinated by the gangs, were operating on the bridge. Of the people CCHR interviewed who were on the bridge that night, 10 per cent said that the panic started due to the involvement of gangsters. An additional 17 per cent said that the cause was a mixture of gangster involvement and rumours that the bridge was collapsing.

The possible explanations above, are based on what was reported in the media, and the information gathered from our interviews of witnesses. However, it seems likely that the panic was the result of a number of different factors, and also that we will never know the true sequence of events. However, when the number of people within a confined area increases to over six per metre squared, people become uncomfortable and try to escape. The panic and resulting crush could simply be due to the fact that there were too many people within the small area of the bridge.

Responsibility

The comments made by the various RGC officials about the crush and the possible responsibilities of the authorities involved varied considerably. Some spokesmen accepted a certain lack of preparation by the authorities in charge. For example, the RGC admitted it had overlooked issues of crowd control at the event: "We were concerned about the possibilities of boats capsizing and pick-pocketing . . . we did not think about this kind of incident" said Information Minister Khieu Kanharith. Prum Sokha, Secretary of State for the Interior Ministry who headed the investigation into the cause of the crush, also acknowledged that the RGC had not looked into whether the bridges could handle the expected crowds: "If there had been a study, we would have been able to avoid this." When asked why the study had not happened, he said "your question is too hard."

It is evident that the preparations for the Water Festival were focused on terrorism and dissenter prevention, injuries in the water, or preventing petty criminal activity. From the published information CCHR has been able to identify, there do not appear to have been detailed or specific measures relating to crowd management and control (other than a reference to "preserve public order and arrangements" on the Phnom Penh City Hall website), or the possible risks associated with the large number of visitors to the city. After the incident, police officials conceded there were a number of short-falls in handling the crowds. National Police spokesman Kirth Chantharith accepted that the police were overwhelmed by the crowd, that there were too few police at the scene, and that the police that were present may not have been prepared or properly trained.

Despite this, the police and authorities did not take ultimate responsibility for security on the bridge. No one was held accountable for the tragedy, and the RGC maintained that it was an unforeseen accident. Prime Minister Hun Sen and the police officers con-sidered the tragedy was an unpredictable event: "We did not expect that people could fatally collide with each other like motorbikes and cars. If anybody expected it and had told us and we ignored it, I as Prime Minister would ask all the ministers to resign." Kep Chuktema was quoted as saying: "I am truly responsible for the security and order preparations, but if you imagine that in the entire city of Phnom Penh, there was no less than 4 million people who came in to see the Bon Om Touk festival, there was no incident whatsoever. This year, we are very happy to see that the preparation was done the best possible [sic]. But, it was unintentional that we did not think this tragedy could take place". This quote appears to marginalise the scale of the disaster at Koh Pich, and implies that it could not have been avoided with adequate crowd control procedures.

In local and regional media the police came under criticism for a failure of crowd management and for an inadequate and incompetent response to the disaster. Some reports went as far as to say that "military and police attempts to control the crowd may have exacerbated fear and confusion and caused further fatalities." One police officer said that only half the officially reported numbers of police officers were actu-ally deployed. One report said 106 private security guards and 12 police officers were on Koh Pich that night, apparently jointly responsible for crowd control compared to the 2,838 officers which were reportedly supposed to be assigned to the district which included Koh Pich.

The Asian Human Rights Commission summed up the situation by saying: "while the exact cause of the stampede last night remains unclear, with contradictory reports indicating it may have been instigated by either crowd antics or poor construction of the bridge to Koh Pich, the failure of the state to control the crowd and limit the damage from the stampede is clear."

The full report is available from the Cambodian Center for Human Rights: **www.sithi.org**.

References

Barrucho. L. (2013) 'Could Brazil's club fire have been avoided?', BBC Brazil, San Paulo. Online. Available HTTP: <http://www.bbc.com/portuguese>, 1 February 2013.

Brooks. B. (2013) 'Brazil nightclub fire: Police point to cheap outdoor flares'. Brazil nightclub Associated Press. Online. Available HTTP: <http://hosted.ap.org>, 29 January, 2013.

Cambodian Center for Human Rights (2011) *The Koh Pich Tragedy: One Year on, Questions Remain.* CCHR. Khan Chamkar Mon, Phnom Penh, Kingdom of Cambodia.

Helbing. D. & Mukerji. P. (2012) *Crowd Disasters as Systemic Failures: Analysis of the Love Parade Disaster.* EPJ Data Science

Kilman. S. and Merrick. A. (2011) 'Indiana State Fair Stage Collapse', *Rolling Stone*, October 2011.

Loveparade (2012) Video: *Loveparade 2010.* Online. Available HTTP: <www.documentation-loveparade.com>

Index

Abbink, H. 260
acceleration forces in crowds 73
access 113, 128–9; emergency services
    113–14, 116; service 112, 128
accident protocols 39
accountability 21, 22
age identification wristbanding 193–4
agent-based models of crowd behaviour
    72, 74–5
aggressive crowds 51, 92
ALARP principle 4, 28
alcohol 98, 108, 161, 187–98; adverse
    health and social effects 188–9;
    advertising 194–5; age restrictions
    193–4; breathalysers 197–8; and
    crowd control 191; designated areas
    192–3; and drugs 198–200; and food
    availability 194; harm minimisation
    benefits/considerations 189, 197;
    licensing requirements 182, 190;
    monitoring for intoxication 195;
    refusing to serve alcohol to intoxicated
    guests 196; removal of intoxicated
    patrons 196–7; responsible drinking
    strategies 189; responsible service of
    190–1; safe partying policy 186–7; sales
    staff 190–1; seized 219; spiking 206;
    time period for availability of 192; and
    tobacco 200
alcohol-free events 191
ambulance services 144
ambulatory crowds 92
amphetamines, and alcohol 199
approvals, site use 110
'assumption of risk' 13
audience number estimations 107–8
audiovisual (AV) equipment 175–6
auditorium 126–7, 155

auditorium protocols 40
Australia 4; National Building Technology
    Centre 48; National Occupational
    Health and Safety Commission Act 5
Australia—New Zealand Counter-
    Terrorism Committee 231, 232
Australian National Council on Drugs 202
authority 21, 22

backstage 129–31; entrances/exits 112;
    see also green room areas
bag checks 218
barriers and fences 124, 133, 152
basic protocols 37–8
Berk, R. 53
Berlonghi, A. 67–8, 81, 92
Big Valley Jamboree stage collapse,
    Camrose, Alberta (2009) 292
biomechanics 164
Boddy, N. 201, 202, 203
body searches 218, 219
'boids' model of crowd behaviour 72
bomb threats 162–3, 239–40
bottlenecks 84, 85, 90, 112, 118
box office protocols 40
Bruinsma, G. 260

Caldicott, D. 201–2
campgrounds 138–9
cancellation of events 94, 96, 97, 153,
    170, 253–4
cannabis, and alcohol 198
Canter, D. 55, 56, 268
case examples: Big Valley Jamboree stage
    collapse, Camrose, Alberta (2009) 292;
    Ibrox Park soccer stadium incident
    (1971) 48; Indiana State Fair stage
    collapse (2011) 292–3; Jamarat Bridge

disaster, Mina, Saudi Arabia (2006) 48; Kiss Nightclub fire, Santa Maria, Brazil (2013) 107, 293–5; Koh Pich Bridge disaster, Phnom Penh, Cambodia (2010) 25, 107, 296–300; Love Parade music festival disaster, Duisburg (2010) 48, 57, 107, 295–6; Musikfest festival, Bethlehem, Pennsylvania (2011) 293; Ottawa Bluesfest 205, 293; Station nightclub fire, Rhode Island (2003) 55

casual crowds 50

causal analysis of incidents 285–6

CCTV (closed circuit television) 93, 98–9, 237

celebrations, crowds at 50

celebrity security 223–5

cellular automata models of crowd behaviour 72, 74

certification, equipment operators 171

Challenger, R. 46, 50, 65, 66, 68, 71, 268

chemical, biological or radiological (CBR) terrorist attacks 246

chemical storage 185

Chen, R. 259

chill-out space 204

chlorine 175

cleanliness: food contact surfaces 184; hand washing facilities 137, 182, 183; of venue/infrastructure 68

cocaine, and alcohol 199

Cocking, C. 57, 58, 266

codes of practice 9, 11–12, 12; compliance/non-compliance 11

cohesive crowds 92

communicating with crowds 100–3; in an emergency 257–8, 266, 269–70; during event 102; on-site communication systems 103; pre–event 101–2, see also information provision

communicating with staff see staff communications

communications in an emergency see emergency communications

complacency 23

compliance: with codes of practice 11; public health 156

comprehensive protocols 40

compressive asphyxia 46, 48

computer aided design (CAD) 117

concert crowds 50

confiscation of prohibited items 219

consultation 8, 23

contractors/sub–contractors 9, 115; insurance 14; management of 152; security 219–20; security checks for 223; selection of 14, 219–20

control risks 29

conventional crowds 50

'corner hugging' 70, 84

Corporate Homicide Act (2007), UK 2

Corporate Manslaughter Act (2008), UK 2

counter terrorism security advisers (CTSAs) 232–3, 235, 236

Crompton, J. 51

crowd behaviour: causes of poor 67–8; DIM-ICE model of 75–6; factors influencing 90; monitoring 90–3, 97–8; simulation modelling 69–75

crowd behaviour in an emergency 270–1; affiliation and normative approaches to 56, 57–8; and habitual behaviour 55–6, 270–1; leadership and 58; mass panic theory of 56–7; social identity approach to 56, 57–8

crowd behaviour theory 46, 52–6; crowding perception 53–5; deindividuation 52; group mind theory 52; mob sociology 52–3; place scripts 55–6; social identity model 53

crowd control 81, 90–3; and crowd management distinguished 67; in designated drinking areas 191; factors triggering need for 67; staff 58, 93–7, 100, 215–16

crowd crush 46, 47, 48, 81, 296, 297, 298

crowd demographics 90

crowd density 47, 48, 50, 53–4, 73, 81, 82–3, 90, 267

crowd disasters 48; death and injury in 46; factors raising probability of 65–6, 81; panic stampede view of 46, 56–7; see also under case examples

crowd dispersal strategies 99

crowd flow 81, 82–3, 84–6, 155

crowd forces 48–9, 54, 65, 70, 73, 81

crowd jams 84–5

crowd management 24, 81, 90, 155; and crowd control distinguished 67 crowd management planning 65–79; and DIM-ICE model 75–6; manuals 69; simulation modelling 69–75; 'What if' exercises 75

crowd monitoring 90–3, 97–9

crowd mood 51

crowd numbers/size 50, 90, 97–8, 107–8

crowd pressure detectors 98

crowd processing 86–8; early opening and delayed closing 86–7; ticketing 86, 87–8

crowd surfing 96

crowd turbulence/quake 47–9

crowd volunteers 58, 94

crowding perception 53–5; expectancy 54; social interference 54, 55; stimulus overload 54

crowds: aggressive or hostile 51, 92; ambulatory 92; at celebrations 50; at concerts 50; casual 50; clusters within 83; cohesive 92; collective purpose 50; communicating with 100–3; conventional 50; criteria characterising 50; defining 49–52; demonstrator 93; dense or suffocating 93; different crowds within 51–2, 92; disability or limited movement 92; emotional intensity 93; escaping or trampling 93; expectations 101; expressive or revellous 51, 92; group behaviour within 93; individual behaviour with 93; participatory 92; rushing or looting 93; self-organisation 52, 85–6; separation of group members within 84; social identity 50, 51, 52, 53, 57–8; spectator 92; and traffic separation 112, 118; types of 49, 50–1, 51–2, 91–3; violent 93

crush/crushing 46, 47, 48, 81, 296, 297, 298

deaths 46

debriefing 288

deindividuation 52

demographics of crowds 90

demonstrator crowds 93

density see crowd density

design 75; inappropriate 65; versus operational practicalities 23–4; see also site layout and design

Dickie, J. F. 65–6, 81

Dillon, P. 203

DIM-ICE model 75–6

disability or limited movement crowds 92

disabled access and facilities 24, 127, 128

dismantlement of a site 159

dispersal of crowds 99

documentation 28; see also hazard registers; incident reporting and investigation

Donald, I. 55, 56, 268

doors and windows 134

drink: sales 108; spiking 206; see also alcohol

drinking water 139, 204

drugs 98, 161, 186, 198–204, 212; and alcohol 198–200; deterrence-based approach to 203–4; overdoses 200–1; pill testing 201–4; safe partying policy 186–7; seizing of 219

Drury, J. 53, 57, 58, 266

due diligence 7

duty of care 2–4, 11, 12; compliance so far as is reasonably practicable 3, 4

duty of care holders 3, 4, 8

e-ticketing 87–8

ecstasy (MDMA) 203; and alcohol 199

Elaborated Social Identity Model 57–8

electrical equipment, weather/ waterproofing of 175–6

elimination of hazards at source 35

Elliott, D. 65

emergency communications 255–6, 257–63; between agencies 259–63; and evacuation 266; planning 258–9; with the public 257–8, 266, 269–70; with staff 258

emergency equipment 110, 155, 276

emergency exercises or drills 276

emergency exits/entrances 110, 112, 118, 127, 156, 271–2

emergency grab bags 263–5

emergency lighting 110, 257

Emergency Operations Centre (EOC) 93, 102, 113, 254–7; communications system/procedure 255–6, 262–3; documented procedures 255–6; situational awareness 256; staff 255, 256

emergency power 256–7
emergency protocols 39–40
emergency response 252–80; cancellation of events 253–4; equipment 110, 155, 276; leadership and 272–3, 275; post-emergency recovery phase 274–5; staff training 275–6; see also emergency communications; evacuation
emergency services 22, 23; access 113–14, 116; site maps for 115; vehicles 115, 116, 144
emergency signs 114, 122, 272
emotional intensity of crowds 93
entrance points 81, 97–8, 111, 112, 124, 125; dispersed 113, 125; emergency 112, 113; restricted areas 128–9; service 112, 128
entrance protocols 40
entrapment theory of panic 56
Environment, Health and Safety (EHS) software 35
environmental hazards 110
equipment 170–6; emergency 110, 155, 276; guarding controls 172, 173; hazard identification and assessment process 171–2; lock out/ tag out protocols 40, 174; locking switches 173–4; modifications 174–5; operational controls 172–4; registration, licensing, certification, permit to work 171; systems of work 171–2; weather/waterproofing of 175–6
ergonomics 164–6
escaping or trampling crowds 93
evacuation 231, 262, 265–70; assembly areas 114, 155, 265–6, 273–4; decision to evacuate 267–8; delayed warnings 268–9; exercises or drills 276; guidance 271–3; instructions to the public 269–70; and leadership 272–3; planning 265–7; protocols 39, 226; signs 114, 272; simulation software 73–5
event breakdown 149, 159
Event Safety Guide: A Guide to Health, Safety and Welfare at Music and Similar Events 82

Event Safety Management System (ESMS) 19–44, 253, 283, 284, 287; and event safety policy 20–1, 25–6; general structure 19; hazard control 35–7; hazard evaluation 29–5; hazard and risk management process 26–8; health and safety officer 22; identifying activities 26; monitoring and evaluation 41–2; multi-agency teamwork 24–5; organisational structure and allocation of responsibilities 21–2, 24; partnerships 22–4; post-event review of 287–9; protocols 37–40; software 35
event safety policy 20–1, 25–6
evidentiary standards 11
exit points 81, 97, 111, 112, 116, 125; dispersed 113, 125; emergency 110, 112, 118, 127, 156, 271–2; service 112, 128
EXODUS evacuation model 74
expectancy theory of crowding 54
exposure standards 10–11
expressive crowds 51, 92

falling from height 10
'faster is slower' effect 70
fences and barriers 124, 133, 152
Festinger, L. 52
fire protocols 39
fire safety 177–8
firearm attacks 241–4
fireworks and flares 177
first aid 110, 114, 116, 141–4, 152, 275
first aid attendants 160
flooring 156
flow see crowd flow
flow charts 88–90
fluid dynamics models of crowd behaviour 72
food/food safety 128, 182–5; and alcohol consumption 194; catering licenses 182; cleaning and sanitising food contact surfaces 184; food handling 182, 183, 184, 185; gas cylinders 185; hand washing 137, 182, 183; storage 182, 185; supplies 184; thawing, cooking, heating and cooling 184; vans or stalls 128, 182–5; waste disposal 139–40, 183

force effects in crowds 48–9, 54, 65, 70, 73
front-to-back communication 101
Fruin, J. J. 47, 48, 54, 65, 81, 82, 93, 126
fun runs 114

Galea, E. 268
gangways 126, 155, 156
gas cylinders 185
Getz, D. 112, 118
Goffman, E. 84
Graefe, A. R. 53
green room areas 131; media access to 217–18; VIP 226
greenfield sites 111, 159
group mind theory 52
guardrails, leaning force on 48
Guide to Safety at Sports Grounds 82

habitual behaviour in a place 55–6, 270–1
hand counters 97
hand washing facilities 137, 182, 183
hazard, defined 26, 27, 28
hazard audit 28
hazard control 35–7
hazard evaluation 29–34; impact effect/description 33; likelihood description 33; priority 34
hazard identification 29–30, 108; checklists 30–3
hazard management 27; definitions 27–8
hazard registers 28, 171
hazardous substances 176–7
Hazardous Substances Information System 176
hazardous waste 140
health; definition of 6; promotion 204–5
Health and Safety at Work Act (1974), UK 2
Health and Safety Executive, UK 163
health and safety officers 22
hearing protection 204
heavy vehicle terrorist attacks 246–7
Heberlein, T. A. 54
Helbing, D. 47–8, 73, 84, 296
Henein, C.M. 49, 73
herding 70, 73, 82
heroin, and alcohol 199

high profile events, security provision for 225–7
hostile crowds 51, 92

Ibrox Park soccer stadium incident (1971) 48
improvement notices 12
improvised explosive devices (IEDs) 237–40
incident reporting and investigation 13, 282–91; causal analysis 285–6; gathering information 284–5; incident protocols 282–3; record–keeping 283; written report 286–7
incident(s): defined 28; injury-causing 46, 282; near misses 282
Indiana State Fair stage collapse (2011) 292–3
infection control 205
information management, hazard 41, 42
information provision 75, 100–2; and evacuation 266, 269–70; lack of, and crowd disaster probability 65, 81, 100; lack of, in emergency situations 259–60; overload, in emergency situations 260
infringement notices 12
injury-causing incidents 46, 282
inspections 12–13
insurance 15; cancellation 254; contractors 14
Integrum QHSE Risk & Compliance Software 35
investigation notices 12
IP rating 176
isolation of hazards 35

Jamarat Bridge disaster, Mina, Saudi Arabia (2006) 48
'just in time' (JIT) schedules 151

Kilman, S. 292
Kiss Nightclub fire, Santa Maria, Brazil (2013) 107, 293–5
Koh Pich Bridge disaster, Phnom Penh, Cambodia (2010) 25, 107, 296–300

lane formation 70, 85–6
Langston, P. A. 81, 107

language issues 101
lawlessness, crowd 92
Le Bon, G. 46, 52, 56
leadership: and crowd behaviour 58; in emergency situations 272–3, 275
leaning forces in crowds 73
Lee, H. 53
'legal highs', and alcohol 199–100
legislation 2, 9; administration of 12
liability, release and waiver 13–15
licenses/licensing regulations 152, 171; alcohol 182, 190; catering 182
lighting 68, 112, 118, 132; emergency 110, 257; of emergency entries/exits 113; external 124; outdoor rated 175–6; stage 169
likelihood, defined 28
litter management 140–1
local authorities 152, 182
looting 93
lost-time injuries 282
Love Parade music festival disaster, Duisburg (2010) 48, 57, 107, 295–6

machinery and equipment see equipment
McKay, S. 51
manuals 40, 69
marijuana (cannabis), and alcohol 109
marshals, parking 113, 120–1, 160
mass panic theory 56–7
Mecca pilgrimage disaster (Jamarat Bridge), (2006) 48
media passes 217–18
medical facilities/personnel 110, 114, 116, 141–4; see also emergency services; first aid
Merrick, A. 292
minors 14–15
mob sociology 52–3
mobile phones 258
Molnar, P. 73
Momboisse, R. 50–1, 52
monitoring: crowd behaviour 90–3, 97–9; hazard management processes 41–2
motives for attending events 51
Mukerji, P. 296
multi-agency teamwork 24–5

Musikfest festival, Bethlehem, Pennsylvania (2011) 293

Najman, J. 203
National Building Technology Centre, Australia 48
National Counter-Terrorism Security Office (NaCTSO), UK 231
National Occupational Health and Safety Commission Act, Australia 5
National Police Chief Council (NPCC), UK 230–1
natural disasters 67
near miss incidents 282
Netten, N. 259
no lost-time injuries 282
noise 11
notification of incidents 13

occupational health and safety (OH&S) 2–3, 4–7; consultation element 8; defining 5–6; information sources 6–7; objectives 6; responsibilities of managers 7–8; suppliers and contractors 9; workers rights and duties 8–9
occupational overuse syndrome (OOS) 165–6
on-the-spot fines 12
operations management see site operations
Ottawa Bluesfest 205, 293
overcrowding 47
overflow areas 110

panic stampede or flight 46, 52, 56–7
parades/processions 114
parking 108, 111, 114, 116, 120–1; emergency services 113; marshals/officials 113, 120–1, 160; overflow 110; secure 121, 226
participants, liability 13, 14–15
participatory crowds 92
partnerships 22–4
passes 216–18; media 217–18; staff 216–17, 227; temporary 218; VIP area 226–7
Pauls, J. 101, 125
penalty notices 12

perception of crowding levels *see* crowding perception
performance areas: design 127, 131–2, 133; safety measures 168–70
performance-based standards 10
performers: actions/misbehaviour of 96–7, 170; backstage access 112; green room areas 131; security 223–5
perimeters 124
permit to work procedures 171
personal hygiene 205; *see also* toilet and washing facilities
personal protective equipment (PPE) 35, 166–8
persons conducting a business or undertaking (PCBUs) 7–8
pictograms 101
place scripts/schema 55–6, 270–1
places of mass gathering (PMG) 231
police 22, 23, 92, 159, 160, 211, 212, 224, 226; counter terrorism security advisers (CTSAs) 232–3, 235, 236; and crowd control 67; first responders to terrorism incidents 231, 243–4; notification of event 212; security co–ordinators (SecCo) 236
police intelligence 69
Police Tactical Group (PTG) 231
post-event hazard control review and report 287–9; debriefing 288; recording issues 287–8; revising plans and procedures 288–9
postponement of events 153, 254
power supply 132, 155, 175; emergency 256–7
process standards 11
production *see* site production
prohibition notices 12
Project SoundCheck 205
property damage 92
protocols 37–40; basic 37–40; communications 157–8; comprehensive 40; firearms/weapons incidents 242–3; improvised explosive device (IED) incidents 238–9; public 37; specific 40
Proulx, G. 269
psychological aspects: of human behaviour 70; of work health 6

public address systems 115, 257–8
public health 205; compliance 156; hazards 110
public order 5
public protocols 37
public transport 108, 111, 114, 121–2, 159
pushing forces in crowds 65, 73, 81

queuing 70, 73, 85, 113, 237
queueing theory 88

Radio Frequency Identification (RFID) 216–17
ramps 126
re-scheduling events 153, 254
record-keeping 283
reduction of hazard 35
registration, equipment 171
regression models of crowd behaviour 72
regulations 9, 10, 12, 152
Regulatory Enforcement and Sanctions Act (2008), UK 2
Reicher, S. 49–50, 52, 53
release *see* waiver and release
repetitive strain injury *see* occupational overuse syndrome (OOS)
repulsive forces in crowds 73
residual risk, defined 28
resource supply scheduling 151
respond hazards 29
responsibilities, allocation of 21–2, 24
restricted areas 128–31
review, post–event 41, 287–9
revising plans and procedures 288–9
RF Safe-Stop system 247
rigging 152
risk: avoidance 14; control 29; defined 26, 27, 28; residual 28; transfer 14–15
Ritter, A. 202
roadways: closure of 110, 114; restricted access 113
route choice models of crowd behaviour 72
rubbish collection hazards 36–7
rule-based models of crowd behaviour 72

safe partying policy 186–7
safe sex messages 204
safety, concept in legislation 6

safety culture 20
safety data sheets 8
safety evaluation 108–11
safety hazard, defined 28
safety management software 35
safety policy 20–1, 25–6
sales staff 160; alcohol 190–1
searching of persons 218–19; bag
    checks 218; body searches 218, 219;
    confiscated items 219; staff for 219;
    warning notices 218
seating 127, 134; temporary raked 135
security 5, 68, 152, 211–28; and crowd
    control 67, 91, 215–16; 'early and
    often' techniques 216; high profile
    events 225–7; performer, celebrity and
    VIP 223–5, 226–7; procedures 215–16;
    searches see searching of persons;
    see also terrorism
security contractors 219–20
security managers 235–6, 256
security passes 216–18, 226–7
security screening of staff 221–3;
    contractor staff 223; criminal
    convictions 223; employment checks
    222–3; identity verification 222;
    pre-employment screening 221–2;
    qualifications and employment history
    222
security staff 92, 93–4, 129, 138, 160, 196,
    197, 211, 213–15; briefing of 214–15;
    co-operation with ushers/stewards 214;
    general duties 213–14; identification
    213; passes 217; patrols 214; qualities
    required of 213; for searching persons
    219
self-categorisation theory 53, 58
service access 112, 128
sexual activity 204
sexual molestation/assault 96, 205–6
Shelby, B. 54
shockwaves 82
shut down see event breakdown
sign-on sheets 130
signage 68, 101–2, 110, 111, 112, 118,
    122–4, 156; alcohol advertising 194–5;
    colours 123–4; electronic message
    123; emergency/evacuation 114, 122,
    272; language issues 101; location and

orientation 122, 123; special needs
    128
Sime, J. D. 56, 81, 100, 169, 257, 269
simulation modelling of crowd behaviour
    69–75; evacuation 73–5; and force
    effects 73; macroscopic models 71, 72;
    microscopic models 71, 72–3
SIMULEX evacuation model 74–5
site administration office 93, 102
site construction: precinct control 151–2;
    sub-contractor management 152
site construction scheduling 150;
    production scheduling 150–1; resource
    supply scheduling 151
site inspection 108, 109–10
site layout and design 107, 111–14, 128–9;
    access entry 113; and audience number
    estimations 107–8; auditorium 126–7;
    backstage area 129–31; campgrounds
    138–9; computer aided design (CAD)
    117; crowd/traffic–related issues 112;
    doors and windows 134; emergency
    services access 113–14; entrances/exits
    and perimeters 124–5; green room
    areas 131; lighting 110, 112, 113, 118,
    132; medical facilities 110, 116, 141–4;
    power supply 132; restricted areas
    128–31; safety evaluation 108–11;
    seating 127, 134, 135; separation
    issues 112; signage 110, 111, 112,
    114, 118, 122–4, 128; special needs
    127, 128; stages/performance areas
    126–7, 131–2, 133; stairways, gangways
    and ramps 126; stalls 128; street and
    unconfined events 114–15; temporary
    structures 134, 135; toilet and washing
    facilities 108, 128, 135–8; vehicle
    traffic management 117–22; waste
    management 108, 128, 139–41
site management: ergonomics 164–6;
    event breakdown 159; fire safety
    177–8; fireworks and flares 177;
    hazardous substances 176–7;
    occupational stress 162–4; performance
    area and stage safety 168–70; personal
    protective equipment (PPE) provision
    166–8; staff communications 40, 157–9;
    violence 160–2; see also equipment;
    site operations; site production

site managers 154
site maps 115–17
site operations 149, 154–9; immediate pre-opening activities 154–5; public health compliance 156; staff communications 40, 157–9; supervision of event operation and venue services 155–6
site production 149–53; safety monitoring 153; weather impacts 153, *see also* site construction
slipping hazards 156
Smith, D. 65
social facilitation theory 55
social forces model of crowd behaviour 72, 73
social identity of crowds 50, 51, 52, 53, 57–8
social interference theory of crowding 54, 55
software: computer aided design (CAD) 117; evacuation simulation 73–5; safety management 35
Someren, M. van 259
sound equipment 175–6
space 81, 82; inadequate 65; occupancy levels 54
special needs 127–8; *see also* disabled access and facilities
specific protocols 40
spectator crowds 92
spreadsheet modelling 71
staff: alcohol sales 190–1; crowd control 58, 93–7, 100, 215–16; Emergency Operations Centre (EOC) 255, 256; food handling 185; groups most affected by violence 160; medical/first aid 110, 142–3, 160; numbers 94–5; passes 216–17, 227; sales 160; security awareness 237; stewards and ushers 58, 95–6, 103, 160, 214; stress 162–4; toilet attendants 138; volunteer 58, 94, 100; *see also* security screening of staff; security staff; staff communications; staff training
staff communications 40, 157–9; in an emergency 258–9; example protocol for 157–8
staff training 26, 35, 100, 237; for emergencies 275–6

stage managers 169–70
stages 126–7, 131–2, 133; break-away skirt 133; safety measures 168–70
stairways 126, 155, 156
stakeholders, defined 28
stalls 128; food 128; tattooing and body piercing 186
Standard Emergency Warning Signal 257
standards 9, 10, 12; performance-based 10–11; prescriptive 10; process 11
Station nightclub fire, Rhode Island (2003) 55
statistical analysis 71
stewards 58, 95–6, 103, 160, 214
Still, G. K. 65, 69, 72, 75–6, 266–7
stimulus overload 54
Stott, C. 53
street events 114–15, 159
stress 54, 70; occupational 162–4
sub-contractors *see* contractors/sub-contractors
suicide bomb attacks 240–1
sun protection 204
suppliers 9, 112, 115
suspending events 254
swimming areas 111
Synergi Life software 35

task saturation 252
tattooing and body piercing stalls 186
teamwork, multi-agency 24–5
technical rehearsal 169
temporary structures 134, 135
terminology, consistency of 25
terrorism 2, 114, 221, 224, 230–50; bomb threat 239–40, 262–3; chemical, biological or radiological (CBR) attacks 246; and evacuation planning 267; firearm attacks 241–4; heavy vehicle attacks 246–7; hostile reconnaissance 247–8; improvised explosive devices (IEDs) 237–40; police response to 231, 243–4; and proportionality in prevention measures 232; protected spaces 244; protective security advice 230–2; response levels 234–5; risk management 232–4; security planning 235–7; and staff security awareness 237; suicide bomb attacks 240–1;

suspicious deliveries 245; threat levels 234, 235
ticketing 86, 87–8, 108
time factors 65, 81
time-based strategies 86
tobacco, and alcohol 200
toilet and washing facilities 108, 128, 135–8; attendants 138; campgrounds 139; food vendors 137; maintenance 137–8
Toohey, J. 282
traffic management *see* vehicle traffic management
training *see* staff training
Treuille, A. 71
tripping hazards 156
turnstiles 97–8
two-way radio (WT) 40, 157

Understanding Crowd Behaviours report (2010) 46
USA (United States of America) 4; Department of Homeland Security 232, 234, 242; National Bureau of Standards 48
ushers 95–6, 160, 214

vehicle traffic management 117–22, 156; crowd/traffic separation 112, 118; New South Wales control regulations 118–20; *see also* parking
video equipment 175–6

violence 10, 92, 160–2; response to 162; risk assessment 161; zero tolerance policy 161
violent crowds 93
VIP security 223–5, 226–7
virtual reality modelling 71
volatility, crowd 92
volunteer staff 58, 94, 100

waiver and release 13–15
warning sirens 257
waste management 108, 128, 139–41; food 139–40, 183
water, drinking 139, 204
water areas 111
weapons: confiscation of 98, 219
weather factors 67, 90, 115, 153, 253, 292–3
welfare 6
Wertheimer, P. 293
White, T. 49, 73
windows and doors 134
Wodak, A. 201
work at heights 10
workers: rights and duties 8–9; *see also* staff
workplace health and safety *see* occupational health and safety (OH&S)
World Health Organization 5
wristbanding, age identification 193–4
WT channels 40, 157